A KING'S RANSOM

A King's Ransom

*The Life of Charles Théveneau de Morande,
Blackmailer, Scandalmonger & Master-Spy*

Simon Burrows

continuum

Continuum UK, The Tower Building, 11 York Road, London SE1 7NX
Continuum US, 80 Maiden Lane, Suite 704, New York, NY 10038

www.continuumbooks.com

Copyright © Simon Burrows 2010

First published 2010

British Library Cataloguing-in-Publication Data
A catalogue record for this book is available from the British Library.

ISBN 978-0826-41989-7

Typeset by Pindar NZ, Auckland, New Zealand
Printed and bound by MPG Books Ltd, Cornwall, Great Britain

Contents

Illustrations

In memory of
Danalee Burrows

La calomnie, Monsieur, vous ne savez guère ce que vous dédaignez, j'ai vu les plus honnêtes gens prêts d'en être accablés.

Calumny, Sir, you hardly know what you are disdaining: I have seen the best of men laid low by it.

BEAUMARCHAIS,
THE BARBER OF SEVILLE

Prefatory note

For readability, I have used English versions of French book and manuscript titles and editions wherever a suitable equivalent exists. Where feasible I have consulted English language editions and used their translations. Other translations, save where indicated, are my own.

Where no translation is given for a French phrase or title, it is because the wording is too close to the English equivalent to require one. In a few cases, it has been necessary to use French or eighteenth-century English terms that are unfamiliar and lack precise modern English equivalents. Most are explained at first use. A short glossary is also provided.

Noble titles have been anglicized. However, in order to distinguish between the two titles, vicomtesse and marquise have been rendered as viscountess and marquise respectively rather than as marchioness.

There were approximately 24 French *livres* to the pound sterling; 20 *livres* made a Louis. British money equivalents for French figures are usually given in the text.

Prologue: Auto da fé

On a late April evening in 1774, a cart stacked high with freshly printed books turned out of Duke Street. It wound a few hundred yards through the streets of London and took the road to Mary-le-Bone, then still a village on the city's outskirts. There, in the kiln of a glasshouse hired for the occasion, the volumes were burned. That very night in Versailles King Louis XV of France fell terminally ill. Within a fortnight he was dead: poisoned, according to one satirical report, by toxic fumes wafted across the English Channel from the bonfire of malodorous books. Just one copy of the fatal text was saved from the flames, to be ritually dismembered and distributed among the six men who witnessed or recorded this strange *auto da fé*.[1]

This select crowd contained some of the most extraordinary, celebrated and notorious Frenchmen of their era. It included the renegade diplomat, the Chevalier d'Eon, a French agent who had helped to negotiate for the suppression of the books.[2] In the mid 1760s, d'Eon had stunned Europe with his unprecedented exposés of French diplomatic life and startling allegations that the ambassador to London had conspired with the foreign minister to kill him. Subsequently, even more extraordinary rumours had begun to circulate about him: it was said that he was a woman.

The second witness was Marie-Félix Guerrier de Lormoy, a one-time cavalry officer and Captain of Hunts to Louis XV's grandson, the Count de Provence. Lormoy was famous for his large horse-breeding establishment, which had been founded with government encouragement. Unfortunately, Lormoy's business acumen was no match for his horsemanship; his enterprise collapsed, and he fled to London. There, he too attempted to negotiate the book's suppression.

The third witness was the dramatist Pierre-Augustin Caron de Beaumarchais, the rising star of French theatre. His comic creation and *alter ego*, the wily intriguer Figaro, would soon establish him as the acknowledged successor to Voltaire. Beaumarchais had been sent to London by Louis XV himself to suppress the book and hoped his mission would restore him to favour after suffering two disastrous legal judgments. As cunning as his *alter ego*, Beaumarchais had succeeded where other negotiators had failed. The books were burned as part of a deal he had brokered.

Accompanying Beaumarchais was his secretary, Paul-Philippe Gudin de la

Brenellerie. As Beaumarchais' first biographer, Gudin would one day chronicle these events.

Then there was the aristocratic Count de Lauraguais, a playboy pamphleteer, who had introduced the sport of horse-racing to France. Lauraguais' family was among the most prominent in France: it supplied the court with both royal mistresses and government ministers, including the Duke de Choiseul, France's leading minister in the 1750s and 1760s. However, to his contemporaries Lauraguais was best known for his stormy on-off love affair with the actress Sophie Arnould, a celebrated wit and courtesan who was perhaps the most talked-about French woman of her age. Their antics provided endless copy for gossipy newsheets such as the *Mémoires secrets* for more than a dozen years.[3] However, Lauraguais was also a bosom companion of Louis XV, who had scandalized Europe by taking to his bed in close succession four of Lauraguais' aunts, the aristocratic Nesle sisters. The scandal was not just about morality: it had serious political and religious repercussions. As the Church considered sexual relations with sisters to be incest, many of Louis' subjects believed subsequent political and military disasters were divine punishment for the king's sin.

The concern of Louis' subjects only worsened when the king abandoned tradition by taking his last two long-term mistresses from beyond the charmed circle of the aristocracy. It was bad enough that one, Madame de Pompadour, was the wife of a wealthy financier. But most of the royal court found his last mistress, the young, stunningly beautiful but decidedly plebian Jeanne Bécu, known to history as Madame du Barry, completely beyond the pale. For if she had not exactly been a streetwalker, she had certainly been a courtesan, working her way up through noble lovers with the assistance of her ambitious pander, the Count du Barry. Eventually she caught the eye of ambitious courtiers, who slipped her into the royal bed and married her to du Barry's destitute good-for-nothing brother, the Viscount du Barry, in order that she could be named official mistress, an honour reserved for the nobility. In a society where power was determined by proximity to the king's body, her elevation infuriated the powerful Choiseul clan, the aristocracy and most of the royal family, many of whom snubbed her publicly or spread malicious rumours about her. Thus the royal sex life fuelled widespread discontent at all levels of society. By 1774, Louis XV was probably the most unpopular king in French history.

Lauraguais was among those who risked the king's wrath over du Barry, particularly when he audaciously nicknamed Laurence Lefebvre, the serving-girl he had just taken as his mistress, *la comtesse du Tonneau* [the Countess of the Tun]. This sarcastic word play on the wits' punning nickname for du Barry, *la comtesse du Baril* [the Countess of the Barrel], did not amuse the king.[4] As Lauraguais' opposition extended beyond such drollery to writing pamphlets against du Barry's ministerial allies, he found it prudent to remove himself from court. So it was that he found himself in self-imposed exile in London and able to play a part in suppressing the malodorous book. This might help to win back the favour of the king and Madame du Barry, for the book concerned them.

The final witness was the author of the books. His name was Charles-Claude Théveneau de Morande and he is the subject of this biography.[5] After his dissolute youth and a life of crime and debauchery, Morande came to the attention of the French government and public in 1771 as the author of *Le Gazetier cuirassé ou anecdotes scandaleuses de la cour de France* [*The Armour-Plated Gazetteer or Scandalous Anecdotes of the French Court*]. This satirical and sexually salacious pamphlet attack on the French government brimmed over with anecdotes attacking government ministers, courtiers and high society. Chief among its targets were Louis XV and Madame du Barry. The work enjoyed a *succès de scandale*, selling like hot cakes to English aristocrats and underground bookdealers in France. The French secret police considered it one of the most toxic libels they had ever encountered.

Flush with success, Morande turned to blackmail, threatening to publish revelations concerning some of the most distinguished people in France. And because he wrote from the haven of London there was little that they could do to stop him. In 1772, Morande turned his attentions to Madame du Barry, who had every reason to fear his pen, particularly since his insinuations that she had jumped straight from brothel to royal boudoir by reinvigorating the jaded sexual appetite of the libertine monarch were not so far from the truth.

Morande's writings had already shown that he was familiar with the *demi-monde* of Parisian courtesans in which she began her career, even if rumours that he was once her lover are probably a later invention.[6] Indeed, the very title of Morande's new work – *Secret Memoirs of a Woman of Pleasure, or Historical Researches on the Adventures of Madame la Countess du Barry from her Cradle until the Bed of Honour* – threatened more intimate revelations than any previous biographer had dared. Already in the *Gazetier cuirassé* Morande had 'revealed' that she had turned tricks in the celebrated brothel of Madame Gourdan and perfumed her genitals with an amber douche to keep herself fresh for her royal lover. No wonder then that du Barry was worried about further 'revelations' and persuaded the king and his foreign minister, the Duke d'Aiguillon, to try to stop Morande's work seeing the light of day.

At first the negotiation went slowly. The blackmailer demanded more than the French government had expected, and so a plot was hatched to kidnap him instead. This was a time-honoured way for the French to deal with scandalmongering authors, but this time it went spectacularly wrong. The kidnappers were thwarted and had to flee England and, in the aftermath, Morande was paid off by the royal treasury. In April 1774, he agreed to destroy every copy of his work and associated manuscripts and never again to publish or contribute to printed attacks on the royal family, ministers or servants of the French Crown. In return the monarchy paid him a large lump sum and a life annuity. For the French government this was a shameful transaction, and it soon became notorious. A traitor who had tarnished the reputation of the French crown and its ministers had extorted riches beyond the dreams of most of Louis XV's subjects. For Morande it was a spectacular coup. As he watched the last books being thrown into the kiln, he was entitled to feel a mixture of satisfaction and trepidation. He had blackmailed a monarch. But how much longer would he live to tell the tale?

This was the defining moment of Morande's life and reputation. For contemporaries and historians it established him as the most notorious and successful blackmailer and scandalous pamphleteer of his age. The Chevalier d'Eon denounced him as 'nothing but a vile libeller, an infamous Aretin,[7] and the basest coward that ever existed in the kingdom of scoundrels'. To Beaumarchais he was 'a monster who has never known any sense of gratitude but to knife me if he were able to'. And in the words of the prominent revolutionary Girondin, Pierre-Louis Manuel, 'he was a thief even before he became a libertine, and first visited a brothel in order to steal a gold box'.[8]

Historians have treated Morande in much the same way. He has been variously described as 'the incarnation of an eighteenth-century rogue', 'a minor king among blackmailers', and 'a flesh and blood Figaro, so devious that he exploited Beaumarchais himself'.[9] This is not to say that he has been universally dismissed as a mere criminal. The influential American historian Robert Darnton reserves a more important role for him. He thinks Morande's *Gazetier cuirassé* served as the prototype for the scurrilous works of a generation of hack pamphleteers who dragged the reputation of the French monarchy through the gutter, stripping it of political legitimacy. He thus supplied one of the sparks from which the French Revolution exploded.[10] According to Darnton's figures, Morande was also one of the five best-selling authors supplying France's extensive clandestine book trade. In the 1770s and 1780s, his works supposedly outsold those of every *philosophe* except Voltaire and the Baron d'Holbach.[11]

Yet Morande was much more than a petty criminal and pedlar of popular infamies. In his efforts to make a pretty penny and rehabilitate himself with the monarchy he had besmirched, he was to turn his hand to many other activities. He was by turns a secret police agent, spy, journalist, political theorist, practical reformer, and apologist for constitutional monarchy. Such activities had a considerable, though often concealed, influence, particularly as he was associated with many of the most colourful and influential literary, political and criminal figures of his day. Thus Morande's life-story serves as a means both to discover the seamier side of life and letters in the eighteenth century and to follow the tumultuous political developments on both sides of the English Channel in the Age of the Revolutions.

The Sins of his Youth

On 10 November 1741, Louis Théveneau and his wife Philiberte Belin baptized their first-born child in the parish church of Saint-Laurent in the small Burgundian town of Arnay-le-Duc. They named him Charles-Claude in honour of his uncle, Claude Théveneau, and his godfather and paternal grandfather Charles.[1] As was customary, a crowd of friends and relatives gathered to welcome the day-old infant into the family of Christ and worldwide Roman Catholic communion. Among them were Philiberte's cousin, Claude Bauzon, a lawyer and local attorney, and his wife Claudine Ravier, who was the child's godmother. Had they the gift of prophecy, the godparents might have renounced responsibility for bringing up the little devil by the font. For in later life this same Charles-Claude Théveneau would be described as 'the greatest scoundrel in three kingdoms'. His name, in a century notorious for dissolute morals, would become a byword for immorality.[2] But for now, all that lies in the future.

There is nothing in the child's background to hint at such a destiny. His family are solidly bourgeois and impeccably respectable members of Arnay's tightly knit, small-town élite. Louis Théveneau is a notary [*procureur du roi*], and Charles Théveneau senior a master surgeon. Claude Théveneau, also a surgeon, holds an MA in medicine. The baby's maternal grandfather is a merchant, as are the child's great uncle Guy Théveneau and several of his cousins. Other relatives are successful tanners, while his uncle Claude Riambourg is another lawyer. In short, Charles Théveneau's relatives are big fish in a small pond; they are also pillars of their little community.[3]

Although upwardly mobile for several generations, no one in this extended family enjoys noble status and the taxation and legal privileges that go with it. Doubtless it is something they dream of, but for now it remains a distant aspiration. Nevertheless, by 1765, Charles-Claude Théveneau will have awarded himself the noble title Chevalier de Morande. As a lie is always most effective when it contains a grain of truth, he takes his 'title' from a small parcel of family land, one of several the Théveneaus rent to peasant farmers. Such fraudulent titles were a common conceit among those who aspired to move up in the world. Before the revolution of 1789 did away with nobility, even prominent future Jacobins, including 'Georges d'Anton', 'Maximilien de Robespierre' and 'Jacques-Pierre Brissot de Warville', gave themselves airs in this manner. In Morande's case, however, the title is taken as a criminal alias and a means of rubbing shoulders with the nobility in search of a better class of dupe. Only after his identity is rumbled by the police will he start calling himself Théveneau de Morande.[4] But as Morande is the name we find most often in contemporary sources, it is also the name we shall use.

In 1741, Arnay-le-Duc was a small provincial town of a little over 2,000 inhabitants, strategically placed on the river Arroux on the road between Autun and Dijon. As the largest community between these two regional centres, it served as a commercial and social centre for the surrounding farms and villages. It hosted the local market every Thursday, and a fair six times a year. Due to its strategic position, it had also been heavily fortified. By the time Morande was growing up, its ancient walls were falling into disrepair, but during the wars of religion in the sixteenth century, the protestant champion Henri IV won his first battle under the town's ramparts.

In its small way, the Arnay of Morande's youth was a vibrant community, home to small-scale manufacturing and several important local institutions. Situated away from the main wine-growing regions of Burgundy, it depended on other industries, particularly the cloth trade, which employed Morande's merchant relatives. Arnay was also a religious centre, the site of an Ursuline convent where Morande's cousin Rose-Nicolle Théveneau would take the habit in August 1767. It was also home to a Capuchin monastery; the eleventh-century priory of Saint-Jacques; a sixteenth-century hospital; and a *collège* [high school]. The town was also the seat of a royal *baillage* [local court], where Morande's father practised law. These institutions all attracted people and business to the town, bringing the townsfolk into contact with the wider world and oiling the wheels of commerce. During Morande's youth the townsfolk were prosperous enough to rebuild their ancient parish church.[5]

Arnay's social elite tended to mix and marry among themselves. The tight, family-orientated focus of their social world is clearly evident in the records of the town's baptisms, marriages and deaths. The Théveneau clan appear regularly as the witnesses at one another's weddings, as godparents to one another's children, and mourners at family funerals. Marriages between cousins or those already related by marriage are not uncommon. The complex web of their family connections can be revealed by considering some of the guests who sign the marriage register at the wedding of Louis Théveneau and Philiberte Belin on 10 January 1741. Among the bride's relatives is Jeanne Ravier, who in 1745 will marry the groom's brother, Claude. On the groom's side, Louis Théveneau's cousins Dominique Noirot and Louise Théveneau are already married to each other. The next two generations of the family will also witness marriages between first cousins.[6] This is doubtless partly a strategy to keep property within the family, but it also indicates a lack of suitable marriage partners in the neighbourhood.

Louis Théveneau was a widely respected man of integrity, who dreamed his son would follow him into the legal profession. The Chevalier d'Eon, who knew the family, describes him as 'honest', as do several other literary and police sources. Morande's own memoirs depict a stern but loving father, driven to his wit's end by a dissolute and uncontrollable son. Morande's mother, Philiberte, was devoted to her brood and warmly welcomed Morande's wife and children when they visited her in the 1780s, but for many years she disowned him and resisted his increasingly desperate appeals for money. Philiberte was in later life deeply religious and strongly influenced by her spiritual advisors. Shortly before she died, she was reconciled with Morande, and there was enough evidence of her change of heart for her will to be quashed in his favour.[7]

Louis Théveneau and Philiberte Belin had a large family. The mid eighteenth century was a period of economic growth and good harvests, and they and their affluent relatives were spared the worst of the devastating visitations of infant mortality that plagued the poorer sections of the community and earlier generations of their own families.[8] By 1754, Philiberte had given birth to Morande; Rose-Antoinette (born in July 1743); Jean-Claude (February 1745); Antoine-Claude (July 1746); Françoise (November 1748); Louis-Claude-Henri-Alexandre (February 1751) and Lazare-Jean (September 1754). Of these, only Jean-Claude and Antoine died in childhood.

Morande's two surviving brothers had distinguished careers. Louis entered the legal profession, remained in Arnay and rose to local prominence. Morande considered him a feeble, well-meaning 'sot'. Lazare-Jean by contrast travelled widely and was a young man of considerable talents. Through Morande's recommendation, he was employed as a secretary by Beaumarchais and visited London and the nascent United States, where he channelled money and weapons to the American revolutionaries. Thereafter he was appointed *conseiller-secretaire du roi* and *contrôleur de la chancellerie*. Of all his siblings, Morande seems to have been closest to Lazare-Jean, in spite, or perhaps because of, the 13-year age gap. Lazare-Jean was only about 10 when Morande fled the family home, and perhaps this made it easier for him to forgive or romanticize his wayward brother. In any case, Lazare-Jean, who styled himself Théveneau de Francy, seems to have been Morande's temperamental opposite. He was admired for probity and honesty as well as for his application and administrative talents.

Morande's sisters seem to have been two very different characters. Morande describes Françoise as 'honest', 'religious', 'tender' and generally well-disposed towards him, though lacking strength of character. However, her piety was a stumbling block: Morande believed that she was prejudiced against his children merely because his wife was not a Catholic. His other sister, Rose-Antoinette, who was of a different mettle, married Jean-Bernard Villedey, a lawyer from Autun. Morande claimed to hate them both, and in his correspondence regularly disparaged them. He described Rose-Antoinette as devious, malevolent and grasping, 'the worst shrew that ever lived'.[9]

Morande developed a malicious, spiteful and imaginative sense of humour at a young age, as is clear from his youthful pranks. One day, while still a schoolboy, he visits the marketplace and finds a peasant selling a basket of eggs and butter from a large pot. As if to check that the eggs are fresh, he takes the basket from the unsuspecting yokel, makes him fold his arms across his chest and, having carefully examined each egg in turn, places them on the man's arms. Once the peasant is laden with eggs and dares not move, Morande nimbly undoes the buttons on the man's breeches, pulls them down to his knees, and retreats into the crowd with the pot of butter. The peasant attempts to give chase, but falls. The eggs tumble everywhere and break, and there is much merriment at his expense. Meanwhile, Morande spreads the butter on his bread, all the while laughing at his victim.

On another occasion he is crossing the market carrying half a hollowed-out baguette when he spies a peasant woman selling pots of cream. He asks the price, takes some cream and pours it into the hole in his bread, then hands the woman half the agreed sum and walks off. When she shouts after him demanding the rest of her payment, he turns with a grin and announces 'since you are not content, give me my money back and take back your cream'. With that, he snatches back his coins, pours the cream back into her pot, and saunters off with his bread nicely soaked in cream and the laughter of the market traders ringing in his ears.

However, Morande's favourite targets were not hapless peasants but the local Capuchin monks. According to local legend, he would sneak into the monastic kitchen whenever it was unguarded. Once there, he would slip the lid off the large stockpot of bubbling soup and add whatever new ingredient took his fancy, whether the cat snoozing by the fire or an old wig. Such pranks rapidly became public knowledge and survived in Arnay's folk memory for decades afterwards. However, as he grew older, they might also get him into serious trouble. This is precisely what happened when he decided to pick on the monks' Father Superior.

The rules of their order required Capuchins to grow their beards only from the point of their chin and to leave only a narrow ring of hair below their tonsure. In consequence, they had to have both their face and the top of their heads shaved regularly. Morande learns that the monks are shaved by their barber in a special cell containing a heavy wooden armchair. The Father Superior always goes first. One day, he is already seated in the cell waiting to be shaved, with a heavy cloth napkin wrapped round his neck and the chair, when he hears a commotion. It is Morande, who has been lying in wait, shouting and knocking over furnishings in the great cloister. The Father Superior, alarmed, sends the barber out to discover the cause of the disturbance. As he awaits the barber's return, Morande creeps into the cell behind him, grabs the corners of the napkin, twists them tightly and fastens them securely to the back of the chair with a gimlet. Before the Superior has realized what is happening, Morande has left the cell, locked the door, and slipped the key into his pocket. He steals out of the monastery while the Capuchin, firmly pinned to his chair, desperately spins around and crashes about in a bid to free himself. Meanwhile, outside his cell, the hapless barber cries at the door, unable to free the prisoner inside.[10]

This escapade soon became the talk of the town, but Morande was no longer a schoolboy and his father feared serious repercussions. He therefore decided to send the boy to Dijon to continue his education, reckoning emotions would soon simmer down. He still hoped that his son would pursue a legal career and eventually succeed him as *procureur* at Arnay. Morande was almost certainly a pupil at the prestigious *Collège Godrun*, where he was, if we can believe his memoirs, something of a prodigy, excelling particularly in logic. Both of Dijon's *collèges* were run by Jesuits, a dedicated teaching order, and the *Collège Godrun* was perhaps the finest school in Burgundy. It was there, doubtless, that Morande acquired his erudition, making good use of the magnificent library – now Dijon's university library – which had been bequeathed to the school in 1708. Thereafter, he probably continued his studies in the University of Dijon's law faculty.[11]

Exposure to Jesuit teachers probably helped to nurture the rebellious teenager's innate anti-clericalism and religious irreverence. Both are features of his later work, and the Jesuits come in for particularly heavy criticism. Morande was not alone in his antipathy to the Jesuits, which had political ramifications. Founded at the height of the Counter-Reformation to reclaim souls for Catholicism, the Jesuits were by the eighteenth century a force to be reckoned with. Many Catholic rulers had Jesuit confessors and their order was extremely rich. But it also had many enemies. These included the *parlements*, sovereign law courts who claimed to represent the people against the Crown, and the Jansenists, advocates of an austere, simplified form of Catholicism, whom the Jesuits and the Crown were determined to stamp out. During Morande's youth, the political struggle between the Jesuits and their enemies was reaching a climax. The result was a total victory for the Jansenist-*parlement* faction. In 1764, the Jesuits suffered a disastrous legal judgment and Louis XV reluctantly permitted their dissolution.

Louis Théveneau lived to regret sending his son to Dijon. Compared to Arnay, the Burgundian capital was a veritable metropolis. With a population approaching 20,000, it offered undreamed of distractions and illicit pleasures for Morande, as well as a protective anonymity. Morande quickly ran up large debts, doubtless from his first encounters with the delights of gambling, fast women, and debauchery. Soon Louis Théveneau was receiving reports of his son's misbehaviour. At his wit's end, he refused to pay off Morande's debts and decided on drastic action. He could have applied to have his son locked up indefinitely by a *lettre de cachet*. This was an order bearing the royal seal and the standard way for dealing with wayward wives and children in eighteenth-century France. Instead, according to Morande, his father summoned a friend who was a captain in the dragoons and asked him to enlist the boy in the French army. On 15 April 1760, Morande enlisted for six years service as a common dragoon in the Prince de Bauffremont's regiment. The regiment had a long and proud history and was at that time campaigning in Germany. Thus, at the age of 18, Morande found himself heading off to war.

Regimental records describe Morande as five foot three inches, a respectable height for the period, with chestnut hair, blue eyes and a large nose. They also reveal that he enlisted with two other lads from Arnay-le-Duc, one of whom, Claude-François Bouillotte, would later desert. Morande's company commander was Laurent le Bas de Claireau d'Egremont, a career soldier from an aristocratic background, who was described by his superiors as 'a very good officer with a fine unit. Full of valour . . . an excellent subject, [who] has kindliness and lots of willpower' and 'in every respect made to be at the head of a *corps*'. Both company and regiment seem to have been well-led and they suffered surprisingly light losses in the campaigns in which Morande participated in 1760 and 1761.[12]

Despite his rebellious nature, Morande found himself well suited to the rigours of military life. He was physically large, powerfully built and well aware how to use his bulk to intimidate and bully. In terms of sheer strength, few soldiers could match him. It is generally supposed that the rank and file of old regime – that is to say, pre-French Revolutionary – armies was composed of desperate men: criminals who joined up to avoid punishment, knaves with no prospects, vagabonds, and the destitute. However, the French army, comprising over 200,000 men in wartime, was too large to conform to this image. This was particularly true of dragoon regiments, which travelled by horse, though they sometimes fought on foot. Dragoons needed to be competent horsemen, and a high proportion of the Bauffremont regiment were also literate. Even so, few of Morande's comrades were bourgeois. This probably mattered little to Morande, who clearly enjoyed their camaraderie.[13] Their coarse language, manners and entertainments were also to his taste.

Morande was less impressed by the majority of the army's exclusively noble officer corps and wrote with disdain of their incompetence. He once asserted that not four in two hundred knew even the basic rudiments of their trade. These allegations had serious implications because the French nobility claimed to be a military caste. They justified their privileged place in society through their leadership on the battlefield. The suggestion that they were unfit for this role undermined their entire *raison d'être* and with it their position at the top of the social pyramid. Morande had looked at the army and found it wanting. The army had begun to shape him into a *patriote* reformer.[14]

Morande was not alone in criticizing the army's performance, for the war in which he was fighting ended in the most disastrous military defeat the Bourbon monarchy ever suffered. For a country that had aspired to be the dominant European and world power for over a century, this was a terrible shock, especially as defeat stripped France of colonial possessions in Canada and India. Moreover, many Frenchmen believed the war was fought on behalf of an unworthy ally, the Austrian Empire. Austria and France were traditional enemies, so when the two powers signed an alliance in 1756, it sent shock waves through Europe. Nor did it seem a short-term shift in alliances, since the treaty was sealed by the promise that an infant daughter of the Austrian Empress would marry the future Louis XVI of France, who was then a small child. The ruler who had most cause to be alarmed by these developments was Frederick the Great of Prussia. In 1740, Frederick had seized the Austrian province of Silesia, unleashing the Wars of the Austrian Succession. Despite their best efforts, the Austrians had been unable to win Silesia back, and in 1748 an uneasy peace had been agreed. Now Frederick feared that the Austrians and their French and Russian allies were encircling him. He therefore launched a pre-emptive attack, precipitating the Seven Years' War. Three years later, after a brief period of basic training in drill and the mass manoeuvres required by the tactics of the day, Morande and his comrades were sent to fight in Germany.

If we may believe his memoirs, young Charles Théveneau was excited by the prospect of action, and dreamed of nothing but glory. However, his ardour was quickly cooled by a bullet in the leg and the sight of friends lying dead beside him. He was found in agony several hours later and stretchered to a nearby farmhouse. There he found 'kindness, virtue, fresh straw and soup'. A barber-surgeon from the nearest village applied a dressing to his wounds. Having survived the night, he was taken to a military hospital in the French base at nearby Lippstadt. Six months later he hobbled back to his regiment before limping home to Arnay-le-Duc. In January 1763, before he could return to active service, the war ended and Morande was decommissioned. His brief and inglorious military career was over.[15]

That, at least, is Morande's account. Assuming it is true, Morande must have received his wound during the summer of 1761, while his regiment was campaigning with the Army of the Upper Rhine on the river Lippe. It was probably inflicted during July 1761, after the French advanced out of Lippstadt during the Vellinghausen campaign. Most likely, it was at the battle of Vellinghausen itself, a bloody defeat for the French fought on the river Lippe close to Paderborn on 15 July 1761. In all, the French suffered some 5,000 casualties and were forced to beat a hasty retreat, while the allies' official death toll was 434. Fortunately for the Marshal de Broglie and his forces, and particularly for Morande, the allies were slow to follow up their victory. This renders the tale of Morande's rescue from the battlefield a little more credible.[16]

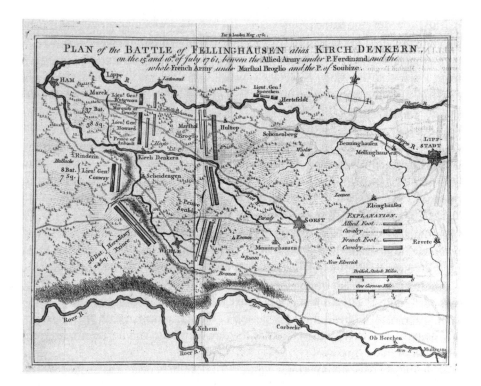

Plate 1. Contemporary British Map of the Battle of Vellinghausen. Courtesy of the Brotherton Collection, Brotherton Library, University of Leeds.

Morande's enemies, above all the Chevalier d'Eon, tell a more picturesque tale. They say Morande deserted from the French army and served under the banners of both Russia and Prussia's Black Hussars.[17] These allegations emerged at a time when d'Eon and his friends were trying to provoke Morande into fighting a duel and are probably false. They are not mentioned in police dossiers, which record that he served with the Bauffremont regiment, nor by his enemies during the revolution. A regimental register of troops, which was maintained thoroughly until at least June 1762, makes no mention of his leaving the regiment, whether through desertion or discharge. His name does not appear in the next register, which only starts in March 1763. As the regiment retreated into France in late 1761 and played no part in the 1762 campaign, Morande's version of events, though impossible to confirm, is consistent with surviving registers. Equally, the charge that he fought for the Russians, who withdrew from the war early in 1762, appears chronologically incompatible with the documentary record.[18]

Morande's counter-claims that he transferred into an elite cavalry regiment, the Carabiniers, and was promoted to the rank of sub-lieutenant, through the patronage of its commander, Monsieur de Poyane, also appear to be false. The surviving records of the Bauffremont and Carabiniers regiments contain no evidence that he was ever promoted. The French police doubted the story and a letter from Poyane to the *Morning Chronicle* denied it outright.[19] There is, however, evidence that he suffered a serious wound, as later physical descriptions suggest that he walked with a pronounced limp. It is quite possible, of course, that his long absence from his regiment gave rise to rumours of desertion. If this is the case, d'Eon, who came from the Burgundian town of Tonnerre, could well have got to hear them. However, d'Eon frequently spread lies and distortions about his enemies. His colourful version of Morande's military career is probably just one more example.

If Morande's family hoped that the rigours of a military career would reform his morals, they were sadly deluded. No sooner had he returned to Arnay than he resumed his gambling and womanizing. In an age when a young woman's reputation was often her only asset, he was every mother's worst nightmare. A wounded war hero, he was worldly, handsome, strong, witty, well-educated and came from a good family. No wonder the local girls fell at his feet. Soon, he was writing poems in praise of those who encouraged his advances and maligning those who scorned him.[20] Such tactics were intended to inflame the social aspirations of his conquests as well as their vanity and passion, for poetry writing was a mark of gentility. Not surprisingly, Morande's memoirs hint that he debauched several girls at this period; local folklore insists he also got away with murder.

Among Morande's most devoted conquests, according to local legend, is the pretty young daughter of Madame Finel, who runs the local coaching inn. Morande seduces her, abandons her, then cruelly mocks her foolishness. Mortified and crushed, the girl fades away and dies of a broken heart. Unfortunately, she has a brother in the army. He learns what has happened, comes home on leave, confronts Morande, and forces him into a duel.

They meet alone, swords in hand, at La Flenne, a secluded hillside field above Arnay's Faubourg Saint-Jacques. They fight for several moments, then Morande's sword snaps. Finel agrees to abandon the combat until Morande can get a new sword. They descend the narrow track from La Flenne in single file, Morande still carrying his broken sword-hilt. Suddenly, Finel loses his footing and stumbles. Morande seizes his opportunity. He thrusts the stub of his sword into his rival with all his might, wounding his own palm as he does so. Finel staggers a few steps and dies, gurgling incoherent accusations. Morande, too, cries out, bewailing his wounds and the death of his adversary. But when the townsfolk arrive, the evidence speaks against him. It is clear that Finel was stabbed in the back; Morande's own wound is further evidence. Powerful voices speak out in Morande's favour, but the authorities are informed. Morande flees to Paris, where he is unknown and anonymous. Meanwhile, his father intrigues to protect him and calm things down. But the judgement of the townsfolk is inflexible: he cannot return.[21]

This, at least, is the version of events given by César Lavirotte in a short unpublished biography of Morande. A nineteenth-century mayor and historian of Arnay-le-Duc, Lavirotte in his youth had long conversations with Morande. Thus, parts of his manuscript appear to draw on Morande's recollections, while others draw on Lavirotte's memories, published sources or local tradition. His account of the duel was clearly part of Arnay's folklore and, in the absence of other evidence, unreliable. Indeed, the records of baptisms, marriages and burials for Arnay-le-Duc appear to contradict the tale conclusively.[22] However, several of Lavirotte's details chime with Morande's own version of the 16 months he spent in Arnay between January 1763 and May 1764. Morande, too, speaks of a duel over a girl; a broken sword; wounding a rival; legal proceedings; and fleeing to Paris to escape the consequences. If Lavirotte's version is false, it apparently offers a distorted reflection of real events, which were no less interesting.

The heroine of Morande's version is the lovely Hélène. She is beautiful, charming and virtuous, but vain and coquettish. She encourages Morande to pen verses in her honour and he concludes that he has won both her heart and the right to her favours. He is doubly mistaken. Hélène has another swain, a muscular youth who courts her assiduously. Morande grows insanely jealous. One day, he meets the couple arm-in-arm. Though armed with just a riding crop, he insults his rival, who unsheathes his sword. Luck is with Morande. He disarms his opponent. The sword snaps and cuts a serious gash in his adversary's head.

Morande's wooing of Hélène ends in a lawsuit for damages. Louis Théveneau decides his son is not to blame. He acquitted himself with honour, having been attacked. He allows Morande to defend the case. The court finds in his favour. And there things should have ended.

Unfortunately, Morande's rival is a soldier. His comrades insist he should avenge the affront to his honour. He acquiesces and returns to Arnay-le-Duc. He seeks out Morande and challenges him. Morande accepts. A time and place is agreed. Before the combat, Louis Théveneau is informed. Distraught, he storms into his son's room, seizes his pistols, his sword and his clothes and locks them up. He leaves Morande only his dressing gown and slippers, assuming this will prevent him from leaving the house.

A few days later, Louis Théveneau learns that his son has been climbing out of a window at night and appearing around town dressed in a lady's riding coat. He does not know what to do. Determined to prevent a duel, he redoubles his vigilance and applies for a *lettre de cachet*, just in case. But he hesitates to use such severity. Instead, he pleads with Morande. Morande listens in silence. He does not wish to appear to be avoiding his opponent.

In late 1763, Louis Théveneau allows Morande to accompany him to Autun.

The ancient representative body of the province, the Estates of Burgundy, is meeting there and he has much business to attend to. But before long Louis learns that Morande is frequenting gambling dens and that his rival is in town. Still he does not enforce the *lettre de cachet*.

Morande loses money at the gaming tables night after night. He grows desperate. One day, he calls on a business contact to try to arrange a loan. To his horror his father walks in from a neighbouring room. He has heard everything. It is the final straw. Morande is arrested that very night and taken into the custody of the local Franciscan monks. He is placed in a cell on the ground floor in solitary confinement.

Immediately, Morande starts trying to dig through the thick walls. He succeeds within eight days and hurries to a house of ill repute to celebrate and boast of his escape. His secret soon reaches the monks. Their Master, a giant of a man, comes after him, accompanied by his deputy and six other brothers. The posse bursts in while Morande is eating and drags him back to prison. He is placed in a more secure cell, whose barred windows are surrounded by wooden joists. The walls are 18 inches thick. Morande rises to the challenge. He loosens one of the beams and softens the stone around the bars with water. He removes two of the bars and, after just 12 days, escapes for a second time.

This time, Morande is more cautious with his liberty. He is convinced that his second escape will soften his parents' hearts, by proving his character and determination. Instead, an unexpected revelation overturns his hopes: he has a child. The unfortunate mother, whom Morande never names, had concealed the identity of her baby's father throughout her pregnancy, but on learning of Morande's arrest she became inconsolable and let her secret slip. The news shocks Morande's parents and particularly strains his relationship with Philiberte. His escape only makes matters worse.

Morande takes refuge with a female relative who attempts to broker a reconciliation with his father. They meet. Louis receives him warmly, but the meeting is not a success. At 11 in the evening, Louis leaves the house unplacated and tearful. Morande, too, is disappointed. He reflects on how he handled their meeting. Had he not shown enough remorse? Had he not seemed submissive enough? There is only one thing for it. He will write his father a letter. He scribbles until two o'clock the next morning then tumbles into bed.

Morande is still not asleep when he hears the door open gently. In the shadows he can make out four armed men creeping up on him. Suddenly he surges for the door. He makes it in a single bound. Surprise is on his side. Two swords are raised against him. They do not stop him. The man closest to him attempts to seize him mid stride, tearing at his shirt. Morande fells him with a single punch. He takes Morande's shirt with him. Morande lunges for the open door. He slams it behind him and locks it on those charged with arresting him.

He is naked but for a shirt sleeve. It is early January. The ground is frozen solid. Somehow adrenalin carries him. He scales a ten-foot wall; he crosses the little river Arroux, breaking the ice as he goes. After covering a mile and an half, he finds himself at the house of a friend of his father. He wakes the household and is lent some clothes. His host agrees to help broker a truce. The mayor of Arnay and Monsieur Godard, father of one of Morande's college friends, negotiate on his behalf. Louis Théveneau capitulates and accepts Morande's submission. The *lettre de cachet* is annulled. He is welcomed back into the parental home. For four months Morande lives there, tormented by the idea of following a legal career and in perpetual fear of new attempts on his liberty or his person. At last, in May 1764, he slips away from home and takes the road to Paris.[23]

We will probably never know how much of Morande's tale of thwarted love, libertinage, family rows, imprisonment and miraculous escapes is true as, apart from Lavirotte's brief rival version, we lack accounts of his youth. However, a relative, Juliot, a lawyer in the Paris *Parlement* who served as Louis Théveneau's legal representative, has left a summary of events. It is contained in a letter written in about May 1768 to the chief of the Paris Police, Antoine-Gabriel de Sartine, to ask for a new *lettre de cachet* and confirms that much of Morande's testimony is at least loosely based on fact. Juliot discloses that Morande had caused Louis Théveneau 'all kinds of grief'. He continues:

> He [Louis Théveneau] did all he could to correct him; he had him locked up in several prisons [*maisons de force*] . . . But as soon as Charles Théveneau was released . . . he gave his father new, ever more serious, causes for disappointment. The different means . . . used to bring his son back to his senses have never had any effect. Charles Théveneau found ways to escape . . . and he always announced his liberation with excesses that made his family tremble. He disappeared several years ago and came to Paris. The supplicant [Louis Théveneau] has learned recently that his behaviour has been no better than it was in Burgundy and that he survives . . . only by his intrigues, having neither employment nor revenues. Charles Théveneau is routinely found with prostitutes; police Inspector Marais is fully informed about this.[24]

There is no reason to doubt Juliot's testimony that Morande had been arrested more often than he admits, especially as Morande himself seldom lied outright. He preferred to play the arch-hypocrite, masking the extent of his wrongdoing behind partial revelations, or making candid confessions while feigning contrition. These stratagems often allowed him to name respectable witnesses who could vouch for what he had said.[25] Fortunately, after his arrival in Paris we have more solid evidence about Morande's activities.

Paris in the 1760s was a genuine metropolis, the second largest city in Europe and home to over 500,000 people. In the late seventeenth century Louis XIV had moved his court to Versailles, some 13 miles away, to place himself at a safe distance from the tumult of the capital, but most leading noblemen kept palatial townshouses in Paris, as well as residences at Versailles. As a result, Paris gradually replaced Versailles as the country's cultural and social centre. Increasingly Paris was a centre for fashion, artists, literature and recreation. It was Europe's capital of pleasure, replete with theatres, the *Opéra*, fashionable boutiques and coffee houses to suit every pocket. It also boasted pleasure gardens, libraries and reading rooms, gambling dens and some of Europe's most celebrated brothels. The notorious police of Paris watched over all this with a jaundiced eye, often tolerating cafés, bars, brothels and gambling dens to remain open only in return for information on the opinions and activities of their clientele. Much of what they learned was written up into weekly reports by Inspector Marais, who was charged with overseeing public morals, and sent to the king for his information and amusement.[26]

In many ways Paris was a medieval town. Running alongside the gated palaces of the aristocracy – built defensively around courtyards with their windows facing inwards – were cramped winding streets and tall apartment buildings where the poor and middle classes daily rubbed shoulders. The most affluent apartment dwellers lived in spacious lodgings on the first floor, above the hubbub of the street. The poorest faced the daily drudgery of carrying water, firewood and food up the worn wooden stairs to tiny garret rooms nestled on the fourth, fifth or sixth floors where entire families shared a bed. Many lived from hand to mouth, going without food and firewood in hard times, keeping one step ahead of the rent collector and changing address frequently. Gambling and prostitution – usually a temporary measure rather than a lifestyle choice – were rife. Some estimates suggest that Paris had as many as 10,000 prostitutes, though this total includes a small army of courtesans and kept mistresses, as well as those who occasionally supplemented their meagre income by selling sex. At the top end of the scale of vice were the girls of the *Opéra* and actresses at the *Comédie française*, whose celebrated talents and beauty attracted wealthy admirers and protectors. The most legendary of them consumed the fortunes of a parade of wealthy lovers.

Morande arrived in Paris with about 4,500 *livres* (£185) in borrowed or stolen cash.[27] In the mid eighteenth century this might just support a modest gentleman's lifestyle for a year, including the rent on a town house, small coach, and a handful of servants. It would not long support a life of luxury, libertinism and debauchery. Morande thus needed to find ways to support his lifestyle. This meant finding patrons and protectors. They alone might supply him with a position and honest income, the appearance of respectability, and rich contacts to be pumped, fleeced or robbed.

According to his own account, Morande soon gained admission into the best homes in Paris. But in the process he needed to spend money, to maintain appearances and keep up with his associates. As his money ran out, he resorted to gambling, getting ever deeper into debt. Once again, this is not the whole story. By January 1765 he was well known to the police and had teamed up with a certain Sieur Daubigny. Together they preyed on young gentlemen fresh from the provinces, luring them to gamble in Daubigny's house, where they would fleece them or steal their money and watches. In some cases they imprisoned them, too.[28] Those who protested were threatened with violence. Perhaps there is more to it than that: Inspector Marais suspected that Morande was also an enthusiastic sodomite ['entiché du pêche antiphysique'].[29] This was a very serious allegation. In theory men found guilty of sodomy might be strangled by the public hangman and then burned. However, this punishment was only meted out nine times by the Parisian executioners across the entire century, and in seven such cases the victims were guilty of other capital offences. By the 1760s the police almost winked at the offence, imprisoning commoners for a couple of weeks and letting nobles off with a warning.[30]

Marais does not give reasons for his suspicions. However, much circumstantial evidence lends weight to the charge. Morande's writings show that he was well acquainted with the homosexual underworld and several of its most celebrated denizens. Moreover, some of his favourite haunts were popular with *antiphysiques*, particularly the brothel and gambling den of Madame Hecquet in the rue Feydeau, at the heart of a district notorious for its male prostitutes. Although Hecquet's establishment was a favourite resort for many heterosexual libertines and had a large stable of girls, it also employed more pretty young boys than most Parisian brothels. Yet even if he did have sex with other men, we should be cautious about labelling Morande a bisexual or homosexual: sodomy was often part and parcel of an eighteenth-century libertine lifestyle. It could even be seen as masculine behaviour, so long as one played the active, penetrative role, rather than that of the passive *bardache*. There is no proof that Morande visited *la Hecquet*'s bordello to have sex with men. However, one evening in early February 1765, he and Daubigny call in to play cards. Morande loses heavily. At the evening's end he owes Daubigny 280 *livres*. It is a debt of honour, but that means little to Morande. Later that night, he goes to Daubigny's house armed, drags him out of bed, and threatens to kill him if he ever mentions the debt or tells the police.[31]

By this time Morande is suffering from syphilis, the scourge of eighteenth-century libertines. The disease can be slow torture over many years. At the outset, it has few visible signs, but eventually it disfigures its victims, drives them insane, and often kills. The only hope lies in a treatment almost as bad as the illness itself: a course of mercury is applied to the body across several days. Not for nothing is the process of applying it called 'frictions'. Morande submits to a course of frictions in the days following his attack on Daubigny. Eight days into his treatment he visits widow Longpré's brothel. While he is there police Inspector de La Janière arrives with orders to arrest a scoundrel called Charles-François Lebeau. Dame Longpré, who has heard whispers of Morande's treatment of Daubigny, denounces him, too. Both men are dragged off to Fort l'Évêque prison. La Janière boasts to Sartine with some satisfaction that Morande is well known to him as Daubigny's accomplice, a 'crapulous libertine' and 'brute' who falsely claims to be employed by the Prince de Limbourg.[32]

Fortunately, Morande has a real protector, a wealthy Burgundian gentleman named La Saule. La Saule probably first met Morande in 1763 in Autun while a member of the Estates of Burgundy. At the time of his arrest, Morande is living under La Saule's roof in the rue du Batoir in the Faubourg Saint-Germain. On learning of Morande's arrest, La Saule pleads with Sartine for his release, asking him to excuse the follies of youth. He adds that Morande's condition is visibly deteriorating due to the interruption to his treatment and will soon be without remedy as 'the mercury works so horribly on him that a longer stay in Fort l'Évêque will inevitably prove fatal'.[33] Sartine proposes that Morande be sent to the prison infirmary, but La Saule begs that he be spared from the 'horror that reigns in that place, which is only inhabited by the dregs of humanity'. He adds that if Morande's imprisonment continues, it will inevitably become known in Burgundy, where his father fears dishonour more than death. La Saule finishes by contradicting allegations made against Morande. Morande is not without resources. His family regularly send him money and he is also supported by the Prince de Limbourg who has promised him a position. He even suggests that his quarrel with Daubigny was not occasioned by his debt, but by Daubigny's cheating. If only Sartine will release him, La Saule promises to support Morande through his convalescence then send him away from Paris.

Struck by La Saule's assurances, Sartine intercedes with the Count de Saint-Florentin, the Keeper of the Seals, to secure Morande's early release. He tells Saint-Florentin that Morande 'is ill and requires care promptly. His liberty is requested by people of consideration. He promises to cease visiting gambling dens and appears to have been sufficiently punished'. On 14 March 1765, Saint-Florentin gives the order to set him free.[34]

Why did La Saule go to such lengths to secure Morande's release? At first glance, it seems that he was blinded by affection for the young reprobate and completely taken in by Morande. Morande claims that La Saule and his wife always treated him like a son because they were childless. Was La Saule, who knew much of Morande's history, really taken in? It seems more likely he endorsed Morande's untruths because they were lovers. If so, the relationship was largely commercial: Morande provided sex in return for large sums of cash, the price of his silence and acquiescence. Needless to say, Morande never took a job with the Prince de Limbourg; his family were not supporting him; and no other source mentions Daubigny's cheating. Nor does La Saule send Morande away from Paris when he is recovered. Instead, over the next four years, he does all he can to keep him there.[35]

If Morande does not now mend his ways, he at least changes his operating methods and stays out of gaol. He continues to insinuate himself with the wealthiest aristocrats: one hapless creditor reports that both the Duke de Bethune and Duchess de Châtillon vouched for his *bona fides*.[36] Judged creditworthy, he continues to borrow large sums. By mid 1768 he has amassed a staggering 52,000 *livres* (about £2,150) of debt with Parisian merchants, as well as allegedly squandering 30,000 *livres* of his father's money and large sums advanced by the ever-indulgent La Saule.[37] More astonishing still, until late 1767 he even pays many of his bills.[38] With this much money, Morande cuts a fine figure in society. He has a coach and a light cabriolet and keeps five horses.[39] He runs up bills of 1,784 *livres* on fancy lace cuffs and fine Pekin cloth embroidered with flowers; 2,069 *livres* on jewellery; and over 700 *livres* on four coats for himself and his manservants.[40]

He funds his lifestyle and services his debts largely by vice.[41] Where once he spent his money in brothels, he now lives from the earnings of high class courtesans and kept women. He insinuates himself into their lives by feigning passion, then exploits and bullies them without scruple. He so terrifies one of his early conquests, *la petite Desmares*, the one-time mistress of Prince Camille de Rohan, that she flees home to Bordeaux to escape his rage. And this was a girl so compliant, energetic and vigorous in her love-making that more than one customer was said to have been unable to remount his horse after having 'ridden her too much'. Another of his conquests was *la Beauchamp*, a former lover and travelling companion of Casanova. Beauchamp's brothel in the *rue des deux portes* was a magnet for aristocratic libertines: on one occasion Paulmy d'Argenson, the son of the foreign minister, was serviced there by no less than five girls. In *la Beauchamp*, Morande meets his match. When his depradations become too much, she escapes his clutches by telling the police that he stole her watch during a trip to the royal palace at Fontainebleau. Morande is arrested and briefly imprisoned, probably in Bicêtre, a gaol for common prostitutes and criminals, but manages to secure his release.[42] He then sells his services to visitors to Paris, offering to show them around Paris and sneak them into the homes of the leading courtesans and mistresses of aristocrats, who, he claims, are under his 'protection'.

By 1767, Morande is attempting to worm his way into the affections of the mistresses of some of the richest men in France. Among them was Mademoiselle Souville, the mistress of Monsieur de Bourgogne, who the police said 'was known to all the world'. Souville had worked her way round most of the most notorious brothels of Paris. She began her career *chez la Montigny* before plying her trade in Brissault and Hecquet's establishments, even while she was being 'kept' by Monsieur de Vauvray, a one-time Master of Requests at Versailles. By 1767, she was keen to abandon a life of '*guerluchonnage*'[43] to devote herself entirely to Bourgogne, with whom she was besotted. Indeed, when Bourgogne took back a promissory note for 20,000 *livres*, Souville's response was to redouble her caresses. Morande apparently got nowhere with her.

Morande apparently had more luck with Mademoiselle La Cour, a flame-haired beauty celebrated for her libertinism. La Cour, mistress to the Prince de Lamballe, was known as *palais d'or* [gold palate] because her palate was reputedly so ravaged by the effects of Dr Keyser's pills, a celebrated treatment for venereal disease, that she replaced it with a new one constructed of precious metal.[44] This little dampened the ardour of Lamballe and Morande, both of whom were already infected. Morande may briefly have wooed La Cour away from Lamballe, but soon afterwards he was forcing his way into the houses of both Souville and La Cour by violence.[45] When they attempt to bar their doors, he threatens to have them imprisoned in Bicêtre. Thwarted in his designs, he revenges himself in anonymous letters to Lamballe, which are passed to the police. Several years later, he publishes anecdotes about La Cour in his *Gazetier cuirassé*, including a cruel epigram, which plays on the ambiguity of the French word '*palais*', which means both palate and palace:

> Let's fear Dr Keyser's secrets
> And their deplorable effects
> La Cour, alas, is an example;
> Wishing to purify her temple [of Venus, i.e. vagina],
> She demolished her palace/palate.[46]

However, upsetting women with powerful protectors is dangerous: Morande is making powerful enemies.

La Cour is not the only female *acquaintance* Morande denounces: he also tells Inspector Marais 'horror stories' about a certain demoiselle d'Oppy, with whom he had 'close relations'. Just how close is a moot point, for d'Oppy, a well-born married lady and mother, was accused of adultery by her husband, who embroiled her in a notorious divorce case. d'Oppy's troubles began on 15 April 1768, when she was arrested at Madame Gourdan's bordello in the *rue des deux ponts*. While this might appear damning evidence against her, d'Oppy claimed that she had been tricked into going to the brothel by a friend of her husband's family. He had introduced her to Madame Gourdan, assuring her that Gourdan was a lady of quality, and across the next two years d'Oppy visited her three times. d'Oppy insisted that she had never suspected that she was frequenting a place of prostitution, but Gourdan accused her of 'debauches worthy of the most degraded of her own infamous pupils'. Denying all such accusations – which were presumably corroborated by Morande's testimony – d'Oppy asserted that she was the victim of a conspiracy whereby her in-laws hoped to have her locked away permanently in order to gain control over her property.

Amazingly, after many legal twists and turns, the divorce petition was quashed and, in June 1776, d'Oppy was acquitted through lack of evidence. For her part in the mysterious affair, Gourdan, who had fled Paris, was sentenced in absentia to be led through the streets riding backwards on an ass. Two of her accomplices were gaoled. What we make of Morande's involvement depends on whether we accept d'Oppy's defence. If she was innocent, Morande was part of a conspiracy to ruin her reputation, strip her of her property, and have her falsely imprisoned for life. However, we must draw a different conclusion if, like some contemporary commentators, we refuse to accept that d'Oppy could live for two years in blissful ignorance of Gourdan's profession and dine innocently in a brothel with a crowd of male strangers. In that case, Morande is guilty only of debauching and perhaps corrupting an adulterous lady of quality who was willingly led astray.[47]

By this time rumours of Morande's behaviour are trickling back to Burgundy. Morande concludes that one of his servants has been bribed to pass reports to Louis Théveneau, who comes under intense pressure from his family to have Morande locked up for good. At the end of January 1768, Louis yields and sends a power of attorney to Juliot, instructing him to apply for a new *lettre de cachet*. This time, Louis Théveneau suggests that Morande should be imprisoned at Charenton, a prison for the insane, then sent into penal servitude *aux îles* [i.e. the West Indies].[48] However, nothing is done to execute the *lettre de cachet* for several months. Perhaps Louis is still reticent? Perhaps Juliot is waiting for an opportunity to ensure that it will be granted? Maybe it is shown to Morande and held over him as a threat? Or maybe the old regime bureaucracy just acted with characteristic slowness? Indeed, it might never have been enforced but for an *Opéra* girl known as Mademoiselle Danezy.

Like most *Opéra* girls, Danezy is a lady of easy virtue and extremely pretty. Originally from Lyon, she had married a certain Derigny, who was transported to the West Indies shortly thereafter. Forced back on her own resources, Danezy went to Paris where for two or three years she survived from her '*galanteries*'. She became the mistress of Monsieur Rollin, a wealthy tax farmer, whose fortune she consumed with her lover and pimp, the Chevalier Delamotte. Unfortunately, Delamotte was arrested, and Rollin, on learning of her inconstancy, abandoned her. Subsequently, she had a number of amorous adventures, and between lovers occasionally serviced clients *chez La Brissault*.[49]

Danezy first encounters Morande at a ball at the *Opéra* in about January 1768. They speak and she gives him her address. Soon, he is both her favoured lover and her pimp. She uses different names and has a succession of paying lovers, yet struggles financially. She sells off her furniture a piece at a time. When her dressmaker hires a bailiff to pursue her for a 55 *livre* debt, Morande promises to pay it, fearful that he will lose her. On 1 March he signs a paper to that effect. The bailiff, Desmoulins, calls frequently at Morande's house over the following weeks, but Morande always fobs him off with empty promises. Early in the morning on 8 April, Desmoulins calls once more, determined to collect the debt, but the servant tells him that Morande is not at home. He asks to leave a message. He is shown to the study. As he enters, he is ambushed. A frenzied Morande sets about him with a pair of heavy metal tongs. A visitor intervenes to protect his head, but Morande continues to beat Desmoulins across both legs. Desmoulins escapes and immediately writes to ask Sartine's assistance.[50]

Soon afterwards Danezy flees her appartment in the *rue Saint-Florentin* and takes up lodgings near the Palais Royal. Morande accuses an older woman, Madame de Clermont-Arnoul, an architect's wife, of turning Danezy against him. He becomes aggressive. Madame de Clermont-Arnoul says she will report him to the police and warns him never to approach Danezy again. Morande writes to the police himself, denouncing Madame de Clermont-Arnoul as a malicious and dishonest old procuress who arranges 'intrigues' for 'women who do not give their names'.[51] He threatens to denounce her to her husband and the wider world unless she stops bad-mouthing him. He turns up at her house and creates a disturbance.[52] Is this just a dispute between pimps for control of *la Danezy*? Not according to the lady herself, who complains of his obsessive behaviour.

Danezy grows more and more alarmed. She recruits friends and relatives to solicit protection from the most powerful official in her home province, Jacques de Flesselles, the Intendant of Lyon, who is in Paris. He responds positively, perhaps motivated initially by revenge: Morande is said to have seduced Flesselles' mistress Mademoiselle Cressy.[53] On 12 May, Flesselles writes to Sartine asking for Morande to be banned from Danezy's house. Inspector Marais speculates that Flesselles fancies her for himself. It is certainly strange that he should trouble himself for a woman of her reputation. Flesselles provides Danezy with a little house and garden near the *barrière de Mousseau*. It appears that she has become his mistress.[54]

Somehow, Morande discovers Danezy's refuge. On 22 May he scales her garden wall and begins shouting for her. Perhaps he hopes to win her back: his memoirs claim he wished to rescue her from Flesselles' custody. Danezy shuts herself up in the house. Morande gives up and departs. Two days later, early in the morning, he returns and forces his way past her doorman. He storms up the stairs to her bedroom 'like a madman' but she barricades herself inside. She is terrified that he will break down her door. In desperation Danezy threatens to go to the Lieutenant of Police. Morande replies that he has already written to Sartine himself. His bluff frightens Danezy, but her threats calm him and he leaves. At once, Danezy scribbles a semi-literate account of events and sends it to the police chief. The following day, Sartine commands that provisional orders be drawn up for Morande's arrest.[55]

Although Saint-Florentin signs the order to arrest Morande on 27 May, he is not picked up for nearly a month. The delay apparently stemmed from a technicality: before they can act the police want the original of Louis Théveneau's request for a *lettre de cachet* and to know where he wishes Morande to be gaoled. The last consideration is a serious one: as the family has solicited his imprisonment, they will bear the costs. In the interim, Morande realizes something is afoot and desperately attempts to forestall punishment by intimidation. He calls on Juliot, whom he suspects is his father's informant, and threatens to 'wash his hands in his blood'. Inspector Marais learns of the incident and takes pre-emptive action, even though Louis Théveneau's wishes are not yet known. On 25 June, he arrests Morande and takes him to Fort l'Évêque, where he is held 'in secret', in a fourth-floor cell with just a bed and a window smaller than a fist.[56] As far as his associates and creditors are aware, Morande has simply disappeared. But he is not prepared to vanish quietly.

By 6 July, the prison concierge, Duvergé, has had enough. He is weary of Morande's incessant shouting and alarmed by the crowds that gather daily outside the prison, drawn by the commotion. He decides he must speak to the prisoner to discover what is going on. Accompanied by a turnkey, he climbs the long winding staircase to the fourth floor and unlocks the door. As they enter they spot a suspicious bulge beneath the prisoner's trousers. Morande refuses to explain what he is concealing, but after a brief struggle several fragments of paper covered in writing tumble from his breeches. Mystified, his gaolers search his room. In his bed they discover a rope made of shreds of blanket two inches wide and long enough to reach the ground. Morande has been using it to smuggle messages in and out of the prison via his window.[57] The Duke de Bethune probably learned of his imprisonment by this means, for he has already written to Sartine petitioning for Morande's release.[58]

Morande is now transferred to an isolation cell, where he can cause no further problems. However, several days later Louis Théveneau requests that he be held in the monastery of Armentières, or any other similarly priced prison where he can be prevented from communicating with other prisoners. Morande is duly transferred to Armentières on 22 July, together with instructions that he be closely watched.[59]

Such surveillance proves unnecessary. Morande has realized that his liberty depends on his ability to convince the Superior, his family and the Lieutenant of Police that he is a reformed character. He writes to Sartine protesting that his crimes have been magnified by his enemies. He also asks permission to write – without giving his whereabouts – to reassure his creditors and to appoint someone to look after his financial affairs. Sartine, who has been receiving letters from Morande's creditors almost daily, readily agrees.[60] Inside the monastery, Morande's behaviour remains exemplary over many months. His family are informed and Louis Théveneau, always indulgently optimistic, relents and requests his son's release. However, the final decision rests with Sartine.

On 4 May 1769, Bernard Croquison, the Superior at Armentières, writes to Sartine to inform him of Morande's reformation, enclosing a letter from Morande. It expresses sincere repentance and promises he will mend his ways. Sartine, who sees many petty crooks, needs to be reminded of the details of Morande's case.[61] However, he soon learns of more pressing reasons to release him: Morande's health is deteriorating rapidly. He is unlikely to survive if he is confined much longer and needs to convalesce in the open air. Sartine responds quickly: on 7 June he asks Saint-Florentin to order Morande's release. Five weeks later Morande is free.[62]

When he feels well enough, Morande writes to thank Sartine and repeats his promises of good behaviour. Nevertheless, on 3 August Sartine orders that Morande should leave Paris. Morande responds with a request to stay, arguing that he must remain to clear his remaining debts, which total 22,000 *livres*. His presence is essential because La Saule, who has already paid off 30,000 *livres* for him, has given him a stake in several enterprises and agreed to act as his guarantor. In return, he wants Morande to manage several of his business interests. By these means Morande expects to clear his debts within three years. Morande's letter supplies names and details so that Sartine can verify his story. After quizzing Morande and conferring with Marais, who presumably confirmed some of Morande's claims, Sartine grants his wish.[63] Morande's relationship with La Saule cools rapidly thereafter. There is no evidence that he took up La Saule's offer, which was doubtless just a ruse to keep Morande near to him, and La Saule's name disappears from Morande's correspondence.

Within three months, Morande is up to his old tricks. He slips into the home of a rich lawyer, Monsieur de Bignicourt, and extorts a loan of 60 *livres* from the terrified magistrate. He gives a false address and, when Bignicourt starts making enquiries, sends him threatening letters. The police are informed and Sartine approaches Saint-Florentin again, but somehow Morande is not arrested.[64] He is not so lucky the following May, when the Count de Narbens approaches Sartine for help retrieving money he has lent Morande. Narbens gives Sartine worrying intelligence: Morande is gambling in the Venetian and Danish embassies every evening. This raises questions about what else he is up to and Sartine immediately orders his arrest as a 'bad subject'.[65] Inspector Marais finds Morande at Versailles in the *Grand Common*, a barracks for palace servants. Morande, forewarned, warns Marais that he is armed and will not be taken. He runs off and Marais gives chase. Marais is short of breath and heavy. Morande, fleet of foot, soon outpaces him.[66]

Morande suspects the game is up. The next day he sets out through Champagne for Liège, then an independent archbishopric. From there he travels to Brussels and Ostend, where he embarks on a ship for England. He will not set foot in France again for 21 years.[67]

2

The Armour-Plated Gazetteer

Morande was intoxicated by London, which he found 'the most fascinating and dangerous place in the whole universe'.[1] When he arrived, he intended to stay in England only for a short while, but exposure to the British capital soon changed his mind.[2] Britain was, Morande wrote approvingly, 'a land where the great are but the equals of the least citizen, where the prince is the first observer of the laws, and one can speak without fear of all the powers of the earth'.[3] He could reinvent himself there as a victim of French ministerial persecution. He therefore claimed that he fled to Britain to avoid a *lettre de cachet*, having written an ode denouncing the tyranny and inhumanity of the Count de Saint-Florentin, who had just received the title Duke de La Vrillière.[4] This was a tale well calculated to appeal to British prejudices concerning their own liberties and French despotism.

London in 1770 was a bustling commercial metropolis, the largest city in Europe, home to around 850,000 people. Britain's capital had grown rapidly across the previous century in tandem with her global mercantile empire, and was now the emporium of the world. Into the docks to the east of the city sailed ships laden with tea, coffee, textiles, porcelain, lacquerware and spices from Asia and the East Indies; sugar, tobacco and raw cotton from the Americas; timber and naval supplies from Russia and the Baltic; fish from the North Sea and North Atlantic; wines and manufactured goods from Europe. Underpinning this prosperity was the might of the Royal Navy and the East India Company and the most sophisticated banking system and financial exchanges in the world. Crucially, too, the British landed interests were partners of the merchants, and freely invested in East India Company stocks, mercantile fleets and colonial estates. The profits from these ventures funded the aristocracy's frenzied building of great country houses and the purchase of elegant new residences in the freshly laid out squares of London's West End.

London was vibrant culturally, too, with theatres, pleasure gardens, lending libraries, society rooms and hundreds of coffee houses. It had the freeest and most extensive daily press in Europe and a publishing industry free from the censorship that was pervasive on the continent. It was also cosmopolitan enough to have businesses that catered specifically for foreigners, such as the Spring Gardens and Orange Coffee houses, where French exiles gathered. The entrepreneur John Boosey had recently established a lending library of works in French, German and other European languages; and several book shops and publishers also catered for a French-speaking clientele.[5]

The biggest culture shock facing a French visitor was not the sheer size and economic vibrancy of London, but the political freedom its inhabitants enjoyed. Lacking an effective police force, the city seemed anarchic to foreign observers. The coffee houses, taverns, theatres, gambling dens and brothels were not crawling with spies. There was a representative system of government, elected on an uneven franchise it is true, but which nevertheless could be said to reflect the various economic interests in the country. Britain also had the law of *habeas corpus*, which prevented prisoners' being held without a stated charge. Most important of all, Britain had liberty of speech and expression. Morande approved of many of these liberties, which he studied and exploited to his own ends.

Morande found lodgings with Jane Rowe, the widow of a lawyer named Charles Sinclair. She had a teenage daughter, Elizabeth, known as Eliza, who very quickly caught the debauchee's eye. The polished, sophisticated Frenchman soon captivated Eliza, and before long, as the Chevalier d'Eon puts it, the teenage English rose and the French libertine 'were both making and unmaking his bed' together. Within a year of Morande's arrival the couple married in the Parish Church of Saint-George, Hanover Square and set up house in Half-Moon Street off Piccadilly.[6] The bride, not yet 20, fell pregnant within days of the ceremony. She gave birth to a son, George-Louis Théveneau, on 21 January 1772. Two other children, Elizabeth-Nicolette and Harriet Hannah, known in French sources as Henriette-Anne, who were born on 21 February 1779 and 1 September 1780 respectively, also survived to adulthood. At least four more died in early infancy.[7]

Eliza Morande was a kind, charming and quietly courageous woman, who inspired lasting admiration, deep devotion and not a little sympathy in the hard-nosed *politiques* Beaumarchais and d'Eon. Unfortunately, our only detailed description of her comes from César Lavirotte and dates from the 1790s, when she was about 40 years old. It reveals that Eliza was 'a little stout; with an artless countenance; remarkable for her extreme gentleness, patience and resignation without limit, and the deepest devotion to her husband, before whom she always seemed lost in admiration.[8] Eliza herself described her husband as 'the man to whom I cling by the bonds of duty and affection', and even the brutish Morande conceded that she was 'a virtuous wife'.[9] Francy's observation that she had 'a very feeble heart and mind' therefore seems rather uncharitable.[10]

The marriage of Morande and Eliza was a genuine love match, and for several years the French *roué* was tamed by his 'virtuous wife'. During the early years of their marriage, d'Eon, who socialized with them, assured the Count de Broglie that Morande loved his wife deeply, and wits joked that 'Monsieur de Morande is a husband of a rare stamp, in that the only wife of whom he ever speaks well is his own.'[11] Morande could indeed play the caring husband and devoted father.

On one occasion he was so anxious about his wife's health that he declared that her latest pregnancy would be her last. Only later would Eliza learn what a brutal man she had married. Hints of Morande's violence towards her arise by degrees. In 1774, he jokes that d'Eon may beat his wife. By 1776, albeit in a challenge, d'Eon suggests that things have gone further, writing of his pity for Eliza Morande 'in being married to so corrupt, hot headed and violent a man, who nevertheless is only terrible to women and children'.[12] While it was considered acceptable in eighteenth-century England for a man to chastise his spouse, Morande apparently went too far.

By the mid 1770s, Morande had probably reverted to his libertine habits, although our only evidence is colourful slurs by his enemies. D'Eon told the uxorious and straight-laced Count de Vergennes, who served as French foreign minister from 1774 to 1787, that Morande had in a single month fathered children by his wife, his two domestic servants and several neighbours. Moreover, whenever Beaumarchais was in London, he and Morande frequented the brothels of Covent Garden three times a week and hired streetwalkers to dance naked and serve their pleasures. This, d'Eon asserted, was public knowledge in London, and he named witnesses to the facts.[13] D'Eon's claims concerning Beaumarchais may well be malicious falsehoods, but his are not the only tales of Morande's infidelities.[14]

Several years later, the scandalmonger Anne-Gédeon La Fite de Pelleport alleged that Morande had met a certain Madame Maurice, a comely French *marchande de modes*, in a London brothel where she had called to sell ribbons and other fashionable trinkets. Finding her pleasing, Morande promised her a house in the country and a 50 guinea down payment if she would become his mistress. As this was more money than her husband, a mere clerk, would earn in a year, she succumbed to Morande's solicitations and he debauched her on the spot. His lust sated, Morande took his conquest into the city in his carriage, promising to collect her money from his bank. Instead, he set her down and abandoned her. Thereafter, through sheer malice, he set out to frame her cuckolded husband, implicating him in the production of pamphlets against the French monarchy.[15]

Such tales blur with fiction, another genre that features Morande. The sexually liberated heroine of the libertine novel *Julie philosophe* (1791) seeks Morande out and surrenders herself to him while he tries to procure a rich lord as her lover. Predictably, the lord never appears and Morande abandons her after borrowing her last remaining jewels.[16] Likewise, in his allegorical novel *Les Bohémiens* (1790), Pelleport depicts the villainous Mordanes – who is clearly based on Morande – attempting to rape Félicité, the newly pregnant wife of the feckless *philosophe* Bissot (who is intended to represent Jacques-Pierre Brissot). Unable to resist Morande's strength, she diverts his attentions away from her vulva to her anus, and thus protects her husband's claim to be father of her unborn child. In a particularly malicious twist, Pelleport implies that Felicité actually enjoys being sodomized. Being forcibly debauched by the libertine Mordanes is more satisfying than sex with her husband. Pelleport's main target here is clearly Brissot rather than Morande.[17]

By the early 1780s, Morande's mistreatment of Eliza, aggravated by the stress of his financial problems, had become almost intolerable. In 1783, when she travelled to France without him, Eliza contemplated abandoning him altogether. As she mulled over her decision, she extended her stay by several months, aided by Beaumarchais, who gave her a small monthly allowance. However, when Morande persuaded Beaumarchais to intercede with her and promised a moral reformation, she began to waver. In a heartfelt letter to Beaumarchais, she poured out her despair and sad experience of marriage:

> You counsel me, Monsieur, to make another attempt [at reconciliation]. I resign myself to it. I dare not hope for a happy outcome . . . but I am disposed to sacrifice myself to the tranquillity of those whose interests I hold dear. All my wishes would be fulfilled if my return to a man who was once very dear to me could only contain him and prevent all the horrors which I have suffered, but twelve years of the most cruel experience lead me to doubt the change of which you assure me.[18]

Nevertheless, she did not return home at once. Instead she travelled to Burgundy to see her brother-in-law, Francy, who reported: 'Ever since the question of her return to England arose, she has wasted away visibly; and she appears to fear the impending reunion more than death itself'.[19]

After months of prevaricating, Eliza finally returned to London in April 1784. She arrived in such poor health that Morande seems to have taken to heart Francy and Beaumarchais' strictures that 'he should nurture her feelings if he wished to keep her'.[20] His sentiments on Eliza's return seem to have been dictated by fear of losing her, and perhaps even genuine remorse:

> I am really worried that in the state she is in I will be unable to save her; I froze when I saw her and could think of nothing but my own sins; hers do not stem from a bad heart and it was weakness of mind that made her take the unfortunate route that made me lose my senses and commit so many stupidities. I have been sufficiently punished. No man ever passed eighteen months in a state comparable to me.[21]

This was as close as Morande ever came to a genuine apology, but the reconciliation was permanent. Eliza remained alongside her husband for the rest of his life and accepted her lot without complaint. There are no more hints of impending separation or spousal brutality. Perhaps, faced with her loss, Morande really did mend his ways. Certainly Eliza was more to him than an emotional crutch: she also often served as his agent and provided leverage in his dealings with his family, Beaumarchais and others. When begging money or favours, he frequently tried to evoke sympathy for Eliza and his children. Beaumarchais implies that Eliza also became a reliable advisor and confidante to her husband, as well as a moderating influence: 'It is she, my dear fellow,' – he assured Morande in 1788 – 'who saves you from very real evils in this world and damnation in the next'.[22] Perhaps, then, Lavirotte read their relationship correctly when he noted Eliza's admiration and devotion towards her husband. Or perhaps her cowed behaviour was that of a psychologically crushed and severely battered wife?

Morande arrived in London ignorant of the country's language, laws and culture. He also lacked contacts and, in all likelihood, funds. He therefore found himself, as he puts it, 'exposed to make bad acquaintances, like any man who moves country without knowledge of the places he is going to live'.[23] How he survived the early months of his exile, while learning the local language and customs, is not entirely clear, but his enemies allege that 'he earned a few guineas from secret liaisons with clapped out aristocratic *roués* who had renounced women'.[24] Having infiltrated this debauched homosexual subculture, he turned on his clients and threatened to expose them. Since sodomy was a hanging offence, this might conceivably result in their execution. Such blackmail leaves little trace, so the truth will probably never be known. However, the allegation fully fits with what we know of his character. He probably had homosexual inclinations; blackmail and extortion were his stock-in-trade; and he was intimately familiar with the worlds of vice and prostitution.

Morande also tried to tap into London's Burgundian networks. One of his first targets was the Chevalier d'Eon. D'Eon was a magnet for French refugees, and with good reason, for he was the most notorious renegade in London. He had arrived there as a diplomatic envoy towards the end of the Seven Years' War, with orders to assist the Duke de Nivernais in negotiating peace. Once a treaty was signed, d'Eon stayed on as minister plenipotentiary awaiting the appointment of a new ambassador. Although he came from the lowest ranks of the nobility, d'Eon harboured hopes that he would be given the post. Such hopes were entirely unrealistic. Instead, the honour was given to the Count de Guerchy, an aristocrat with no diplomatic experience whose sole qualifications for the job were his title and his friendship with the foreign minister, the Duke de Praslin. D'Eon was expected to stay on as Guerchy's secretary and, as was customary, to find a property to serve as his embassy.

D'Eon took this humiliation badly. Even before Guerchy reached London, the pair were arguing about the sums d'Eon had spent on the ambassadorial residence. Once Guerchy arrived, matters deteriorated rapidly, as d'Eon refused to obey a letter of recall and began demanding reimbursement of monies he claimed to have expended in the service of France. From October 1763 the dispute took a spectacular turn as d'Eon published allegations that Guerchy had tried to poison him. In March 1764, he went further still and published a selection of his diplomatic papers, which heaped ridicule on Guerchy and his allies in France. This was a breach of protocol verging on treason, for foreign policy was considered 'the king's secret'. Educated Europeans had never seen documents like these, and many were deeply scandalized by d'Eon's actions.[25]

D'Eon's behaviour, while idiosyncratic, was not without a rationale. In effect, he was sending the French government a coded warning of what to expect if they did not meet his financial demands. For among the papers that d'Eon did not publish was a brief note in Louis XV's handwriting ordering him to spy out potential invasion routes between the South Coast and London. This secret order showed that even while making peace, the French were preparing an attack on Britain. If it were published, it might both damage Louis XV's diplomatic credibility and provoke Britain to launch a pre-emptive attack on a recently defeated France. Moreover, d'Eon had only received the order because he was party to a further secret. D'Eon was a member of a clandestine espionage and diplomatic network known as *Le Secret du Roi* [The King's Secret], which had for decades been pursuing a secret policy diametrically opposed to that of the Foreign Ministry. At the very moment that d'Eon went renegade, Louis XV was attempting to dismantle the *Secret* and pension off its agents and orchestrator, d'Eon's patron, the Count de Broglie. It was not unnatural therefore for d'Eon to fear abandonment.

D'Eon's battle with Guerchy spread from pamphlets into the English courts. In October 1764, d'Eon's claims gained sensational support when Pierre-Henri Treyssac de Vergy offered sworn testimony that he had been involved with Guerchy in a conspiracy against d'Eon. In consequence, a Grand Jury at the Old Bailey lodged a bill of indictment against Guerchy for hiring Vergy to 'kill and assassinate d'Eon'.[26] Such an allegation against an ambassador was deeply embarrassing to the British government, who ensured that the case remained in limbo. In retaliation, the ambassador brought and won a criminal libel suit against d'Eon, who wisely failed to turn up for sentencing. Instead, he went into hiding in Byfleet in Surrey, where he spent a year disguised as a woman under the alias of Madame Duval.[27] He only re-emerged when Guerchy was recalled in 1767. By that time he had been completely vindicated. The indictment against Guerchy was still active; the reality of the plot was broadly accepted; and in 1766 a French agent paid d'Eon to surrender his secret papers.

These events made d'Eon the darling of British opposition politicians and something of a celebrity, having apparently overcome attempts of despotic French ministers to kidnap, murder or otherwise silence him. He thus had much in common with the British radical politician John Wilkes, who in the mid 1760s faced libel prosecutions, expulsion from Parliament and arbitrary arrest by 'general warrant'. Forced to flee into exile, Wilkes eventually emerged triumphant and secured the abolition of general warrants. Not surprisingly, British opposition MPs were quick to draw parallels between the two renegade heroes, who became friends and allies. But they also courted d'Eon because they erroneously believed that his papers might prove that French agents had bribed British ministers into agreeing a lenient peace settlement during the peace treaty negotiations. Thus opposition politicians made overtures to buy his papers and organized mobs to rally to his defence or stone Guerchy's carriage.[28]

By the time Morande arrived in London, d'Eon was also starting to attract attention for another reason. Rumours had begun to circulate that he was really a woman. At first few people believed them, but gradually the idea began to take off. Eighteenth-century Englishmen would gamble on anything, and the possibility that d'Eon was female seemed sufficiently credible that a few reckless souls were prepared to wager money on it. However, such gambling was technically illegal and so had to be carried out by means of insurance policies on the chevalier's sex. The earliest known policies were taken out in March 1770 at a rate of 10:1 against d'Eon being a woman. By June the odds were much shorter and some speculators had already made considerable sums playing the changing prices.[29] However, for as long as d'Eon kept quiet about his sex, no one was likely to collect on the original policies. A number of unscrupulous individuals therefore tried to persuade or force d'Eon to reveal his secret, either publicly so that they could collect their winnings, or privately, so that they could corner the market, which was rumoured to be worth over £100,000. From the very start of their friendship, this was probably what Morande had in mind.

Morande courted d'Eon assiduously, sending him numerous letters and calling frequently at his house.[30] D'Eon tried to keep him at a distance, but found this impossible. His account of their relationship, which he sent to the Count de Broglie makes instructive reading:

Monsieur de Morande is my countryman and boasts here that he is related by marriage with part of my family in Burgundy. As soon as he came here . . . the first thing he did was to write to me that he was arrived, that he was an officer in the Carabiniers . . . and that he desired to see and befriend me. For two months I refused him my acquaintance. Since that time he has knocked on my door so often and so tormented me with his letters, that I let him enter my home from time to time in order that I do not turn him against me. He is a young man with a good heart in many respects, but one of the most turbulent and impetuous of minds, who knows neither limits, nor measures, nor ranks, nor dignities, nor sacred, nor profane when he is in the effervescence of his writing, which resembles a fever. His actions are generally good when he follows the natural inclinations of his heart, but the particularities of his speech and his writings and even his gestures are always satirical and reprehensible when he listens only to his wit, his head and the vengeance to which he is given. He would already have faced transportation or prison, if I had not counselled him on how to avoid it . . . He is a very imprudent and very dangerous subject . . . it is for that reason that I hold him in reins a certain distance from me, without either breaking off or allying myself with him too closely, despite all his efforts to persuade the credulous of our friendship.[31]

In this summary, d'Eon is attempting the impossible. He wishes to suggest to Broglie that he is the perfect person to deal with Morande, yet deny a culpably close friendship with him. The result is a stunningly frank exposé of their relationship. The same letter explains that d'Eon is the only well-known French expatriate in London to have escaped Morande's bitter satire:

doubtless because I have always sought to oblige him and give him good advice, which he has scarcely heeded, and because he knows by example that I am not of a patient disposition and that, if he attacks me, I will not rely on litigation as my means of defence. Over two years ago he asked me for an explanation of the tone I adopted towards him, because I did not wish to receive him as often as he desired . . . I gave him this explanation immediately. He . . . made his excuses and asked me to burn his letter. I did so at once, being as easily appeased as irritated. Since then he has not ceased to speak highly of both me and my family. I allow him to do so without paying much attention to his praises or his stupidities. I continue only to allow him to enter my home once or twice for every ten of his importunings.[32]

There is little doubt that d'Eon found his charismatic young compatriot intriguing and entertaining company, yet dangerous and unreliable. Likewise, Morande sensed that d'Eon would make a useful friend and dangerous enemy.

Morande's letters to d'Eon were a seductive mixture of requests for interviews, news, amusing poems and anecdotes and scandalous gossip, many of which were calculated to appeal to d'Eon personally. Like most well-educated French noblemen of his generation, d'Eon had been brought up to prize wit above almost any other quality. He particularly loved humorous or scandalous anecdotes, word plays, *double-entendres* and especially puns, however bad. These Morande was more than happy to supply. For example, one of his earliest letters contains a poem ridiculing d'Eon's old enemy, Guerchy, and satirizing virginity, another of d'Eon's obsessions. It also offers a characteristic, if laboured, swipe at the continence of French aristocratic ladies:

I don't know whether fruits grafted legitimately are better, but it is certain that the same trunk frequently bears pears and apples . . . This miracle sometimes extends to ten different varieties according to the agronomist Patixillo [sic?]. We have several duchesses who without being able to read are as enlightened as him by practical experience.[33]

However, d'Eon soon discovered that Morande was writing up his scandalous anecdotes and titillating gossip into *nouvelles à la main* [manuscript newsletters] and reading them aloud at gatherings in private homes around London. His hosts included aristocrats and confidants of George III, whom he amused at the expense of the French, but it is unlikely that Morande was merely singing for his supper.[34] He was probably running a commercial operation and selling regular instalments to a select clientele on the continent by post, especially as his correspondence with Paris and Versailles involved high costs and considerable risks, particularly for his informants. Several writers and newsmongers in Paris and abroad supported themselves like this, providing exclusive uncensored news by subscription to wealthy clients. However, clandestine *nouvelles à la main* were not always what they seemed, for the Paris police kept a keen watch on known *nouvellistes* and frightened them into imposing a rigorous self-censorship. Morande's newsletter, produced in London with the assistance of unknown correspondents, was hence far freer than most. When Morande showed d'Eon drafts of one of his manuscripts, he was horrified and spent two days trying to persuade Morande to burn them, warning of the potentially 'fatal' consequences of his 'unbridled licence . . . in speaking so unworthily about the person of our August King'.[35]

Despite his reservations, d'Eon was unable to resist the occasional pleasure of Morande's company. Besides, in his role as a French agent, he probably felt it would be more useful to watch Morande closely than to ignore him, although it is suggestive that he did not report on Morande's activities until ordered to do so. Over several years he did Morande small services, inviting him to lavish dinners, exchanging cooks and servants, and lending him books from his extensive personal library. D'Eon probably also introduced Morande to key figures in British society, particularly opposition politicians, and to a Burgundian *grande dame*, the Countess de Courcelle and her husband. If so, he played a decisive role in shaping Morande's career.

The Courcelles had been settled in England for several years, and the family were on intimate terms with d'Eon, who dined with them almost every day. The Count de Courcelle, a French army officer, probably got to know London while on parole as a prisoner of war and decided to stay on after the peace, whereupon his wife and four children joined him. The countess even dreamed that d'Eon might marry her daughter, Constance. Indeed, she seemed to think that he had agreed to do so.[36] In return, she and her husband volunteered to serve as d'Eon's agents at the French court.

The Courcelles originally rented a large house in Petty France, close to the Queen's Palace. However, by early 1771 they were living in straitened circumstances, first in a second floor apartment in Suffolk Street, and thereafter in the Warwick Street home of Joseph de Vignoles, the defrocked priest who headed d'Eon's masonic lodge and became his secretary. All was not as it seemed, however, for Courcelle was an intriguer and had probably lost a fortune on the stock market as a result of dodgy insider information supplied by the French ambassador's secretary, Barthélemy Tort. In 1770, Tort was paid substantial sums by corrupt investors to divulge diplomatic secrets at a moment when the British and Spanish governments were at loggerheads over the Falkland Islands. Unfortunately, he failed to predict the French mediation that resolved the crisis, and the investors lost a fortune. Courcelle appears to have been among those who got burned.[37] By the time Morande met them, the Courcelles were living beyond their means and struggling to keep up appearances. They ran up vast bills on wine, pawned jewels, and had increasing difficulties raising loans and cashing letters of credit. Some of their activities were bordering on the criminal.

In Morande's case, the Courcelles incited near treason. In their home, Morande read out his *nouvelles à la main* to a dozen friends and fellow exiles. According to Morande, the Count de Courcelle, a skilled manipulator of people, incited him to express his resentment towards France and the 'persecutions' he had suffered there in ever stronger language. Courcelle then went further, suggesting that Morande's anecdotes deserved to be printed, and encouraged others of the company to contribute material. This, according to Morande, was the origin of his notorious *Gazetier cuirassé*, which was conceived, written, copied, printed and published within 17 days.[38]

Thus, if Morande may be believed, five or six people collaborated in the writing of the *Gazetier cuirassé*. The tenor, if not the detail, of Morande's claim is supported by no less a person than the French ambassador, the Count d'Adhémar. In June 1783, d'Adhémar told Vergennes that 'according to the details and many proofs he [Morande] supplied, his book is in truth less his own work than that of a class of persons whose correspondence with this wretch is criminal by nature'.[39] According to d'Adhémar's underling, the Count de Moustier, these 'criminal correspondents' supplied Morande with materials so that he could attack the Duke d'Aiguillon, France's foreign minister from 1771 to 1774, under the pretext of writing against the du Barrys.[40] D'Eon, too, implies that Morande's work became more extreme in the editing process, though admittedly he wished to dispel suspicions of his own involvement. He claims that between early drafts and the final version, the *Gazetier* 'was enlarged by more than one-half, particularly with insults to the King which were not in the early sheets brought to my house'.[41] Pelleport adds that much of Morande's raw material came from the Countess de Courcelle, who reputedly continued to send him intelligence from Versailles for many years after her return to France in September 1771.[42] Nevertheless, Morande undoubtedly bore primary responsibility for compiling, editing, printing and publishing the pamphlet, which he peddled around the homes of the British aristocracy for a guinea per copy. This was an astronomical price for a pamphlet and allegedly Morande earned £800 by this means alone.

Nor did *Gazetier*'s success end there. Between July 1771 and 1785, it went through at least five editions, making it one of the most successful clandestine works of the era.[43]

Morande's pamphleteering debut came at an opportune moment, for France had just plunged headlong into her most serious political crisis in over a century. The so-called Maupeou crisis stemmed from the accession of a new ministry and the resulting change in government policy towards the *parlements*. For most of the 1760s, France's *de facto* chief minister Choiseul had sought the acquiescence of the *parlements* to a policy of reconstruction following the Seven Years' War. Hence Choiseul forged a tacit partnership with the *parlements* and did nothing to prevent their dissolving the Jesuits in 1764. However, the *parlements*' triumph proved short-lived, and by the late 1760s Choiseul's grip on power was weakening. This was largely due to the emergence of Madame du Barry, who formed an unholy alliance with the pro-Jesuit '*dévot*' party and resented Choiseul's open enmity and attempts to place his sister in the king's bed. Hence, du Barry allied herself closely with Choiseul's enemies at court, in particular the Chancellor, René-Charles-Augustin de Maupeou; the finance minister Abbé Joseph-Marie Terray; and d'Aiguillon. After Choiseul was dismissed from the ministry by Louis XV in December 1770, power passed into the hands of this triumvirate, which was united primarily by opportunism and self-interest and had powerful motives to crush the *parlements*. Maupeou hoped it would fortify his place in the ministry; Terray wanted to force through radical financial reforms; and d'Aiguillon sought to avenge himself on the Breton and Paris *Parlements*, which had tried to impeach him while he was governor of Brittany in the 1760s.

Once Choiseul was out of the way, Maupeou felt strong enough to strike. In January 1771 he set about remodelling the Paris *Parlement* and sent dozens of its magistrates into internal exile. This measure resulted in a wave of remonstrances from the remaining *parlements*, several of which were now reformed or abolished; retaliatory judicial strikes; and a flurry of oppositional pamphleteering on a scale unseen since the Fronde rebellions of the mid seventeenth century. This in turn provoked an official clampdown on the unauthorized publication both inside and outside France of news concerning the *parlements*' resistance.

Although newspapers produced inside France were heavily censored, French subjects could follow the developing crisis and read about the *parlements*' protests during the early months of 1771 in the international French-language gazettes produced in the Netherlands, Germany and Avignon, then a Papal territory. As long as they did not offend the government, these gazettes were usually permitted to circulate inside France, where they were highly valued and accounted for about a third of all newspaper sales. However, by late March, after a concerted diplomatic offensive and threats of exclusion from the lucrative French market, even these beacons of eighteenth-century journalistic liberty had resorted to rigorous

Plate 2. Chancellor Maupeou. Contemporary engraving. Courtesy of the Brotherton Collection, Brotherton Library, University of Leeds.

self-censorship. As a result, political news was at a premium and rumour rife. Not for nothing did Morande call his pamphlet *The Armour-Plated Gazetteer*.[44]

Maupeou's attempts at reform proved explosive because of the pretensions of the *parlements* and their role in French political life. As well as serving as the highest courts of appeal, the 13 *parlements* also had to consent to and register royal edicts, including those establishing new taxes, before they could become law. In practice this power was relatively limited, because the monarch had considerable coercive measures to ensure the *parlements'* eventual compliance. In particular, the king could call a royal session or *lit de justice*, at which he would order the registration of an edict. If that failed, the king could exile or arrest truculent magistrates by *lettres de cachet* until they changed their minds.

Nevertheless, the power to enregister edicts made the *parlements* the only real institutional check on the power of the king and his ministers and, because they also had a right of remonstrance, the only forum for quasi-legitimate opposition. Thus the decades preceding the Maupeou crisis witnessed a series of clashes between the *parlements* and royal authority.

Over the course of the eighteenth century the *parlements* had begun to adopt the language of representative government in their struggles with the Crown. Although the *parlementaires* held their positions by purchase or hereditary right, they began to claim to represent the French people and to embody 'public opinion', a new and amorphous concept with growing political resonance. For the king and his agents these pretentions represented dangerous attempts to constrain their freedom of action. However, for many French subjects, the purging and silencing of the *parlementaires'* opposition overthrew the accepted political balance, which many considered tantamount to an unwritten constitution. This offered proof that there was no institutional body in France capable of checking unbridled royal or ministerial despotism. In the ensuing furore, the supporters of the *parlements*, or patriot party, portrayed themselves as the representatives and defenders of the people in the face of unaccountable absolutist power and ministerial tyranny. Among the many pamphlets denouncing the burgeoning ministerial despotism, the *Gazetier cuirassé* was undoubtedly the most virulent.

The *Gazetier cuirassé* was Morande's masterpiece. It offered a heady mixture of pithy invective, informational soundbites and political satire, together with scurrillous gossip, innuendo and sexual defamation. It was instantly recognized as a uniquely scandalous, toxic and dangerous pamphlet, and for many years its very title was a term of opprobrium. Voltaire, a partisan of Maupeou and enemy of the old *parlements*, who was then at the height of his literary and moral author-ity, spoke for many when he announced:

> There has just been published one of those works of darkness where everyone from the monarch to the least citizen is furiously insulted, where the most atrocious and absurd calumny distils a frightful poison over all that is respected and cherished.[45]

The *Mémoires secrets* announced in astonishment that Morande did not conceal his authorship of the pamphlet, since 'It is a work to disavow because of the dangers that the author runs in attacking the King himself, Madame the Countess du Barry, the Chancellor [Maupeou], the Duke d'Aiguillon, Mr Bourgeois de Boynes, the Abbé Terray, etc.' The Chevalier d'Eon found it so dangerous that he renounced all connection with Morande.[46]

French officials also reacted with horror on learning of the work. Alerting the Duke d'Aiguillon, the foreign minister, to the *Gazetier cuirassé*'s appearance, the royal censor Marin wrote:

A very reprehensible book entitled *The Armour-Plated Gazetteer or Scandalous Anecdotes of the Court of France* . . . has been printed in England. It is a rather thick volume in octavo divided into three parts and printed in large characters.[47] On the frontispiece [see plate 3] there is a print representing an armoured man seated on cannons and above a barrel [the satirical symbol for Madame du Barry], a Medusa's head bearing the initials of the Duke of La Vrillière, and a wigged head with the initials of the Chancellor [Maupeou]. The book is written in the style of a gazette and . . . contains horrors against the most respectable people and does not spare the King himself. This book sells at a guinea in London. Several Englishmen newly arrived here have brought copies . . . and there are perhaps three or four . . . circulating from hand to hand. As I have . . . more contacts than anyone, I have managed to read this audacious work that no-one wished to show me.

Such a work required an extraordinary response from the authorities, as Marin made clear:

I have alerted Mr Sartine who gave the most rigorous orders, but I imagine that we must not limit ourselves to police measures. This work is surely by a Frenchman and a man who has lived in good company and bad. I could well guess the author, but it is necessary to make sure of his identity and to punish his dreadful but criminal audacity in order to ensure his future silence. He does not spare your person and speaks of you in several places in a most reprehensible manner.

Marin recommended that the French ambassador in London should attempt to discover the book's author and that parcels and packetboats arriving from England be searched. The French ambassador in The Hague might also push for measures to prevent copies entering France via the Netherlands.[48]

Official vigilance paid dividends. The *Gazetier cuirassé* was among the works most often confiscated by the French police and Paris customs service across the next two decades.[49] Even beyond France, publishers and book dealers recognized it as supremely dangerous. In far-off Switzerland, rows occasioned by Samuel Fauche's marketing of the *Gazetier cuirassé* even led to the dissolution of his business partnership with the celebrated Typographical Society of Neuchâtel.[50]

It is easy to see why contemporaries saw the *Gazetier* as a uniquely reprehensible and daring text. Irreverent and libertine in tone, sacrilegious in content, and contemptuous in its irony, the *Gazetier* blasphemed against all the idols of French old regime society. The king, Roman Catholic Church, Christian faith, clergy, great lords and their ladies, the nobility, French army, courtiers and government ministers, the justice system, learned and cultural institutions: none were spared. To be sure, French enlightenment writers made frequent and effective use of light-hearted social satire, and many *philosophes* had long considered Catholicism fair game. But Morande's corrosive iconoclasm knew no limits. It presented his society's upper echelons as shot through with degeneracy, incompetence and sexual and political corruption.

The sheer range of Morande's attacks on the French elite and its most cherished institutions is breathtaking. When d'Eon produced an 'Alphabetical list containing the names of the Princes, Princesses, Lords, Ladies and other Persons, whom the sieur Théveneau de Morande has insulted and abused in his Infamous Libel entitled *The Gazetier cuirassé*', it enumerated no fewer than 256 individuals, groups or corporations. Alongside (and frequently beneath) political figures and leading courtiers, it features *Opéra* girls, courtesans and *femmes galantes*; leading members of the clergy; literary and cultural figures; lesser noblemen; army officers; and a host of sodomites and tribads (the contemporary term for lesbians).[51]

The Roman Catholic Church was near the top of Morande's hit list, and his assault was as political as it was sacrilegious. In a divine right monarchy, any attack on religion or the established Church undermined one of the main ideological and political supports of the monarchy. The bulk of Morande's attacks on religion were bawdy anti-clerical jokes about monks and nuns, priests and bishops, who are satirized as sexually licentious hypocrites who habitually break their vows of chastity. Sometimes his criticism is generalized and light-hearted. 'Fecundity has slipped into the convent of the Daughters of the Immaculate Conception, where the Holy Spirit worked ten miracles in a single night'; to prevent incest among the clergy, priests are 'to be permitted to take wives in order to spare their sisters'. Just whose wives is left ambiguous. Elsewhere Morande names individuals. A Chartreux monk has been discovered on his nightly visits to 'minister to' the Superior and Mistress of Novices of the Port Royal convent. The Abbé Grizel is a paedophile who abuses the confessional to blackmail young boys into sex. And the Bishop of Saint Brieux suffers from near permanent erections after a lady wounded him while he attempted to rape her.[52]

Morande insinuated that sexual corruption went to the very heart of the Church. Hence the French ambassador to Rome, Cardinal Bernis, had been 'naturalized as a Roman by Cardinals Pallavieino and Acciaioli, who treated him as an altarboy in a nocturnal assembly of the Sacred College'. As Morande's contemporaries called sodomy 'the Italian sin', his *double entendre* was transparent. Nor was the darker side of clerical pretensions forgotten. Hence Morande announced a forthcoming book of 'observations on the charlatanism of the Court of Rome, the bad faith of priests, the roguishness of monks, and the horrors of the inquisition'. As the Spanish Inquisition continued to root out supposed religious offenders throughout Morande's lifetime, this was a particularly damning angle of attack.[53]

The Church's alliance with the French state was also ridiculed. Morande challenged the Kings of France to produce the contract by which God had instituted the French monarchy. He also 'revealed' that Louis XV was searching for the confessor who would be easiest on his conscience. More sinisterly, he alleged that confessors were being recruited as police informants. This charge revived memories of the 'refusal of the sacraments' scandal of the 1750s, when the Archbishop of Paris had ordered that priests should only administer the last sacrament to persons able to produce a certificate testifying to their spiritual orthodoxy and, by implication, rejection of Jansenism.[54]

Morande does not limit himself to anti-clericalism and attacks on the Church's political role. He also mocks the human cost of delays in the administration of providential justice and slanders the Virgin Mary, whom he claims was descended from four prostitutes.[55] Shocking and repulsive though this blasphemy must have been to devout Christians, Morande's insinuations were not particularly original in either style or content. Indeed, freethinkers had been using the techniques of literary criticism to challenge fundamentalist Catholicism and the *Bible*'s historical accounts since the days of Pierre Bayle (1647–1706). The most brutal such critique, Voltaire's *Philosophical Dictionary*, had appeared in 1764. Moreover, the *Gazetier* was published at the height of the anti-Christian propaganda war waged by d'Holbach, whose materialist *Système de la nature* denied the existence of God and the soul. Both these works outsold the *Gazetier cuirassé*, and both presented a more systematic and corrosive challenge to religion. Lacking the subtlety and system of his more philosophic contemporaries, Morande's blasphemies are more shocking for their crudeness than their cogency.

Morande also tore into the nobility. Joke after joke, anecdote after anecdote stresses their sexual corruption and deviancy. To preserve family honour, he announces, incest is rife among Parisian aristocrats. Such inbreeding led to physical as well as moral degeneracy. Hence, aristocrats wishing to see a family resemblance in their children 'adopt the system of Rousseau and have them march on all fours'. This was also a fashionable swipe at Jean-Jacques Rousseau, whose insistence on the corrupting effects of civilization and the superiority of 'a state of nature' were widely derided as a call to return to an ape-like existence. Morande further suggests that the French nobility are so enfeebled by inbreeding, disease and homosexuality that their wives have to look elsewhere for sexual fulfilment and sires for their children. Hence 'robust fellows are beyond price' and 'a lackey starting out in Paris is as expensive as a racehorse in England'. Elsewhere, in a smutty *double-entendre*, he reports that a troop of skilled Savoyard chimney sweeps have arrived in Paris, much to the delight of the ladies of the court, who wish them to clear out the old '*croutes*' ['crusts' or 'fossils'] stuck in their 'flues' due to the 'feebleness of their French sweeps'. However, lackeys and Savoyards are not the only resources available to sexually frustrated ladies of quality. Such, indeed, was the inconstancy of aristocratic wives that an insurance company offering policies on their fidelity was charging premiums starting at 50 per cent and rising steeply for ladies with good looks or bad reputations.[56]

The *Gazetier* argued that many members of the aristocracy and clergy were useless as well as sexually corrupt. It suggested that contemplative monks would be better employed as soldiers and that monks, dervishes and Brahmins were all rogues. Likewise, the French officer corps, which was monopolized by wealthy aristocrats, was entirely incompetent.

> There are in France around 200 colonels – wrote Morande – of which 180 know how to dance and sing fashionable songs, about the same number wear lace and red heels [a fashion then associated with fops], and half at least know how to read and sign their names . . . not even four know the elements of their trade.

He went on to ridicule the performance of French generals in the Seven Years' War, particularly at Minden and Rossbach. Given that the nobility justified its social pre-eminence through its claim to be a military caste, these slurs had wider ramifications. In some ways they seem to prefigure the arguments of the Abbé Siéyès and subsequent revolutionary demagogues that the nobility were parasitic on the nation and should form no part of it. However, Morande's main point was that the army stood in need of meritocratic reform, or as he put it: 'in every country in the world military rank is the prize for talent or for brave actions; but there are corps in France where high rank arrives like white hairs. You only need to wait.'[57]

Contemporaries probably found Morande's disrespect for the monarch and his mistress even more shocking than his treatment of clergy and aristocracy. Much of the *Gazetier*'s most memorable material comprised scurrilous or satirically exaggerated allegations against Louis XV and his consort. Its raciest passages tell how Madame du Barry maintains her ascendancy over the king by a daily application of her amber douche and a sexual technique 'that is not made use of in respectable company'. Morande adds that the lost royal sceptre of France has been found in the boudoir 'of a pretty lady called "countess", who uses it to amuse her pussy', a *double-entendre* which works equally well in French as English. He further satirizes Madame du Barry's sexual career by 'reporting' that she is to be the Grand Mistress of a new Order of Saint Nicole. To qualify for membership, men need to have enjoyed her favours, while women need to have lived with at least ten different lovers. Naturally, this new order of chivalry will be much larger than the old Order of Saint Louis, which it replaces. Less pleasant was the symbolic tale of the discovery of 'an equestrian statue of one of our kings covered in ordure coming from a barrel which adorned him as a hat right down to his shoulders': the barrel was normally used to dredge the gutters of Paris. Such puns represented much more than puerile scurrility. French absolute monarchy was underpinned ideologically by the theory of divine right. Louis XV ruled because God had appointed him to do so. Any form of disrespect for the monarch was a crime of *lèse-majesté* and a sin against God: all legitimate political criticism was aimed at the king's ministers, who could be replaced, rather than the king himself. Morande broke these taboos. The message of the shit-bucket adorning the king's head was as stark as it was vile. Du Barry, a whore from the gutters, had Louis XV wallowing in putrid filth.[58]

This was heady and dangerous stuff. In the eighteenth century serving royal consorts were rarely subjected to salacious pamphlet attacks, still less reigning monarchs.[59] Nor had anyone had the courage to prise open the door of the royal boudoir and imagine the king and his lover *in flagrante delicto*. This was a step even Morande hesitated to take, and with good reason. Libellous attacks on Louis XV seldom went unpunished, and exiled scandalmongers had a habit of meeting sinister and unpleasant ends. The fate of one such dissident, Dubourg, was the stuff of legend. Snatched from Frankfurt by French agents in 1745, he was taken to Mont Saint Michel where he died in agony after spending a year suspended in a cramped metal cage in which he could neither sit outstretched nor stand upright. Seven years later, on Good Friday 1752, the Marquis de Fratteaux, author of a scandalous manuscript attacking the royal family, ministers and Madame de Pompadour, was arrested in the streets of London by a corrupt bailiff, delivered to French agents, and spirited away to France. He was imprisoned in the Bastille and died there 27 years later. In the mid 1760s the London press frequently invoked Fratteaux's name when they reported rumours of French agents come to seize the Chevalier d'Eon. Whether such reports were true remains uncertain, but d'Eon evidently felt that his life was in danger, and Louis XV certainly gave instructions that he should be seized if he could not be silenced by other means. Morande knew these tales: the *Gazetier* refers to both d'Eon and Fratteaux.[60]

Morande responded by brazenly flaunting the *Gazetier*'s illegality and daring. He predicts that the *Gazetier* will be burned publicly, like 'all good books' in France, and celebrates the British liberties which shield him.[61] The *Gazetier*'s title page boasts that it is published 'One hundred leagues from the Bastille at the sign of liberty', while an explanation of the armour-plated Gazetteer depicted on its frontispiece [plate 3] describes:

> An armed man . . . seated tranquilly under the protection of the artillery which surrounds him . . . the leaves of paper which flutter across the lightning above the armed man are *lettres de cachet*, against which he is guaranteed by the smoke of his artillery, which prevents their reaching him; the mortars whose fuses he lights are designed to spread the truth about all vicious persons, crushing them to make an example.[62]

In a mock 'Dedicatory epistle' addressed to himself, Morande advises himself to 'enjoy your glory' without worrying about 'the risks you run' from du Barry

Plate 3. Frontispiece from Charles Théveneau de Morande, *Le Gazetier cuirassé* (1771). An armour-plated writer uses cannons to ward off the thunder and lightning issuing from Madame du Barry, the Abbé Terray and Chancellor Maupeou, who are represented symbolically by a barrel, a Medusa's head and a wigged man respectively. From the author's collection.

and her ministerial allies, whom he describes as 'the enemies of your country', a terrifying phrase that prefigures Jacobin rhetoric during the Terror.[63] Morande doubtless hoped to insulate himself from kidnapping by exposing the dangers he faced, as d'Eon had done. In the mid 1760s British opposition politicians had mobilized mobs in d'Eon's defence and provided him with a bodyguard after newspapers sounded the alarm.[64] It was not the last time Morande would imitate this technique or set himself up as a champion of liberty.

The licentious and disrespectful manner in which Morande spoke about 'the fair sex' in the *Gazetier cuirassé* was calculated to offend as much as amuse. He invariably portrays aristocratic women as well as prostitutes and *Opéra* girls, as libertine and sexually voracious. Indeed, when he writes of a venereal disease spreading like wildfire from the girls of the *Opéra* to the ladies of the court and thence to their lackeys, he insinuates that the great noblewomen at Versailles are no better than whores. To ram his point home, he compares the famous brothels of Mesdames Brissac and Gourdan, which he claims have refused the services of numerous countesses and marquises, with such 'honest houses' as those of the Princess d'Anhalt and the Countess of Auxonne, 'where strangers are always welcomed with open arms'. Likewise he recounts how several ladies of the highest quality who had been denigrating Madame du Barry were won over to her camp after she angrily instructed them to 'get fucked'. Amused by this 'grenadier's compliment', they thenceforth 'only wished to be guided by her advice'! Finally, as if to offend good taste and public morals to the hilt, the *Gazetier* ends with a 20-page section of *Transparent News* devoted to anecdotes concerning aristocratic homosexuality, in which lesbians feature almost as much as sodomites.[65]

Morande revels in his joyously libertine writing. In a dedicatory epistle addressed to the *Opéra* girls who furnish the bulk of his scandalous anecdotes, he declares:

> My Ladies, if heaven had given you virtues, I would not have the honour of knowing you, [but] my depraved taste never having brought me close to any but corrupt women, your weaknesses were necessary to procure me the *advantage* of being presented to you; receive, my ladies, the tribute of my gratitude, and the homage that my heart owes you.[66]

He goes on to explain that he is performing a public service in 'giving the details of your *galanteries*, which will amuse the public without any danger, and could warn them of those they have to fear on your part'.[67] More improbably, he claims to be embarking on a moral crusade against the vice he reveals:

> If I operate some marvels in demasking famous sinners, if I make virtuous the Villettes and Marignys [famous homosexuals], if I make modest certain women without shame ... if I force evil persons to be just (be it only once), will I not have fulfilled the goal of a man of virtue... It is only ever in making vice blush that it is forced to hide: a man more virtuous than me would perhaps lack my courage.[68]

Some of Morande's scandalous anecdotes were probably motivated by revenge. His treatment of his former lover Mademoiselle La Cour and her gold palate is a case in point. He reports that after her paramour, the Prince de Lamballe, died, La Cour retired to the convent of Saint-Gervais, for fear that otherwise she would be sent to l'Hôpital, a house of correction for prostitutes. Thereafter, she managed to get herself presented to the Duchess de Villeroy – a notorious lesbian – 'by means of a secret of the convent where she had been staying *en pension*'. However, due to 'her deathly voice, her paste teeth, her red hair [which was considered ugly in the eighteenth century] and her bad reputation, even 'the Duchess' troop' refused to receive her.[69]

Morande's treatment of the Venetian ambassador, at whose house he had formerly gambled, also appears vengeful. Morande 'reveals' that the ambassador had been found 'fainting' in the arms of an unknown man in the Luxembourg gardens, a notorious hang-out for homosexuals and prostitutes of both sexes. He was returned to the embassy by two Swiss guards, who refused his offer of hush money and would have locked him up had he not revealed his identity.[70] Such anecdotes were far from harmless fun. Among continental powers an insult to an ambassador was considered a slight to his state and had the potential to cause a diplomatic incident if it went unpunished. Britain was probably the only country in Europe where Morande would have dared to print such a story. Even his slurs on the fragile reputation of a courtesan or prostitute, by accusing her of harbouring disease or cheating her lovers, could prove devastating, for courtesans were as reliant upon their 'reputations' as women of spotless honour.

Yet beyond its libertine, anti-clerical, anti-aristocratic rhetoric, the *Gazetier cuirassé* was primarily an attack on ministerial despotism. Its main targets were Maupeou and d'Aiguillon, who together enjoy such an ascendancy over Louis XV, that 'they only leave him the liberty of sleeping with his mistress, stroking his dogs and signing marriage contracts'. They, along with La Vrillière and Terray, are accused of establishing an unprecedented despotism because they have abolished the *parlements*, banished the *parlementaires* who protested, and greatly increased the political use of *lettres de cachet*. They are also accused, with considerable rhetorical licence, of widespread kidnappings and secret executions for, according to Morande, Maupeou defines a monarchic state as one where the king has power of life and death over his subjects and owns all their property. Hence Maupeou intends to introduce a machine capable of hanging 100 men at a time, while d'Aiguillon is said to have poisoned all Brittany.[71]

The Maupeou regime is also accused of plotting to reintroduce the Jesuits into France, a charge which explains much of the *Gazetier*'s anti-clericalism. Morande accuses Maupeou of having illicit relations with three Jesuits – who in the satires of the period are invariably associated with buggery – in a 24-hour period. Elsewhere he suggests that Maupeou restored Avignon to the Pope following its occupation by French troops in return for holy objects with the power to absolve him for sins he had yet to commit. These included a set of indulgences and, according to Morande's playful errata, some wax models of the Holy Lamb of God, for the use of grandees who believe in such things. However, his original text read not *Agnus bénit* [blessed lamb] but '*A.nus* [sic] *bénit*' ['blessed anus'].

To fortify his blasphemy he added that these objects had been distributed to the Count de Noailles, the Prince de Bouillon, the Duke de La Vauguyon and the Marquis de Villette, all reputed sodomites. This association of the regime with the religious orders is specific to the Maupeou ministry. In contrast, Morande claimed that Choiseul had aspired to overthrow all religious orders in France, as well as to end pointless expenditure on aristocrats' sinecures and pensions.[72]

Choiseul's parsimony and religious reforms are juxtaposed to a very different tableau of France under Maupeou. With a whore like du Barry in the royal bed and abetted by the ministry, sexual corruption has reached endemic proportions. Du Barry has banned the police from raiding the brothels of Paris, where she once worked, and infected the king with venereal disease. She is a danger to public health, good morals and the body politic. She endangers the king's very life. Ministerial corruption is also a threat to every subject. This is exemplified by La Vrillière, who abuses his power by using *lettres de cachet* to imprison his lover's husband and the fathers of half the *femmes galantes* in Paris. In the context of the Maupeou crisis, these were much more than opportunistic satirical attacks: they contained the *Gazetier's* essential political message. Morande contends that the French government has succumbed to a despotism against which the subject has no defence. France has strong tendencies towards such despotism, but is not inherently despotic, as the example of Choiseul proved.[73]

Yet for all his withering critique of the French polity, Church, army and aristocracy, Morande believed that the Bourbon monarchy might reform itself. Despite its close rhetorical resemblance to many revolutionary texts, the *Gazetier* is not itself revolutionary. An ephemeral product of the Maupeou crisis, it shares common goals with the most advanced 'patriot' supporters of the *parlements* and opponents of the Maupeou ministry. Nevertheless, Morande appears to have written independently of the Choiseulist and *parlementaire* factions. His informants at Versailles may well have had Choiseulist or *parlementaire* leanings, but the *Gazetier* does not spare members of either faction. Among those he satirizes are the princes of the blood, who, with the exception of the Count de La Marche, publicly supported the *parlements*. Likewise he derides Choiseul's cousin, Praslin, who according to Morande had died of rabies contracted from biting his own nails. Equally, the *Gazetier* grudgingly praises one aspect of the Maupeou reforms – the abolition of the old custom whereby litigants had to pay their judges. The *Gazetier cuirassé* must therefore be considered primarily the work of an angry young maverick lacking powerful protectors inside France. This left Morande dangerously isolated.[74]

3

A King's Ransom

In his *Questions sur l'Encyclopédie*, Voltaire advises would-be Morandes:

> May the young fools who are tempted to follow such an example and, lacking in talents and science, have the fever of writing, realize to what such a frenzy will expose them. They risk the noose if they become known, and if not they live in the gutter and in fear. The life of a galley slave is preferable to that of a writer of *libelles* [scandalous pamphlets] ... There is not a single example of a *libelle* that has done the least good to its author; one will never receive any profit or glory from that shameful career.[1]

For Morande, Voltaire's advice came too late. Before the *Gazetier cuirassé* the authorities viewed him as just another petty criminal. Now he was a fully fledged renegade. He had offended powerful individuals in every faction at court, and many others besides. From time to time this realization pushed him to despair. But it also emboldened his writing and drove him to turn his hand to blackmail.

In his pamphleteering, Morande now expanded his attack on Bourbon despotism. The *Gazetier cuirassé* had already suggested that the monarchy was degenerating into tyranny. Early in 1773, Morande raised an advance subscription for a new work that would expose the despotic nature of the French penal system. Its subject was that most notorious of state prisons, the Bastille. The provocatively titled and anonymous *Rémarques historiques sur le Château de la Bastille & l'Inquisition de France* was based on serious research and finally appeared in late 1774.[2] The information it contained so impressed the prison reformer John Howard that he translated and published it as *Historical Remarks and Anecdotes on the Castle of the Bastille* and adopted it as his standard reference work on the French penal system.[3]

The *Historical Remarks* differs from previous and subsequent exposés of the Bastille, which tend to offer sensational narratives of a single prisoner's experience and sufferings. Morande's pamphlet offers instead a detailed description of the physical layout, furnishings, daily routine, menus, procedures and personnel of the Bastille. It discusses the rituals for the reception of new prisoners, interrogation techniques, and procedures for prisoners wishing to communicate with their gaolers or the outside world. It even gives the salaries of the Bastille's employees and methods of documenting prisoners, together with a detailed plan of the fortress.

Yet for all its apparent empirical rigour, the *Historical Remarks* had a clear political agenda. This is evident from Morande's opening remarks:

> Since the mortal wound was given to French liberty, Despotism, that scourge of human nature, which it debases and dishonours, has acquired strength by striking at all ranks, and spreading a general terror. Nothing is heard of but banishments, proscriptions, and prisons; of which last the Bastille is undoubtedly the most formidable.[4]

By dating the 'mortal wound' to liberty to 1770 and 1771, Morande indicates that his primary target is the Maupeou ministry. From a political perspective, the *Historical Remarks* is a natural sequel to the *Gazetier cuirassé*.

The *Historical Remarks* presents a brief history of the emergence of French despotism. It asserts that it was Cardinal Richelieu who first 'began to fill castles and prisons' with 'victims' under Louis XIII (1610–1643). Thereafter, Louis XIV (1643–1715) had been 'nothing but a despot without principles, dominated by his passions, vain, ambitious, turbulent and often cruel'. Finally, under Louis XV, who died shortly before the *Historical Remarks* was published:

> ministers erected despotism into a law. *Lettres de cachet*, vexations of all kinds, were their engines. They obstinately combated the Laws of the kingdom; and concluded with dispersing and proscribing all who administered them [i.e. the *parlementaires*]. It may therefore truly be said, that imprisonment, and exile, were the great instruments of government in the last, as well as in the two preceding reigns.[5]

Despite this schema, few horror stories in Morande's pamphlet were of recent origin. Indeed, the most chilling dated from the reign of Louis XI (1461–1483), when Tristran the Hermit allegedly murdered 4,000 people in the castle's *oubliettes*. When talking of his own time, Morande is more cautious. Although he calls the penal regime a 'cruel and odious inquisition', he does not mention physical torture, which, although not formally banned until 1788, was by then little used.[6]

Instead, the Bastille subjects prisoners to cruel mental torture and perpetual surveillance. Everything they say is reported to the police, and prisoners are often unaware of the charges against them. When they receive visitors, a guard always sits between them. All sorts of ruses, tricks, distressing lies, threats and mendacious promises of freedom are used to extract confessions or torment prisoners. Some of the castle's personnel also act as *agents provocateurs*. Prisoners are isolated from each other and walks are only allowed once a day, always under escort. Prisoners are kept in total isolation from their arrival until their interrogation, which may occur weeks later. Thereafter they are allowed to communicate with the outside only via the governor, whose permission is required for even mundane acts, like being shaved by the prison surgeon. The rules governing prisoners' lives are applied inconsistently, because 'all that is done in this castle is arbitrary'.[7] Thus prisoners are treated differently according to influence, rank and the caprice of their gaolers. This regime is calculated to drive prisoners mad.

There are also hints of scandal. Most prisoners are summoned for interview by the Lieutenant of Police, but 'sometimes he goes to visit them in their chambers; especially the ladies'.[8] And because the governor can keep the surplus from the prisoners' meal allowances, the food is so awful that the prisoners' health suffers.

The *Historical Remarks* ends with seven case histories of inmates, each designed to reinforce a different point about despotism. Predictably, there is the enigmatic 'man in the iron mask', who was even stripped of his identity. There is also François de Bassompierre whose 'good conduct', 'courage' and 'lofty reputation' were no defence when Richelieu took umbrage against him. Under a despotic government no one is safe and virtue is no protection. The Chevalier de Rohan, by contrast, was a victim of duplicity. He confessed his guilt when promised a pardon, but was beheaded anyway. An unnamed 13-year-old boy was confined for 31 years for composing a blasphemous Latin epigram mocking Louis XIV and his Jesuit schoolmasters, who betrayed him to the authorities. He was only released because the Jesuits, having learned that he had inherited a fortune, petitioned for his release to win his family's favour. Alongside this tale of Jesuit hypocrisy, Morande denounces the pernicious effects of having appointed Jesuits to serve as confessors to the prisoners: 'This position, of little importance in other hands, was in theirs a means to make discoveries which shaped the deep-seated designs of their infernal politics'. Morande had not forgotten his old enemies and teachers.[9]

Nor had he forgotten another, more recent, detractor. For his final case study, of Thomas Arthur, Count de Lally, served primarily as a pretext to attack Voltaire. Voltaire recognized Lally, an Irish Jacobite with an abrasive personality and notorious temper, as the victim of a miscarriage of justice. In 1761, Lally had been the French commander at Pondicherry when the city surrendered. Subsequently, while a prisoner-of-war in England, he learned that he was being accused of treason, and asked permission to return to France to defend his conduct and reputation. Once in Paris, he was arrested and imprisoned. Though his only offence was to have surrendered a city, he was found guilty by the *Parlement* of Paris on 6 May 1766, refused a royal pardon, and executed. In 1773, following an approach from Lally's family, Voltaire launched a campaign to rehabilitate Lally and remind his readers of the iniquity of the former *parlements*.[10] This was as a red rag to a bull to Morande. 'We behold with a contempt mixed with indignation', he wrote:

that this old man, who boasts of loving the truth beyond every thing . . . has only touched upon the pleas offered by the condemned party in his justification. That is sufficient to give M. de Voltaire a handle for declaiming against the *Parlement* of Paris, and for reproaching them at random with occurences of two hundred years standing . . . without having the good sense to reflect, that all honest minds would revolt against the iniquitous baseness of taking advantage of the dispersion and exile of this body, the victims of their patriotism, to insult them without shame.[11]

This slur on Voltaire's integrity, made in Morande's characteristic insinuating style, was the sole personal defamation in the pamphlet. It was an indulgence he ought to have foregone, but Morande seldom let ideological consistency get in the way of malice or moneymaking. Thus a pamphlet dedicated to denouncing Bourbon despotism ends with a sordid attack on a campaign to rehabilitate a victim of French arbitrary justice.

Nevertheless, the *Historical Remarks* was arguably Morande's most influential work, for as Rolf Reichardt and Hans Jürgen Lüsebrink have noted, it marks a decisive shift in the literature on the Bastille. With the publication of the *Historical Remarks*:

anti-Bastille journalism became increasingly fundamental and radical on the subject of changing the system . . . . Increasingly politicized, Bastille journalism went from covering sensationalistic scandals to making a fundamental critique of the system and finally reached its prerevolutionary sharpness . . . in the 1780s.[12]

Ironically, the key anti-Bastille works of the 1780s were written by Morande's enemies Simon-Nicolas-Henri Linguet and the Count de Mirabeau. However, it was Morande who pioneered this new style critique of despotism as a system of government.

Morande received help with his research from an unexpected source: the Chevalier d'Eon. D'Eon admitted that he allowed Morande the run of his extensive library and 'not only lent, but gave him, all that I had on the inquisition of Spain and of France'.[13] D'Eon had split with Morande in July 1771 following publication of the *Gazetier cuirassé*, but they were reconciled by the following September, when they teamed up to rescue the Countess de Courcelle from arrest and disgrace, after her husband took 'precipitous and necessary' flight from London. Courcelle fled shortly after pawning several valuable pieces of jewellery, leaving behind considerable debts.[14] The sole creditor to recover something from the wreckage was d'Eon, who, on learning of the count's imminent departure, had most of the Courcelles' goods seized and sold.[15] However, Courcelle was running from more than debts. He also feared criminal charges, for the pawned jewellery did not belong to him, and its rightful owner, Madame de Lormel, was on his tracks. By this time, neither Morande nor d'Eon cared much for Courcelle, but both were alarmed for his wife, whom they considered a valuable ally.

The challenge facing d'Eon and Morande was to recover the jewellery while protecting Madame Courcelle and her children from gaol, total destitution and criminal charges. To a large extent they succeeded. On 15 September 1771, just prior to Courcelle's flight, Morande signed a declaration which suggested that the jewellery had been received by the Courcelles in good faith from a third party. D'Eon then helped to redeem the jewellery and on 23 September lent the Countess de Courcelle enough money to travel to France. She fled that very evening, abandoning her two youngest daughters with their wetnurse.[16]

Morande kept in touch with the Countess de Courcelle after her return to Paris, while her husband descended into gambling, poverty and crime.[17] Courcelle's death in late 1775 was thus a release for the countess, who confessed that he had been 'jealous of his own shadow'.[18] Morande, too, shed no tears. He had long since blamed Courcelle for leading him astray.[19] Nevertheless, Morande and d'Eon remained committed to the rest of the family. In 1775 they even concocted a comical conspiracy to smuggle the two youngest Courcelle girls and their wetnurse's husband [père nourricier] into the French embassy via the kitchens. They hoped that the sight of two tiny innocents might melt the ambassador's heart and persuade him to intercede on their behalf to persuade Courcelle's friends to pay the wetnurse and repatriate the children. The plan apparently failed. D'Eon's account books record that in March 1776 he gave 'the père nourricier of the little Courcelle girls' two shillings 'through charity'. However, mother and daughters were eventually reunited. By 1785 they were living together in Paris, whence the Countess de Courcelle probably continued to supply Morande with information.[20]

While working on the Historical Remarks, Morande resorted to blackmail. His self-justificatory letters to d'Eon claim that he did so through pressing financial need, and by July 1773 he was certainly in financial difficulty. His problems may have stemmed from mercantile speculation rather than gambling and fast women, for by the mid 1770s he was importing French goods on a large scale: in 1776 he insured a single shipment for £2,030.[21] By 1774, he lived in a smart house in fashionable Duke Street, but his debts amounted to over £1,000, and any hopes of help from his family had been dashed by his father's death on 30 September 1772. Although Louis Théveneau's will acknowledged the customary and legal rights of all his children over his inheritance, he left all the family property to Morande's mother, who was poorly disposed towards him.[22]

Morande's blackmail systematically targeted individuals he had attacked in the Gazetier cuirassé, particularly those he had accused of homosexuality. One source describes his method thus:

> For several years he has made the greatest Lords in France pay him, by means of menacing letters in which he informs them 'that he has received secret intelligence . . . containing scandalous anecdotes relating to their lives and morals; but that he believes he has a duty . . . to inform them, in order that they might be in a position to suppress them; and that it is within their power to spare themselves the distress of seeing them . . . in the pamphlet that he has just printed, and which they are at liberty to suppress should they so wish, by paying him a certain sum' which he always takes care to state and to fix according to the degree of their fortune.[23]

His threats left his victims with few options. It would be tricky to bring a libel case against Morande in England, as this required the presence of the complainant. Even then, the plaintiff would have to establish both that they had a reputation in England and that it had been harmed before any damages would be awarded. Nor could he be convicted of blackmail, because the law only protected British residents. Not surprisingly, some of his victims chose to pay, to avoid any scandal. Among them, apparently, was a certain Monsieur Collet d'Hauteville, the sole known victim not to appear in the *Gazetier cuirassé*, and the Duke de Bethune, Morande's former friend and protector, whose peccadilloes were doubtless well known to him.[24]

One of Morande's most lucrative targets was Madame de Pompadour's brother, the Marquis de Marigny, who was Director of the Royal Buildings and Counsellor of State. He made a particularly attractive target because Pompadour's family were known to have paid off other blackmailers, including an exiled former nun Marianne Agnès Pillement de Fauques de Vaucluse.[25] Although Morande accused Marigny of 'tastes contrary to nature', he was also fond of prostitutes.[26] So fond, according to Parisian gossipsheets, that he was delighted when his wife left him for the notoriously lecherous Cardinal Rohan, since it freed him to pursue his own pleasures. Marigny's name appears several times in the reports of Inspector Marais, which recount that he once enjoyed an intimate 'supper' at *la Brissault*'s brothel with Mademoiselle Souville, subsequently one of Morande's infatuations.[27]

Whether Marigny was a sodomite is less clear. Morande certainly insinuated as much. The *Gazetier cuirassé* told how Marigny, having lashed out 300,000 *livres* on a classical sculpture of Ganymede, had been 'surprised in meditation at the feet of the statue by his wife . . . who ran up piously with a cup to receive his incense, which was about to be spilt'.[28] The symbolic significance of Marigny's kneeling and masturbating before one of the most celebrated homosexuals in classical mythology would not have been lost on educated eighteenth-century readers. However, Morande also targeted Marigny in other ways. In November 1773, Broglie reports that despite her death almost a decade earlier, Marigny was negotiating with Morande to suppress a scandalous pamphlet about Pompadour.[29]

It seems therefore that Marigny paid to silence a whole series of threats to his family's honour. Contemporary sources allege he gave Morande 10,000 *livres* on three separate occasions, and that his family continued to pay Morande a pension after his death. Morande denied these allegations, but as so often the evidence speaks against him.[30]

The Marquis de Villette, a minor poet and the most notorious French sodomite of his time, showed rather more spirit than Marigny when faced with Morande's threats. Villette had been the butt of many of the *Gazetier cuirassé's* most puerile anecdotes, *bon mots* and homosexual jokes. It announced the invention of a carriage that could only be mounted from behind: it would be called a coach *à la Villette*. Villette was a coward: on over ten occasions he had turned his back in public. He did so even more frequently in private. He was, in addition, the most zealous user of the Pope's aforementioned 'blessed anuses'. Morande also reported that the Marquis had finally given up plucking his facial hairs in order to appear younger (so he could play the *bardache*), and accepted that he must henceforth take the role of the older man. In other words, Morande informed his classically educated readers, Villette had metamorphosed from Alcibiades into Socrates.[31]

More intriguingly, the *Gazetier cuirassé* told of Villette's adventures with women. The notoriously bisexual Mademoiselle Clairon had 'supped' with Villette in order, she said, 'to taste a little of everything'. Morande even reported that Villette had taken a mistress. Asked why, Villette retorted with unsurpassed impudence 'because she has two sphincters'.[32] A man reputedly capable of so flaunting his homosexuality and social convention cared little for Morande's threats. Villette recounts how when Morande offered to sell his silence for 50 Louis, he responded by 'asking him for 100 Louis for other yet more secret and curious anecdotes that he could append to his manuscript'.[33] The libel never appeared.

Villette's friend Voltaire reputedly also negated Morande's threats. The *Gazetier cuirassé* had reported (correctly) that Voltaire and the journalist Elie Fréron made allegations of homosexuality against each other. However, when Morande threatened new revelations, Voltaire supposedly published the blackmailer's letter and was left in peace. At least, this is how the story has always been told.[34]

This is ironic, because Voltaire was apparently the only victim of Morande's blackmail campaign who failed to silence him, whether by cash or other means. For in his autobiographical *Réplique de Charles Théveneau de Morande à Jacques-Pierre Brissot*, Morande confesses that he wrote an anonymous libel against Voltaire, published by his close associate, the London-based Genevan-born bookseller David Boissière. Here is what he says:

A little pamphlet entitled the *Tocsin des Rois* [*The Alarm Bell for Kings*], which preached a crusade against the Turk, was printed in London; I produced a response ... intitled

Mendement [sic] *du Muphti*, which condemned the *Tocsin des Rois* to be burned, and Voltaire, (who was said to be the author), to be impaled. I presented him with a stake, and he sent me back a noose; it was a fair exchange.[35]

While this summary gives the essence of the exchange, it does little justice to an unashamedly mischievous and scathing satirical attack on Voltaire. For the *Mandement du Muphti* [*Muphti's Decree*] poured scorn on Voltaire's reputation as a prophet of toleration, opponent of persecution and indefatigable campaigner against the Roman Catholic Church.[36]

Posing as the chief cleric of the Ottoman Empire, the *Muphti*, Morande accused Voltaire of seeking to revive the crusades, associating him with some of the worst atrocities ever committed in Christ's name, many of which Morande describes in delicious detail. Such a conceit allowed Morande to describe Voltaire's writings as 'bizarre' and 'monstrous'; to suggest that he only defended victims of intolerance and injustice through vanity; and that he had turned on Islam to attract fresh public acclaim because his attacks on Christianity had become repetitious and stale.[37] Morande's rhetorical position even allowed him to portray Voltaire as a defender of the detested Papacy:

> You claim, Tocsinist firebrand, that it would be a great evil to see the true believers [i.e. Muslims] in Rome; [but] what would Christendom lose by this event? An impostor of a priest [i.e. the Pope] . . . a skilful charlatan who fleeces his neighbours, in giving them blessings, bulls and indulgences of no value in return for gold.[38]

If such charges were less than compelling given Voltaire's lifelong struggle against intolerance and fundamentalist fanaticism, they doubtless raised many a malevolent smirk, even among the sage of Ferney's admirers. Nor did Morande miss the opportunity to flaunt his own philosophic and atheist credentials. In an ambiguous aside worthy of Gibbon or Voltaire himself, he declared 'If religion were only a political convention to lead and direct the nations, the adept who instructed them ought to be delivered up to public indignation! He would be the common enemy of society.'[39] This is, clearly, precisely how Morande wished his audience to see priests.

In short, the *Mandement du Muphti* delivers a Voltairean attack on both Christianity and organized religion while deriding Voltaire personally and tarring him with the brush of intolerance. At the same time, it sought to refute the case for an anti-Turkish alliance, by arguing that while the Ottoman Empire offered no external threat, it was stronger internally than often believed. Moreover, victory for any such alliance would result in a dangerous consolidation of Russian and Austrian power. Voltaire, who had tried to allay such fears in the *Tocsin des Rois*, was thus a dangerous and bellicose traitor, particularly as France and the Ottoman Empire were allies. He was also, Morande implied, working as a propagandist for his old friend the Russian Tsarina Catherine II, who was at that moment embroiled in the first partition of Poland and wars with the Turks and the Swedes.

Morande doubtless intended the *Mandement du Muphti* as an act of retaliation against Voltaire for his insults in the *Questions sur l'Encyclopédie* and for refusing to succumb to blackmail. It is probable that Voltaire, who died in 1778, never knew the identity of his attacker, for as Morande wished to maximize the impact of his calumny, he guarded his anonymity for almost 20 years. If the *Mandement* did little, if any, lasting damage to Voltaire's reputation, it is nevertheless valuable as the sole example of a published personal libel from this stage of Morande's career. The text is testimony to Morande's inventiveness and ability to cast aspersions on almost any act or virtue. Since the pamphlet went through at least two printings, it also demonstrates Morande's talent for turning the most improbable and calumnious material into a commercial success.

The most celebrated and damaging response to Morande's defamation campaigns came from the dashing aristocratic pamphleteer and playboy, Lauraguais. The first stone in their quarrel was thrown by Lauraguais, who had come to England in the spring of 1771 to proclaim his opposition to the Maupeou ministry. The result was a pamphlet entitled *Du Droit des français* [*Of the Laws of the French*], which argued that the French monarchy was based on a voluntary social contract between the monarch and his subjects. French laws were therefore valid only with the consent of both parties. By implication, a king who infringed the rights of his people could be removed. This was potentially explosive, particularly in the context of the Maupeou crisis. It marked Lauraguais as an outspoken supporter of the *parlements* and critic of the ministry. Not surprisingly, the French authorities seized a consignment of 1,500 copies *en route* for Paris.[40]

Lauraguais set up house in Brompton, where he lived with his servant-girl mistress, Laurence Lefebvre. Wishing to conceal their liaison, he pretended that Laurence was his maidservant and arranged for her to marry his secretary, Drogard. Drogard initially connived in the count's wheeze, but in early 1773 he sued Lauraguais for adultery and kidnap, hoping to make his fortune. Lauraguais answered Drogard's charges in a spirited judicial memoir. Lauraguais admitted he had lived with Laurence for several years but alleged that Drogard had beaten her savagely, ravished her against her will, and blackmailed her into marriage. She had therefore fled to a convent in France, but Drogard, on learning of her impending departure, had done nothing to stop her. This surely negated the kidnap charge.[41]

Morande was apparently a stranger to the Drogard case, but Lauraguais denounced him in an aside nevertheless:

> There is a scoundrel who claims to speak well of me in a libellous pamphlet where he rips into all that I love and respect; who believes he passes for a bright wit in good company because several whores call him the Chevalier de Morande, instead of Morande; and because he has printed a scandalous hotchpotch, which has the appearance of being written by a coachman based on the memoirs of Madame Gourdan's cook.[42]

Lauraguais had multiple motives for this attack. He was genuinely incensed by the *Gazetier cuirassé*'s attacks on the monarchy, aristocracy and many of his friends, relatives and former lovers. He may also have been upset by a passage concerning himself, though it was opaque and comparatively anaemic. It announces Lauraguais' self-imposed exile thus:

> France has just lost a man of the highest quality ... who has decided to renounce ... the peerage and the Paris Opera, to complain in freedom and teach the French that he knows how to think in the real meaning of the word.

By way of explanation, Morande reveals that this man (Lauraguais is never identified by name) was once asked by the king what he had got up to in London. 'I learned to think' came the reply. 'Yes, of horses!' retorted Louis XV, turning his back.[43] Above all, Lauraguais wished to distance himself from rumours that he wrote the *Gazetier cuirassé* or had helped in its compilation. As Lauraguais believed, erroneously, that Morande had encouraged these tales, his anger is understandable.[44]

Morande retaliated to Lauraguais' provocation with what d'Eon described as 'the bloodiest libel you could ever read'.[45] Morande mistakenly believed that if he concealed Lauraguais' identity, he would be immune from the British libel laws. Thus, he styled Lauraguais the Count de Brascassé [broken arm], an allusion to his family name of Brancas. However, the count's description, residence, writings and adventures were so transparent that there could be no doubt who was intended.[46] Morande compounded his error by reading the proofs of his pamphlet to some friends of the count, who informed him of its content. Lauraguais immediately instituted proceedings for criminal libel.[47] Disconcerted and frightened, Morande sought d'Eon's advice. Seeing a chance to serve both parties, d'Eon advised Morande to stop publication and guard the entire print run in his home. This would impress his judges and might encourage Lauraguais to negotiate an out-of-court settlement.

D'Eon's calculations were overthrown by the publication of a pseudonymous French verse in Woodfall's *Morning Chronicle* of Wednesday 23 June 1773. It was addressed 'To the anonymous author of a Scandalous Libel, entitled "Le Gazetier Cuirassé"; who intends (as it is said) to publish a false history of the Bastille' and read:

(Self-styled) great wit, you once again threaten us
With a satirical, boring, defamatory pamphlet
You claim to be well-informed: like a man in disgrace,
You come to a foreign country to invent heinous crimes
Instead of the Bastille, where you have never been;
Speak therefore of Bicêtre, where you found a place
As a bad subject living everywhere from gambling,
Swindling one and all, and lying not a little?
The Englishman is an enemy, but he is not unjust.
Stigmatized by your country with just reason,
He will see in you only a vulgar impostor,
A despicable scribbler, a vile adventurer.

For the benefit of English readers, two footnotes explained that the Bastille was a 'state prison where people who are well born, rich or witty are locked up', while Bicêtre is 'a house of correction where the anonymous author knows (by experience) that they lock up crooks, gamblers, vagabonds etc.'

The public did not have long to wait for Morande's response. The very next day the *Morning Chronicle* carried an 'Answer of the *Gazettier Cuirassé* [sic] to the Imposter who signs himself *Virtutis Amicus*, in your paper of Wednesday last'. Like the original offence, this reply was written in French verse:

I read the verses manufactured at Brompton
By a rhymer whom they call Count,
Who lacking honour, courage, or reason,
Must die sooner or later under the rod
(Always provided he does not perish of shame.)
I read them without being moved;
Although the author claims that I was once
Sent to Bicêtre on account of my wickedness.
If anyone asks how that can be?
I will reply that the author lied;
And that a lie never angers:
To which, I loudly add, a challenge
To prove to me how I was condemned.
I'll stop there; the author is a coward.

These lines were accompanied by defamatory footnotes explaining that Brompton is a village outside London which manufactures 'court cases, marriages and all kinds of infamies'. New provocations were added the very next day (25 June), when the poem was republished with different notes. These asserted that

Lauraguais had been imprisoned in Dijon in 1766 for cheating Villette over a gambling debt and added that Morande never slept without weapons by his side and was always ready to fight a duel.

Several near contemporary accounts assert, incorrectly, that Morande was forced to confess publicly that he wrote both poems, posing as Lauraguais and attacking himself in print in order to have a pretext to retaliate. This act of fraudulent hypocrisy became central to the legend of Morande's depravity. It allowed his enemies to portray him as a liar, libeller and impostor so base, devious and hypocritical that he denounced himself in order to defame Lauraguais. This became the accepted version of events.

The allegation that Morande defamed himself first surfaced in a letter to the editor of the *Morning Post* on 30 June 1773. However, the following day's *Morning Chronicle* contained a letter from 'Impartial' refuting such an absurd notion and thereafter the charge was forgotten for several years. It resurfaced in 1776, when d'Eon began disseminating a wilfully distorted version of Morande's confession.[48] It seems unlikely that d'Eon really believed Morande to be '*Virtutis Amicus*', for in a letter to Broglie written on 13 July 1773, when he was advising Morande and familiar with the cases of both litigants, d'Eon asserted that Lauraguais was the author of the first poem.[49] He would not have done so had Lauraguais accused Morande of writing the poem. At this stage d'Eon was evidently dismissive of the allegation in the *Morning Post*. In consequence, it seems likely that the mysterious '*Virtutis Amicus*' was a malevolent third party, as Morande would later claim.[50] But it is also possible that he was Lauraguais.

Meanwhile, Lauraguais, maligned and (probably) falsely accused, put on a brave face. When George III – himself a celebrated victim of the press – asked him how he found British liberty, Lauraguais replied 'I have no complaints: I am treated like a king'. Such sarcastic indifference masked his true feelings: Lauraguais responded to the second poem by bringing a further libel case against Morande and the printer of the *Morning Chronicle* at the Court of King's Bench.[51] He pressed the case through the courts as quickly as possible, and as Morande puts it, 'the attack was conducted better than the defence'.[52] Within 20 days Morande had lost, but, as was customary, sentencing was deferred until the end of November.

During this respite, Morande took advice from his friends and legal advisors. They warned that the judgment was likely to 'reduce him and his family to the depths of beggary'.[53] It might also put him behind bars. D'Eon advised that the only hope was to broker a peace with Lauraguais. According to Morande, their lawyers cut a deal by which it was agreed to burn Morande's pamphlet.[54] This is probably not the whole truth. Another source reports that Lauraguais only agreed to drop the case after vigorous lobbying from d'Eon, Morande's friends and Eliza, who called on Lauraguais with her infant children.

[They] came, tears in their eyes, to prostrate themselves at the knees of the Count and implore his clemency in favour of their father and foolish husband, whose criminal errors had so justly provoked his indignation, and whose punishment, merited as it was, could not but cause the ruin of the innocent supplicants.

This lachrymose and pathetic scene, so calculated to appeal to enlightenment sensibility and Lauraguais' gallantry, 'had its desired effect on the Count's sensitive and generous soul', though not immediately.[55] When the count finally offered terms in mid November, he sent them by messenger from Brussels. Morande was deeply unhappy with Lauraguais' conditions, which required a humiliating public apology, but d'Eon convinced him that he had no choice.[56] Later reports record that shortly afterwards Morande appeared before the count on his knees to deliver his submission and, according to one account, receive a sound thrashing.[57] Thereafter, he published a humble apology in the Morning Chronicle, which declared:

Count Lauraguais having been pleased, on my humble submission, to drop the prosecution he lately commenced against me for several false and groundless assertions against him, which I was the author of, in some verses printed in this Paper on the 24th and 25th of June last, entitled "Answer of the Gazetier Cuirassé", I request you, Mr Woodfall, through the same channel that my verses were made public, to communicate to the world my sincere contrition for having so injuriously traduced the Count, and my most grateful thanks to him for accepting my submission and dropping the prosecution. DE MORANDE, 26 November. 1773.[58]

Similar humiliating notices appeared in several other newspapers. None mention the first poem attacking Morande, which was published on 23 June. The suggestion that Morande confessed to writing it thus appears devoid of truth. Nevertheless, Morande's violent talk had been exposed as the hollow bravado of an inveterate coward and his humble submission was a scene his enemies would never forget. Nor did it take much prescience for d'Eon to predict, 'it will not be the last folly he commits in London'.[59]

In fact, as d'Eon well knew, Morande was already engaged in a breathtakingly foolhardy campaign to blackmail Louis XV and Madame du Barry. We do not know how Morande first announced his demands, but we do have a fellow scandalmonger's best guess. It appears in a spurious blackmail note published by Mathieu-François Pidansat de Mairobert, which names a price and hints that Morande's manuscript contained insinuations that du Barry was 'cuckolding' the king with d'Aiguillon. It reads:

Madam

As I live in a country where men have not given up the faculty of thinking for themselves; which faculty they are at liberty to exercise, without the least risk . . . I can with confidence avow myself the author of a small work intitled *Le Gazetier cuirassé*. If this work . . . has afforded you the least amusement, I shall applaud myself for being the author of it; your approbation must be esteemed its greatest praise. I am just now going to print another work, intitled, *Secret memoirs of a woman of pleasure; or an Essay on the adventures of the Countess du Barry from her cradle to the bed of honour*. I do suppose, madam, if I had not added the second part of the title, you would easily have discovered by the first whom I meant. I thought it however but right to communicate my design to you . . . because, as you have . . . shewn a peculiar taste for arts, and sciences, you might wish to be the sole possessor of a manuscript which I have endeavoured to render interesting to the public, and which may appear to you of great value. If you think so, it will not cost you above 50,000 livres. Though this price may seem high, it is yet very moderate. You would scarcely believe, madam, what expense I have been at to procure the necessary materials. The anecdotes of the latter part of your life have been purchased at an immense price. I have bought with hard gold the particulars of your amusements with his most christian majesty, and of the methods you used to deceive his spies, when you consoled yourself for his Majesty's deficiencies with your good friend the Duke d'Aiguillon; and when he failed with little Zemoro [i.e. Zamoro, du Barry's black servant boy], with whom you tried all [the sexual techniques] that Aretin has taught, and even outdid that ingenious Italian. In short, madam, you may be assured that this work is very compleat, and that it is furnished with everything which can insure it a rapid sale . . . I am with the greatest respect &c

The Chevalier de MORANDE.[60]

Du Barry had good reason to fear Morande's revelations, for he had already provided a blueprint for his *Secret Memoirs of a Woman of Pleasure* in the *Gazetier cuirassé*. It 'reveals' that du Barry is the daughter of a monk called Père Ange Picpus and:

a peasant-girl servant (his cook), who brought her into the world in a small priory in Brie, where that beloved monastic product was brought up until she was 10 years old. At that age a wandering agent seized from this holy man the fruit of his exertions in order to take her to the centre of libertinage, where all France has seen her plunged for so long. Her debut was in the most modest sphere, and has undergone strange revolutions during the last 15 years. First she was seen to walk on foot beneath the street-lights of Paris; from there to the Palais Royale, *which has been the seminary for so many marquises*; from there she acquired a few furnishings and an accommodating lover, who began to enlighten her with his advice; from there she associated herself with the Count du Barry to play at twenty-one . . . and attract a crowd to his establishment; from there she had 100,000 livres of debts and a coach which began to give her some importance in the world; from there she was linked to Madame de St***d **** who brought M. Lebel [sic – Le Bel], the faithful valet de chambre of a great prince with whom she took a journey to Versailles *during the night*; from there she at last emerged as a *Countess, has been formally presented at Court,* [and] *lodged in the palace,* whence she has chased *a princess, two ministers, and all the respectable people* that she could find.[61]

This exposé contained plenty to upset Madame du Barry, not least because it came much closer to the truth than the only pamphlet biography then in circulation, an absurd erotic fantasy entitled *Authentic Memoirs of Madame De Barre,* published in 1771 by Sir Francis N., which identified Madame du Barry as one Emily Palmer. The *Authentic Memoirs* claimed she was the child of a French servant girl married to a certain Mr Palmer, an Irish language teacher in Paris. The exact identity of Emily's biological father remained a mystery, however, for Palmer allowed his wife to take two paying lovers, an Abbé and a wealthy financier. Most of Francis N.'s novel is concerned with young Emily's sexual awakening and libertine adventures with the Chevalier de M——, a soldier, and Monsieur de C——, the well-endowed and sexually voracious husband of her compliant best friend. These, according to the *Authentic Memoirs,* were her only two lovers prior to Louis XV. There is no suggestion that she had been a prostitute or courtesan. Only at the very end of the novel, when Emily encounters the Count du Barry does the tale begin to offer anything approaching genuine biographical details. Readers, naturally, were disappointed: Mairobert's review concludes 'nothing is as dull and disgusting as this pamphlet . . . The few facts found therein could equally well apply to the heroine as any other public woman [i.e. prostitute]; there is not a single anecdote that can be considered remotely true.'[62] Clearly Morande's illustrated history would be far more 'authentic'.

Du Barry had reacted to previous libels with disdain and even amusement, but she was understandably alarmed at Morande's threats. According to Mairobert she wrote at once to d'Aiguillon to demand action, saying:

> I have just now received, my Lord Duke, a most abominable letter from London. You will judge yourself of it; I send it to you herewith. Lose not an instant to employ every possible means to prevent the publication of this execrable libel, with which we are threatened. You are as nearly concerned as I am.[63]

Although this letter is probably apocryphal, d'Aiguillon did indeed work closely with the countess to ensure the work's suppression, trying all imaginable means. The result was a cat-and-mouse pursuit that lasted for almost two years.

D'Aiguillon and Madame du Barry probably learned of Morande's libel in May 1772. By the middle of that month, d'Aiguillon was conducting negotiations

Plate 4. The Introduction of the Countess Du Barre [sic] to Louis XV. Contemporary
British print. Courtesy of the Brotherton Collection, Brotherton Library, University
of Leeds.

with Morande's envoy, an ageing adventurer, merchant and fraudster named
François Benavent. Benavent claimed, improbably, that he met Morande in
London by chance, learned of his intention to publish the *Secret Memoirs of a
Woman of Pleasure* and believing it his 'duty', persuaded Morande to suspend
publication while he went to Paris to try to negotiate a good price for the suppression.[64] On arrival in Paris, Benavent contacted the Lieutenant of Police, Sartine,
who approached d'Aiguillon. They asked Benavent to continue his correspondence with Morande and dictated his replies.

The negotiation did not progress well. D'Aiguillon found Morande's demands
excessive, though at 24,000 *livres*, they were less than half the figure given in
Mairobert's letter. In addition, d'Aiguillon wanted to see the manuscript, but
Morande refused to relinquish it until negotiations were successfully completed.

Moreover, he demanded to be paid through a London banker in order to guarantee any engagement was kept.

D'Aiguillon and du Barry informed Benavent that these conditions were unacceptable. Ratcheting up the pressure, Morande responded by threatening to 'speak in such a manner as to merit their attention' and berating Benavent for his failure and believing him 'imbecile enough to send his manuscript'. Morande adds that while he would prefer to sell his silence, 'the public . . . pays very well for this type of work'. Indeed, he can be certain of success because even 'a wretched rhapsody in English on the same subject with all its facts contrived [i.e. *The Authentic Memoirs*?] brought its author almost 12,000 *livres* [£500]'. Moreover, his material is based on common knowledge:

> all Paris is aware of the facts I have exposed to the light of day: my only merit is to have compiled them and added a little of the vindictiveness that these sorts of works always need. It is true that I have added some anecdotes of her early childhood and several of the most secret of these latest times. It will be seen that the details I give are from very close.

Morande believes, however, that his price is modest in comparison with the 100,000 *livres* that Madame de Pompadour, with much less reason, allegedly paid for a scandalous manuscript. Benavent passed these demands to d'Aiguillon, who was unimpressed and resorted to more direct means.[65]

On 19 May 1772, d'Aiguillon remarked to Lord Harcourt, the British ambassador, that he had heard that writing threatening letters was 'a Capital Offence' in England. Unfortunately, as Harcourt reported, 'he was not informed at the same time, that the letter must be wrote to some person in Great Britain, in order to make the Crime Capital'. As a result, d'Aiguillon could only ask Harcourt to forward Morande's letters to the British government 'in hopes that some method may by Your Lordships be found to stop the publication'. A true diplomat, Harcourt reassured d'Aiguillon that his superior, Lord Rochford, would do 'everything *in his power* to oblige'. This did not actually amount to very much.[66]

Perhaps d'Aiguillon took Rochford's assurance to mean that the British government would turn a blind eye to discreet attempts to silence Morande by force. Parisian newsmongers certainly picked up (false) rumours that the British 'would not be opposed to someone's coming to kidnap . . . or drown in the Thames, this monster [and] plague on society, . . . provided it is done in great secrecy' at the very moment that d'Aiguillon and the du Barry clan resorted to clandestine means.[67] Their search for a reliable, loyal and expendable agent soon led them to the Chevalier Fontaine. An inveterate adventurer with large debts, he seemed the perfect candidate for such a task. Fontaine had been an officer in the Swiss guards, but was dismissed for scandalous behaviour, and was languishing in prison 'for some roguery or other'. He also knew England, where he had operated as a card sharp. Above all, he was tied to the du Barry faction, for his natural daughter, Madame Murat, was mistress to the Count du Barry, Madame du Barry's brother-in-law [sic], pimp and former lover. It was the count who secured Fontaine's release from prison and provided him with money, a servant, letters protecting him from his creditors and a *post-chaise* to take him to England.

If the French hoped the British would go along with their plans, they were sadly mistaken. Harcourt got wind of the Count du Barry's largesse and was immediately suspicious. He found Fontaine's cover story that he was going to London to buy Canada Bills implausible and on 16 July told Rochford:

> I cannot help thinking that the chevalier's journey may have some other object, and that he may perhaps make some attempt to carry off the Chevalier de Morande, who has made himself so very obnoxious to the Duke d'Aiguillon, who I am of the opinion will leave no stone unturned to prevent the publication of Madame du Barri's [sic] Memoirs.[68]

Once in London, Fontaine posed as a negotiator and approached Morande's latest middleman, the publisher and bookseller Boissière, who ran a lucrative sideline in blackmail pamphlets. Boissière had arrived in England in about 1770 and started his business with funds stolen from his former master, the Russian courtier, privy councillor and gambler Dmitri Mikhaïlovitch Matouchkine. His bookshop was for many years a meeting place for French expatriates and refugees from Bourbon justice, who formed an informal Literary Society. It included all manner of rogues and rakes, army deserters, seducers, spies and criminals.[69]

Boissière took Fontaine to meet with Morande, ostensibly to negotiate. Details of what happened are sketchy, but it seems that Fontaine won Morande's confidence and invited him on a trip to the countryside. On the appointed day, Fontaine, his servant and Morande duly set off in Fontaine's *post-chaise*. Seated either side of Morande, Fontaine and his man struck prematurely. Before even leaving London, they seized upon him with a gag and a garotte. Morande fought back furiously, in fear for his life. Summoning all his strength, he managed to struggle free and shout 'murder', summoning passers-by to his aid. They ripped him from the coach and escorted him home, but Fontaine and his companion goaded their horses onward and escaped.[70]

Following the failure of Fontaine's mission, other adventurers offered to kidnap Morande, but there is no evidence that their offers were accepted.[71] For the next year, while Morande worked on his manuscript, low level negotiations may have been kept alive. By July 1773, the French court realized that time was running out and considered changing tactics. They were concerned that Morande's manuscript was nearing completion and alarmed by reports that one of the

Spanish ambassador's secretaries was collaborating with Morande. This raised the spectre that he might have sensitive insider-information and that powerful political patrons might be deploying Morande against du Barry and her political allies. If so, it might be best to pay him off after all. Broglie was therefore asked to sound out d'Eon as a possible go-between.[72]

D'Eon responded enthusiastically, assuring Broglie that he was the ideal agent because of his close relations with Morande and Eliza. Indeed, he claimed that 'I could even have the wife steal the manuscript, but that would cause a row between them, compromise me, and only result in another, more terrible work'. D'Eon was unable to confirm whether Morande had collaborators. However, he could report that Morande had bought two presses and a set of typographic characters and installed them in his home, because he dared not entrust his manuscript to a publisher.

D'Eon boasted that he would acquire Morande's manuscript for no more than 800 guineas and ensure that Morande did not double-cross him. His plan involved dining at Morande's home and applying high-pressure tactics to cement a deal in a single session. Then he would demand the manuscript and search Morande's house for any other papers relating to the French court. All would be placed under seal. Morande would receive half the sum agreed when these documents, along with a signed declaration that he would never 'compose or have composed any manuscript or printed work' concerning du Barry or the Court of France, were delivered to d'Eon. The second half would be paid once Morande had repeated his declaration as a sworn affidavit. If he broke his word thereafter, he would face the full weight of the law against perjurers.[73]

Louis XV referred d'Eon's plan to Madame du Barry, who in turn consulted d'Aiguillon. Unfortunately, d'Aiguillon considered Broglie a dangerous rival and feared that if d'Eon were successful, Broglie's credit would increase. He therefore persuaded du Barry to use another intermediary. However, by the time du Barry informed Broglie of her decision, several weeks later, d'Eon had won Morande's confidence by defusing a dispute between him and a colonel in the Polish service called Jossecourt, thereby preventing a duel. D'Eon could therefore claim to enjoy Morande's full confidence whereas a swarm of other agents and freelancers had only put him on his guard. Broglie was thus able to persuade Louis XV to allow d'Eon to continue to watch events closely.[74]

D'Aiguillon eventually found a new agent in Marie-Félix Guerrier de Lormoy, who fled to Britain to escape debts of 300,000 *livres* in October 1773 following the collapse of his equine establishment. In London, Lormoy encountered Morande and tried to dissuade him from publishing. On his own initiative, Lormoy opened negotiations and informed his patron, the Duke of Deux-Ponts (Zweibrücken), to whom he sent 12 pages of Morande's printed work. The duke then wrote to d'Aiguillon, who accepted Lormoy's overtures and began to direct his actions.[75]

Neither Morande nor d'Eon knew what to make of this freelancing adventurer, his links to the Duke of Deux-Ponts, and his offer to pay £5,000 for Morande's libel. The enormous size of the sum aroused their suspicions and these were exacerbated when Lormoy consulted d'Eon about the feasibility of a kidnap. Would it be possible, he asked, to get Morande transported to America, then bribe the captain of the vessel conveying him to drop him on the French coast? D'Eon's responses were not encouraging. Kidnapping was too risky and libellers were not subject to transportation.

D'Eon advised Morande to accept Lormoy's offer, if it proved genuine, then retreated to his friend Lord Ferrer's estate in Leicestershire. Morande remained cautious, but met with Lormoy several times. In mid November, convinced he had concluded a deal, Lormoy wrote Morande a promissory note for £5,000. Morande read it then returned it, declaring it 'a good decoration for a wardrobe but a very poor title in a portfolio'. Lormoy blustered back that if Morande did not settle, he would begin legal proceedings in order to placate his master. Morande retorted that he did not fear Lormoy's master, but he wrote at once to tell d'Eon what had happened, declaring that:

> at last everything is going to be resolved and this time my work shall appear. I am very relaxed about this because I shall thereby fulfil two essential duties, the first to the public, to whom I shall make an honorable recompense, the second towards Courcelle, whom I shall crush like a rascal for his roguery towards me.[76]

As Morande no doubt intended, d'Eon wrote immediately to Broglie to pass on this intelligence and scotch rumours that he had impeded Lormoy's 'extravagant' and 'chimerical' projects. He added that Morande's publication was now 'coming on apace' and, unable to resist rubbing salt in the wound, boastfully prophesied that:

> When it is dispersed across Europe, the interested parties will regret not having immediately acquired that abominable manuscript by the means that I proposed and would have executed all alone and without any commotion, and certainly without any personal motive but that of pleasing His Majesty, you, and his ministers.[77]

D'Eon's smugness cut no ice with d'Aiguillon, who now decided on one final throw of the dice. He brought plans to kidnap Morande to the King's Council which, after debating two rival proposals, appointed a police spy called Béranger (or sometimes Bellanger) for the job and provided him with a posse of five policemen, the most noteworthy of which were called Finet and Receveur. A contract was drawn up and signed on 18 December 1773 and Béranger was given an advance of 6,000 *livres*. He would receive a further 24,000 *livres* and the Cross of Saint Louis if he succeeded.[78]

Béranger and his officers set out at once for Calais, where they embark on a packet boat bound for Dover. Among their fellow passengers is Anne (or Marie-Madeleine) de La Touche Gotteville (or Godeville) a roving, ravishingly seductive female adventurer and woman of easy virtue. By the time they reach Dover, the policemen are competing for her attention. With tongues doubtless loosened by alcohol, they begin boasting of their mission and the wealth it will bring them. Encouraged by her response, Finet pushes his luck further, and is, we may speculate, rewarded by her favours. Writing to him several months later, Gotteville teasingly chides 'the hearts of women, who are accused of inconstancy, are much less like weathercocks than those of men: they love more and for longer'.[79] Gotteville's constancy, such as it is, evidently does not extend to secret policemen's confidences, and she duly informs Morande of their plans. He, however, has little need of her intelligence. He had probably been tipped off by sources in Versailles and, in any case, has already encountered Béranger in the gambling dens of Paris.[80]

When he reaches London, Béranger masquerades as an infantry captain, contacts Lormoy and informs him that he has brought the funds to pay Morande. Like Fontaine, Béranger plans to lure Morande to the countryside, then seize him. Lormoy takes Béranger to Morande's home, where Morande reads him 60 pages of his pamphlet. Later, Morande takes Lormoy aside and asks:

> Do you really know who you have brought with you? Béranger is not an infantry captain but a police spy, a recruiting officer [for spies], a holder of the bank in Sormanie's [gambling den], who is a gambler by profession and swindler like him.

Outside, Lormoy warns Béranger that he is recognized. Béranger now admits everything save his kidnap plan.[81]

Although Béranger's cover is blown, some of his officers decide to try their luck. On 4 January 1774, Morande meets two of them in a tavern, where, after some discussion, they each lend him 30 guineas. Their purpose is not merely to win Morande's confidence. They are hoping that when they call in the loan, Morande will be unable to repay them, and hence that they might have him arrested for debt. Once in prison, he will prove more tractable. Perhaps they also dream of bribing the arresting officer to deliver him to them: this was the device used to kidnap Fratteaux in 1752. Morande is, of course, wise to these snares. It is said that he always carries a gold sovereign in his palm. This is double the fee paid to an arresting officer and sufficient to persuade most of them to let him escape.[82] However, Béranger's officers are an entirely different proposition. He must strike before they can spring their trap.

Before the officers can leave the tavern, Morande pounces. To their astonishment, he repeats what they told Madame Gotteville at Dover. Then, before they can respond, he begins a new line of interrogation:

'Do you know M. Tesson, treasurer of France at Lille?'

'No, we don't know him.'

'That's very strange, as I have received a letter saying that you dined with him and that you spoke about me at length in such a way as to all prove yourselves my friends. Thank you for doing so.'

'Monsieur, you are mistaken. We spoke about you but said nothing disadvantageous. You may be well persuaded of it.'

'Messieurs, I have spoken so ill of my compatriots that I do not merit any indulgence from those who dine in Lille while I am in London. But I recall smashing a chair across the kidneys of some fucker [Jean-Foutre] who thought that my hide would fetch a good price in Paris.'

Warming to his theme, Morande rants loudly about duelling pistols and Tyburn, London's place of execution, much to the officers' discomfort. The initiative is now firmly in his hands.[83]

Over the next few hours, Morande contacts the newspapers and tours the taverns and coffee-houses of London attempting to incite a mob against Béranger and his posse. His plan works in part, for at 11 that night an exultant Morande tells d'Eon 'I write to inform you, in grenadiers' language, that I have forced two [police] exempts, four archers [i.e. low ranking officers], and a ship waiting for them on the Thames to bugger off'.[84] Although it is late, he begs d'Eon, who has just returned to London, to call on him after he has dined.

It is well past midnight when d'Eon arrives at Morande's home. There, he is astonished to see all three floors piled high with freshly printed pages of the *Secret Memoirs of a Woman of Pleasure*. Morande now gives him a full account of Béranger's activities. D'Eon replies bluntly that Morande has only himself to blame, since he chose to write about du Barry and French ministers. 'By the Devil!' explodes Morande:

I could not have chosen a better subject to arrive at my intended goal, which is money. Would you have me write novels or sermons? No-one would read or buy me. By the subject I have chosen and the way I have treated it, I am certain to have readers across all of Europe.

Then, with a flourish of bravado he declares:

I don't give a damn about poison and daggers. If I die thus, I will not have been hanged and it will dishonour only my poisoners or assassins. If you like, you can tell the Duke d'Aiguillon and his whole clique that I really couldn't give a flying fuck about him, the whole court, and the entire army.

D'Eon retorts that Morande is no better than a highwayman, before adding caustically 'your pen is only murderous in appearance, and will not kill anyone who knows how to defend themselves against you'. It is two in the morning, but as he leaves d'Eon aims a parting shot at Eliza: 'Watch out for your husband. He is a hothead. On behalf of you, him and his children, I am concerned about his state.'[85]

Four days later, Morande informs d'Eon that he has received a new approach from a clerk at Versailles, but is fed up with 'little negotiators'. He will respond by publishing his work 'which is being printed day and night and is not far from completion'. If Morande is hoping that d'Eon is still empowered to make offers, he is disappointed. Instead d'Eon tries to reason with him:

'May God bless you and your work my dear Morande. Do what you wish. You only listen to your current needs, without considering what the future holds for you, your wife or your children.'

'I know nothing' – replies Morande – 'but my pressing needs and the roguishness of the folk at Versailles, but Devil take me, I will unmask them even if they kill me one hundred times.'[86]

While d'Eon is reporting these events back to Versailles, Béranger and his men are still at large. Morande's initial efforts to expose them had met with only limited success, for none of the newspapers was keen to run his story. On 6 January, the editor of the *Public Advertiser* refused Morande's copy, remarking: 'If the case of the foreigner, who imagines himself liable to be kidnapped, is a fact, why does he not authenticate it? The printer of every paper in London will readily ring the alarm bell on such an occasion.'[87]

On 9 January, in an obvious state of agitation, Morande and Eliza consult d'Eon again. They read him an article that they hope to publish in the newspapers and ask for legal advice on how to defend themselves against Béranger. This time, d'Eon refuses his help, saying he will not offend the French ministry by offering legal advice or recommending a lawyer. As for the best means of protection, d'Eon notes that 'in defending myself, I always took care to put the law and public opinion on my side. You, in contrast, attack first. It is thus up to you to know your counter-measures.'[88]

Abandoned by d'Eon, Morande and Eliza carry the day alone. They get their paragraphs identifying the policemen's lodgings inserted in the *Morning Post* of 11 January, and lay a complaint before Sir John Fielding, the blind magistrate with responsibility for policing London, who issues a warrant for the arrest of Béranger and his fellow officers.[89] Faced by the wrath of the law, the policemen depart precipitously. Lormoy, deeply compromised, also takes flight. The Parisian rumour mill claims that the policemen were driven from their hotel by an angry mob and fled for their lives. It is said that two were lynched and Receveur, apprehended by the mob, was tarred and feathered and thrown in the Thames. Although he was fished out, he spent several weeks in Bedlam recovering his wits.[90]

After this defeat and faced with the imminent publication of Morande's book, du Barry begins to consider a pay-off. Morande also seems to have forced d'Aiguillon's hand, sending him accusatory letters comparing him to a bandit, which he threatens to publish unless d'Aiguillon lays them before the king. This leaves d'Aiguillon an unpalatable choice between a pay-off, humiliation before his master and the court, or allowing Morande to publish a detailed exposé of his involvement with the Béranger mission. A new negotiation is therefore entrusted to Préaudeau de Chemilly, the treasurer of the Maréchausée, the French mounted police force, but it proves fruitless.[91] Then Louis XV and du Barry's eyes alight upon a new agent: Pierre-Augustin Caron de Beaumarchais.

In the spring of 1774, Beaumarchais is facing financial oblivion and disgrace, following two disastrous court judgments. The first found him guilty of forging his benefactor's will. This gave rise to the second case, in which Beaumarchais accused his judge, Goëzman, and his wife of failing to return a small cash gift. It was standard in old regime France for judges to receive such gifts from litigants, but customary to return them if a litigant lost. To back his case, Beaumarchais published four witty judicial memoirs, which the public bought avidly and read as scathing attacks on the Maupeou *parlement*. The judgment in the case ordered his memoirs be burned by the public hangman. It was little comfort to Beaumarchais that it also ordered Goëzman struck off. His acceptance of a mission to London to suppress the *Secret Memoirs of a Woman of Pleasure* is thus a means of restoring his fortune and rehabilitating himself in the eyes of Louis XV, du Barry and the ministry.[92]

Like the rest of the French public, Morande was closely watching the outcome of the case, which cemented Beaumarchais' fame as a writer. He also identified with Beaumarchais as a fellow critic of the Maupeou *parlements*. On 9 March 1774, while informing d'Eon of the *Parlement*'s judgment, Morande adds a parallel observation about himself: 'They hang me [in effigy] in Paris, they burn me, they erect altars to me. At last, they are as keen to buy my book as I am to sell it.'[93] Thus, when Beaumarchais arrives to negotiate with him a fortnight later, Morande is delighted. Once Beaumarchais convinces Morande that he acts in good faith, the two men quickly develop a *rapport*. After their first encounter Morande tells d'Eon:

> I have Beaumarchais in hand, he is adorable . . . I'd subscribe my neck to a promissory note testifying he is innocent; I would bet my head on it . . . He writes so beautifully that

I could hang myself. Voltaire never equalled his style. You may judge tomorrow.[94]

In a single meeting Beaumarchais persuades Morande to let him take a copy of the *Secret Memoirs of a Woman of Pleasure* back to Versailles for Louis XV and du Barry to inspect. The work causes such panic that Beaumarchais is given full powers to deal with Morande. His mission is now urgent. Morande's books are already packed in crates and waiting to be sent to booksellers in Amsterdam, Brussels, Rouen and Paris. He is holding them back only as a gesture of good faith.[95]

D'Aiguillon, vengeful as ever, presses Beaumarchais to reveal the names of Morande's collaborators, but he refuses. He has no wish to compromise the king's interest or his negotiation, or to see anyone punished solely on the basis of Morande's denunciation.[96] Meanwhile, d'Aiguillon is simultaneously pressuring the British, still hoping to avoid a pay-off. Informed of the imminent publication, British ministers finally make efforts to deter Morande. With rebellion brewing in their North American colonies, they are keen to placate the French. According to French diplomatic sources, Rochford even proposes buying Morande's silence, but Chief Justice Mansfield vetoes the idea. Instead, the British decide to intimidate him.

Thus, in early April, Morande is summoned to a meeting with Sir John Fielding, who lectures him on the dangers of producing reprehensible works. However, Morande denies that he is the author of the *Secret Memoirs of a Woman of Pleasure*. He insists that he is writing a political work and promises to show it to Fielding five days later. Presumably Morande intended to fob him off with his *Historical Remarks*, but there is no evidence that this second meeting took place. Such initiatives only rile d'Aiguillon, who believes that the British insistence on positively identifying the author and refusal to employ *force majeure* are mere prevarication. In fact, British actions reflect the requirements of the libel laws and the problems the government faces if it wishes to deal with Morande without violating liberties the British populace hold dear.[97] As a result, d'Aiguillon has little alternative but to accept the 'repugnant' necessity of Beaumarchais' mission, and authorize the necessary payments. These are to be overseen by Lauraguais, who assists Beaumarchais in his negotiation.[98]

Beaumarchais and Lauraguais are old friends. They first met through Lauraguais' one-time paramour, Sophie Arnould, and together they explore the seedier side of Britain's capital. Beaumarchais also makes common cause with d'Eon and Lormoy, who has returned to London, but is in desperate financial difficulties. Beaumarchais thus presents Morande with a united front and hence a single channel for negotiations. But he also seems to have absorbed the previous negotiators' ideas and advice. As a result, the final settlement he negotiates on 26 April closely resembles that suggested by d'Eon several months earlier.[99]

Thus, on 27 April 1774, Lauraguais, Lormoy, Beaumarchais, Gudin, Morande, and possibly d'Eon, watch as 6,000 volumes of the *Secret Memoirs of a Woman of Pleasure* are burned at Marylebone. Only one copy is spared the flames, and it is torn in two 'in such a manner that the sense and meaning of no part of it could be made out ... without the help of the other'. One half is given to Morande, the other to Lauraguais. Before that is accomplished, the first four pages are detached. One is given to Lormoy. It was intended that the other three would be attached to three copies of a memorandum recording the event. Sadly, they were subsequently mislaid and no trace of the work survives.[100]

The legal contracts by which Beaumarchais secured the suppression and destruction of Morande's work, plates and related manuscripts were carefully designed to ensure his future good behaviour. By a contract with the British banker Sir Joshua Van Neck dated 29 April 1774, Morande confirms that he has delivered his entire print-run for burning and promises never again to libel the French monarch, his court, his ministers, or his servants. In return, Van Neck is to pay his debts of 32,000 *livres* (just under £1,400) and ensure payment of a life-long annuity of 4,000 *livres*, provided that Morande keeps his promise. Morande also insists on a clause stating that in the event of his death, a reduced annuity should continue to be paid to Eliza and his children. Morande informs d'Eon that this condition is essential because he still fears assassination. By a second contract, Morande promises that he shall never 'directly or indirectly cause or procure to be written, published, divulged, printed, reprinted or continued' the *Secret Memoirs of a Woman of Pleasure* or further '*libelles*' against the French court or monarchy, and contracts to pay 32,000 *livres* to Lauraguais should a British law court ever determine that he has done so. Evidently Lauraguais was chosen because he was trusted by the French court and because, due to the bad blood between them, he could be relied upon to sue Morande in case of recidivism.[101]

For Morande the suppression of the *Secret Memoirs of a Woman of Pleasure* represents a major coup. After two years of cloak and dagger negotiations, court skullduggery, and repeated attempts on his life and liberty, he has been paid a fortune greater than he originally demanded, cleared his debts, and been granted an annuity that, in more prudent hands, might have secured his future. He still fears the assassin's dagger, but for now he can afford to crow about his success. And crow he does, calculating that the more he publicizes the dangers he faces, the safer he will be. Thus, details of Béranger's mission and his pay-off appear in most of the best-selling works of the so-called 'Mairobert corpus' as well as British caricatures [see plate 5] and later exposés of the French secret police.[102] Such notoriety and success swiftly spawn imitators, and this, too, serves his interests, as we shall see.

Beaumarchais is not so lucky. He arrives back in France to learn that Louis XV is on his deathbed. Three days later the king is dead. With Louis gone, Madame du Barry consequently exiled from court and d'Aiguillon's days in power

THE FRENCH LAWYER *in London*.

THE BODY SOUL & MIND OF THE GAZETIER CUIRASSÉ

Plate 5. The French Lawyer in London (1774). British caricature of Morande, depicting him in French lawyer's robes with animals' paws and ears. The serpents among the open writings on his head probably allude to the Medusa's head in the frontispiece to the *Gazetier cuirassé* (see Plate 3). Courtesy of the Department of Prints and Drawings at The British Museum. © Copyright The British Museum.

numbered, Beaumarchais' hopes of immediate preferment vanish. In the event, he does not even receive his expenses.[103]

According to the historical record, Louis XV died of smallpox. However, as noted in the prologue, a letter appended to the 1777 edition of the *Gazetier cuirassé* suggests that in reality he was slain by Morande and the *Secret Memoirs of a Woman of Pleasure*. For miasma from the *auto da fé* had been blown across the channel to Versailles, where it had poisoned the king, bringing on his final illness. The moral of this parable was plain to all. The toxic stench of corruption would prove fatal to the monarchy.[104]

4

Figaro's Nemesis

How did Beaumarchais succeed in securing Morande's silence when so many others failed? His trump card lay in some additional sweeteners. Beaumarchais did not just pay Morande off. He also hired him as his agent and spy. Morande was instructed to assist Beaumarchais' 'secret inquisitions' against 'those infamous libels to which his own notorious example had begun to give rise' and give him 'secret intelligence on England, her naval forces, her ministers, the decisions of the government offices where he claimed to have friends etc.' This provided Morande with increased security, new moneymaking opportunities, a powerful new ally and, Beaumarchais hinted, the hope that one day, on account of his services, he might be allowed to return to France without fear of arrest.[1]

In Beaumarchais, Morande tied himself to a rising star in both literature and international politics. Following the first public performance of *The Barber of Seville* on 23 February 1775, Beaumarchais and Figaro, his play's wily servant hero, became cultural figures of European significance. Beaumarchais' political influence, though hidden, was even more profound.

On his trips to England in 1774, Beaumarchais became acutely aware of the growing tensions between Britain and her American colonies, where discontent with Britain's imperial preference policies, revenue collection, and government heavy-handedness was reaching boiling point. Beaumarchais first arrived in London within weeks of news of the protest known as the Boston Tea Party, during which American patriots threw a cargo of tea into Boston harbour, and Parliament was already discussing the punitive retaliatory measures that became known as the Coercive Acts. These included the Boston Port Act, which closed Boston to trade, and the Massachusetts Government Act, which severely curbed local political autonomy. Rather than isolating Massachusetts and cowing the other colonies, as the British had hoped, these repressive measures terrified the colonists into creating the First Continental Congress to orchestrate resistance and underline their insistence that they would resist taxation until given Parliamentary representation. From there, despite attempts at conciliation, it was only a matter of time until the Americans' struggle flared into open conflict. The first shots were fired at Lexington in April 1775.

Beaumarchais saw these developments as a once in a generation opportunity. He therefore began pushing the new king, Louis XVI, and his foreign minister,

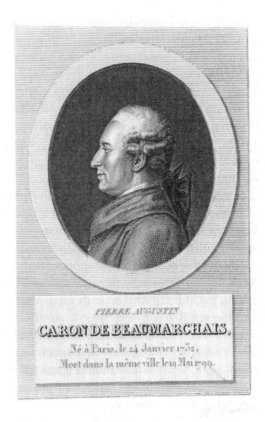

PIERRE AUGUSTIN

CARON DE BEAUMARCHAIS,

Né à Paris, le 24 Janvier 1732,

Mort dans la même ville le 19 Mai 1799.

Plate 6. Pierre-Augustin Caron de Beaumarchais. Courtesy of the Brotherton
Collection, Brotherton Library, University of Leeds.

Vergennes, to support the Americans. At first, they were only prepared to do so
clandestinely. Thus from 1775 to 1778, they used Beaumarchais as their secret
channel for sending much-needed French arms, supplies and money to the
Americans. Throughout these years, Beaumarchais pressed for France to support the Americans openly. His wish was granted in stages. In February 1778,
the French government, encouraged by the surrender of General Burgoyne at
Saratoga, signed an alliance with the Americans. Five months later, on 10 July
1778, they declared war. Until that moment, London was the key venue for
contacting the insurgents' emissaries and their British sympathizers. For the
American revolution was, particularly in its early stages, a British civil war. Even
after the Americans declared independence on 4 July 1776, there were both
loyalist and rebel sympathizers aplenty in both the colonies and the mother
country.

Thus Louis XVI's accession coincided with a remarkable transformation in Morande's fortunes and apparent loyalties. He was suddenly an agent in France's secret war on behalf of the Americans and a spy in London's French exile community, who between 1774 and 1776 denounced several scandalous anti-Bourbon pamphlets. By June 1775, Beaumarchais could assure Sartine that 'He is . . . a poacher whom I have turned into a good gamekeeper, and in many cases is, and will be, very useful to the interests of the King.'[2] However, despite Beaumarchais' recommendation, Louis XVI preferred not to employ Morande directly. He remained Beaumarchais' agent alone.[3]

Morande and Beaumarchais were difficult men to contain. Across the next few years they dreamed up several schemes to make money and advance Beaumarchais' political credit. Foremost among them were a conspiracy to extort a final blackmail payment from the French court and an attempt to corner the market in wagers over d'Eon's sex. But, as Beaumarchais was to learn to his cost, even sweeteners like these could not tame Morande forever.

The bargain between scandalmonger and playwright was an uneven one. In Morande, Beaumarchais met his match. Morande provided valuable services as a co-conspirator and spy in the late 1770s and as editor of Beaumarchais' mouthpiece, the London-based French-language *Courier de l'Europe* newspaper, from 1784 to 1791. However, in both roles he proved impossible to control. Nor was he always successful in lesser endeavours. True, he tracked down Beaumarchais' missing nephew, Eugène Salzédo, when he absconded to London in 1787. More often, however, Morande's efforts were counter-productive. His drawn-out attempts to export a printing press designed by the French royal printer Anisson-Duperron but manufactured in Britain foundered over problems with expiring export licences and petty quarrels between agents, manufacturers and Anisson himself. His interventions in furnishing and later selling Beaumarchais' London townhouse almost certainly lost Beaumarchais money. And his attempts to translate Beaumarchais and Salieri's opera *Tarare* for performance on the London stage were abandoned in the face of English competitors, criticisms of his lack of local allusions, and his reluctance to truncate Beaumarchais' original text.[4]

Morande's least ambiguous services perhaps lay in the introductions he provided, notably to Francy, who sailed for America in September 1777 to serve as Beaumarchais' agent with Congress, and Madame de Gotteville, whose sensual four-year affair with Beaumarchais revolved around congress of another kind.[5] By the 1780s, Morande's services were certainly not worth the price Beaumarchais had to pay. For that price included endless payments in response to begging letters and threats; serving as an intermediary with Morande's relatives; mediating endless family squabbles; and even overseeing George's education. Morande was to sap Beaumarchais' finances and peace of mind for the rest of his life.

Morande perhaps even helped mould Beaumarchais' *oeuvre*. In the *Barber of Seville*, Bartholo's line 'Calumny, Sir, you hardly know what you are disdaining: I have seen the best of men laid low by it' may be a veiled reference to the suppression of *The Secret Memoirs of a Woman of Pleasure*, accomplished shortly before Beaumarchais completed his manuscript. More intriguingly, the shift from the light-hearted carefree Figaro of the *Barber of Seville* to the darker, more cynical, slightly malevolent Figaro of the *Marriage of Figaro* (completed in 1778) coincided with the years when Beaumarchais and Morande enjoyed their closest working partnership. Does this reflect the injection of Morande into a character usually perceived as Beaumarchais' *alter ego*? It is tempting to think so. If so, paradoxically, Morande can be considered both Figaro and Figaro's nemesis.

One of Morande's first services, Beaumarchais hints, was to denounce the impending publication of a pamphlet entitled *Avis à la branche espagnole sur ses droits à la couronne de France, à défaut d'héritiers* [*Advice to the Spanish Branch* (of the Bourbon family) *on its Rights to the Crown of France in the Absence of Heirs*]. The pamphlet, which was being prepared in London within weeks of Louis XVI's accession, claimed that the new king was impotent and that his Austrian-born Queen, Marie-Antoinette, was taking lovers to produce an heir. It appeared designed to undermine the queen's position and hence the Franco-Austrian alliance, by casting doubts on the legitimacy of her future children and encouraging Louis XVI to repudiate her. Beaumarchais duly informed Sartine, who, despite Louis XVI's misgivings, despatched Beaumarchais to London to suppress it.[6] Strangely, Beaumarchais took a German-speaking servant with him to London. This was part of a premeditated plan.

According to Beaumarchais, the author of the *Avis* was Guillaume Angelucci, an elusive Venetian Jew who used the improbable alias William Hatkinson [sic]. However, Beaumarchais' narratives of events call this into question. For his various accounts include many bizarre and improbable details, a wild goose chase across half of Europe, and significant discrepancies. In combination with the other surviving evidence, they offer compelling proof that the *Avis* was produced as part of a conspiracy involving Morande and Beaumarchais. Morande would thereby extort a final blackmail fee from the French monarchy and Beaumarchais would increase his political credit with the rulers of France and Austria. He would also justify an exorbitant expense claim for over 72,000 *livres* (£3,000).[7]

Beaumarchais claims he burned 4,000 copies of Angelucci's pamphlet outside London on 23 July 1774, before going to Amsterdam to suppress its continental edition. He says he paid Angelucci £1,400 (35,600 *livres*) for the pamphlet, but the perfidious Israelite held back a copy and fled to Nuremberg, intent on reprinting it.[8] Beaumarchais somehow learned his plans and caught a mail coach to Nuremberg. He reports that he caught up with Angelucci in a wood near Neustadt, but Angelucci spotted him and plunged into the trees on his pony. Beaumarchais stopped the coach, told the coachman that he needed to relieve himself, descended, and gave chase, pistol in hand. He caught Angelucci and forced him to surrender the pamphlet. Then, suddenly, a band of robbers appeared. They set upon Beaumarchais, wounding him in the arm and chin. Fortunately, he was saved by the sound of the coachman's horn, which caused his assailants to flee.

The first person to hear this tale was Beaumarchais' coachman, George Dratz. He did not believe a word of it. He had neither noticed Angelucci nor heard a struggle. Nor had he ever seen brigands on that particular road. He concluded that his passenger's wounds were self-inflicted with a razor, and his suspicions intensified when Beaumarchais refused to see a doctor or report the affair until they arrived in Nuremburg, 60 miles further on. He concluded that Beaumarchais was a madman or economic saboteur and denounced him to the authorities.[9] They ordered extensive police searches but no trace of the brigands, the pamphlet, or Angelucci was ever found. Nor is this Beaumarchais' only account of what happened. Over the following weeks he described the ambush on several occasions, with significant discrepancies concerning people and events.[10]

Breaching Sartine's orders, Beaumarchais continued to Vienna, where he requested an audience with Marie-Antoinette's mother, the Empress Maria-Theresia. He read her the pamphlet and then made an astonishing suggestion. He asked to edit and reprint the pamphlet, stripping it of references to Marie-Antoinette's being unfaithful so that he might present a copy to Louis XVI. He assured the Empress that his subterfuge would never be discovered because he possessed the only copy. Yet when refused permission, Beaumarchais changed tack and insisted that Angelucci must be discovered before he could print his new edition.[11]

By now the Austrians smelt a rat. They put Beaumarchais under house arrest, but to their astonishment, Sartine confirmed he was a French agent. They thus had little choice but to release him, compensate him and send him on his way. Sartine blamed Beaumarchais' behaviour on an excessive zeal to please the Empress. Amazingly, this has also been the judgement of most of Beaumarchais' biographers.[12]

Equally amazingly, the Angelucci affair did Beaumarchais' credit little damage. After a short inquiry, Sartine exonerated him and paid his inflated expense claim. Yet Sartine was secretly tormented by doubts and gradually ruled out all other suspects. In all probability, he eventually concluded that Beaumarchais was implicated in the production of the *Avis* and other scandalous pamphlets. Others shared his suspicions, including the new Lieutenant of Police for Paris, Jean-Charles-Pierre Lenoir; the Austrian ambassador, Mercy-Argenteau; and the long-serving French minister, Malesherbes.[13] However, Sartine preferred a face-saving cover-up to reopening the affair. Besides, a man like Beaumarchais could be useful.

Sartine's misgivings were surely well founded, for there are simply too many suspicious circumstances. Why did Beaumarchais take a German-speaking servant to London unless the trip to Vienna was premeditated? And why were his arrangements with Angelucci so lax? It beggars belief that Beaumarchais, who ensnared Morande and later d'Eon in binding webs of contracts, should have failed to take the most elementary precautions to prevent Angelucci's recidivism. Why, too, in marked contrast to the *auto da fé* for Morande's work, are there no independent witnesses or contemporaneous accounts of the burning of the *Avis*? And why is there no corroborating evidence of Angelucci's existence and activities? The obvious inference is that neither he, nor the sylvan brigands, nor the continental edition ever existed. Beaumarchais' copy of the pamphlet was probably the only one ever printed and Angelucci was a figment of his imagination, carefully designed to exploit his audience's anti-semitic prejudices.

Moreover, the *Avis* was evidently completed and printed only after Beaumarchais' departure for London on 26 June 1774, as it refers to the successful innoculation of Louis XVI and the royal family against smallpox. The innoculation took place on 18 June 1774 but its success was only confirmed a week later. In addition, the text of the *Avis* appears designed to serve Beaumarchais' interests. Beaumarchais knew that no one but its main targets, Marie-Antoinette, Louis XVI, Sartine, Maria-Theresia, and the Austrian Chancellor, Kaunitz, was ever likely to read it. And these were the very people whose patronage Beaumarchais sought.[14]

Who, then, could have printed the *Avis* in total secrecy in London after Beaumarchais' arrival? The finger of suspicion points strongly at Morande. It was Morande who first denounced the pamphlet. It was Morande who served as Beaumarchais' main contact in the London publishing scene. Morande is known to have had a printing press in his house and thus means of producing a *libelle* in secrecy. Indeed, if d'Eon can be believed, Beaumarchais had already used Morande's press to print a clandestine edition of his judicial memoirs against Goëzman. Moreover, Morande had a track record of producing scandalous works. And Morande was the sole person in London on whom Beaumarchais could depend for total secrecy, for he faced massive financial losses if his involvement were ever discovered, due to his bond with Lauraguais. This implies that Beaumarchais was party to the plot at the moment it was hatched. It also explains why, several years later, when faced with financial ruin, Morande was able to threaten to hit the 'self-destruct' button and blackmail Beaumarchais with threats to implicate them both in the production of *libelles*. And it would also explain Beaumarchais' willingness to pay to silence him.[15]

As if this were not evidence enough, Beaumarchais protected Morande when he again turned his hand to libel. For in July 1776, Morande wrote an anonymous 'Letter from Marly' to the editor of the newly established *Courier de l'Europe*.

It insulted and satirized French government ministers, members of the royal family and the armed forces. But above all, it suggested that French policy was forged out of a perpetual and bitter struggle between Marie-Antoinette, who dominated the king in the bedroom, and the wily old minister Maurepas, who reigned supreme in the Council chamber.[16]

The 'letter from Marly' provoked outrage at Versailles and the *Courier de l'Europe* was immediately banned from France, its main market. Beaumarchais, seeing the paper's potential either to disseminate mischief or serve as a French propaganda organ, lobbied against the ban on behalf of the paper's owners. In September 1776, he arranged for one of them, Samuel Swinton, to meet with Vergennes, who was persuaded to request a royal privilege for the paper. Shortly afterwards, Swinton gained permission to print a continental edition in Boulogne, thereby evading Britain's heavy newspaper stamp duties.[17] The result was a publishing sensation. By late 1776 the Americans' struggle had transfixed the attention of the European public: it was the great news story of the day. Thus, a paper written from London and able to give the freshest political news of both Britain and her rebel colonies in the *lingua franca* of the day was virtually guaranteed to be a runaway success. Within a short while the *Courier de l'Europe* was outselling all other international gazettes and Swinton's first editor, Alphonse-Joseph de Serres de La Tour, could boast in astonishment that his one-third share in its profits made him more money in a year than Jean-Jacques Rousseau had earned in a lifetime.[18]

As the price of this favour, Swinton informed Vergennes that Morande was responsible for several articles offensive to the French government and supplied him with the original draft of the 'Letter from Marly'. It is written in Morande's highly distinctive scrawl. Nevertheless, there was no comeback. Presumably Beaumarchais persuaded Vergennes that rather than unleashing Lauraguais, he should use the 'Letter from Marly' as a means to control Morande. Doubtless Beaumarchais feared that, were Morande to be convicted in court, he might also reveal the truth about the Angelucci affair.[19]

Despite the Angelucci fiasco, the French government was soon entrusting Beaumarchais with suppressing further pamphlets discovered by Morande. By April 1775 he was back in London to suppress a scandalous newsheet produced by d'Eon's sometime secretary, Vignoles. 18 months later he paid a certain Madame Vernancourt to prevent 'a political work against all the current government'.[20] As Morande socialized with both Vignoles and Vernancourt, it seems likely that he was an *agent provocateur*, inciting others to produce works that he denounced.

While Beaumarchais was in London to suppress Vignoles' news-sheet, he received an unexpected visit from d'Eon. Several months earlier, d'Eon had attempted to negotiate a full and final settlement of his financial claims with the French court in exchange for surrendering his diplomatic and espionage correspondence, much of which he had secretly held back in 1766, after the conclusion of his previous settlement. Unfortunately, discussions proved abortive due to the extravagance of d'Eon's demands, which were doubtless inspired by the size of Morande's pay-off. The silence that followed alarmed d'Eon, but he lived in daily expectation of fresh overtures. These hopes were not unreasonable. D'Eon was aware that when Louis XVI, on his accession, learned of the continuing existence of the *Secret du Roi*, he had quickly decided that it should be closed down, its operatives pensioned off, and all documents relating to its existence gathered together for safe-keeping. As a spy for the *Secret*, d'Eon could legitimately expect his due. Moreover, Louis XVI viewed d'Eon as a special case, because of the secret orders in his possession. Thus d'Eon naturally assumed that Beaumarchais – who had indeed lobbied unsuccessfully for the task – was charged to open a new negotiation.[21]

When d'Eon learned that Beaumarchais had no such instructions, he tried to recruit him as an intermediary regardless and showed him some of his secret correspondence.[22] This was a shrewd move. Louis XVI and Vergennes would conclude that d'Eon had confided everything to Beaumarchais, rendering it necessary to employ him in negotiations at once. It also reminded them of the harm that d'Eon might do by selling his papers to British opposition politicians or publishing his correspondence. D'Eon had already done this in 1764 and now hinted that he was preparing a new volume. Indeed, on 3 April 1775 he hired Vignoles to compile it.[23]

Neither side in the ensuing negotiation placed much trust in the other. Beaumarchais knew that having already been paid to surrender his papers once, d'Eon had held back the most sensitive documents. Equally d'Eon knew of Beaumarchais' legendary cunning. Perhaps this explains why Beaumarchais employed Morande as an agent, calculating that, due to his friendship with d'Eon, he might smooth relations between them. Hence in the second half of 1775, Morande socialized frequently with d'Eon and Beaumarchais, sometimes accompanied by Eliza or Francy. They had dinner parties together and pleasure trips to Greenland Dock, Woolwich Arsenal, Hammersmith and Fulham. In October 1775, d'Eon even presented Eliza with a small enamelled heart.[24]

There was more than money at stake in d'Eon's negotiations with Beaumarchais. He was also bargaining about his gender status, dress and civil existence. As we have seen, d'Eon had been cross-dressing in private since the late 1760s, if only as a disguise, while from 1770 his sex had been a matter of public speculation. D'Eon himself had done nothing to confirm or deny rumours that he was really a woman, although he had never worn female dress in public. Nevertheless, by 1775 he seems to have wished people to perceive him as female. Thus, to avoid appearing personally duplicitous, he promoted two rumours to suggest that a male gender had been imposed on him unwillingly. The first rumour asserted that although he had been born female, his parents had brought him up as a boy to avoid dividing the family inheritance. The second story stated that Louis XV had employed him as both a female and male spy during missions to Russia in the 1750s. Both tales were completely false. Anatomically speaking d'Eon was fully male.[25]

D'Eon's motives for crossing the gender divide were idiosyncratic, ultimately inexplicable, and remain a matter for debate. They apparently had nothing to do with sexuality: indeed, d'Eon had almost no interest in sex – perhaps due to a physical impediment – and probably died a virgin. Instead, he believed a retreat into womanhood would allow him to escape the corrupt world of male politics and a dead-end career, while redeeming his immortal soul. Hence, as he later put it, 'from a bad boy' he was transformed into 'a good girl'.[26] To explore and justify this unique motivation, he would from the 1780s develop a unique, proto-feminist, 'gendered theology'.[27]

However, in 1775, d'Eon's thoughts were in an embryonic stage, and his gender identity in crisis. He also still had worldly ambitions for his gender transformation, for it would bring him celebrity and security.[28] By adopting a female persona, he would transform himself from a man with some claim to renown into the most celebrated woman of his age. He also hoped to embarrass the French government into recalling him at once and on his own terms. Finally, he would marginalize himself politically and thereby reduce the risk of assassination. Yet at the same time, d'Eon did not wish to abandon male dress, behaviour and many other benefits of masculinity. Female dress was imposed upon him by Beaumarchais and the French court during the labyrinthine negotiations as a condition for meeting some of his demands.

Beaumarchais and d'Eon concluded their secret agreement, known as the Transaction, on 4 November 1775. It stipulated that d'Eon must surrender all his secret and diplomatic papers to Beaumarchais; stay silent regarding his old enemy Guerchy; and return to France as soon as possible, where he would adopt female clothes. In return, the king would grant him an annuity of 12,000 *livres*; safe passage to France; recognition of his female status; a trousseau of female clothes; and pay d'Eon's main creditor, Lord Ferrers, a significant – but as yet unspecified – portion of the 318,477 *livres* (£13,933) d'Eon was claiming in compensation and expenses.[29]

Once the Transaction was signed, Beaumarchais moved quickly. He at once paid Ferrers a first instalment, totalling £4,625, and sent Morande to Ferrers' London townhouse to retrieve a large, sealed iron chest of d'Eon's documents. This was a serious test of Morande's loyalty, for he realized that the chest contained a treasure trove of blackmail material. D'Eon was livid that Beaumarchais had taken such a risk. He was even angrier when he learned what had happened at Dover, where he claims Beaumarchais suffered an attack of 'the pox' he had contracted from 'some whores his dear trusty Morande had procured for him'. There, poorly and distracted, Beaumarchais left the chest of papers on the deck of the wrong ship. Fortunately, some attentive sailors tossed it after him and it reached Versailles safely. Beaumarchais' haste disconcerted d'Eon, who was furious that Ferrers had surrendered his correspondence without being paid in full. Fortunately, d'Eon had secretly held back some papers as security.[30]

Beaumarchais and Morande had good reason to stipulate that d'Eon should adopt female attire. It was part of a ruse to win a fortune by cornering the market in policies on d'Eon's sex. Beaumarchais and Morande were by this stage convinced that d'Eon was a woman, but to make sure they offered him £7,000 or £8,000 to reveal his true sex.[31] Once he refused, they needed a public demonstration. This is why it was so important to Beaumarchais that d'Eon adopt female garb. Once d'Eon began dressing as a woman and was recognized as female by the French government, the question would appear decided and their fortunes would be made. Even if some gamblers still refused to settle, the odds on the policies would shift decisively, ensuring them a massive windfall. D'Eon realized what was afoot when the *Morning Post* of 11 November 1775 announced:

> A new policy is preparing in the city *to do* the *she* Chevalier d'Eon [sic]; betts [sic] now run 7 to 4 a woman against a man; and a nobleman well known to the turf, has pledged to bring the matter to a clear decision before the expiration of fourteen days.

D'Eon, concluding that Morande had placed this announcement, exploded in indignation.[32] This speculation on his person infringed his privacy and put him in physical danger, since gamblers seemed willing to resort to violence to uncover his sex. He therefore wrote at once to the *Morning Post* to beg the British people 'not to renew any policies on his sex'. He warned that powerful men and bankers in France, perfectly aware of his true sex, were conspiring with financiers in London to profit at the gamblers' expense. He also alerted readers that he had 'recently refused great sums of money, which have been offered to him to be concerned in such policies'. As a result 'he declares that he will never manifest his sex, till such time as all such policies shall be at an end' and 'if that is impossible', will quit the country.[33] This letter was intended to prevent a betting frenzy, but it also incensed Morande. D'Eon reports that within hours of its publication, Morande called on him to warn him that 'Beaumarchais would be furious with me [d'Eon] because of this announcement; that it would wreck all the fine plans he had for me; and that I was nobody's friend and my own worst enemy'.[34]

Yet even now d'Eon did not break off relations. Instead, on 28 December, with Beaumarchais still away in Paris, he hosted a sumptuous dinner party for Morande, Eliza, Francy, Vignoles and Mesdames Cecil and Vernancourt.

This was a veritable blackmailers' feast, for d'Eon, Morande and Vignoles had all recently been paid off by Beaumarchais, while Vernancourt's turn would soon come. Perhaps d'Eon hoped that by bringing together so many blackmailers in one convivial gathering, he might loosen tongues and confirm who was behind the offensive newspaper advertisements? Whatever the case, by the time Beaumarchais arrives in London the next day, the stage is set for a showdown.[35]

Beaumarchais spends the day of his arrival closeted with Morande. On the morrow he summons d'Eon to dine at Morande's house. D'Eon finds Beaumarchais 'in the gayest spirits, laughing and joking with the two Morande brothers'. He congratulates Beaumarchais on his restored countenance, to which Beaumarchais replies indelicately 'my malady was not in my face and was not at all dangerous to men'. To d'Eon's horror, Beaumarchais goes on to perform a satirical love-song that he has composed, in which d'Eon plays the male role and Beaumarchais the lady. It is one among many doing the rounds in Paris, where Beaumarchais has been claiming that d'Eon is going to marry him. Then the conversation turns to d'Eon's letter to the Morning Post.

D'Eon tells Beaumarchais that he should never have written his letter 'if persons Beaumarchais knew well had not, in previous paragraphs, deliberately tried to start up a new blaze of speculations and wagers on my sex'. Beaumarchais responds furiously, roaring that d'Eon's letter was 'ill-written, humourless, unpolished, stupid and irrelevant from beginning to end' and that d'Eon had 'broken his word of honour'. D'Eon tells Beaumarchais to 'go fuck himself' and leaves in a fury. The next day he departs secretly for Ferrer's country estate, where he takes to his sick-bed and lies low for two months.[36]

Beaumarchais realizes that he has gone too far. The following day he writes to d'Eon in the hope of a reconciliation. However, the tone he adopts, at once jovial, patronizing, insinuating, hectoring and chiding, is ill-suited to this purpose. 'My dear chevalier, or all that it pleases you to be with me . . .' he begins playfully, using the masculine form, 'you must search elsewhere, my child, for those who toady or dissimulate to you'. He assures d'Eon of his friendship, then chides him for his letter in the Morning Post which 'ran contrary to the efforts that I was making on your behalf in France'. Nevertheless, Beaumarchais promises 'to forget with all my heart the things which escaped you, not against me, but against reason, in your lively and feminine anger yesterday morning', and invites d'Eon to dinner. He gets no reply and, unable to learn his whereabouts, asks d'Eon's landlord to forward the letter.[37]

D'Eon's response, when it comes, is long and scathing. It condemns Beaumarchais' 'revolting' and 'despotic' behaviour and his thoroughly bourgeois lack of honour (Beaumarchais was, after all, a mere clockmaker by trade). It boasts of d'Eon's long years of spotless service to the king and reiterates that he would never indulge in shameful trafficking in the policies on his sex. Finally, it accuses Beaumarchais of holding back the money promised for his trousseau.[38]

On 18 January, Beaumarchais raises the stakes by insisting that d'Eon abandon his 'scandalous' 'cross dressing' at once and don female attire. He gives d'Eon just eight days to capitulate and concludes with some naked threats: 'If you ignore this salutary and final advice . . . I will . . . acknowledge at the feet of His Majesty that I was terribly blind, when I guaranteed the good sense, honour, and loyalty of the Chevalier d'Eon.' In addition, he threatens to sue d'Eon for failing to hand over all his papers.[39]

D'Eon calls Beaumarchais' bluff.

> I grant you permission – he replies – to do as you threaten; to go throw yourself at the feet of all the kings and ministers on earth, in order to depict me, following your words, as an 'extravagant maiden', and at the same time as the shrewdest maiden in Europe.

Fully embracing his new female persona, d'Eon laments 'that men are only good in this life to deceive girls and women' and upbraids Beaumarchais 'Monsieur, you must stop taking advantage of my condition and wanting to profit from my misfortune to make me look as ridiculous as you'. He mocks Beaumarchais' recent attack of venereal disease 'which was probably given to everyone in Paris', and scolds him for making d'Eon look stupid with his talk of a marriage. Finally, d'Eon insists that once he has received his trousseau, dowry and expenses, 'harmony will be restored between us. Then . . . I will return to London to embrace you'.[40] However, instead of doing d'Eon's bidding, Beaumarchais leaves town, leaving Morande as his agent.

On 23 February, Morande placed a sensational article in the *Public Ledger* entitled 'The Discovery of Sex'. D'Eon had no doubt of the story's source, for its revelations exactly matched what French ministers and Beaumarchais knew, or thought they knew, about his sex and career. Only one man in London could have been privy to these secrets. The article said that when Louis XV died, a secret correspondence with d'Eon, dating from the 1760s and 1770s, including periods when he was supposedly a renegade, was found among his papers. It revealed that while exhorting his ministers to apprehend d'Eon, Louis XV had secretly alerted him to their projects because he wanted to protect d'Eon's secret, *viz* that he was a woman raised as a boy. When Louis XVI had learned of this, d'Eon had confessed the truth and been persuaded to sign the Transaction, the key clauses of which were printed in the article. D'Eon was incensed by this breach of faith, particularly because it exposed him as a spy, but there was little he could do. He was still dependent on Beaumarchais as a middleman.[41]

Thus in March, d'Eon approached Morande again. There was even a reconciliation of sorts when Morande and Eliza invited him to dine. D'Eon had every incentive to attend this and subsequent meetings, convinced that it was his best chance to recover the £9,308 that he was adamant France still owed him. He had no intention of surrendering his remaining papers for less.[42]

At a dinner party on 11 April, in front of several witnesses, d'Eon forced an astonishing admission out of Morande. Morande confessed that the previous October he and Beaumarchais had indeed attempted to involve d'Eon in a conspiracy to buy up the policies on his sex, but d'Eon had refused. He added that they considered putting the plan into action regardless, but, 'wishing to leave nothing to fortune', consulted several of London's leading lawyers. Their unanimous advice was that no one could be forced to honour such policies. As a result, Morande claimed the project was abandoned. D'Eon clearly doubted this.

This confession was dynamite for d'Eon, who now took the offensive. His first step was to refuse to meet Morande while Beaumarchais' behaviour towards him, which he blamed on Morande's perfidious advice, remained so 'extraordinary'.[43] Next, he got the witnesses to Morande's confession to swear an affidavit confirming what Morande had said.[44] Finally, on 27 May, he sent a long list of his complaints against Beaumarchais to Vergennes, accompanied by a dossier of documentary proofs. He sent further copies to about a dozen leading figures at the French court.[45]

D'Eon's narrative of events was colourful, to say the least, and must have shocked Vergennes. It recounted Morande's past adventures, his relations with Beaumarchais, and their attempts to traffic in policies on d'Eon's sex. Nothing was spared to paint Morande as a monster of mythical proportions. It contains d'Eon's first allegations that Morande had spent three years in Bicêtre, caused his father's death of chagrin, habitually impregnated his neighbours and servants, and posed as Lauraguais to attack himself in print. D'Eon also asserts that Beaumarchais and Morande combined to produce pamphlets for suppression, a clear allusion to the *Avis à la branche espagnole*. Finally, he accuses Beaumarchais of living at the French government's expense, cynically spinning out negotiations for months, when in reality he had spent only four or five hours in face to face discussions with d'Eon. Instead he passed his time with Morande at 'sordid and exotic orgies', catching the pox in the brothels of Covent Garden. Beaumarchais and Morande are therefore hardly the sort of men to 'restore the reputation of a man who has fallen victim to the passions of the great, still less that of a virtuous maiden'. In consequence, d'Eon demanded that Vergennes replace Beaumarchais with a more appropriate intermediary.[46]

D'Eon's request went unheeded. Instead Vergennes advised him to be patient and continue to deal with Beaumarchais. This was not something d'Eon was prepared to do, especially after Beaumarchais laid his own complaints before the foreign minister. D'Eon's door remained firmly closed against Beaumarchais and Morande.[47]

Things were beginning to turn sour for Morande. It was bad enough that both Beaumarchais and d'Eon now blamed him for the rupture.[48] Worse still, Morande's associates, and in all probability Morande himself, had tied up a great deal of money in wagers on d'Eon's sex. But it now seemed unlikely that they would be able to collect their winnings in the near future. Morande's plans had backfired. A public acknowledgement of d'Eon's sex was less likely than ever.

On 4 June, Morande came up with a scheme for a reconciliation that might also resolve the gender issue publicly. He offered to become d'Eon's biographer:

> I have had a project for a long time . . . It is to be your chanter, your historiographer and to hand you down to posterity with all your virtues, all your qualities without the false colours that the minor shortcomings in your honour and in politics have been able to cast over your entire life . . . I do not flatter you. Without any doubt, you have some distinguished talents, but they have their nuances, and they are what a friend never allows to be seen. It is well said that there are no heroes for the *valet de chambre* and the intimate friend . . . and that part of my project which I have already completed will make you see by its execution my sincere attachment to your person.[49]

We should not take Morande's words at face value, for they contain a chilling implicit threat. D'Eon must co-operate with Morande in producing an authorized biography or fall victim to a muckraking memoir.

D'Eon ignores this threat until 3 August, when Morande sends him a 38-page manuscript 'full of calumnies and impertinences' addressed to 'Mademoiselle d'Eon'.[50] D'Eon reads it 'with equal pleasure and contempt', before delivering his reply:

> All Europe knows, that the Sieur de Morande has no other means of subsistence in London, but what he derives from the mud of his libels . . . the Sieur de Morande may make vain endeavours to live at the expense of Mademoiselle or Chevalier d'Eon. No one will be very surprised at such atrocious proceedings: but the Sieur de Morande may rest assured that he will gain nothing by it, except contempt; and that the friendship he offers is considered a heavier load than the hatred he threatens.
>
> Mademoiselle d'Eon, as she already told the Sieur de Morande . . . can't [sic] grant him audience only in Hyde Park on whatever day shall be convenient to him. She will come thither accompanied by her brother the Chevalier d'Eon, who . . . always undertook to defend his sister's honour.[51]

The blackmail has failed. So has Morande's attempt to get a public statement on d'Eon's sex. And now he faces a challenge from d'Eon, who is reputedly one of the finest swordsmen in Europe. Morande refuses to fight, saying that 'it is impossible for him to meet d'Eon anywhere but on a bed.'[52] D'Eon is incensed and promises to beat him with his cane instead.

On the morning of 7 August, bearing pistols and swords repaired and sharpened for the occasion, d'Eon and his brother-in-law, the Chevalier O'Gorman, call at Morande's house to force him to fight. O'Gorman beats at the door, but when Morande fails to come, he is maladroit enough to deliver d'Eon's challenge to a heavily pregnant Eliza, who becomes distraught. By way of reply, Morande sends an insolent note, stating that:

> he has not a hand so vile or a heart so base to fight against a woman who has lifted her shirt to him, shown him what she has got, and to make him more certain of the facts, made him touch it.

He will, however, defend himself if attacked.[53]

Such pretended gallantry and bravery convince no one. In response, d'Eon sends a second 'billet', full of comically extravagant insults. It opens:

> Sir,
>
>   Your discourses concerning me, your behaviour . . . and the letters or rather libels which you have sent me, together with your persevering and reiterated refusal of giving me . . . either with sword or pistols that satisfaction which is due to injured honour, will convince the whole world . . . that you are nothing but a scurrilous *libeller*, an infamous *Aretin*, and the basest *coward* . . . in the kingdom of scoundrels . . . Henceforth you must expect no other treatment from me but that drubbing which the asses of your country meet with, to wit, canings and kicks in the breech [?]. Away, away beast and live with the hogs, your only fit companions, poor *Gazetier cuirassé*. Now put on your breastplate, lest the wasps issuing from the mire from which you sprung should sting you amidst the thistles you herd upon.

Warming to his theme, d'Eon's hyperbole becomes yet more absurd:

> Remember and never forget that you were the cause of your honest father's death, that you were imprisoned . . . with the Banditti at Armentières, and that you escaped from thence to England, with the perfidious and cruel design of bringing to the gallows your innocent mother, already too unfortunate in giving birth to so unnatural a monster.
>
>   Remember too, that you were forced to deliver into the flames of Sodom and Gommorah in Marylebone all the productions of your infernal brain. This is but the forerunner of the fate that awaits your infected carcass.[54]

And so it continues, a tirade of insults pouring down upon Morande's head. D'Eon will live to regret stooping to Morande's level.

Three days later, d'Eon tries again. This time the challenge comes from O'Gorman, who wishes to avenge Morande's affront to his family's honour. It is delivered by the Chevalier de Piennes, a French dragoon captain. For 24 hours Morande evades him, but eventually Piennes catches him at home and reads out the challenge. Morande responds wrily that 'even my character requires me to meet him'. All he asks is time to settle his affairs, make a will and find £46 that he owes to d'Eon. Piennes assures him that d'Eon will gladly excuse the debt if Morande will meet O'Gorman in combat. Morande accepts. He proposes that the duel take place the following Saturday and promises to give Piennes an exact time and place on Friday.[55]

However, come Friday, Morande has gone to ground. Piennes searches for him fruitlessly for five hours. Finally, at 10.30 p.m., Morande sends d'Eon a note requesting to see Piennes. Piennes rushes to Morande's house and asks him to settle the time and place. Morande replies that he is 'firmly resolved, neither to mention a place for a duel, nor to consent to meet for any such purpose . . . unless compelled to it by being attacked in the streets of London'.[56] Finally, to secure his safety, he and Eliza call on Lord Mansfield, the Chief Justice, to swear that Morande's life is in danger. In consequence, on Wednesday 21 August 1776, d'Eon is bound over for £200 to keep the peace.[57]

Morande has chosen life and dishonour over possible death. In the eyes of his contemporaries this proves he is no gentleman. Hence, although duelling is technically banned in both France and Britain, d'Eon and O'Gorman have no hesitation in sending a documented account of events to Vergennes. Their purpose, they say, is to make known to the foreign minister 'what sort of man' Beaumarchais has employed, and to show that Morande 'only has the courage to insult the king's, the ministers, the grandees and the ladies of the French court. He is the basest coward when it comes to rendering satisfaction arms in hand to men or women whom he slanders'.[58]

This extraordinary dispute was followed by a newspaper war, as Morande attempted to flush out d'Eon's sex and persuade the public 'that there is not a single instance of truth in all the transactions of her life'.[59] It was an uneven battle, in which Morande commanded the support of the *Morning Post*, *Public Ledger* and, above all, the *Westminster Gazette*, a newspaper in which Morande probably had a stake. D'Eon's sole mouthpiece was the *Public Advertiser*.[60]

Morande had opened with a warning shot in the *Westminster Gazette* of 6–10 August, which announced that the paper had been promised 'a full, genuine . . . account of the epicoene [sic] d'Eon, containing the principal anecdotes of *its* life, and a full detail of its artful behaviour in regard to the policies which were done on its sex'. This was clearly intended to make d'Eon back off and perhaps reconsider his refusal to bow to blackmail. Morande only unleashed his full broadside two weeks later in a pseudonymous letter signed *Quos Ergo*.

Quos Ergo's letter boasted that Morande had brought Beaumarchais and d'Eon together. He attributed their quarrel to d'Eon's fury at Morande's rebukes, first for holding back his papers, and then for writing to Vergennes and reading his letter 'to many gentlemen here in London.' The letter added bluntly that d'Eon's conduct was all the more blameworthy because Morande knew all 'her private history' including 'the whole fabrication of those awful affidavits against *le comte de Guerchy* and . . . her part in the scandalous business on the policies on her sex'. This was combustible material. Morande was suggesting not only that d'Eon had encouraged and profited from the policies, but that he had conspired in perjury to implicate a French ambassador in attempted murder. These allegations were all the more dangerous because many facts in the affidavits against Guerchy had indeed been fabricated.[61]

Worse was to follow. A letter in the *Public Ledger* of 24 August complained that the public were being 'pestered' over a 'dispute between a parcel of renegade French SPIES' and concluded that the dispute was probably 'all a hum' designed 'to cover their rascally designs'. The writer went on to label d'Eon an impostor:

> She may or may not have been the best SPY that the French ever had in England. At any rate, this is not the age for the English to be bamboozled by any foreign impostor, who prefers breeches to petticoats.

The letter then suggested a solution to the problem of d'Eon: the authorities should enforce England's ancient sumptuary laws concerning clothing.

> As there is not any doubt of her being a woman, the shortest method of dealing with her is, to enforce an Act of Parliament which inflicts a punishment on those who are dressed in a garb improper for their sex.

If this article was not by Morande – and even he might hesitate to label himself a 'renegade French spy' – it certainly served his immediate designs.

Other articles tried to justify Morande's cowardice or make favourable comparisons with d'Eon's behaviour. Whereas d'Eon was 'an absolute impostor' and 'a pensioned spy' wrote François [Morande?] in the *Public Ledger*:

> Monsieur de Morande is, I find, a gentleman of abilities, respectability and honour. HE actually hath made the French Ministry so much his enemies, that it would be dangerous for him to set his foot on French Ground. He is not playing a double game, nor acting in a sinister method, unbecoming of a man.[62]

The *Westminster Gazette* also argued that Morande was the more honourable man: he was a young hothead when he sold his *Secret Memoirs of a Woman of*

Pleasure but kept his word to deliver the whole manuscript. D'Eon acted with the cool calculation of age when he sold his papers and perfidiously held many back. The paper also chided O'Gorman for being 'imprudent enough to challenge Morande's wife now seven months gone with child' and derided d'Eon's courage, which, 'were it real', would not 'become a person of her sex'.[63] Morande, on the other hand, 'must have been blamed by the whole world had he *put her to the sword*'.[64] Ultimately, the paper suggested, d'Eon's challenges were mere smoke-screens to help her to evade the issues Morande raised concerning 'the affidavits, the policies, &c.' for 'in ages of ignorance or superstition . . . it was customary to answer the accusation by the sword; but in this more polished time, fighting does not refute any charge'.[65]

Such logic does little to help Morande when he encounters O'Gorman in the Spring Garden Coffee House late on the evening of 2 September 1776. For, after a brief exchange of words, O'Gorman draws his sword and advances.

We have two radically different accounts of what happened next. According to the *Westminster Gazette*:

> De Morande instantly drew and defended himself against the furious assailant, who finding De Morande determinately getting in on him drew back and put up his sword while some gentlemen interposed and said that a coffee-house was no place for such an encounter.

O'Gorman, the *Westminster Gazette* continues, responded enthusiastically: 'By Jasus', [sic – the writer is mocking his Irish accent] 'we will both set off together this moment in a post-chaise for the country.'

'Sir' replied Morande, 'I am going to walk in St James Square.' However, although he waited there until 1 o'clock in the morning, O'Gorman never appeared.[66]

A more plausible account comes from a correspondent to the *Public Advertiser* of 6 September 1776, who objects to 'the vapouring "Gazetier cuirassé" the hero of his own tales . . . who morning and evening pesters the Papers with his own achievements (not those wherein he valiantly took Lord Mansfield for his second)'. He asserts that O'Gorman drew his sword in front of several gentlemen and officers, whereupon Morande:

> had the impudence, with a pale face and trembling joints, to claim friendship with one of them; but he answered that he was worthy neither of his friendship nor enmity: Whereupon report says, Mons. [Monsieur] Cuirassé got to the door, and run [sic] out, crying out lustily, Watch! Watch! and so ran as fast as his trembling Age would permit him, perhaps to St James's Square, or God knows where.[67]

At 5 o'clock the next morning O'Gorman's second, Captain Horneck, calls at Morande's house to request he attend a 'breakfast party' in the country. Horneck has been branded 'The Military Macaroni' by satirists, on account of his foppish dress and effete mannerisms, and thus strikes an amused Morande as the ideal ally for d'Eon. Morande mocks him as a 'puppy', a 'mere child'. Leaning from his bedroom window, he tells Horneck he will not make up any 'country parties' but walks abroad in London every day, sword by his side. But if Horneck does not leave his door and stop frightening his wife, Morande will 'amuse the mob which Horneck's impertinence had assembled at his expense'. At this, according to the *Westminster Gazette*, Horneck retired 'precipitately, which is the only part of military duty that this *brave* officer has practised'.[68]

At 11 the same morning, Horneck and Morande run into each other again at the Mount Coffee House in Grosvenor Street. Harsh words are exchanged. Both step outside. They are wearing swords, but Horneck says he wants to fetch his pistols and retires, leaving Morande free to ridicule him in the newspapers:

> M. de Morande is very happy to have drawn the vengeance of all the he-she things upon him; Miss d'Eon and her clique were sufficient to alarm every man who is afraid of an assassin, or a poisoner; if all our English Miss Mollys [i.e. homosexuals] join in the confederacy, or even *Captain H——'s* [i.e. Horneck's] acquaintance, all Fielding's men will not be sufficient to prevent the schemes which this *worthy* group are capable of executing.
>
> Yesterday Captain Horneck's sex was done on change at 50 L. per cent. It is imagined from something that happened at Mr de Morande's door, that the policies will be as high as 70 L per cent before night.[69]

When Morande returns home that night he finds two challenges from Horneck and a promise to denounce him as 'the greatest JEAN FOUTRE [fucker] in the universe' if he fails to turn up at Hyde Park at six the next morning. Morande's answer is a brazen and provocative refusal:

> I will not accept a stated rendezvous from, or permit the weapons to be appointed by, anybody. I have declared . . . my resolution in that respect . . . After having refused to go out with Mr O'Gorman, I will not have it laid to my charge that I have chosen for an adversary a child, who calls for pistols when he has his sword by his side, *and when arrived at the field of battle would very likely faint away.*[70]

Horneck does not forget these insults. Six months later, in the early hours of Sunday 2 March 1777, he gets a chance to avenge them. He is sitting in the Mount Coffee House when Morande walks in. Armed only with a cane, Horneck sets about him. Morande draws his rapier. Horneck closes with him to avoid his sword-thrusts. Morande is the stronger man and, according to some accounts, grabs Horneck's head and begins slamming it against the wall. Onlookers intervene and separate them. A new challenge is issued, and a rendezvous set for Hyde Park on Friday 7 March at 5.30 in the morning. The protagonists agree to use both swords and pistols 'and as the affair was of the most serious nature to both parties, *large pistols*, and a very small distance was pitched on'. Seconds are chosen and two surgeons appointed 'as the nature of the offence was such that great danger was inevitable'.

To Horneck's delight, Morande keeps the appointment, though he arrives late. Horneck runs straight to his coach, begging him to follow him at once. But Morande repeatedly calls for Horneck's second, Captain Watson, to come across and instruct him. He seeks clarification about where to go and what to do with his pistols. He is told to put them in his pockets. He is procrastinating, and with reason. Suddenly, Mr Lucas, High Constable of Westminster, arrives and arrests them both. They are taken before Mr Justice Addington, who has been tipped off by Eliza, and each bound over for £200 to keep the peace.[71] Few doubt that Morande approved Eliza's actions in advance, and this time he is the one pilloried in the press:

> Mrs. De Morande, as some atonement to her husband for her late faux pas with Justice Addington, has pledged herself to call out Capt. Horneck, and thus to restore the lost honour of the family, by the prowess of a female arm.[72]

Such ridicule is a small price to pay for his escape.

Unable to deal with Morande on the duelling field, d'Eon decides to attack him in law and consults Sir John Fielding. This shift in strategy is all the more urgent because public opinion is turning rapidly against him. The London mobs that had once defended him are beginning to see d'Eon as an impostor, spy, liar and fraud. Things come to a head on the night of 9–10 August 1776, when metal railings are torn from in front of d'Eon's house and stones thrown through the windows, injuring one of his friends. D'Eon is certain the damage was done by rogues sent by Morande, but the incident shows he is no longer a popular hero.[73]

D'Eon's opportunity to strike back comes on 14 September, when the *Westminster Gazette* carries a long letter from Morande 'to the public'. It outlines Morande's dispute with d'Eon and asserts that Morande has proofs to back his claims. His key allegations are mostly familiar. D'Eon is a woman; 'she' is 'privy to policies opened on her sex'; the key affidavits against Guerchy were mendacious; and 'she' was not entitled to sell 'her' political papers because they already belonged to the French Crown. In short, 'd'Eon is an impostor of the first magnitude; and, if she doth not, in defence of herself, convict me of false-hood she must be a reptile of the most contemptible class.'[74] Naturally d'Eon rises to the challenge. He instructs his lawyers to pursue Morande for libel. For good measure, he also pays Sheriff Whitcombe's men to arrest Morande for his outstanding debt of £46.[75]

D'Eon's information – surely one of the strangest ever to be entered – comes before the Court of King's Bench in late November, amid great public interest. On the day it is due to be heard, it is impossible to get into the courtroom, so great is the throng waiting to learn 'many curious secrets . . . respecting the real sex of the prosecutor or prosecutrix.'[76] Morande's defence is simple. As his counsel, Mr Bearcroft, puts it,

> it has ever been a rule in this Court never to grant Informations where the parties applying for them could be proved to have been guilty of the same offence . . . nay . . . it is deemed necessary that the plaintiffs should be perfectly innocent.

In particular, Bearcroft argues that d'Eon's allegation that Morande had caused his father's death and plotted his mother's demise pre-dated the offences of which he complained.

This was no dry legal argument, for the correspondence of both parties was read and, 'as they contained a variety of ridiculous expressions, the Bench, the Bar, and the auditors, were repeatedly thrown into the most violent fits of laughter.' D'Eon's counsel, Mr Buller, replied that he had already answered at law for his letters of challenge by taking out a bond for good behaviour, and therefore stood pristine before the court, but to no avail. To the general surprise of the crowd of legal students and news correspondents expecting a solemn judgment, Lord Chief Justice Mansfield dismisses the case in five words. This, opined the *Morning Post*, did him great honour, 'as the whole business was of too ridiculous a nature for his more serious attention.'[77]

There was similar mirth on 1 July 1777, when Morande again testified in front of Mansfield, this time in a case concerning wagers on d'Eon's sex. Following the failure of his libel suit, d'Eon had remained in England while redoubling his complaints against Beaumarchais and attempting to bargain directly with the Crown. Meanwhile, many of those who had bet that d'Eon was female now believed the evidence of the Transaction, which Morande had discussed in court, was sufficient to justify claiming their winnings. Among them was a surgeon and mid-wife named Hayes, who claimed £700 against an original £105 stake. When Mr Jacques, who had issued the policies, refused to pay, Hayes took him to court, assisted and probably encouraged by Morande. D'Eon neither attended the court nor made legal representations to prevent his body being discussed by the litigants.

During his opening statement, Buller, who on this occasion was Hayes' barrister, brought 'a good laugh' from the court with his assertion that he would 'prove d'Eon was a woman'. This assurance was supported by perjurous testimony from three witnesses. First came Mr. Le Goux, a French surgeon. He testified that he had once examined d'Eon for a complaint which required an examination of 'the parts from where knowledge of sex arises'. He was thus certain that d'Eon was a woman, but had been sworn to secrecy. Under cross-examination he claimed that he had initially refused to testify, but had been subpoenaed to appear. The third witness, a French physician called Malon, used Morande as his interpreter, and testified that he knew d'Eon to be 'a Woman by *Sight* and *Touch*'. D'Eon was convinced both witnesses had been suborned by Morande.

However, it was Morande's own testimony which attracted most attention. To guffaws of laughter, he declared 'It is a Woman: I say so within my own knowledge', before offering a series of anecdotes and further particulars. Under cross-examination, he added:

> about four years ago I was very intimate with her; she was very lively in her Conversation, and spoke to me with great freedom on the Subject. She one day shewed me her Woman's Cloaths, Ear-Rings, and shewed me her breasts.

Pressed further he said that on the morning of 3 July 1774:

> I was (being myself a married Man) introduced into her Bedchamber; she was in Bed, and with great Freedom bid me satisfy myself of what we had so often been jocular about, for she had often said I was to be Godfather. I put my Hand into Bed and was fully convinced she was a Woman.

The defence did not dispute any of these testimonies. Instead, it suggested that evidence concerning d'Eon's private parts ought to be dismissed as indecent, obscene and demeaning to a court of justice. In addition, it suggested that Hayes had possessed insider knowledge and thus his wager was fraudulent.

In his summing up, Lord Mansfield said he could find no evidence of fraud, particularly as d'Eon had refused to co-operate with any party. While he agreed with the defence's first objection as a moral principle, he concluded regretfully that it had no basis in English law. He therefore directed the Jury to find in the plaintiff's favour. Nevertheless, he declared the whole subject to be distasteful, although 'the indecency arose more from the unnecessary questions asked, than from the case itself'. He found it particularly reprehensible that gamblers could wager on an issue that violated the privacy, security and reputation of a third party.[78] By December 1777, when he heard the same witnesses testify in a further case involving wagers on d'Eon's sex, Mansfield had devised a formula to turn these convictions into a legal principle and so found for the defendant. However, he also made clear that he was not questioning d'Eon's sex, which following the

Hayes-Jacques case was, from a legal standpoint, considered to be female.[79]

Following the Hayes-Jacques case, d'Eon continued to refuse to confirm his true sex and encouraged gamblers to refuse to settle. Finally, in mid August, he returned to France. D'Eon insisted that his departure was the result of the court judgment. In reality, Vergennes and Louis XVI had now paid enough of his British debts that he felt able to leave. Once in France, he finally adopted female attire. He wore it for the rest of his life.

Astonishingly, there is a happy ending to the tale of d'Eon and Morande. In November 1785, d'Eon returned to Britain to fight a court case with Lord Ferrers' heirs. He remained there for the rest of his life. The following March, d'Eon encountered Morande at a friend's house. Morande reports that their interview was 'very peaceful' and, rather more ambiguously, that they 'embraced each other

MADEMOISELLE de BEAUMONT, or the
CHEVALIER D'EON.
Female Minister Plenipo. Capt. of Dragoons &c. &c.

Plate 7. The Female Minister Plenipotentiary. Caricature of d'Eon from the *Town and Country Magazine*, 1778. Courtesy of the Brotherton Collection, Brotherton Library, University of Leeds.

with all the tenderness that you might suppose to exist between us'.[80] Over the next few years, Morande did d'Eon numerous favours, including mediating a financial dispute, tracing the relatives of an abandoned French child, and even, apparently, preparing and translating memoranda on d'Eon's behalf.[81] By 1789, their relations were cordial, and in 1790 and 1791 they met socially or dined together several times.[82] Their mutual back-scratching even extended to their writings. On the first anniversary of the fall of the Bastille, Morande praised d'Eon as 'a good patriot', while later in the revolution d'Eon applauded Morande's belated conversion into a 'good citizen and patriot' who had risked his head for the constitutional monarchy.[83] The two men saw each other for the last time in April 1791, shortly before Morande returned to France. He died apparently still ignorant of d'Eon's sex, which was finally revealed following d'Eon's death on 21 May 1810. His corpse was examined by a professor of anatomy, two of London's top surgeons and several other distinguished witnesses. All attested to d'Eon's perfect masculinity.[84]

On one level, the dispute between the d'Eon and Beaumarchais camps was indeed a struggle between 'a parcel of French spies'. Or rather two rival networks. For, like Beaumarchais, d'Eon had dreamed of channelling aid to the Americans: this made him all the more furious that Morande and Beaumarchais had exposed his espionage activities. On 25 April 1777, d'Eon retaliated by denouncing Francy and Morande to Broglie's secretary. According to d'Eon, Francy kept Morande informed of all the plans Beaumarchais hatched with the French naval ministry, and Morande then relayed this information to Lord North, the British Prime Minister.[85] Similar, more specific, allegations appear in an anonymous letter sent in December 1776 to Benjamin Franklin, the newly arrived American ambassador to France. The letter, which almost certainly emanated from the d'Eon camp, accuses Francy, Morande and Beaumarchais of betraying 'all the transactions of the court of France for America, the ships, description, name, force and cargo of Mr du Coudray's expedition at Havre &c.' to 'Charles [sic – Nathaniel] Parker Forth', principal agent of Lord Stormont, the British ambassador in Paris.[86] At about the same time, Barthélemy Tort, who was then acting as a French agent and was closely linked to d'Eon, repeated these charges in an interview with Vergennes.[87] They also find echoes in Pelleport's Diable dans un bénitier, which alleges that Morande, Beaumarchais and Francy betrayed French and American shipping to the British and vice versa.[88] However, the accusation was evidently discounted by the French and American authorities, who continued to place their faith in Beaumarchais. D'Eon did not dare to repeat the charge in any further letter or publication. It thus appears to be the product of malice.

Further circumstantial evidence that Morande, Francy and Beaumarchais were innocent is found in Stormont's correspondence. It shows that British intelligence concerning Beaumarchais' activities came from surveillance rather than betrayal.

Beaumarchais hoped that his dealings with d'Eon would provide cover for his trips to London, but his frequent comings and goings only raised British suspicions. These were confirmed in August 1776, when Stormont reported that Beaumarchais had been given 3,000,000 *livres* to help the Americans. By November 1776, Stormont knew that Morande was in regular correspondence with Beaumarchais and recommended that his letters be opened, read and resealed.[89] It is unlikely that the British learned much from them. None of Morande's correspondence with Beaumarchais from this period survives, but, as we will see, he was not naïve enough to send truly compromising materials through the post.

Morande was doubtless aware that he was under suspicion. As early as April 1776, the British minister Rochford assured George III that rumours that Beaumarchais was a spy were unfounded. He nevertheless reported their conversation to Beaumarchais, presumably as a warning. Several weeks later, Lauraguais, who was by then one of Beaumarchais' agents, fled London fearing he was deeply compromised.[90] However, lacking certain information, the British merely kept Morande under surveillance. They only moved against him after the outbreak of hostilities with France in July 1778.

Still unsure of their ground, the British tried to flush Morande out using a stalking-horse. This was the Reverend Henry Bate, editor of the *Morning Post*, London's most notorious daily scandalsheet, which was closely aligned with Lord North's government and notoriously corrupt. As a muckraker, Bate was perhaps the only man in London who could hold a torch to Morande. He was, in addition, a well-connected socialite, writer of fashionable operas, and a formidable duellist and fist fighter.[91] Bate was also an agent of Lord Sandwich, First Lord of the Admiralty. Bate's brother was Sandwich's private secretary.[92]

In late August 1778, Bate ran a series of insinuating articles about Morande. At first they were oblique. Morande's identity was concealed behind epithets such as '*the long sided Frenchman – the French runaway – Beaumarchais friend* [sic] – *his protegee* [sic] – *his correspondent – his spy*'.[93] Finally, on 26 August, Bates indicated Morande directly by refering to the Horneck affair.

Morande felt obliged to respond. He at once sent the *General Advertiser* and other newspapers a long list of insinuating 'Queries', which piled provocation on provocation. Morande accused Bate of routinely extorting fees and sexual favours in return for suppressing paragraphs and insinuated that his wife regularly sold her body in Mrs Mullman's brothel. He also suggested that Bate had tried to rape his sister-in-law, the actress Mrs Elizabeth Hartley, and had defended a murderer in return for hard cash. Reaching a crescendo, Morande asked:

Does not that fellow [Bate] daily deserve to be caned and kicked out of all societies; and are you not amazed that in a free country nobody has hitherto *taken the liberty* of knocking out his brains, or breaking every bone in his skin? Could he have expected to live so long when he first started, and to escape as an incendiary the gallows or the barges, or having at least his nose cut off, and his ears nailed to the pillory as an atrocious defamer?

In a covering letter, Morande defended himself, noting that Bate had not been able 'to produce a single fact which might throw but the shadow of suspicion on me'. As a result, he had nothing to fear from Bate's accusations, particularly as his literary pursuits were well known and entirely occupied his time:

> I will therefore give the Editor of the *Morning Post* ample leave to inform against me at the Secretary's of State [sic], to call me a spy . . . without apprehending that the information, and the oath of Henry Bate . . . will ever mislead the public on my account.

Morande concluded with a further taunt:

> in justice to myself, as well as to fulfil my engagements to the public, who nauseate the slanderous *Morning Post*, I cannot finish without openly declaring, that the Editor of that Paper . . . is as great a COWARD, as, to the knowledge of all the world, he is a KNAVE and a SCOUNDREL.[94]

This was fighting talk and Morande knew it. No man of honour could ignore such insults and imputations. If Bate did so, his testimony would be considered false and Morande would be vindicated. This is probably what Morande hoped would happen, for he apparently believed that, in a previous duel, Bate had conspired to charge the pistols with just powder and bran.[95]

Unfortunately, Morande has been badly misinformed. He has also misjudged his adversary. Bate – who soon afterwards became known as 'the fighting parson' – immediately sends a challenge. Morande accepts and, once fortified by alcohol, makes no attempt to evade the combat. Whether through drunken bravado or genuine anger, he is ready to fight to the death.

Bate and Morande meet with pistols in the Ring at Hyde Park, a favourite venue for duellists, at 5 a.m. on 28 August. Morande choses a distance of just 12 paces and they exchange shots. Both miss. Unsatisfied, Morande advances two or three paces and shoots again, but aims wide. Bate's second shot also misses.

The commotion is now attracting passers-by, so the duellists and their seconds decamp and continue in a field off the Edgware Road. There, Morande shoots first, but his pistol misfires. Bate fires back and strikes a hook in Morande's hat. The bullet ricochets and scrapes Morande's skull. The damage is slight and both men fire again.

By now, their seconds are growing alarmed. They beg both men to retire with honour satisfied. Bate refuses. He demands the 'fullest recantation' from Morande, but Morande remains unrepentant. They begin to reload.

In desperation, the seconds threaten to retire. Morande comes to his senses. He assures Bate 'I am now concerned for the attack I made upon your character, Sir, ... and am ready to make all the reparation in my power through the same public channel.' Bate accepts, contingent on the wording. Relieved, they retire to the Turk's Head coffee-house in the Strand to 'adjust the whole to the satisfaction of all parties' and to prepare a report for publication in the newspapers.[96]

On 31 August, the daily papers carry their announcements. Morande declares that Bate has proved himself a 'man of honour' and that his 'Queries' appear, on closer examination, to be undeserving of 'the smallest credit', particularly those regarding Bate's wife. Likewise, Bate declares that he no longer has 'the smallest doubt' of his rival's 'personal courage' and therefore thinks 'this gentleman's character has been misrepresented to me'. Of the allusions to espionage there is not a word.[97]

On reading such puffery, some readers concluded that the whole affair was fabricated by two 'rascals acting in combination' and that the '*honest* and ingenious Morande, is endeavouring to fabricate a second d'Eon's affair ... in which he acted so conspicuous and *honorable* a part.'[98] Such doubts, while natural, seem misplaced. According to Pelleport, Morande's copyist, Jean Goy, reported that he spent the night before the duel plying Morande with *eau de vie* to build up his courage. This detail may also explain his inaccurate shooting. Coming from a sworn enemy of Morande, the tale appears to prove beyond dispute that the duel really took place, although perhaps neither protagonist was quite as bold or foolhardy as their official account suggests.[99]

Nevertheless, Morande now realized the game was up. In all probability, Bate warned him of the government's suspicions. Whatever the case, Morande had a brief interview with Lord North shortly afterwards in which he promised to quit London for the duration of the conflict.[100]

Morande and his family duly retired to Great Stanmore, 10 miles north-west of London. There he rented a modest house and gardens for £12 per annum. The local land tax and highway surveyor's accounts show that he arrived in Stanmore in 1778 and continued his tenancy until 1783, shortly after the end of the war. On 4 April 1779, Morande's daughter Elizabeth Frances was baptized in Stanmore parish church. There also, according to Pelleport, Morande developed some fabulous gardens 'which contained an immense quantity of flowers of great beauty'. However, as we shall see, allegations that these gardens were purchased with blood money are false. Indeed, from 1778 until 1781, as French and Spanish naval aid undermined Britain's maritime hegemony and helped turn the tide of war decisively in the Americans' favour, Morande seems to have lived in quiet retirement and had nothing to do with espionage.[101]

After his interview with Lord North, Morande doubtless calculated that it would be too dangerous to continue in Beaumarchais' pay during wartime. Instead, he decided to extort money from Beaumarchais by threatening to expose him as his collaborator in the production of several 'infamies', including, undoubtedly, the *Avis à la branche espagnole*. Moreover, according to Beaumarchais, he also threatened to inculpate one of Beaumarchais' friends in the ministry. The obvious inference is that Morande intended to accuse Sartine of a cover-up to protect Beaumarchais. To deal with this threat, Beaumarchais wrote to his business agent in London, Samuel Swinton, one of the few men in England who could match Beaumarchais or Morande for cunning. Swinton was probably first introduced to Beaumarchais by Lauraguais, and hence well aware of Morande's history. A former naval officer, soldier of fortune and entrepreneur, Swinton was also married bigamously to Félicité, the sister of Lauraguais' mistress Laurence Lefebvre and had helped to organize Laurence's flight to France.[102]

Swinton reported that Morande could be appeased for just £500, for which price he would deliver up any letters and papers in his possession that might compromise Beaumarchais. Swinton promptly lent him this sum, which Beaumarchais quickly repaid. However, when Beaumarchais opened the three packages of documents sent by Morande, they contained nothing but Beaumarchais' judicial memoirs against Goëzman and a mocking letter saying that because Beaumarchais had only lent him the money, he was only sending '*papilottes*' [twists of paper used to curl hair].

Over the next few months, Morande continued his threats, some of which he even trusted to the post. Alarmed by his recklessness and determination, Beaumarchais therefore decided to bring a legal action, even though this involved a risky trip to England in September 1778. However, instead of dragging Morande before the courts, Beaumarchais forgave him after hearing 'his repentance, the motives he gave for these attacks, made, he said at the instigation of my enemies, the excuses he made me, the tears he shed, the pardon he asked in writing from the minister and me'. Beaumarchais even loaned him a further 3,000 *Louis* to pay off his remaining debts. This would, Beaumarchais suggested, allow him to pursue Morande for debt in the case of any recidivism. In return Morande surrendered some of Beaumarchais' correspondence.[103]

Nevertheless, less than two years later, Morande made new threats. In the summer of 1780, he wrote three letters to Sartine in which he claimed that Beaumarchais had cheated him and threatened to forward a damning commentary on Beaumarchais' trip to London in 1778, unless Beaumarchais paid him the money he claimed he was due. Sartine forwarded the correspondence to Beaumarchais, and there is every indication that he paid.[104] Yet within months, Morande was making new demands, claiming to possess some scandalous verses corrected in Beaumarchais' hand.[105]

Sick of Morande's demands, Beaumarchais decided to fight fire with fire. Sometime around January 1781 he sent Swinton a package of documents incriminating Morande, including 'information that this man has given me by his own hand, written in his own handwriting, on all the secret aspects of the dockyards, navy, [and] administration of England'. Beaumarchais was threatening to expose Morande as his own agent. He also instructed Swinton to begin proceedings for libel and demanding money with menaces. Yet once again Beaumarchais hesitated and offered to pay Morande's debts if he would only surrender any supposedly incriminating documents and acknowledge his own dishonesty and Beaumarchais' probity in writing. Beaumarchais intended to use this confession as evidence in any future litigation.[106]

Clearly Beaumarchais was at the end of his tether. He had hesitated before entrusting Swinton with incriminating documents, and well he might. Unbeknown to Beaumarchais, Swinton was a British spymaster and ran a network of agents out of Boulogne, where the *Courier de l'Europe*'s printshop served as a cover for frequent trips to France. Indeed, when he offered his services to the British government in April 1778, Swinton had boasted of his friendship with Beaumarchais and the access it gave him to French government circles.[107] Neither Beaumarchais nor Morande suspected Swinton's activities, perhaps because Swinton was anxious not to jeopardize his friendship with Beaumarchais. As a result, Swinton kept his own counsel. Moreover, he warned Beaumarchais that Morande had shown him documents and printed works of an alarming nature, before adding 'if I had not known the handwriting perfectly, I would have had difficulty believing that the author [i.e. Beaumarchais] would have confided such things to him'. He advised Beaumarchais to settle at once.[108] Apparently this is what he did.

All this is highly suggestive. For although Morande's attempts to blackmail Beaumarchais are known primarily through a single letter of Beaumarchais to an unknown correspondent, in which he protests his innocence, he nevertheless admits to paying Morande off repeatedly and willingly purchasing supposedly incriminating documents. In a probable allusion to the Angelucci affair, the same letter suggests that Morande threatened to accuse himself of a crime in order to name Beaumarchais as his accomplice.[109] Although blackmail victims in the eighteenth century, as now, sometimes chose to pay to suppress false allegations, the spectacle of Beaumarchais repeatedly bowing to blackmail, together with the circumstances surrounding Morande's allegations, suggest that there were concrete reasons for him to fear exposure. And if Morande's blackmail ceased after 1781, it was probably because he had thrown himself into a lucrative espionage career once more.

5

On His Majesty's Secret Service

At a quarter past 9 in the morning on 27 July 1781, Henri de La Motte was conveyed on a sledge from Newgate prison to Tyburn. There, he mounted a cart beneath the gallows. After praying briefly, he signalled his readiness to the executioner and was hanged. Mercifully, he was spared the full horrors of his sentence. Instead of being drawn down while still alive and having his bowels cut out and burned before his face, his corpse was left dangling for an hour. Only then did the executioner chop it down, 'sever the head from the trunk', and remove and singe his heart. It was the first time in a generation that a man had been hanged, drawn and quartered, and Londoners turned out in record numbers to watch.[1]

La Motte was a career spy. A French nobleman and officer of moderate means, he had been court-martialled and disgraced in 1757 for retreating without orders. To restore his fortunes, he agreed to serve as a secret agent in England for the duration of the Seven Years' War. Thereafter, he spied for the Parisian police.

In 1777, La Motte returned to England as a secret agent on a stipend of just £8 per month. His fortunes changed in 1778, when he met and hired Henry Lutterloh. Lutterloh, a German mercenary, had served with the British in North America. A nobleman, gambler, adventurer and habitual womanizer, he was at ease among the British gentry and military officers. While La Motte ran their network out of London on an increased salary of £50 per month, Lutterloh established himself in a country house at Wickham in Hampshire. There, he kept a pack of hounds and entertained naval officers from nearby Portsmouth at his frequent hunts. In their company, he was able to visit the naval docks and magazines, apparently without arousing suspicions.

According to newspaper reports, La Motte's network fell apart as a result of greed. In June 1780, La Motte hired Stephen Radcliffe (or Ratcliff), a boatman from Rye, to carry packages from Dover to Boulogne, promising a monthly bonus of £100 if they were delivered on time. However, when Radcliffe attempted to claim the bonus, La Motte refused, saying that his parcels often arrived late. Angry and sensing the danger he was in, Radcliffe then confessed everything to the British authorities. La Motte was duly arrested at his Bond Street home on 5 January 1781 and became a scapegoat for British reverses. His arrest coincided with a moment of national panic, for at midnight on 6 January the French invaded British soil by landing in Jersey.

The arrest of La Motte caused a sensation among the British public, as revelations about his activities followed thick and fast. Within days the newspapers revealed that La Motte was the 'person who has so indefatigably and industriously been the immediate means of coming at the knowledge of our signals, which the French have of late, with so much success, made use of'.[2] According to newspaper reports, the source of this intelligence was a certain Ryder, who worked at Plymouth. Moreover, La Motte's papers were discovered to contain lists of every armed ship in British ports and dockyards and their complements. There were even lists of seamen in hospital in Portsmouth and Plymouth.

When interrogated, La Motte panicked, told the British about Lutterloh and confessed everything, hoping to turn king's evidence and save his neck. Lutterloh and the rest of the network were swiftly rounded up, but it was they, not La Motte, whom the British spared for cooperating. In court, Lutterloh confirmed that La Motte had paid him 50 guineas per month to spy on the dockyards and, according to the prosecution, papers found hidden in Lutterloh's garden proved that there never was 'a more industrious, ingenious and able spy than Mr de la Motte'.[3]

The British decision to sacrifice La Motte but pardon Lutterloh and the rest of his gang was a calculated move. They had evidence enough to damn both men, but preferred to sow mistrust and fear among enemy agents. It was an effective gambit. Several years later, in peacetime, the French *chargé d'affaires* and future politician François Barthélemy lamented that, owing to La Motte's grisly fate, he found it impossible to recruit agents for a new network.[4]

Morande seized this opportunity. Shortly after La Motte's arrest, he wrote to an old acquaintance, Baudouin, to offer his services. Baudouin, who masterminded the naval ministry's espionage efforts, was acquainted with Morande during the late 1760s and knew of his espionage work for Beaumarchais prior to 1778. Baudouin consulted the Marquis de Castries, the naval minister, who duly hired Morande to take over many of La Motte's duties.[5] For the next seven years Morande corresponded with the naval ministry via Baudouin and, following Baudouin's death in 1783, the Marquis de Launay, governor of the Bastille, and the Count de La Touche. From December 1786, he also corresponded with the Foreign Ministry, which from 1788 employed him exclusively and paid his stipend.[6]

Morande's enemies allege that he betrayed La Motte. Manuel asserts 'it was believed and even said in the public prints that he had been the principal informant against the unfortunate Delamothe [sic] and that he received 200 guineas on that occasion'.[7] Pelleport adds:

> The poor La Mothe [sic] who we saw hanged in London was one of the victims of their [Francy, Beaumarchais and Morande's] horrific betrayals, and it is believed that it was from his blood-price that he [Morande] established the famous garden of Standmore [sic].[8]

According to Manuel, French ambassadors did not blush to consult Morande in these 'scandalous gardens'.[9]

There is not a shred of documentary evidence to support these allegations. The papers concerning the La Motte case in the Treasury Solicitor's files make no mention of Morande. Nor do any of the English newspapers in the Burney collection or any other known newspaper report. Neither does Morande's name appear in the official transcript of the trial. All these sources provide credible and broadly consistent accounts of La Motte's downfall, and in the absence of compelling alternative evidence, there seems no reason to doubt them. Pelleport's allegation also falters on the issue of timing, for Morande moved to Stanmore three years before La Motte was arrested. Moreover, contrary to the 'official' reports in the press, British agents had been monitoring his network since before La Motte even joined it. They had been opening his mail since 1778.[10] Thus the allegations of Pelleport and Manuel appear to have stemmed from malice.

Pelleport was on firmer ground when he asserted that Morande spied primarily for money to fund his 'gambling and debauchery'.[11] For despite receiving huge sums in blackmail payments, loans, pay-offs and debt write-offs, Morande dissipated cash faster than he could make it. The sums involved were immense.

Despite receiving 32,000 *livres* (approximately £1,400) cash down from the crown and a life annuity of 4,000 *livres* (£175) in 1774, Morande was soon in financial trouble again. In 1775, after Beaumarchais gained him royal permission, he cashed in half his annuity for 20,000 *livres* (£875). Beaumarchais agreed to pay off a further £300 of debts in 1779 and by 1781 Morande had extorted further sums from him by blackmail.[12] To excuse this behaviour, Morande claimed that he had lost his head after losing 6,000 guineas (£6,300), but he does not say how or when he lost it. Perhaps it was through a disastrous commercial speculation? Gambling probably also contributed. In the 1779 lottery alone he lost almost £1,000 to a single broker betting on individual numbers via insurance policies. He also continued to enjoy card games, particularly *Pharoan*. Or he may have lost money playing the Stock Exchange, as in December 1782, when he gambled that Lord Shelburne's peace overtures were insincere and lost a fortune. This perhaps calls into question both his judgement and the reliability of his sources.[13]

Morande's debts might have destroyed him but for a new saviour: his brother, Francy. By the early 1780s Francy had grown spectacularly rich through serving and speculating with Beaumarchais, using his personal contacts with American politicians to good effect. Francy began bailing out Morande in July 1783, when he paid £3,589 to clear his heaviest debts. In return, Morande signed an indenture making him liable for twice this sum if he did not repay Francy within a year. Francy's aim was not to bankrupt Morande; rather, he wished to coerce him into good behaviour and, perhaps, emigrating to America. Across the next 22 months Francy provided another £700 and Beaumarchais £325.[14]

Between 1774 and 1785, the aforementioned revenues alone brought Morande over £6,800, but he also drew an income from his publishing, commercial and other ventures. From 1781, he also received around £1,050 a year for spying for the French crown, although this was halved from 1 May 1787 as part of the government's financial retrenchments. Moreover, from January 1784 he earned £200 per annum to edit the *Courier de l'Europe*; and in both 1784 and 1787, Louis XVI approved additional gratuities of 100 Louis (approximately £105).[15]

Additionally, when Francy died prematurely of consumption on 27 May 1784, and childless, he left Morande, Eliza and their children annuities worth a total of 5,000 *livres* (about £238) per annum. These were to be administered by Beaumarchais, as Francy's executor. According to Beaumarchais, Francy wished to leave everything to his wife. It was Beaumarchais, who had every interest in securing Morande's financial future, who persuaded him on his deathbed to make provision for Morande's family. This forced Beaumarchais into a lasting financial relationship with Morande.[16]

Nevertheless, the bulk of Francy's fortune of 505,000 *livres* (£24,100) plus an American plantation, went to Francy's cousin and widow, Philiberte Guichot, whom he had married while already ill. This angered the Théveneau clan. They complained that their debt-ridden Guichot cousins had cheated them out of Francy's fortune and accused them of coercing Francy into a marriage his health could not sustain! They considered litigation, but Francy's widow generously settled one-third of the real estate on Morande's mother. This, the family lawyer assured Eliza, would be 'sufficient to make a very material difference after her death to the fortune of her four children'.[17]

In his 21 years in London, Morande's verifiable income came to around £21,300.[18] Then there were loans from Beaumarchais (over £3,000) and further earnings from his mercantile ventures, secret blackmail receipts and writings, which, we might speculate, probably came to at least £10,000. This suggests that Morande's average income was in excess of £1,500, and perhaps considerably more. To put this in context, a generation later, after war and agricultural inflation had doubled landed incomes, Jane Austen's heroines would consider a man who enjoyed £5,000 per annum an extraordinary catch. Such sums put them among the most eligible bachelors in an entire county. In real terms, Morande's income was almost in this league, though he lacked the landed estates and gentlemanly *mores* of an Austen hero.

Equipped with such sums, even Morande was able to reduce his debts once he put his mind to it. That point was reached around July 1783, when he owed £7,500. Payments from Francy and Beaumarchais reduced this to £3,500 by September, and thereafter Morande gradually reduced the sums he owed. By mid

Lenain sc.   A.Quantin Imp Edit.

THÉVENEAU DE MORANDE

Plate 8. Charles-Claude Théveneau de Morande. From the author's copy of Paul Robiquet, *Théveneau de Morande* (Paris: Quantin, 1886).

April 1784, his debts were only £1,400, not including legally unenforceable debts to lottery keepers. Thereafter progress was painfully slow, but by the late summer of 1789 only £800 was outstanding.[19]

Even now, the threat of imprisonment remained. Indeed, as Morande's creditors grew fewer in number, the delicate game of borrowing from one small creditor to pay another became more difficult. Hence, his worst financial crisis arrived in late 1789, when his credit dried up as he was being pursued for a mere £51. On 15 December he implored Beaumarchais: 'I have just been arrested and write to you from prison, where I will sleep tonight; my wife is plunged into the greatest despair, and if I am not yet torn apart, it is because I still dare to turn my eyes towards you.'[20] Tired of his importuning, Beaumarchais turned a deaf ear, as did everyone Eliza begged for help. Yet somehow, by 24 December, Morande had secured his release and two months' grace from his creditors 'through incredible efforts and nearly 40 guineas of expenses.'[21] It was, apparently, the last time he was gaoled for debt.

Was money Morande's only motive for throwing in his lot with Beaumarchais and the monarchy? Some historians have concluded that Morande cynically turned coat because with the accession of the uxorious Louis XVI, the French court offered blackmailers scant pickings. This interpretation ignores two crucial facts. First, Morande faced bankruptcy and prison if he broke his bond with Lauraguais by once more attacking the French court. Second, in the wake of Morande's pay-off, the first years of Louis XVI's reign saw a bonanza for black-mailing pamphleteers.[22]

Morande's motives were, in fact, rather complex. True, money was, as always, a major consideration, but he was neither a mere mercenary nor a complete cynic. There were, after all, significant dangers involved in serving as a secret agent, so his statements of motive deserve serious attention. On one level, Morande clearly had to balance risks. He still feared assassination by royal agents or bounty-hunting freebooters, and changing sides might reduce that danger. He also sought rehabilitation and permission to return to France, and he could only achieve these goals if he atoned for his crimes.

Ideological and political considerations may also have contributed to Morande's *volte face*. They certainly made it possible. By the spring of 1775, when Beaumarchais first commended Morande's services to the French government, Morande's old enemies were in retreat and the political outlook had changed significantly. D'Aiguillon resigned as foreign minister in June 1774 and was replaced by the Count de Vergennes. Du Barry was in disgrace. Maupeou remained Chancellor, since the position was held for life, but he was marginalized in government following Louis XVI's decision to recall the old *parlements*. In his place, the preponderant voice in government had passed to the ageing Count de Maurepas, whom Louis XVI had recalled from the political wilderness to be his mentor.

Maurepas was notable for his insouciance and consensual style. He served as a minister under Louis XV but was dismissed for showing disrespect to Madame de Pompadour. One probably apocryphal tale claims his offence was to remark that he had 'always known that Madame de Pompadour would give the king white flowers' on seeing her present Louis XV with a bunch of hyacinths. As 'white flowers' was slang for venereal disease, this insult was intolerable. Other reports say he distributed verses attacking the favourite. He was certainly an avid collector of political epigrams, songs and slanderous *libelles*, even those written at his own expense. In Maurepas' eyes, only printed attacks on crowned heads were beyond the pale. Such a minister was more likely than a Maupeou or d'Aiguillon to regard Morande with indulgence.

The elevation of two other ministers, Turgot and Malesherbes, added to the impression that the new government would be less hostile to the Morandes of this world. Turgot, a physiocratic reformer, had an impressive array of proposals for reducing ministerial despotism; Malesherbes, a former *parlementaire* spokesman, had been famously liberal when in charge of the book trade in the 1750s and 1760s. In a society where politics revolved around connections and personalities, these changes were significant. They encouraged hopes that Louis XVI's government would embrace a less 'despotic' style of rule and embark on a programme of reform. This coincided with the desire for patriotic reforms that finds expression in Morande's writings throughout his career. As a realist, his political hopes lay in a regeneration of the existing monarchy. To move from opposition to service of the royal government represented no inherent moral or ideological contradiction under the old regime. Indeed, many *philosophes*, *parlementaires* and government ministers followed the same path. After all, in 1774 no one could foresee the revolution of 1789, still less suspect that by 1793 France would become a republic and execute her king.

Nor was the monarchy's decision to employ Morande so bizarre. It had a long history of taking renegades into clandestine service, though this tendency intensified under Vergennes, who, it has been said, 'ran a curiously informal and unsystematic intelligence operation' and 'seemed to set great store by the services of persons of checkered and unsavory backgrounds'.[23] Yet although this involved risks, the policy had benefits, too. Renegades usually had strong political links with France's enemies and were less likely to be suspected of collaboration with the French government. Moreover, it made sense to buy off dangerous critics, many of whom were talented and keen to redeem themselves. Hence the French re-employed d'Eon in the late 1760s and hired Morande (albeit indirectly through Beaumarchais) in the mid 1770s. Similar motives led them to employ Beaumarchais and his adversary, the disgraced magistrate Goëzman, as agents. Besides, after Henri de La Motte's demise, they had few options. Hence, when Sartine – who knew rather too much about Morande's past – was replaced at the naval ministry by the Marquis de Castries in 1780, the last obstacle to Morande's direct employment was removed.

The testimony of French diplomats suggests that from 1781 Morande was a loyal servant. In March 1787, the Count d'Adhémar recommended to the new foreign minister, the Count de Montmorin, that Morande be granted a gratuity, with the words:

> This Frenchman, who after having been a scandalous writer on the streets of London, has shown me so much remorse and been so well behaved towards his country since I have been in London, that I believed it my duty to intercede for him with Vergennes.

Nevertheless, d'Adhémar was well aware of the ambiguity of the relationship, for he added: 'That minister [Vergennes] was always generous to him. He knew how, without showing fear, it is vital not to embitter these sorts of people, who by their skill at writing, can do much harm.'[24] Likewise, Barthélemy considered Morande 'a detestable instrument full of vices and indiscretions', but thought it good to support him. He valued Morande's journalism and his knowledge of Britain and was convinced that he desired to repair the sins of his youth.[25] Moustier was even more cynical. Unaware that Morande was already working for the naval ministry, he recommended him to Vergennes as an agent, adding:

> God forbid that I should suggest employing him or placing any confidence in him. But he is a man to be treated carefully and who should not be irritated . . . He has not done any harm until now; he has even sought to make himself useful; but he knows a lot about the correspondence that the [French] ministry has conducted in this country. It is necessary to give him some crumbs, and by taking lots of precautions, without letting him sense them, we could get something from him. It would be helpful to have him on our side.[26]

As a spy, Morande's most arduous and dangerous task was to prepare lists of the Royal Navy's ships and despatch them to France every six months.[27] Similar lists had been found among La Motte and Lutterloh's papers and were considered some of the most damning evidence against them. In accepting this role, Morande was literally risking his neck. To discover what this task involved, we can examine the 'State of the British Navy' that Morande sent to the foreign ministry on 24 August 1788, which although particularly heavily annotated is otherwise typical.[28] It comprises five lists of ships, together with analytical summaries. It extends across 23 folio pages and provides frequent cross-references to previous memoranda. In sum, it provides an analytical overview of the number of ships; the rate of naval expansion; British shipboard technology, armament and practice; and naval preparedness.

Morande's first list offers a 'State of the British navy from Ships of the First Rank down to Vessels of 50 Cannons'. For every ship he gives the number of guns, current location, whether it is armed, its state of repair and seaworthiness, and in many cases further annotations. Second comes a list of frigates and smaller vessels. It notes the frequency with which ships return from overseas and movements of ships on the Antilles station between Jamaica, Antigua and, in the storm season, Halifax, Nova Scotia. By a strange quirk, the three smallest ships are among the most famous. The 10-gun *Sirius* and 8-gun *Supply* under Captain Arthur Philips were with the First Fleet at Botany Bay, while the 8-gun *Bounty* under Captain Bligh was in the Society Islands. The third list identifies every armed capital ship in seaworthy condition and all ships-of-the-line that were ready for service, or could be armed immediately. It is accompanied by a list of vessels needing only light repairs to become seaworthy.

The final table offers a comparative summary of capital ships broken up, built or repaired since the end of the American Revolutionary War. This made uncomfortable reading for French ministers. For while 29 obsolete or heavily damaged capital ships had been destroyed, 38 new ones had been built and 41 fully repaired. Seven more were under construction. The effective strength of the Royal Navy had increased by 50 capital ships, the vast majority ships-of-the-line. Morande concluded that 'the British navy has increased considerably and in every sense, the rank of vessel that it has built and has under construction being very superior to those of the vessels that have been dismantled'. Britain had never been more energetically occupied with her navy, and had so over-compensated for war losses that he feared a sinister purpose. However, in reality, Britain was locked in a 'remarkable arms race' with the combined fleets of the two Bourbon powers, France and Spain. While her naval growth between 1785 and 1790 easily outstripped each of these powers in isolation, the combined tonnage of the Bourbon navies, already superior in 1785, was expanding at a faster rate. By 1790 they had achieved parity of numbers as well.[29]

In the short term, too, Morande raised reasons for concern. The current level of activity in British ports suggested that something serious was afoot, and he promised that, since his friends in the navy expected orders within ten days, he would soon discern what. There were in fact no major international crises or British operations in 1788. Instead, Morande was detecting the results of heightened tensions caused by British fears of French intentions in India, Britain's concomitant build-up of forces in the Indian Ocean, and France's counter-measures. Morande's reports undoubtedly fed such tensions.[30]

Alongside broad conclusions, Morande's annotations offered a huge range of information, both on the navy and how he compiled his lists. He explains that his report represents the cumulative improvement and correction of his information over several years of research. His most basic information about the British fleet was in fact available in the public domain, in the naval lists regularly published by the Admiralty. However, according to Morande, these printed lists are so riddled with errors that their only practical use is to verify ships' names and dates of construction. The information they give concerning a vessel's station, state of repair and even whether they are under construction, is frequently erroneous or incomplete. Morande speculated that these errors were a deliberate attempt at disinformation and tried to compensate for them by frequent conversations with naval officers. A more likely explanation is that no list could accurately capture the precise condition and seaworthiness of a ship or predict its exact readiness, as that depended on supplies of men, munitions, victuals and money. Indeed, there are considerable discrepancies between the lists kept by the Navy Office and the Admiralty.[31]

Morande also discusses numerous British technical innovations, some of which had long been known to the French. He describes patent pulleys that require considerably less manpower than ordinary pulleys and ventilation systems that use leather tubes and water vapour to pipe fresh air around ships on long haul voyages (Sutton's tubes). He reports on experiments with wind pumps at Deptford; emergency valves to control the flow of water onboard ship; and iron galley kitchens (Brodie's firehearths) which greatly reduce the risk of kitchen fires but are very heavy. For a ship of 100 guns they weigh three tons. Such kitchens, he adds, are routinely supplied with a still for the emergency desalination of sea water for drinking. Astonishingly, Morande reveals that he acquired one of these galleys and sent it to Brest for installation on the explorer La Pérouse's ship for his voyage to the Pacific. Unfortunately, it proved impossible to load and install, but Mr Brodie, the manufacturer, had promised to send a worker to put it together.

Morande's annotations also offered intelligence on British innovations in gunnery and their rates of adoption on warships. He reports that the Royal Navy had started mounting naval cannons on a new type of guncarriage, which used leather buffers and ropes to return guns to the firing position. This system, developed by Sir Charles Douglas, one of Morande's closest associates in the navy, prevented dangerous and random recoil and hastened the return of cannon to a shooting position, thus improving safety, accuracy and speed of fire. Morande explained that the new system allowed guns to be repositioned as they recoiled, though it is unclear whether he appreciated the full implication, 'that this allowed guns to be fired when canted well before or abaft of the beam, thus allowing fire to be developed when the ship was not broadside to the enemy'. Morande noted that only a few such carriages had yet been made, but an officer had already promised him a diagram.[32]

Morande also described royal navy sighting systems and reported that many cannons now used a gunlock [batterie] resembling those on rifles. In fact, the British had been using gunlocks since at least 1745, but as late as the 1780s, as Morande's testimony clarifies, few ships were universally equipped with this innovation. Before gunlocks, guns were fired by applying a linstock (a burning slowmatch attached to a stick) to priming powder in a touch hole in the gun's side. This was a slow and dangerous process and impeded accuracy, as the gunner had to stand beside the gun. In contrast, a gunlock was safer and more accurate, as there was no match, no delay in lighting the powder and, as long as he stood beyond the recoil, the gun captain could look along the barrel and fire with a lanyard (cord). This also meant that broadsides could be fired simultaneously. Unfortunately, the older style Armstrong guns could not be fitted with gunlocks, and it took many years for the British to replace their entire stock of cannon. In France, progress was even slower. As the naval historian Nicholas Rodger has noted, this 'important aid to fast and accurate firing' was 'still not generally adopted in the French navy at the time of Trafalgar', more than 17 years after Morande revealed that it was becoming general in the British fleet.[33]

Morande also announced that the British had improved rather than abandoned carronades – described by Rodger as 'short light guns with large calibres but a very small charge' which 'could easily be handled by a few men' and, due to their low recoil, might be placed on a 'simple swivel mount'. Four to eight were being mounted on ships to supplement their ordinary gunnery. Morande adds, probably erroneously, that smaller carronades were also being mounted in tops to dispense grapeshot in combat at close quarters. Carronades were originally developed to defend merchant shipping during the American war. They were only belatedly adopted by the Royal Navy, which found that they could have a devastating impact at close range during boarding operations. However, if ships were exclusively or mainly armed with caronnades, as was tried during the American war, they became vulnerable to long range fire, and thus there was some scepticism in the Admiralty about their utility. In fact, Rodger concludes, caronnades were 'a considerable addition of strength' to British ships and, because French gun foundries could not match them for 20 years, gave the Royal Navy a long-lasting technological advantage. Morande grasped their significance. Indeed, he sent Baudouin their design specifications within days of their securing their first major victory, the capture of the frigate *Hébé*. He also noted that British ships habitually carried large numbers of blunderbusses to supplement the output of grapeshot in boarding actions.[34]

Morande's appraisal of the Royal Navy also emphasizes the importance of naval discipline and cleanliness to British shipboard practice. Such details were hardly closely guarded secrets: it is the sort of information provided by a modern military attaché. The same was true of Morande's revelation that sailors garrisoning moored ships were routinely employed in naval shipyards. This facilitated the expansion of the Woolwich docks and thus British shipbuilding capacity, reducing the navy's dependency on private shipyards, which had proved costly during the American war. On top of this, Morande claims, the British had perfected the art of equipping and provisioning vessels. The speed with which they could put ships to sea depended only on the rate at which they could assemble crews.

In addition to updating his 'States of the Navy', Morande sent regular despatches to France. He estimates that between 1781 and 1787 he sent some 400 packets of advice to the naval minister Castries via Baudouin and Launay, but few survive. In contrast, the archives of the French foreign ministry contain some 79 spy reports that Morande wrote to Vergennes and Montmorin between 25 December 1786 and 8 April 1791, most of which are signed only '#'. Almost all date from 1787, 1788 or the first half of 1789, when Britain and France were at peace.[35]

A note of 27 July 1788 clarifies what Montmorin wished Morande to include in his reports. They should relate occurrences in the ports and the admiralty and give all available information on the Foreign Office's intentions. Morande should limit himself to simple facts and indicate their degree of certainty in cases of doubt. Any observations should be made in the margin or on a separate sheet of paper.[36] In fact, Morande's reports usually contain a mixture of military intelligence, political information, miscellaneous news, gossip and speculation of varying quality, as well as frequent insights into his sources and methods. His staple topics include the movements of ships, naval preparations, diplomatic developments, British dispositions, news from India, plus British domestic politics, espionage and communications.

A characteristic spy report is Morande's letter of 1 July 1787, sent as the international crisis precipitated by the Dutch patriot revolution was coming to a head. This was a key moment in the unravelling of French international power: the Dutch crisis laid bare the full extent of the financial problems that eventually precipitated the French Revolution of 1789. In essence, the Dutch patriot revolution was a decade-long attempt by democratic (patriot) elements within the Dutch Republic to entrench a more republican form of government. This involved excluding the rival power of the Princes of Orange who, in times of crisis, were habitually invested with emergency powers and the title of Stadholder. For well over a century the Dutch constitution had thrived despite, or perhaps because of, the uneasy tension between the patriot party and the Stadholderate, but by the early 1780s things were beginning to unravel. And as the Stadholder was tied to the British and Prussian monarchs by religious and family bonds, all three made common cause against the French-backed patriots, who were, in due course, decisively defeated.

Morande's report begins by reporting that the British government had just received two couriers from Holland. The first brought news that delighted George III: the Stadholder's party had just regained a majority in the Dutch Estates-General in The Hague. This would put him in the political driving seat. However, despite spending several hours in the 'Club' at the Mount Coffee House, which he described as the 'centre of all political news', Morande had been unable to learn what intelligence was brought by the second courier. All he knew was that it was disagreeable. Only two days later did he learn that the courier brought word that the King of Prussia's sister, the Princess of Orange, had been detained by patriot forces.[37] This action proved decisive, giving the Prussians a *bona fide* pretext for decisive military intervention, backed-up by British mobilization. However, on 1 July, all Morande could report was British ambassadorial revelations that the Stadholder's troops were starting to desert.

Morande then turned his attention to Britain's naval armament, reporting that ten ships-of-the-line were being commissioned for action. Having learned from their captains that they were arming, he deduced from the supplies being prepared that at least three were being equipped for a long voyage. He concluded that they were destined for India, where the British were alarmed by the activities of the ruler of Mysore, Tipu Sultan. However, although he had reported the armament a week earlier, on 1 July he was still unable to give any precise details, other than to name the ships involved and to refute rumours that 'press warrants' had been issued for conscripting sailors.[38] The only certainty was that orders for provisions indicated that some of the ships would sail via Penzance, Cork and Lisbon.

The French government considered such up-to-the-minute naval intelligence essential for gauging British intentions. However, Morande's reliance on conversations with ships' captains suggests that neither he nor his employers had, at that time, reliable, high-placed sources in the naval administration. Thus, during the Dutch crisis, the French ambassador hired special agents to watch Portsmouth and the Thames ports. Among them were an Irishman named Elliott and Robert Pellevé, a former merchant seaman from Normandy, who was married to Charlotte Butts, whose father had been Bishop of Ely.[39] Pellevé had good connections in the British elite and the Royal Navy and lived in Chichester, conveniently close to Portsmouth. He had served as a spy during the American war and been denounced to Lord Shelburne, but extricated himself with consummate skill. Employed again by the French ambassador in 1783 on Morande's recommendation, he insisted that the ambassador tell Morande that he was not up to the job. Pellevé had no wish to be betrayed.[40] Such agents implicitly supplemented and verified Morande's intelligence, but this does not mean that it was suspect: on the contrary, in 1787 some of the information he supplied was copied out in a fair hand, presumably for circulation among ministers.[41] Moreover, from the onset of the crisis, Morande stressed that the British were ready to back the Prussians militarily in support of the Orangists. Such perspicacious advice was one more small factor behind France's humiliating decision to abandon her patriot allies.[42]

Morande's letter of 1 July 1787 also reported that he had been told by Captain Taylor, whom he styled the new head of the Royal Navy's secret intelligence, that 12 French ships-of-the-line were being prepared at Brest to aid the Dutch patriots and defend Dutch possessions in the Indies. Whether such reports were accurate was immaterial, Morande remarked. What mattered was to learn the identity of Taylor's correspondent, who lived at Roscoff in Brittany. Quite how Morande got this information remains a mystery, but it may have come from Irish smugglers employed to communicate with Brittany during the American War.[43] Nor was Taylor the only British agent Morande denounced. In June 1788, he provided a description of a British spy named Mills whom he believed to be in Paris and intent on visiting the ports of Nantes and Rennes. In June 1789, at the start of the French Revolution, he noticed that the British agent Nathaniel Parker Forth had ducked out of sight and concluded that he had returned to France. According to Morande, he would probably be found with the Duke de Fitzjames and Monsieur

Ducrest, hiring firebrands and rabble-rousers. Thus even before the fall of the Bastille on 14 July 1789, Morande was party to rumours that 'Pitt's gold' was fomenting discord in France.[44]

In other reports Morande pays more attention to British domestic politics and financial questions. He routinely dissects the state of political parties in Parliament, the dispositions of the cabinet and Prime Minister William Pitt's preference for economy above warfare. He reports the attempts of Wilberforce and the abolitionists to end the slave trade; dwells on George III's supposedly visceral hatred of the French; alleges that Britain was perfidiously manipulating the provisions of their commercial treaty with France; and argues that Britain's finances were far less healthy than official figures suggested. However, the most significant British political issue discussed in Morande's surviving spy reports was the Regency crisis, occasioned by the onset of George III's madness late in 1788. In the winter of 1788 to 1789, Morande made energetic attempts to unravel the secrets of George III's health. According to modern specialists, George's insanity was probably caused by intermittent porphyria, but this was a disease unknown to eighteenth-century science. As a result, Morande had to penetrate barriers of official secrecy and medical ignorance to reach a realistic assessment of the disease, the chances of a royal recovery, and the likely political outcome of the crisis.

For the French government, Morande's assessments of the king's health were a useful and informative supplement to the reports of Barthélemy, their *chargé d'affaires*. Barthelémy's first mention of the king's illness appears in a despatch of 21 October 1788, which reports that George III is suffering from an attack of gout. This was the official line. The same day, Morande penetrated much closer to the truth as the government perceived it. The king's health, he asserted, was far worse than ministers were admitting, for a friend of the royal doctor, Sir George Baker, had informed Morande that scrofulous humours and gout were combining dangerously. This was worrying for France. If George III were to remain incapable, the Prince of Wales would become regent and replace Pitt as Prime Minister with Charles James Fox, who, despite francophile cultural tastes, was deeply hostile to France in international politics. Morande had no need to explain that the throne commanded the instinctive loyalty of sufficient Members of Parliament and voters that the prince would be able to appoint the Prime Minister of his choice.[45]

In these assertions, Morande was at least a day ahead of Barthélemy. On 22 October Barthélemy reported that the king's illness was more serious than had generally been believed, but he was now recovered, for the time being at least.[46] However, optimism about the king's recovery proved premature and as the crisis developed Barthélemy relied on Morande to penetrate the walls of British secrecy and misinformation. When rumours of the king's death began circulating in the small hours of a Saturday morning, it was Morande who briefed Barthélemy, after spending the night trawling London's clubs hoping for verification. In the end the news proved false, but Morande's informants confirmed that the king had suffered two serious scares. Moreover, his disease must, in Dr Baker's opinion, eventually prove fatal. Despite reports to the contrary, there was no reason for hope. Indeed, the king was completely deranged in all his organs, not merely feverish as had been reported in the press.[47]

As the regency crisis dragged on, Morande also appraised Montmorin of the Parliamentary delaying and spoiling tactics available to Pitt as he clung to power in the apparently futile hope of a royal recovery. These included tabling amendments to the Regency Bill to restrict the regent's power; filibusters in the Bill's committee stage; and proposals to exclude the Prince of Wales from the succession if it could be proved that he had married his Catholic mistress, Mrs Fitzherbert.[48] On 6 January, Morande informed Montmorin that several well-informed men estimated that Pitt might spin out the passage of the Regency Bill for two or three months without having to surrender the ministry.[49] And so it proved. Pitt was still in power in mid February when the king began his faltering and wholly unexpected recovery. Morande chronicles every step of his progress, frequent relapses and, as late as 26 May 1789, lingering doubts as to whether he would survive.[50] Often these are reported with a certain relish. One can imagine his wry smile on informing Montmorin that:

> This prince [i.e. George III] formerly so timid with women continues to make gallant promises, and to boast of having had (as near as) every woman whose name is known to him. Once the most reserved man in his kingdom, today he speaks only of his vigour, of what he has done and what he is in a position to do.[51]

Nor was the reporting of George III's insane outbursts always just innocent fun. What, for example, was Montmorin to make of a tale, confirmed to Morande by the Pittite MP for Leicester, MacNamara, that on catching sight of his device '*Dieu et mon droit*', George III had exploded 'I hate the French; I will have an English motto by God!'[52] Such reports could only reinforce Morande's self-serving assertions that George III remained France's most implacable foe.[53]

Assessing Morande's contribution as a spy is problematic due to the sheer range of his activities. Fortunately, Morande himself lists his most significant achievements in a long letter to Montmorin written on 28 April 1788. As it was sent in the hope of reversing a salary cut, it must be treated with some caution. However, much of the information he provides is verifiable from other sources, some of which Morande indicates himself.[54]

Morande's letter boasts that from 1781 he advised the French government of every warship equipped in British ports, often revealing their destinations long before they sailed. Moreover, he almost handed the French the most spectacular victory of the War of American Independence. In May 1782, he learned that a merchant convoy of 177 ships from the West Indies was returning to Britain under the lightest of escorts – just three ships-of-the-line – and alerted Baudouin that it would head for the South of Ireland. A French force was sent to intercept them, but the British eluded them under the cover of fog.

The letter also reveals that Morande discovered the overland route taken by British secret communications from Madras to Alexandria, from whence they were forwarded to Sir Robert Ainslie, the British ambassador in Constantinople. This route passed via Basra, whence it was organized by Baldwin, the British Consul. Morande suggested a means for intercepting this correspondence, arguing that several couriers could be seized before the British realized the danger. When Baldwin moved to Cairo and began organizing a new route via Suez, Morande uncovered this as well. In both cases Morande's intelligence was accurate. However, the British eventually abandoned their experiments with both routes due to the monsoon and Ottoman suspicions that they might favour the beys' pretentions to Egyptian independence.[55] In addition, Morande alerted the French to a secret correspondence between George III and his brother-in-law, the Duke of Brunswick, the Prussian commander during the Dutch crisis, and revealed how Dutch patriots might intercept it.

Following the Peace of Versailles (3 September 1783), which granted British recognition to the United States and ended the American Revolutionary War, Morande also provided the French government with commercial information, much of it painstakingly compiled from published sources. During 1783 and 1784, he prepared memoranda on Britain's commercial relations and whale fisheries. He drafted a comparative study of the manufactures of France and England and – by his own admission – a 'very inexact' survey of the tonnage of the merchant navy, which he later had verified against the registers of Lloyds by Pereyra, a Jewish merchant from Bordeaux.[56] He also sent studies of the British national debt (whose extent was then unknown) and statistics concerning the number of British sailors. Several of his memoirs on Britain's trade, fisheries and manufactures had, he claimed, received written approbation from French ministers, and they undoubtedly informed negotiations over the Eden trade treaty with Britain.

Morande was also involved in industrial espionage and the transfer of technicians and skilled workers to France. Much of this related to naval innovations. As we have seen, he acquired a naval galley stove for La Pérouse and sent descriptions of royal naval gun carriages. In 1786 he also seconded the attempts of the engineer and industrial spy Le Turc to acquire the technology, skilled workers and a foreman to manufacture patent pulley blocks. These pulley blocks were first developed by the Taylor family in Southampton in the 1750s, patented in

1762, and subject to continual improvement. The French government had been aware of the superiority of British pulley technology for well over a decade and saw acquiring it as a key priority. However, such a project involved significant risks, particularly as aiding the unlicensed export of technical equipment and emigration of skilled artificers from Britain was illegal. The French government was thus delighted when Le Turc returned to France with his workmen, began manufacturing pulleys at Lorient in government-owned premises and started training French pulley-makers.

Unfortunately, the initiative fell victim to its own success, rapid expansion and Le Turc's desire to develop other manufacturing projects elsewhere. Operatives could not be trained as quickly as the navy desired and in Le Turc's absence discipline and standards among the workers slipped. The enterprise collapsed into chaos. Moreover, the pulleys were not adopted, a misfortune Morande blamed on opposition from existing naval suppliers. The full extent of Morande's involvement in the affair is unclear, but he was certainly familiar with the workmen Le Turc recruited and procured him embassy funds to pay their recruitment bounties and travel costs. He also seems to have lent some of his own money for this purpose. Moreover, Morande recommended Le Turc to Beaumarchais and suggested introducing him to the French finance minister Calonne in October 1785. Clearly, then, Morande was trusted to collaborate with, and perhaps direct, the most militarily important and sensitive operation of an 'immensely active and generally successful' fellow spy. In this he apparently succeeded. No suspicion of Le Turc's activities has been traced in British sources.[57]

However, it was in the civilian sphere that Morande felt that he had nearly pulled off his most spectacular coup. For he asserts it was he who first dreamed of persuading the celebrated engineers Matthew Boulton and James Watt to visit France and serve, in effect, as technological consultants to the French crown. There was always an element of wishful thinking in this enterprise. Boulton and Watt's trip to France in 1786 on the pretext of examining the obsolescent Machine de Marly, which pumped water from the Seine to supply Versailles, is well documented. So, too, is the welcome they received and their equivocal behaviour (they seemed more inclined to recommend an aqueduct than a steam engine to replace the hydraulic pumps supplying water to Paris).[58] What is less certain is Morande's claim that it was he who incited the inventor Aimé Argand, a friend of Boulton, to propose the trip. However, he cited as witnesses the diplomats d'Adhémar and Barthelémy, who apparently first advised the Calonne ministry that Boulton and Watt might be recruited. Probably, then, it was no idle boast when Morande claimed that he had potentially procured for France 'the two most skilful mechanical engineers in the whole world'.[59]

Morande's reports also alerted the French to British attempts to acquire workers at France's expense. In 1789, for example, the Member of Parliament for Newcastle-Upon-Tyne, Sir Matthew White Ridley, told him of his involvement in developing a Dutch-style herring industry in Scotland. Morande then questioned a Monsieur de Baume, whom he had seen calling on Ridley, who told him that he was going to French Flanders to recruit refugee Dutch fishermen. Morande immediately alerted Montmorin and sent him a physical description of Baume.[60]

Morande even suggested acts of industrial or commercial sabotage. In May 1788, he learned that some leading cotton merchants had gone bankrupt owing £500,000. The financial repercussions threatened several large banks and might drag down 'half of Manchester'. The British feared bankruptcies would surpass £3,000,000. Morande therefore suggested that French customs contractors be ordered to find pretexts to delay the sale of English textiles, thereby exacerbating the British cotton industry's cash flow problems.[61] There is no evidence that the French followed his suggestion, but Morande certainly damaged the credit of another enemy of the government. In late 1789, Louis XVI's cousin Philippe, Duke d'Orléans, visited England seeking to borrow large sums of money. D'Orléans' leading role in opposing royal policies was so notorious that by October 1789 some observers believed that he was fomenting revolutionary turmoil in the hope of supplanting Louis XVI. Thus, with the ambassador's approbation, Morande put a notice in British newspapers saying that d'Orléans was paying an astronomical 18 per cent interest on loans raised in France. Needless to say, d'Orléans' negotiations collapsed.[62]

Finally, Morande's letter of 28 April 1788 noted that he had alerted the French government to some of Britain's most significant colonial ventures, especially plans to establish a penal colony at Botany Bay in Australia. According to Morande, Australia was seen as a springboard for attacking Spanish possessions in the Moluccas, Philippines and the Pacific seaboard of South America, following a plan suggested by the naturalist Johann Reinhold Forster on his return from Cook's second voyage.[63] Morande was largely correct. The strategic attraction of Australia as a base for controlling the Pacific and attacking Chile certainly played a part in British long-term planning. However, he overlooked a more immediate advantage: from Australia they could acquire New Zealand timber (kauri and totara, the world's largest hardwood trees, were potentially invaluable for masts) and flax (used for sailcloth).[64] However, strategic priorities were forgotten when the first reports from the colony reached London in March 1789. Then Morande focused on reporting Australia's inhospitable climate, the colony's struggle for survival, and rumours that convicts and colonists might yet be evacuated.[65]

Morande was a valuable agent primarily because of his connections. He was particularly well-connected in naval circles, where his commercial speculations and journalistic activities provided cover for information gathering. In June 1788, he summarizes his knowledge, contacts and sources in a letter to Montmorin, which claims that there is not a government department in which he does not know at least one official.[66] Among the most important is an unnamed contact in the Bureau of Ordnance. As this bureau deals with munitions, Morande is forewarned of any major armament or expedition several months in advance.[67] In addition, he is friendly with 20 naval officers, five or six of whom he has met daily for over 15 years. He also knows the proprietors of every major London newspaper and many brokers, whom he considers 'ferrets' for rooting out political information. He has several acquaintances in Parliament, who often inadvertently verify information or supply papers tabled in the House of Commons. Finally, he boasts many friends among naval suppliers, insurance brokers and people who deal with the East India Company, whose information is often as useful as that direct from government offices.[68]

While such sources could be useful, there was sometimes no substitute for visiting the dockyards. Morande did this on various pretexts. In August 1787, he discusses a forthcoming dinner engagement with an artillery Colonel who lives close to Chatham. Having visited Chatham eight days earlier to observe the ships at anchor, Morande promises to suggest a pleasure trip by boat and take a closer look surreptitiously. He also undertakes to accompany André Saiffert von der Molde, the doctor and putative lover of Marie-Antoinette's favourite, the Princess de Lamballe, on a trip to Portsmouth. Saiffert was fêted throughout England and his celebrity would afford a suitable pretext for visiting the docks. Morande would have only six hours to look round, however, as Portsmouth was almost 70 miles from London and the demands of editing his newspaper prevented his ever being away more than three days.[69]

Morande identifies several important sources by name. His most valued political contact was probably the Pittite MP Chalmers, who served as Parliamentary secretary to Lord Hawkesbury, whom, until 1789, Morande considered 'the soul of the ministry'.[70] He shared this conviction with many high-ranking members of the British opposition, who believed Hawkesbury wielded secret influence due to his friendship with George III. Morande befriended Chalmers in the late 1770s and claimed he could read him like a book. They often conversed for hours at a time and occasionally dined together.[71] In August 1788, Chalmers was Morande's authority for asserting that the British had no intent of allying with the Swedes. The British had incited Sweden to fight Russia because they calculated that when the Russians 'had received a good licking' they would embrace Britain as an ally with open arms.[72] Other government MPs with whom Morande records conversations include Morton Pitt, MacNamara and Evan Nepean, at that time under-secretary to Lord Sydney at the newly-created Home Office. However, none appears to have revealed anything of real substance. Generally, Morande struggled to penetrate the secrets of government, which he claims were the preserve of a very small and tight-knit group, particularly after the regency crisis.[73]

Morande had better contacts in the Whig opposition.[74] Among them were the playwright turned politician Richard Brinsley Sheridan, whom Morande had known since at least 1776.[75] However, opposition politicians were unlikely to be party to political secrets and so rarely appear in Morande's surviving spy reports. One exception is Edmund Burke, who was so volatile that Morande thought he could be used as an unwitting marionette. If stirred up with indignation about the vexations and abuses habitually practised by British custom officials, he might well propose a Parliamentary motion to inquire into such practices.[76]

Morande also sought out well-placed foreigners, particularly foreign diplomats, such as the disgruntled Hessian envoy, the Baron de Kutsleben, who told him in April 1789 that misunderstandings between Russia and Prussia had been exaggerated.[77] He could be highly imaginative at finding sources. In 1789 he traced the doctor of the Brabant revolutionary Van der Noot to learn how his overtures had been received by British ministers when he had visited London.[78] Morande maintained particularly close contact with the Spanish embassy, where he attended at least one ambassadorial fête.[79] He was acquainted with the ambasador, the Marquis del Campo and friendly with his secretary and confidant, Crivio, whom Morande considered an 'imbecile' who could be pumped for information. However, Morande considered del Campo's anglophile leanings dangerous to France. He therefore offered to use the *Courier de l'Europe* to expose his political naivety in hoping to persuade the British to surrender Gibraltar and in ignoring the geostrategic threat of Botany Bay.[80]

Among Morande's most useful friends was Captain John Salisbury of the Royal Navy, whom he had befriended in the 1770s. Salisbury was a distinguished commander and highly regarded by his peers and his protector, Admiral Lord Hood. He had spent several years in France and in about 1782 moved to Cherbourg to observe the construction of the sea barriers there. These barriers, which were being sunk onto the ocean floor to create a new deep sea harbour for the French fleet, were one of the wonders of the eighteenth-century world. As France's northern coast previously had no port large enough to take a fleet of warships, Cherbourg was a serious strategic threat to England's south coast. In consequence, the work there was closely monitored by British agents and warships.

In Cherbourg, Salisbury fell in love with the Viscountess de Perrochel, a lady of English origin. The couple married on a trip to London in October 1783, but unfortunately the Viscount de Perrochel, still very much alive, learned of his wife's bigamy. In December 1783, Perrochel travelled to London to procure a copy of the Salisburys' marriage certificate as evidence for a lawsuit against the couple. There, he consulted Morande, who was well known as a 'fixer' for Frenchmen in London. Morande duly acquired the certificate but wrote to warn Salisbury and his 'wife' to flee France to avoid prosecution. The tip-off proved unnecessary. Salisbury was already *en route* to England and Madame de Perrochel had been forewarned, but the couple was grateful for his efforts. As a result, Morande became their confidant and legal adviser. Morande therefore ignored Perrochel's instructions to begin legal proceedings should the couple return to England. He preferred to secure the goodwill of 'a naval officer lacking delicacy and scruples' than to serve as the instrument of a husband's wrath.

The most useful thing about Salisbury was his wife, who was vulnerable to blackmail. Unknown to Perrochel or Salisbury, she had once worked as a 'common prostitute' in London using the name Miss Percy. Thereafter she travelled to Paris under the alias Madame Tuite, masquerading as the widow of an Irish army officer. She became Perrochel's mistress and when they married brought a large dowry (allegedly £30,000), most of which had been extracted from another of her lovers. Morande was fully aware of her history. Perhaps he first encountered her in a brothel? However, Salisbury was smitten with the lady who, as Morande delicately put it, 'enjoyed a complete ascendancy over him'. Morande therefore assured his paymasters that he could blackmail Madame Salisbury into extracting from her husband any information they wished.[81]

At Salisbury's house, in 1784, Morande learned of a report by General Green on Cherbourg harbour and his contingency plan for disabling it. The topic arose in a conversation about storm damage to the 'cones' that the French were sinking onto the ocean bed. These cones were to be filled with ballast then linked to form a sea wall. When a certain Captain Wallace observed that General Green had reported that the harbour would never be tranquil or even tenable until the sea wall was complete, Morande challenged him, claiming to have received news that the damage was slight and that the port would soon rival Portsmouth. In the debate this provoked, Morande elicited key information about the British assessment of the harbour; weaknesses in its defences (the harbour mouth was too wide to allow accurate bombardment of its centre from the fortresses to either side); and how to disable it by sinking old hulks. Morande reported these findings to the ministry and offered to acquire the original report.[82]

In mid 1788, Morande placed his son, George, into the Royal Navy as an unwitting mole. Again Salisbury was vital, for in early 1788 he was appointed commander of HMS *Termagent*, a corvette based at Plymouth and charged with observing construction work at Cherbourg and intercepting smugglers off Cornwall and the Channel Islands. Morande seized the chance to enrol George as a midshipman under Salisbury's command and get direct intelligence from Plymouth, the port which, for logistical reasons, he knew least.[83] He assured Montmorin that the boy was intelligent and observant and would identify British naval practices that were unknown to the French.[84] Nevertheless, he enlisted George with some reluctance, not least due to the money he had to pay Salisbury for his equipment and maintenance.[85]

George's entry into the navy appeared to resolve the problem of the boy's future. George had little aptitude for study and Morande's decision to educate him in Paris, due to a disdain for English pedagogy, had backfired spectacularly. Despite the attentions of Beaumarchais and the best efforts of the prestigious *Collège de Navarre*, where he studied from 1784 to 1787, George made little progress, particularly at Latin and the sciences.[86] He was homesick and his health deteriorated, much to Eliza's anguish, and by 1785 Morande (of all people) was complaining that he was a spendthrift.[87] George's behaviour was boisterous – his itemized school bills include the cost of two broken chairs – and his headmaster, du Bertrand, was unhappy about the riotous young Englishmen who came calling for him.[88] Thus, in 1787, his parents bowed to the inevitable and recalled George to England for an education more suitable to his talents, focusing on maths and writing. Morande hoped this would equip him for a career in commerce, finance or the civil service, though to Eliza's horror George insisted he wished to go to sea.[89] They therefore enrolled him in a boarding school four miles outside London run by a Mr Serani, where he also learned French, geography, history, drawing, dance, arms and even Latin.[90]

Although George's progress improved in England,[91] he probably only overcame parental opposition to his chosen career due to an unforeseen event. On 19 May 1788, as he returned to school after visiting his parents, he was attacked by a rabid dog, which sank its teeth into his index finger before running off. After consulting surgeons, Morande had the flesh stripped from the finger to just above the wound, hoping to prevent infection. Three weeks later, when he wrote to tell Dr Saiffert of the operation and its apparent success, he also asked about the efficacy of mercury baths should George develop symptoms. His despairing plea 'I have a broken heart, my dear doctor, have pity on my unfortunate son' suggests that he agreed to let George enter the navy while emotionally vulnerable, reassured that he would be under Salisbury's command.[92]

Salisbury was a brave and effective commanding officer. Indeed, in the first few months that George served with him, the *Termagent* probably saw more action than any other ship in the Royal Navy. For, as Morande informed his readers on 20 August 1788:

> None of the Royal Navy vessels destined to run after smugglers has had as much success as the *Termagent*. One can get an idea of the activity of Captain Salisbury, who commands, by his success. In less than two months he has already taken five prizes. The *Termagent* is the terror of the islands of Jersey & Guernsey.[93]

Over the next few months, Morande assiduously chronicled his swashbuckling friend's achievements. Whenever Salisbury took a prize, ran a smuggler onto the rocks, boarded a merchantman to quell a mutiny, or went ashore to raid a smugglers' den, Morande ensured that the world read about it, having doubtless been informed of events by George and Salisbury himself.[94]

In June 1789, having seized yet another smuggling vessel, Salisbury returned these favours, putting George in command of his latest prize. Thus it was that the son of a French spy found himself, however briefly, in control of His Majesty's newest ship. Indeed, he even saw action in this capacity. As they sailed for home, George's ship was attacked by another smuggling vessel. In the ensuing engagement, George acquitted himself with intelligence and *sang-froid* until the *Termagent* arrived and captured the second smuggler. Eliza and Morande were, for once, delighted with George, and particularly with reports that his crew were calling him 'Captain Morande'.[95] Sadly, this proved the high-point of George's career, for in early 1791, as Britain armed for possible war with Spain, Morande ordered him to leave the navy.[96]

Later the same year, Jacques-Pierre Brissot suggested that Morande was a British spy because George served in the Royal Navy. This rather curious logic was, along with charges that he had betrayed La Motte and sold out French or American merchantmen, one of several apparently malicious accusations that his revolutionary enemies used to suggest he had betrayed France or was a double-agent. Pierre-Louis Manuel adds:

> He was strongly suspected of having served the British ministers, particularly the [fourth] Duke of Bedford [sic] and Lord North; it was even claimed that the latter went secretly to his house, to give him notes that he placed in the public prints, on the alleged divisions between the French troops, their generals, those of the Americans and their own.[97]

Despite these allegations, there is little reason to believe Morande was really a double-agent or deliberately feeding the French false information. Indeed, some of Manuel's evidence was clearly false, for as Morande pointed out, Bedford retired from politics and died before he arrived in England.[98] Morande did place paragraphs in British newspapers clandestinely, but frequently this was in the service of France. No evidence yet found in British archives implies that he worked for the British, and French diplomats never voiced the slightest suspicion that he might have betrayed his country in the ways his enemies suggested. Nor did they credit allegations of double-dealing. Instead, the French government continued to place confidence in both Beaumarchais and Morande. In the 1780s Morande was an agent of enormous energy and resourcefulness who rendered several services of the first importance. How, then, did he manage to keep his most valuable activities and communications with the French government a closely guarded secret?

This question is particularly intriguing because Morande was under surveillance from 1776 to 1778 and, from 1783, made little secret of his links with the French embassy. Moreover, while Swinton was his boss at the *Courier de l'Europe*, (i.e. from January 1784 to June 1785 and January 1788 to May 1791), he was working for a former British agent. To cap it all, Morande was denounced several times in print, notably by Henry Bate in 1778, Pelleport in 1783 and Lord George Gordon in 1786. In effect, Morande used his work as a police agent (the subject of the next chapter) and as an advisor to the ambassador to mask his much more dangerous political and military espionage. This duplicity was facilitated by his financial speculation and editorship of the *Courier de l'Europe*, activities which legitimized his information-gathering. His (carefully crafted?) reputation for indiscretion was also calculated to dispel suspicion. But above all, Morande developed a remarkable arsenal of methods for transferring information to France.

The biggest risk Morande faced was the need for collaborators to prepare materials and convey them to France. Above all, he needed a full-time copyist to reproduce documents and convert his near illegible scrawl into a fair hand. The copyist he chose was the elderly French publicist and sometime sub-editor of the *Courier de l'Europe*, Jean Goy, who was renowned for his discretion, had lived in London for over 30 years, and wrote English well.[99] Goy was infirm and his eyesight was beginning to fade, yet these very disadvantages were also attractions. When Morande forwarded details of British plans to attack Cherbourg, he assured Vergennes:

> The person who copied it is an old man aged 78 who has lived with me for more than ten years and I have assured myself of his loyalty by a salary that has attached him to me in such a way that I can be sure of his silence. He is, moreover, a man without a memory, lacking in spirit and who never leaves his bedroom. Such a confidant is not dangerous.[100]

The loss of Goy, who by mid 1789 was terminally ill, was thus a major blow to Morande.[101] Possibly Morande's correspondence with the foreign ministry largely dried up at this point due to his inability to replace him.

Morande also had to be circumspect about his use of couriers. As any individual travelling frequently between London and France would soon become suspect, the use of multiple messengers was vital, but this increased the risk of betrayal. During peacetime Morande was also sometimes able to use the ambassador's regular weekly diplomatic bag. However, this caused delays and might also cause suspicion, were he to be observed entering the embassy too often. He therefore used several other methods.[102] These included couriers specially chosen by Baudouin. The most important was a Boulogne-based merchant called Louis Pocholle de Menneville, whose profession afforded cover for travel between France and London, even in wartime.[103] During the American Revolutionary War either Menneville or his wife visited London every month to liaise with

Morande, making the trip alternately to allay suspicions. Thereafter, one or other continued to come every six to eight weeks. Eliza also played a part, carrying packages to Boulogne for Menneville on five occasions during the war. Unlike George, Eliza was fully aware of her husband's espionage and hence complicit in treason.[104]

Carrying secret messages to France, particularly in wartime, was fraught with danger, as travellers were liable to be stopped and searched. However, Morande describes an ingenious means to avoid detection, developed with Eliza's assistance:

> A false lining of the finest taffeta overwritten with an ink that I prepared specially, was sewn into the clothes of the bearers [of my messages] by my wife, which allowed me during open warfare to speak totally freely without running any of the risks involved in a correspondence by letter.[105]

Morande also sent letters by post, although this was too risky unless sensitive information was concealed by invisible ink or written in a cypher crude enough to escape notice. Morande used both methods, but rarely, and never for really significant or urgent information. His invisible ink was made from milk, while one of his cyphers mischievously refers to Montmorin as his sister-in-law.[106] Likewise, two of his early letters to the Foreign Ministry are disguised as mercantile correspondence. One begins:

> Monsieur,
>   Until now, affairs relating to the commerce of your [mercantile] house having not required me to have written the outcome of what has occurred, I have contented myself with sending you news on the day of each courier,[107] the current state [of affairs] putting off until the next journey of your agent [i.e. Menneville] to furnish him with the accounts ['états' – i.e. states of the navy] that I have felt obliged to make in addition to those for which you pay me for the instruction of your associates.[108]

The stilted and restricted language of such correspondence was potentially opaque or ambiguous even to the intended recipient. It was also inherently limiting with regard to subject matter, because while it legitimately allowed discussion of politics, economics and a degree of shipping news, it left little scope for including sensitive, detailed or nuanced secret intelligence.

Morande found a more effective and reliable means for communicating coded messages in the *Courier de l'Europe*, which, at Beaumarchais' instigation and with Baudouin's approval, he edited from early 1784 until May 1791.[109] Ironically, the *Courier de l'Europe* was widely denounced in Britain for its 'public espionage' in covering Parliamentary politics and shipping news, as well as its dissemination of American propaganda (including the first French translation of the American Declaration of Independence).[110] However, not even the paper's most vehement detractors suspected the full literal truth behind the spying allegation. Nor, until now, have historians. As we have seen, the *Courier de l'Europe* was a cover for Swinton's British espionage network. Thus, once war broke out, the government very publicly banned the export of the paper, but connived in Swinton's efforts to smuggle copies across the Channel to his Boulogne printshop and used the paper as a channel for disinformation. However, the *Courier de l'Europe* also served French espionage.

In 1788, Morande described how he used the *Courier de l'Europe* to transmit messages even before he was on the editorial staff:

> During the war [of American Independence] I secured for myself and had on my payroll one of the collaborators in the *Courier de l'Europe* [probably Joseph Parkyns MacMahon],[111] who inserted into that paper *at least once per week* the articles that I dictated. These articles that I sent first of all to the English newspapers, then translated in the *Courier de l'Europe*, and reported in a form which I had agreed with Mr. Baudouin, kept him always up to date with the everyday events which could be sent in this manner.[112]

Morande's earliest letters to Montmorin, dating from 1787, give an even clearer idea of how the system worked and reveal that much of the information transmitted was far from mundane or 'everyday'.

> If you follow the *Courier* [*de l'Europe*] attentively, note especially the paragraphs where I give news without guaranteeing it. For example, if I wish to say that such and such a force goes from such and such a place, I will begin by putting a made up paragraph in the *Gazetteer* or *General Advertiser* and in translating it I will say 'The *Gazetteer* or the *General Advertiser* claims that . . . [these dots in original] but this news is improbable or not supported by any proof or by details that we can guarantee. When I cite one or other of these papers, I will always . . . ensure that it is from articles that I sent them *and when I conclude without guaranteeing them you can regard them as authentic*, especially if I don't return to them in the following edition. In that case the news will be exact . . . this key will serve always to give you twice a week a summary of events. To ensure these articles are not noticed, I will give several inconsequential articles that are taken from the same papers . . . When there is something . . . of which I am not sure, I will begin them thus: we read in the *Gazetteer* or in the *General Advertiser* that &c. &c. but I will add nothing if I am not certain. I will not offer any doubts except when I am positively sure of my facts. [Emphasis in original].[113]

By these means, Morande was able to send coded signals to French ministers even when he did not have a secure messenger.

The continental edition of the *Courier de l'Europe* also served as cover for the transmission of slightly riskier information direct to France in the general post. For Morande sent letters marked 'note pour le journal' directly to Menneville at Boulogne for forwarding.[114] Indeed, the paper was so useful that when Swinton ran into financial difficulties in mid 1785, Morande arranged for Pierre-Maximilien Radix de Sainte-Foy to buy his stake in the paper.[115] Besides being a friend of Beaumarchais and one of Madame du Barry's former paramours, Sainte-Foy had served as treasurer to the French navy, for whom he was almost certainly acting as a front man.[116]

The involvement of Sainte-Foy is just one more indication of the regard that the French government developed for Morande's services, intelligence, energy and ingenuity. If his information was not always of the highest quality, there is no doubt that over a ten year period he sent a greater variety of intelligence by a greater variety of means than any other spy in London. Moreover, while others were arrested by the British or ditched for being too corrupt, suspect or careless, Morande remained in favour. It was a remarkable triumph for a man whose reputation was so tarnished and who was known to be a French police agent. He was, without a doubt, one of the master-spies of his age.

6

Poacher Turned Gamekeeper: Morande, Police Spy

By the autumn of 1781, Jean-Claude Jacquet de Douai had every reason to be satisfied with life. The former attorney from the Franche-Comté was a rising star of the Paris police and had been appointed an inspector of the book trade as a reward for suppressing a series of scandalous pamphlets attacking the French royal family, especially Marie-Antoinette. As he embarked on another mission to the Low Countries, he was confident that he would not return empty-handed. Further promotion and royal favour beckoned.

The reason for Jacquet's confidence was simple. He had commissioned the very *libelles* he suppressed. They were written in Paris by his accomplices; smuggled out of the country by Jacquet; printed in London and then shipped to Brussels or Amsterdam for him to purchase and transport to the Bastille. It was a straightforward and lucrative scam with no victims but the French treasury. There was only one flaw in Jacquet's calculations. He had reckoned without Morande.[1]

Jacquet's mistake was to take an excursion to London, presumably to discuss the production of further *libelles* with Boissière, while supposedly on mission to Brussels. Morande got wind of his arrival and immediately informed 'a retired police inspector', most likely his old adversary Inspector Marais.[2] Thus began Morande's new career as police spy and informant. His intelligence was passed to the Lieutenant of Police, Lenoir. Jacquet and his accomplices were arrested, and a police inspector sent to Belgium and the Netherlands to search out Jacquet's collaborators and retrieve any remaining *libelles*.[3]

The agent Lenoir chose for this delicate mission was Receveur, a man of private means and veteran of the expedition to kidnap Morande. Receveur was considered above suspicion and did not disappoint.[4] He returned from Leiden and Brussels with enough printed pamphlets to fill several crates. They included a particularly toxic pamphlet entitled *Essai historique sur la vie de Marie-Antoinette d'Autriche, Reine de France* [*Historical Essay on the Life of Marie-Antoinette of Austria, Queen of France*].[5] This sordid little libel offers a chronicle of the queen's supposed sexual relations with lovers of both sexes. It casts malicious aspersions on her most innocent pleasures and suggests that she and her crapulous cronies dictate a pro-Austrian policy to Louis XVI while systematically pillaging the state.[6]

The *Historical Essay* was never intended for publication and was almost certainly unavailable to the public before the French Revolution, because

Receveur seems to have retrieved the entire edition. It was impounded in the Bastille, where most copies were pulped. Unfortunately, a few were held back in the Bastille's secret archives and found when the fortress was stormed. Quickly and frequently reprinted by revolutionary entrepreneurs, who soon added extra material, the *Historical Essay* became a massive best-seller and founding document of the myth of Marie-Antoinette's promiscuity. This myth had no basis in reality, but in revolutionary rhetoric the queen became a monstrous Messalina. Many historians have argued that before the revolution the *Historical Essay* and similar pamphlets were widely read and helped to undermine the monarchy and create a revolutionary mentality. This is improbable because, in reality, such pamphlets rarely, if ever, circulated in any numbers before 1789. Probably they were unavailable to the public.[7] Yet if pamphlets really had such potential power, Morande's new-found role as a police agent charged to keep them off the streets was among his most important services.

Morande was not the only agent involved in chasing scandalous pamphleteers. In the summer of 1781 Lenoir sent Beaumarchais' old rival, the disgraced magistrate Goëzman, to London masquerading as a German baron. While there, he managed to negotiate the suppression of a scandalous erotic poem about Marie-Antoinette and her dashing brother-in-law, the Count d'Artois, entitled *Les Amours de Charlot et Toinette*. Goëzman bought the entire edition from Boissière, including the manuscript, the pornographic illustrations and the print blocks, and smuggled it back to France. Louis XVI and Vergennes were delighted. Goëzman was duly refunded his expenses and sent back to London on a generous stipend with orders to spy on the British navy and keep watch for other scandalous pamphlets.[8]

Goëzman soon began complaining that his salary was insufficient, but his talent for discovering *libelles* remained as strong as ever. He informed Lenoir of a series of new pamphlets, culminating in *Les Rois de France dégénérés par les princesses de la Maison d'Autriche* [*The Kings of France Corrupted by the Princesses of the House of Austria*] and the *Naissance du Dauphin dévoilée* [*The Crown Prince's Birth Revealed*]. According to Goëzman, this last pamphlet was accompanied by lurid, lewd engravings.[9]

By this time Goëzman's success was arousing the suspicions of Lenoir and the spymaster Baudouin. Lenoir told Vergennes delicately that Goëzman's zeal might be inadvertently encouraging the manufacture of scandalous pamphlets and prints. In reality, Lenoir and Baudouin feared that Goëzman was working in cahoots with Boissière and that the British had blown his cover. They believed that he and his mistress were attracting unnecessary attention by their lavish lifestyle and were alarmed at reports that British agents were trying to establish whether Goëzman was linked to David Tyrie, one of his chief informants. Tyrie, who worked in the naval office at Portsmouth, had been arrested for treason and hanged in 1782.[10] Thus, Goëzman might have welcomed a letter of recall in late February 1783. Instead, he brazenly refused to return to France, claiming that his debts prevented his leaving.[11] This only reinforced suspicions against him.

Lenoir was happy for Morande to inform on his fellow pamphleteers, but trusting him to negotiate with them or deal with Goëzman was another matter. He therefore decided to send the indefatigable Receveur to suppress the pamphlets and spy on Goëzman. Vergennes approved the idea and so, although Britain and France were still technically at war, in early March Receveur was despatched to London. His orders instructed him to liaise with the minister plenipotentiary, the Count de Moustier, who would provide useful introductions.[12] Receveur arrived in London on 13 March and met with Moustier, who suggested that 'it would be most desirable . . . to have a man who had practised the same profession [as the blackmailer] at his disposal'. He recommended Morande. Receveur replied that Morande was one of 'the two men he most feared. However, if Morande was disposed to second him, he believed that they would succeed.' The biggest problem would be persuading Morande to work with his one-time would-be kidnapper.[13]

Moustier therefore suggested an ingenious ruse. Some time before, Morande had presented him with a police plan for London, based on that of Paris.[14] The French had long complained of London's lawlessness and how fear of the mob inhibited British ministers from tackling seditious writers and foreign renegades. Morande's plan thus provided both a credible pretext for introducing the two men and suitable cover for Receveur's mission. Moustier therefore informed Morande that the British had been intrigued by his plan and had asked for a police officer to be sent from Paris to confer with them. To prepare the ground for Morande's first meeting with Receveur, Moustier told him that he should embellish his plan with provisions for an extradition convention and punishing libels. Moustier also consulted Morande about what might be done about blackmailer pamphleteers under existing laws. The following day, 16 March 1783, Morande and Receveur were introduced.[15] They spent the next few weeks trying to track down scandalous pamphleteers and conferring on how to deal with them.

Despite Moustier's cover story, Receveur's arrival alarmed London's French exile community. Rumours and disinformation began to fly and some expatriates began to panic. Their fears were understandable. Most refugees knew about the seizure of Fratteaux and attempts to kidnap Morande and d'Eon. They may also have heard whispers of the fate of Jacquet, locked up among the criminally insane at Charenton, or his associate Louis-Claude-César de Launay, who died mysteriously – rumour said by strangulation – in the Bastille.[16] Yet despite these examples, some refugees were still prepared to risk dabbling in scandalous pamphlets. Chief among these budding Morandes was Boissière's protégé, Pelleport.

Although Pelleport had much in common with Morande, he was, by comparison, a second rater. Pelleport was a minor nobleman, a graduate of the prestigious *école militaire* whose brief army career had ended in disgrace. Like Morande, he was suspected of homosexual leanings and his family had him arrested by *lettres de cachet* several times. Like Morande, he, too, married a foreigner, a Swiss chambermaid, whom he met in Neuchâtel, where they had several children. But once her small dowry was spent, Pelleport set out for London to restore his fortunes.[17]

In London, Pelleport met Boissière, who helped him to publish a sexually salacious work entitled *Les Petits Soupers de l'hôtel de Bouillon* [*Intimate Suppers at the Bouillon's Town House*]. This sordid pamphlet told of sexual shenanigans involving the Princess de Bouillon's servants and friends, including various aristocrats, minor royalty and the naval minister, Castries, and culminated in the mysterious suicide of the princess' coachman. A chronicle of adultery, buggery and dysfunctional aristocratic excess, the *Petits Soupers* was almost devoid of wit, puerile and palpably absurd.[18] It seems to have repelled readers and few copies survive. Morande dismissed it as 'badly written, foul, [and] little designed to interest curiosity'.[19] The same might be said of most of Pelleport's *oeuvre*.[20] However, Pelleport's main aim in writing the *Petits Soupers* was not to attract readers but extortion. In November 1782, he wrote to the Princess of Bouillon demanding money. On 3 January 1783, he wrote again.[21] Shortly thereafter he set his sights even higher and demanded money from the monarchy to suppress *La Naissance du Dauphin*.

Justifiably, this title caused alarm at Versailles. For several years after his marriage, it was widely assumed that Louis XVI was impotent. The birth of his first child in 1778 had thus been greeted with consternation by the king's brothers, Provence and Artois, both of whom hoped to inherit the Crown. They and other members of the royal family responded by spreading rumours, songs, poems and manuscript pamphlets calumniating the queen.[22] Such attacks were largely confined to Versailles, the seat of power. However, Pelleport's pamphlet threatened to take rumours of the queen's inconstancy and royal bastardy to a wider public. Such tales could only damage Marie-Antoinette's authority and the Austrian alliance, and had the potential to undermine the succession. Naturally, the monarchy wished to see the pamphlet suppressed.

Receveur was authorized to pay up to 200 Louis for the *Naissance du Dauphin* and 150 for the *Petits Soupers*. This was substantially less than Pelleport, who claimed to be only a middleman, demanded. Pelleport and Boissière therefore published the *Petits Soupers*, hoping to increase the pressure on Receveur. Meanwhile, Morande worked tirelessly, writing a memorandum on *libellistes* [scandalous pamphleteers] and attempting to trace the elusive pornographic engravings described by Goëzman. He soon learned from a certain Abbé Landis or Landine, a Franco-Irish Catholic priest and one-time associate of Goëzman, that Goëzman had supposedly seen the illustrations at Boissière's shop. Landis also claimed that Goëzman had offered his services to Lord Shelburne, the previous British Prime Minister. Moustier took this for confirmation that Goëzman was a British double-agent. In fact, no concrete evidence against him was forthcoming.[23]

On 2 April, Receveur called at Boissière's shop in St James Street and promised to pay well for any pamphlets that 'he did not sell to everyone'. Disconcerted, Boissière denied having any and Receveur left empty-handed. Within hours Boissière had two further visitors. The first was Morande, who asked for a reconciliation. This astonished Boissière. There had been bad blood between them ever since Boissière introduced Morande to the would-be kidnapper Fontaine in 1772. The rift widened when Morande refused Boissière a share of the pay-off for his *Secret Memoirs of a Woman of Pleasure*. Naturally, Morande made no more progress than Receveur. Finally, Boissière was visited by Landis, who, after consulting a scrap of paper, asked whether he had a new poetical work about the queen, containing four lewd prints. Boissière, who thought he recognized Morande's distinctive handwriting on Landis' note, once again issued a flat denial.[24]

Having heard contradictory rumours concerning Receveur's mission, and aware of his links with Morande and Landis, Boissière took fright. He hired a full-time bodyguard, began carrying a pistol, and insisted on negotiating through Goëzman.[25] Pelleport also panicked. On 7 April, he circulated a broadside entitled *An Alarm-Bell Against French Spies*, which alleged that Receveur was constructing prison coaches for the purpose of spiriting away kidnapped Frenchmen.[26]

Pelleport hoped the *Alarm-Bell* would incite the London mob and terrify Receveur into flight. In this it failed, although Receveur did complain to the French ambassador that his life was in danger. Pelleport also used the *Alarm-Bell* to announce the imminent appearance of two further pamphlets, *Les Amours et aventures du visir de Vergennes* and *Les Passe-tems d'Antoinette* [*Antoinette's Amusements*]. Receveur had not heard of these pamphlets before. However, on learning that Pelleport had already written to Marie-Antoinette's favourite, the Duchess de Polignac, offering to suppress them, he concluded that he was the author.[27]

Receveur now lost patience. On 18 April 1783, he issued an ultimatum to Boissière and Goëzman. Either Boissière would deal with him directly or he would return to France. Desperate and alarmed that his cosy arrangement was coming to an end, Goëzman threatened to complain to Louis XVI that Receveur was jeopardizing his operations. However, he also bowed to the inevitable and on 19 April accompanied Receveur to Boissière's premises. There, in front of a trembling Goëzman, Receveur forced Boissière to deny all knowledge of what Receveur wanted. 'So' – replied Receveur:

> 'you deny to Monsieur's face, that you showed him some frightful verses and prints against the Queen of France, about which, with your consent, he advised the ministers of that kingdom? Likewise that you told him that you were in a position to procure for him another horror against that sovereign, the title of which is *Les Passe-tems d'Antoinette* and finally another [called] *Les Amours du Vizir de Vergennes*?'
> 'I did not say that, Monsieur.'
> 'Very well. If you wish to sell me these horrors, I will buy them from you *ipso facto*. I have money for that purpose. If not, I have none.'

And with that, Receveur left. The following day, Moustier and Receveur sent Goëzman to ask Boissière if he was ready to cut a deal. Boissière replied that he had nothing more to say and could not sell the libels, as he had not consulted their authors and dared not seek them out.[28]

As Boissière refused to deal with him, Receveur returned to Paris for further instructions. He could, he suggested, return to London and order Goëzman to drag Boissière before the courts, armed with a written receipt for the suppression of the *Amours de Charlot et Toinette*. Alternatively, the Crown might pay Goëzman's debts and order him to return home. They could then ignore the libels, which, without the oxygen of publicity, would probably not recoup their publication costs.[29]

Morande later boasted that he prevented Receveur from paying off the blackmailer-pamphleteers. If this was misleading, he was more justified when he crowed 'It was I who stopped this branch of commerce.'[30] For, sick of succumbing to blackmailers, the government decided to follow Receveur's advice, which was based on Morande's memorandum on *libellistes*. The results were as predicted. The pamphlets which had alarmed the monarchy never appeared and, as Lenoir noted, for several years the monarchy remained untroubled by scandalmongering blackmailers.[31] Nevertheless, on 12 June 1783, the French government ordered that all consignments of books entering the country should be inspected in Paris by officials of the book-guild. This circumvented provincial customs officials, who could often be bribed, and significantly altered the economics and risks of importing books. As a result, book-smuggling became much more difficult and the cross-border trade of foreign publishing houses went into decline.[32]

Although Receveur's mission failed, French officials were delighted with Morande. From this moment, French diplomatic correspondence begins to contain positive testimony in his favour. Thus, on 15 June 1783, d'Adhémar wrote to Vergennes to plead on behalf of 'a man more evidently culpable than any other, but perhaps worthy of pardon'. D'Adhémar contended that:

his crimes towards individuals are extreme, but he never dabbled in the horrors that have attacked sacred heads. His repentance, his remorse appear sincere . . . he does not ask to return to Paris where he has infuriated too many people. His desire is to retire in safety to America, where his brother [Francy] has a considerable fortune.

D'Adhémar claimed to have seen proof that Morande had had collaborators who were more responsible than he for the *Gazetier cuirassé* and revealed:

He made me feel pity, and I must do him the justice of saying that his zeal for the king's service appears to be extreme. This man is not among the common herd; he has wit and local knowledge. I believe that in taking from him and giving nothing in return save money and a few words of consolation, one could make use of him effectively. He is hated by his former comrades . . . and nothing testifies more in his favour.[33]

Three weeks later, Vergennes responded warmly to his underling's request:

That which you did me the honour of writing, Monsieur, concerning the marks of repentance of this fugitive, accords with the account I have already received from the Count de Moustier . . . This double testimony is well calculated to inspire some confidence in the protestations of Sieur Morande, who moreover has confirmed them by recent proofs of a return to the sentiments that he ought to have always preserved for his former homeland. You know, Monsieur, of his guilt towards the country of his birth and the abuse he has made of his talents in calumnious writings. Despite the enormity of his crimes . . . if he perseveres in the dispositions of a sincere return to himself, I will lend myself with pleasure on the basis of your testimony, to implore the clemency of His Majesty . . . As he had appeared to desire to return to France, M. de Moustier was authorized to tell him that he would not be punished [?] for the past, provided that in future he behaved as a respectful and faithful subject; you, Monsieur, may renew the same promise under the same condition, whether he decides to return to the Kingdom [of France] or follows the plan . . . of going to settle in a French colony in America.[34]

This correspondence suggests that Morande was appreciated even more for his services as a police agent than his work as a military and industrial spy. It also confirms Morande's assertion that he was given permission to return to France at this time and shows that he was unsure whether to use it.[35] Under pressure from Francy and Eliza, he gave serious consideration to settling in the French Caribbean colonies or the United States. In 1786, he even offered to travel to America as Beaumarchais' financial agent.[36]

Pelleport, in contrast, was furious with Morande. He spewed out his rage in a sensationalized pamphlet account of Receveur's mission, suggestively entitled *Le Diable dans un bénitier et le Gazetier Cuirassé transformé en mouche* [*The Devil in a Font and the Gazetier cuirassé transformed into a police spy*]. By far the most interesting and amusing product of Pelleport's pen, the *Diable* offers a highly coloured satirical exposé of Receveur's mission. In particular, it stigmatizes French despotism and the Bourbon government's willingness to employ an agent as tarnished as Morande. Pelleport thus elevated Morande into a symbol of the corrosive rot at the core of the monarchy.

Pelleport depicts Receveur's mission as a despotic initiative to extend French sovereignty over the policing of London: it threatens the liberties of Frenchmen, refugees and Britons alike.[37] Like the *Gazetier cuirassé*, the *Diable* draws connections between vice, corruption and French despotism. However, Pelleport concentrates his ire as much on agents of despotism as on ministers like Castries and Sartine. His chief villains are thus Morande, a loathsome double-agent who sold out all sides in the American Revolutionary War, and the vile Receveur, who revels in sending countless victims to rot in state prisons, or to be broken on the wheel, branded, or flogged.[38]

Pelleport's account of Receveur's mission is detailed and often very accurate. He reveals, for example, the existence of Morande's memorandum on *libellistes* and the advice it contained.[39] He also reports that Morande's police plan had won the approbation of several British MPs, most prominently Morton Pitt, who intended to champion it in Parliament.[40] This was, in fact, true. Moustier's cover story had taken on a life of its own.[41]

Other scenes in the *Diable* are more satirical or defamatory. In particular, Pelleport attempts to implicate Morande in the production of a *libelle* in partnership with a M. de la F. [who appears to be Pelleport himself].[42] Elsewhere, he provides striking and grotesque thumbnail pen portraits of Morande as evocative and faithful as a Hogarth caricature:

> Imagine, reader, a broad, flat face, all the features of which are formed of free-floating and pallid fat, eyes drawn and haggard, expressing fear and perfidy. A flattened nose, some wide and flared nostrils, which appear to breathe the most brazen lechery ... A mouth from both sides of which dribbles a ghastly pus, a faithful emblem of the venom it never ceases to spread; in a word, the face of a tiger which has been skinned and shaved, yet remains unsatisfied by carnage.[43]

Later, he suggests that Receveur developed a rapport with Morande because they shared 'the same hatred for the human race, the same unblushing countenance, the same baseness of spirit'.[44]

The most striking vignette in the *Diable* is its title scene, which also inspired its frontispiece. It parodies Morande's metamorphosis from poacher to gamekeeper, imagining a symbolic baptism in which Moustier and Receveur purge Morande of his past crimes against the monarchy (see plate 9).[45] The outcome of Receveur's mission might almost be seen as divine retribution for such blasphemy. He is thwarted at every turn by Boissière and, above all, by Morande, who bamboozles and misleads him with a series of malicious, false and vengeful accusations designed to deflect suspicion from himself.[46]

Among those Morande allegedly accused was the hapless clerk Maurice, whose wife, according to Pelleport, Morande had seduced and abandoned. In Pelleport's version, Morande informed Receveur that Maurice was the author of the *Petits Soupers* and hired a French officer to procure a sample of his handwriting. When the officer duly passed off a forged letter as Maurice's writing, Receveur and Moustier convinced themselves that it matched the handwriting in the blackmail

Le Plénipot... reçoit l'abjuration de Charlot et R....r lui donne la croix de St André

Plate 9. Frontispiece from Anne-Gédeon La Fite de Pelleport, *Le Diable dans un bénitier* (1783), showing Morande receiving absolution for his crimes by the Count de Moustier (foreground) while Receveur presents him with the Cross of Saint Louis and an enthroned d'Adhémar looks on. Courtesy of the British Library.

letters sent to the Princess de Bouillon. However, the officer boasted of his deed and Maurice got to hear of it. He went to see the ambassador, provided a sample of his handwriting, and convinced him of his innocence. When informed of this turn of events, Morande merely laughed.[47] The most interesting aspect of this tale is that Receveur did indeed leave England convinced that Maurice produced some of the pamphlets he sought. However, there is no evidence that Morande created this impression or fabricated evidence against him.[48] He did, however, frame others in the aftermath of the affair.

Pelleport's pamphlet ends with Receveur exposed, exhausted and admitting defeat. As he sails for France, he curses England and her liberties: 'I have suffered among you the combined torments which I have myself inflicted on so many wretches, but it does not matter. I am sufficiently avenged, cruel Englishmen, [because] I leave you Morande.'[49] This comic ending merely underlined Pelleport's central themes. French government ministers, unaccountable and beyond all control, were poisoning and pillaging the monarchy with their squabbles, feuds, cupidity and ruthlessness. Their behaviour was a threat to every French subject; their agents were as brutal, corrupt, amoral, incompetent and cynical as their masters. And the Mephistophelian Morande, talisman of despotism, had served, manipulated and outsmarted them all.

Pelleport's revelations enraged Morande and angered d'Adhémar. As a result, the ambassador encouraged Morande to bring a libel case, supported apparently by the British Foreign Minister, Charles James Fox, whose mistress Pelleport had also calumniated.[50] This did not impress Vergennes, who curtly informed d'Adhémar that since crowned heads were not attacked, the French government and its representatives should play no role in the prosecution.[51] Morande dragged Pelleport before the courts anyway and encouraged his creditors to pursue him.[52] This was only the beginning. His vengeance would only be sated when Pelleport and most of his associates were safely in the Bastille.

Among the mistakes that led to Pelleport's incarceration, the most serious was his decision to found a new London-based international newspaper.[53] The prospect of a rival to the *Courier de l'Europe* filled its proprietor, Swinton, with dread. He therefore plotted to destroy Pelleport and his newspaper in collaboration with d'Adhémar, a certain Buard de Sennemar, and his newly appointed editor, Morande. Their plan, approved by Vergennes, was breathtakingly simple. It relied on just one thing: Pelleport's gullibility.

Instead of discouraging Pelleport's plans, Swinton offered to reprint his *Mercure d'Angleterre* in the *Courier de l'Europe*'s Boulogne printshop, where it would evade British stamp duties. Pelleport took the bait and in early July 1784 travelled to Boulogne to inspect the premises with Buard, who promptly delivered him to the authorities. He was taken to the Bastille, where he would spend the next four years. Under interrogation, according to Lenoir, he 'was unable to deny that he composed and printed a single one of the many *libelles* that others attributed to him.[54] Pelleport's confession is important because it confirms the innocence of his former associate, the budding *philosophe* and future revolution-ary Jacques-Pierre Brissot de Warville, who was arrested a day after Pelleport, on the basis of trumped-up evidence supplied by Morande.[55]

Brissot had initially brought suspicion on himself. He had arrived in London in 1782, intent on establishing a periodical and an ambitious academic society, the *Lycée de Londres*. However, he panicked when other refugees told him that he had been denounced to Receveur and wrote to Moustier to clear his name.[56] Receveur and Moustier were mystified. They had received no such denunciation, and for a long while Brissot was considered a suspect. Morande was therefore reviving old suspicions rather than making new allegations.[57]

The reasons for Morande's antipathy towards Brissot are complex, but their enmity was enduring, intense and destructive. Brissot described Morande's hatred as 'the greatest torment of my life'.[58] The two men first met in London in 1779 at the home of Swinton, who for six months in 1778 employed Brissot in Boulogne. A clash of personalities between the rakish smutmonger and the priggish young *philosophe*, who was also one of the few true republicans in pre-revolutionary France, was almost inevitable.

In 1783, when Brissot encountered Morande again, he did not even recognize him. Brissot was dining in the Spring Gardens Coffee House when he noticed a stranger staring at him and heard him mutter his name. Only when Brissot expressed surprise at being recognized did Morande approach him and whisper his own name in Brissot's ear. This slightly sinister encounter was, Brissot later speculated, the moment that Morande sized him up as a future victim. However, it was their third encounter, at Swinton's London residence later the same year that cemented the *philosophe*'s ill-disguised revulsion towards Morande. According to his *Mémoires*, Brissot listened in horror as Morande and another journalist 'enrolled under the same banner' (presumably the *Courier de l'Europe*'s sub-editor, Joseph Parkyns MacMahon), boasted of using the press as an instru-ment of blackmail:[59]

'Here is something that merits a thrashing' said one while talking about himself.

'Doesn't this deserve the noose' replied the other . . .

'That merchant gave me this pair of earrings to puff his shop and denigrate that of his rival.'

'That actress sent me a gold ingot to praise her.'

'That excellent wine I gave you to drink was given to me by Déoda, a famous impure [prostitute] who was afraid lest I reveal a nocturnal rendezvous that violates her bargain and a carefully concealed pregnancy.'

'Have you seen my article on that author who is everywhere praised, and who has not sent me copies of his work? Nothing is more amusing than to slate a book you have not read.'

'And I have proved that everything seemed mediocre and detestable at that club where our most famous artists spoke, because they did not send me a ticket.'[60]

Shortly after this conversation, Swinton told Brissot that he wanted him to replace Serres de La Tour as editor of the *Courier de l'Europe*. However, the proposal came with significant strings attached: Swinton wanted Brissot to employ Morande as his sub-editor. Brissot refused, wishing neither to betray his friend La Tour nor work with 'a being I held in contempt'.[61] Disconcerted, Swinton attempted to reassure Brissot that Morande would be at his command, but Brissot retorted indignantly:

> Not at my command nor otherwise. In accepting your offers I would injure both honour and friendship; but to associate myself with Morande, to sully myself by such an alliance, no, never! If I were dying of hunger and you offered me £1,000 a year, I would reject such offers with horror.

He then reminded Swinton that he had once observed himself that Morande deserved to be hanged ten times over and that Hell had never vomited forth his equal. Swinton, piqued, replied: 'All that is true. But Morande is Beaumarchais' protégé and he knows how to turn out a colourful paragraph.' Brissot retorted: 'Too bad for Beaumarchais. Too bad for you. Too bad for whoever is unfortunate enough to transform himself into the bandit chieftain, for those paragraphs are true banditry.'[62] An irate Swinton told Brissot 'you have play'd the foe'; sacked La Tour; and appointed Morande in his stead. Thereafter, Brissot refused to set foot in Swinton's house, saying he did not wish to breathe the same 'pestilential air' as Morande. The latter, informed by Swinton of what had passed, swore vengeance.[63]

There was, however, a practical reason why, having failed to hire him, Swinton and Morande wanted to be rid of Brissot. They saw Brissot's *Journal du Lycée de Londres* as a rival to the *Courier de l'Europe*. The *Journal du Lycée* was just one branch of Brissot's ambitious plans for his *Lycée de Londres*. According to its prospectus, the *Lycée* aimed to create a Europe-wide community of learned men, and thereby to overcome linguistic and cultural barriers to the dissemination of scientific, philosophic, political and literary knowledge, particularly concerning Britain. It would comprise a regular correspondence, a journal, and a weekly assembly.[64] According to the *Lycée*'s founding contract, Brissot was to supply the 'talent', while his business partner, Desforges de Hurécourt, provided some 15,000 *livres* of capital. This money was intended to cover the journal's printing and distribution costs and 'the maintenance of the premises established at

26 Newman Street, London, for the purpose of setting up the *Lycée*, rent of the said house, and feeding and housing the persons associated with this enterprise.'[65] It was scant funding for so ambitious a venture, and when it began to run out, Desforges began to shirk his financial obligations and demanded the break-up of the partnership. Desforges believed that he could invest his money more profitably in ventures suggested by Pelleport and Serres de La Tour. Their seduction of Desforges was encouraged by Swinton and Morande. Indeed, Brissot suspected that it was Morande who first insinuated to Desforges that he had swindled him. Whatever the case, Desforges was soon accusing Brissot of embezzlement and Morande forwarded his allegations to the French authorities.[66] This charge would haunt Brissot for years to come.

In June 1784, desperate to raise new funds for his *Lycée*, Brissot travelled to France. There, on 12 July, he was arrested, taken to the Bastille and accused of helping to compose the *Diable dans un bénitier*.[67] Four days later, Morande forwarded a certificate from a compositor called Lion, which stated that Brissot's brother (Brissot de Thivars) had brought him the proofs of the *Diable* and informed him that Brissot supplied several passages and corrected most of the rest.[68] Moreover, Lion claimed Pelleport and Thivars had told him that Brissot forwarded copies of the *Diable* with his *Journal du Lycée*, and concluded that they were intended for the booksellers Virchaux in Hamburg, Larrivée in Paris and other clients across Europe. Lion even claimed to have seen Brissot putting copies into crates.[69]

Brissot was asked about Lion's allegations during interrogations by Pierre Chénon, *Commissaire* at the Châtelet de Paris. Brissot replied that Lion's accusation was demonstrably false as the *Diable* was printed in the summer of 1783 and Thivars did not arrive in London until the following November. These facts can be verified.[70] Moreover, Lion worked for the *Courier de l'Europe*'s printer, William Cox, who was in dispute with Brissot and dependent on Swinton and Morande. This made him a suspect witness. Nor did Lion dare give his testimony in the proper British legal form as a sworn affidavit, since perjury was a hanging offence. This also explained why Lion had carefully avoided stating that Brissot corrected the proofs, since proofs were customarily left at the printshop and might be recovered. Finally, Brissot observed that neither Virchaux nor Larrivée received the *Journal du Lycée*, and Larrivée would swear that he had never heard of the *Diable*.[71]

The precision, consistency and detail of Brissot's answers impressed his interrogators and convinced Lenoir of his innocence. Thus, on 5 September 1784, Lenoir wrote to the Baron de Breteuil, Minister for the Royal Household, giving his verdict and soliciting Brissot's release. He informed Breteuil that Lion's certificate appeared devoid of authenticity and that Brissot, 'who replied very well under interrogation', attributed it to the malice of his enemies. Lenoir insisted that Brissot's attentions were wholly devoted to the *Journal du Lycée*, and that his liaisons with Pelleport had ended several months previously. He added that Brissot 'has wit; he is a man of letters; he appears to possess [moral] sytems and remarkable principles' and added 'I consider it just to release him'.[72] Five days later, Brissot was released. Pelleport, in contrast, remained in prison until 1788.[73] Thus despite Morande's best efforts, Brissot found himself free again. Nevertheless, there is strong evidence to suggest that he acted as a middleman for Pelleport, forwarding copies of the *Diable* to clients outside France.[74] This made him culpable in Morande's eyes, even if he had not technically committed a crime.

Nevertheless, the damage was done. Brissot was ordered to remain in France and his *Lycée* collapsed.[75] Nor did Morande's persecutions end there. In early 1785, he published a series of unsigned articles in the *Courier de l'Europe* which repeated Desforges' charges and mocked Brissot's claims to probity and writings on the criminal law. In one article, Morande asserted that Brissot was 'mired in the practice, as well as the theory of the criminal law'.[76] In another, he chided 'It is not enough to play the virtuous and act the little Beccaria in writing on Crimes, it is necessary not to commit them'.[77] Brissot, incensed, responded by launching a libel suit in France against Desforges, Desforges' agent, Swinton and the *Courier de l'Europe*'s French censor, the Abbé Aubert.[78] However, his hopes of damages were dashed when Desforges denied responsibility for Morande's articles and Swinton sold his French property and ceded ownership of the *Courier de l'Europe* to Sainte-Foy. Brissot now had no alternative but to drop his case.[79] However, he had not heard the last of the allegation.

If Brissot was innocent of scandalous pamphleteering and blackmail, the same could not be said of another of Pelleport's 'intimate' associates, Jean-Claude Fini, alias Count Hyppolite Chamorand. Fini, a career criminal, was first arrested at Rouen in 1778 for stealing a prostitute's ring. Aware of Fini's past and links to Pelleport, Morande wrote to Receveur recounting his history and asking for further details.[80] According to Morande, Fini had sworn to avenge Pelleport's arrest by writing a pamphlet attacking those who had betrayed him. However, his plans were thwarted when Morande secretly incited a dispute between Fini and Morande's sub-editor, Monsieur de Morgan. Morgan had Fini arrested, presumably for debt, and with Fini at Morgan's mercy, Morande offered to mediate. His price was the suppression of Fini's pamphlet, together with several other manuscript *libelles* that Fini was threatening to publish.[81]

Unable to profit from his manuscripts, Fini dreams up an elaborate and audacious plan to restore his fortunes. On Friday 28 October 1785, Fini's lover, Marie Barbara Mackay, lures one of her rich relatives, who is also named Mackay, to a house in Newington with promises that she will repay a loan. There, he is ambushed by Fini, who draws two pistols and forces him to write a promissory note for £300. The lovers then tie him up and attach him by a cord to the trigger of a pistol which is primed to fire at a barrel of gunpowder. The same trip wire is attached to a window to prevent any rescue. They warn Mackay that if he attempts to struggle free, he will blow himself up. Then they leave to cash his promissory note before returning to extort another. This time Mackay finds the courage to resist their demands and they abandon him.[82]

Fortunately, Mackay's cries are eventually heard and some rescuers manage to enter without tripping the trigger. Fini and his lover have meanwhile fled to Holland.[83] Fearing a murder charge should their victim blow himself up, they send a letter to Mackay's wife from Harwich, informing her of her husband's predicament and advising her to rescue him alone. A second letter, to his lawyer, threatens to murder Mackay if they are pursued.[84] The letters arrive too late, for Mackay has already offered a £40 reward for their capture. Meanwhile, in three successive editions of the *Courier de l'Europe*, Morande publishes a physical description of 'Chamorand' and the numbers of the banknotes he is carrying.[85] Ultimately this will lead to Fini's arrest.

By 17 November 1785, Fini and Marie Mackay have made their way by foot and public diligence from Rotterdam to Brussels to Valenciennes and finally to Paris in an increasingly desperate attempt to exchange their British banknotes. Finally, in Paris, they find a bank willing to accept them and a negligent clerk, who fails to check the numbers. However, the police soon learn of the fugitives' presence and two days later they are cornered near the Tuileries palace by the police officer Longpré. He attempts to arrest them but Fini refuses to give up quietly. He draws his knife and slashes the policeman before fleeing alone towards the banks of the Seine. Finding two boatmen, he grabs his pistols and forces them to ferry him to the other side, where he disappears into the Latin Quarter.

Two days later, Fini takes refuge in the home of a benefactor. Fini tells him that he needs somewhere to lie low until money arrives to pay his creditors and his friend kindly offers to shelter him. This is not his first favour to Fini. He had first encountered him with Marie Mackay when his diligence overtook them trudging along the road from Rotterdam to Brussels. He stopped the coach and offered to pay their fares as far as Valenciennes. On the way he listened spellbound as Fini, evidently a fine *raconteur*, spun him tall tales of adventuring with Captain Cook.

On the second day of his stay, Fini confesses to his adventure with Longpré, and his host, alarmed, tells his uncle. The uncle remembers the description of 'Chamorand' in the *Courier de l'Europe* and, after consulting a copy, contacts the police. The nephew returns home to await the arrival of Longpré and his colleague Surbois, who arrest Fini without any resistance. Shortly afterwards, the uncle writes a pseudonymous letter to the *Courier de l'Europe* telling of Fini's arrest.[86]

Thus, three years later, Morande could boast to Montmorin that he played a vital role in the arrest of Fini and that of Mackay, who was picked up separately.[87] However, this was not the first time that he had used his paper to thwart criminals. On several occasions he had sounded the alarm about international scams to dupe merchants into extending credit to fraudulent commercial houses. He even claimed to have received death-threats after breaking up one such crime-ring.[88] Now, having discovered the effectiveness of circulating descriptions of criminals, Morande used the *Courier de l'Europe* to help apprehend several further villains.[89]

With Fini and Pelleport behind bars and Brissot ruined and confined to France, Goëzman and Boissière were Pelleport's only associates to remain at large. Goëzman certainly did not get away scot-free. Following Receveur's departure, he continued negotiating with Boissière until ordered to return to France in July 1783.[90] He escaped punishment only because conclusive evidence of his complicity was never discovered. Nevertheless, he was received coldly at Versailles, and his requests for further payments proved fruitless.[91]

Boissière was a little more fortunate. For a while the French government considered encouraging victims of Pelleport's *Petits Soupers* to bring a series of ruinously expensive libel cases against him, secure in the knowledge that they could abscond without paying costs if judgment went against them. Such hopes foundered on the question of reputation: if victims lacked a reputation in Britain, there was no hope of damages, and little reason for a defendant to fight the charges.[92]

Although Boissière's gang had been broken up, Receveur and French diplomats remained alarmed about one other desperado: the lawyer turned journalist Linguet. There was no suspicion that Linguet produced sexually scandalous pamphlets. Instead, they were concerned about his journalistic activities, especially his sensational, tear-jerking and largely mendacious *Mémoires sur la Bastille*, which was published in London in 1783 and offered an exposé of the Bastille and the sting operation by which Linguet was imprisoned there between 1780 and 1782. French diplomats examined a number of ways to deal with Linguet under English law. For example, they hoped to persuade the husband of his mistress, who lived with him openly in London, to sue him for adultery. They also dreamed of getting Linguet's former business agent, Lequesne, to sue him for alleging (quite correctly) that he helped to plot the ambush that led to Linguet's imprisonment.[93]

What made Linguet particularly dangerous was his paranoid and highly egotistical style of opinion journalism. It transformed his every experience into a form of victimhood, his every dispute into a personal political crusade. French audiences had never experienced anything like Linguet's periodical *Annales politiques, civiles et littéraires du dix-huitième siècle* [*Political, Civil and Literary*

Annals of the Eighteenth Century]. Despite its premium price, at its peak each issue sold an estimated 30,000 copies, thereby equalling the combined circulation of the entire French newspaper press. Linguet was, then, undoubtedly the most popular and influential French journalist of his age.

For all Linguet's outspokenness, he had fans in high places, including Louis XVI. However, his maverick style and impassioned pleadings in court, pamphlets and periodicals earned him powerful enemies throughout the French legal establishment, literary elite and political hierarchy. In politics, too, his views were idiosyncratic and widely despised. Much to Morande's disgust, Linguet was an outspoken apologist for absolutism, believing it the only means to protect the populace, whose cause he often championed, against powerful vested interests.[94] In 1784, Linguet also enraged politicians at Versailles by writing in favour of reopening the Scheldt river, a move long blocked by France's Dutch allies, who feared competition from the Austrian Netherlands [Belgium]. This was the most explosive diplomatic issue of the day and Linguet's intervention was a blatant attempt to please the Austrian government.[95] Naturally, powerful interests in France were keen to deride and marginalize Linguet. Morande proved to be their champion.

Morande's antipathy to Linguet dated back to the late 1770s, when Linguet took d'Eon's side in his struggle with Beaumarchais.[96] However, if we could believe the date on the title page, Morande's first attack on Linguet appears to be a tiresome tirade of personal abuse published anonymously, purportedly in 1783 in Amsterdam, under the title *Le Bon-homme anglois* [*The Simple Englishman*]. This 30-page pamphlet attacks the claims of the *Mémoires sur la Bastille* and Linguet's talents as a writer, his personal qualities, lack of integrity, and treatment of his mistress, Perrine Buttet. It also denounces his political position as a spokesman for despotism and regrets that he has found asylum in Britain. It even defends the Bastille while criticizing the French government for releasing Linguet.

The *Bon-homme anglois* remains justly obscure. It is Morandian invective at its worst, spurting abuse from its opening sentence. 'I have never, thank God, seen Linguet' it begins. 'If it pleases Him, I never will'. Thereafter, it turns on Linguet's style and influence, his motives and his character, for page after page. The Linguet described in the pamphlet is wicked, avaricious, supremely self-interested and an enemy of public order, particularly in his printed attacks on Vergennes and other French ministers:

> True, Linguet has not killed; but he has calumniated, and by his calumnies he has troubled society, as much as he could, and does not the crime of the perturber of the public peace merit [the same treatment as] that of the murderer? Public peace depends on the respect subjects have for the sovereign.[97]

Moreover, Linguet is vengeful and cowardly:

Wicked without other motive than his self-love or his greed for money, Linguet will do anything to avenge himself on those who have humiliated him or failed to satisfy his avarice: he attacks them, but always from a distance . . . people worthy of faith who have seen him while enraged have assured me that the sight of a sword, a duelling pistol, even a simple riding crop, is sufficient to calm him.[98]

This last passage adds weight to suspicions of the compiler of the *Mémoires secrets*, that the *Bon-homme anglois* was published not in 1783 but in 1785, the year when he acquired a copy. It was also the reason why he was convinced that Morande was the pamphlet's author, a deduction that seems to be supported by both the text and context.[99] For in 1785, Morande and Linguet were involved in a very public dispute. It had reached a climax just after 7 p.m. on 11 September 1784, when Morande encountered Linguet in Piccadilly and spat three times in his face. Rather than avenge this insult, Linguet turned on his heels and fled.[100] The passage above appears to allude to this incident.

At the heart of the dispute lay a dead man: Voltaire. In 1780, two years after Voltaire's death, Beaumarchais set himself up as his literary executor by announcing plans to produce a luxury edition of Voltaire's complete works at Kehl.[101] This massive undertaking would suck up Beaumarchais' money and energy for years to come. As Beaumarchais' agent in London, Morande was involved in liaising with booksellers and clients and championing the project. He thus took a jaundiced view of Linguet's announcement that he intended to produce a rival bowdlerized edition suitable for children, maidens, and other 'delicate readers', who might blush to read Voltaire's notoriously pornographic *Pucelle d'Orléans* [*Maid of Orléans*].[102]

This announcement provoked two letters to the *Courier de l'Europe* ridiculing Linguet's project. Both were probably written by Morande. The letters accused Linguet of sacrilege and wishing to make a Capuchin out of Voltaire.[103] They also turned him into a laughing stock. Consequently Linguet's edition attracted few subscribers and within weeks he was forced to renounce the whole project. In March 1784, Morande wrote to seek Beaumarchais' retrospective approval for the 'holocaust' he had unleashed, gloating that Linguet had abandoned his corrected edition at only page 37.[104] Several weeks later, he gleefully republished Linguet's formal renunciation of the project under the title 'Honourable Restitution to Monsieur de Voltaire's Ghost'. In it, Linguet lamented that while attempting to perform a public service, he found himself assailed from all sides. While the *Courier de l'Europe* accused him of turning Voltaire into a monk, a Luxembourg paper found him insufficiently Christian. He was thus abandoning Voltaire to the *philosophes* and the Luxembourg Christians.[105] Yet even this surrender did not placate Morande.

Linguet initially treated Morande's attacks with disdain. He finally broke his silence only in July 1784, when he published a letter purportedly from a British correspondent in Spa, which defended him against Morande. However, rather than publish the entire letter, Linguet suppressed the key passages, explaining:

> nothing is more convincing than the clarifications that you wish to furnish me with; but the being against whom you wish to defend me is so vile, so completely dishonoured, that he cannot even cause offence. When passing through a place where there are vermin . . . we silently brush off the evil-doing and disgusting insect [sic] which follows its instinct: sometimes we fear contamination in crushing it.[106]

Linguet had named neither Morande nor the *Courier de l'Europe*, but this passage angered his censors and the foreign ministry nevertheless. Although they did not force him to remove it, they held up the distribution of his *Annales* in the post for several weeks, allowing foreign counterfeiters to produce cheap pirate editions and flood the market. The same treatment was meted out to Linguet's next edition, which said nothing about Morande, and there were further delays for two subsequent numbers, which argued for the opening of the Scheldt.[107]

These delays infuriated Linguet, who protested to Vergennes that Morande was permitted to attack him in a censored paper while he, Linguet, was prevented from offering a timely explanation of his reasons for not responding. He therefore concluded that 'it is the Ministry itself which, directly, makes this base and criminal war against me'.[108] At the end of January 1785, having received no reply to this insolent memorandum, Linguet went public with his complaints against Morande, the ministry and his censors in an outspoken and audacious *Advice* to his readers. This set out the reasons for the delays and claimed that numerous readers had urged him to drag Morande before the courts as:

> A universal enemy, one of those beings who live only by the evil they make; of which the venomous ejaculations, dating from the *Gaze . . . cuir . . . [Gazetier cuirassé]*, extend to all orders of society from the lowest right up to the throne; of which the impunity often makes the English blush at the resources which cautious crime finds, or hopes to find, in their constitution.

Nevertheless, Linguet chose not to begin proceedings because:

> To attack him legally would be to authorize the belief that he could have an impact, that he counts for something in the society of respectable people; that one could attach some value to avenging his impostures . . . But there are men who should be left in their obscurity, even when they abuse it, whose names should be treated as Justice will treat their ashes.[109]

Paradoxically, by allowing Linguet's attacks to circulate, the French government spiked his guns. His cries that they were silencing him now rang hollow. Nor did everyone in government stand idly by while Morande poured invective on Linguet's head. In the spring of 1784, Charles-Alexandre de Calonne, the French finance minister, apparently asked his brother, the worldly Abbé Jacques-Ladislas-Joseph de Calonne, to intercede with Morande's patrons and employers and ask them to silence him.[110] Like many ministerial attempts to rein in Morande, this initiative failed. Morande's attacks continued, together, following the incident in Piccadilly, with taunts concerning Linguet's honour and courage.[111]

Morande's harassment of Linguet extended to his domestic affairs. Learning that, after a particularly bitter row, Perrine Buttet had left Linguet, Morande hastened to visit her in her new lodgings. Bonded by a mutual desire to avenge themselves on Linguet, Morande insinuates that they briefly became lovers. Shortly afterwards, Perrine went to see Lord Mansfield, accompanied by the British agent Nathaniel Parker Forth, to allege, among other things, that Linguet had stolen her belongings. Despite his denials, there is little doubt that Morande, who was remarkably well informed about the incident, incited her. But while counting on the fury of a woman scorned, he had forgotten that lovers' anger is often fickle. No sooner had Perrine laid her complaint than she was reconciled with Linguet. And he, Morande, 'was sacrificed like a passing fancy'.[112]

Meanwhile, Linguet also fell out with another refugee pamphleteer, the Count de Mirabeau, the ebullient libertine, pornographer and future revolutionary leader whose fame would soon eclipse that of Morande, Linguet, or even Beaumarchais. In August 1784, Mirabeau fled to London with his pretty 19-year-old mistress, Henriette-Amélie de Nehra. Initially, Linguet and Mirabeau were friends, but two such combustible characters soon quarrelled, rather to the relief of Perrine Buttet, who remarked that when they were together 'no-one else could get a word in edgewise'.[113] The cause of their dispute was probably politics, for in London, in December 1784, Mirabeau published a pamphlet opposing the opening of the Scheldt entitled *Doutes sur la liberté de l'Escaut*.[114]

Shortly afterwards, Mirabeau was summoned before magistrates for beating his servant Jacques-Philippe Hardy so mercilessly that, according to one eyewitness, the whole household came running to his rescue. Mirabeau justified his brutality by accusing Hardy of stealing money and linen and launched a lawsuit against him.[115] Hardy was tried before Justice Buller in the Old Bailey on 26 February 1785. According to Morande, Linguet turned up to defend Hardy, but fled from the courtroom when he saw Morande arriving to testify on Mirabeau's behalf, genuine eyewitnesses having refused to perjure themselves.[116] If this anecdote is true, Morande never got to testify. Faced with scant evidence, Buller stopped proceedings and asked Mirabeau's friend and lawyer, Sir Gilbert Elliot, to drop the case on grounds of insufficient evidence. Mirabeau agreed, but on condition that he could give his reasons for pursuing matters so far.

According to Mirabeau, he had sought a warrant to arrest Hardy on finding his travel bags had been pilfered. However, Hardy absconded before the warrant was served and had Mirabeau arrested for debt to make it appear that his employer acted from resentment. When Hardy was apprehended, he and a female accomplice insinuated that they would defend themselves by slandering Mirabeau. Mirabeau claimed he pursued the affair to refute such calumnies. As a result, Buller told the jury to acquit Hardy for lack of evidence and without a stain on his character. He added, however, that the case was rightly brought and there was no evidence to support the slightest imputation against Mirabeau.[117]

Although Morande did not testify in court, he may have spoken privately to Buller, thus avoiding the risks of a perjury charge. A year later, in a letter to Beaumarchais, Morande confessed that he told the judge everything that Mirabeau wished him to say. In reality, Morande declared, Hardy had taken 30 Louis worth of money and goods, but they were legitimately owed to him as wages that Mirabeau had refused to pay. Morande had thus extricated Mirabeau from the perils of a false accusation.[118]

Morande now set about exploiting the Mirabeau case to his own advantage. Such is the testimony of a witness whose moral integrity is beyond question, the doctor Nicolas Dufriche Desgenettes. Desgenettes was Mirabeau's friend, but refused to give false testimony about the assault on Hardy, which he witnessed. Fifteeen years later, he withstood even Napoleon Bonaparte's browbeating, refusing to administer a lethal dose of opium to plague-ridden troops at Jaffa. Desgenettes tells how, shortly after refusing to testify on Mirabeau's behalf, he was surprised to receive a note from Mirabeau and Henriette de Nehra. They invited him to dinner with them and a certain unnamed 'coquin' [scoundrel]. Intrigued, Desgenettes called on Henriette to learn more. She informed him that the scoundrel was Morande and that Mirabeau 'feared his pen, ill-sharpened as it is' or to meet alone with him. Mirabeau was hoping to persuade Morande not to publish a 'strongly malicious article' concerning the Hardy trial. Thus, they wished Desgenettes to serve as a witness to Mirabeau's discussions with Morande. The negotiation was clearly successful, as the Courier de l'Europe's coverage of the Hardy case is generous to Mirabeau.[119] As for the exact content of the suppressed article, Desgenettes leaves us in the dark. However, several months later Morande offered to send Beaumarchais dirt on Mirabeau, and specifically 'the exact particulars of the trial in London, and on the theft of a certain watch'.[120] Mirabeau had not heard the last of Morande.[121]

As for Linguet, he published Hardy's libellous account of the affair, but left England in the autumn of 1785 to settle in the Austrian Netherlands, unable to bear the ignominy Morande had inflicted upon him in Piccadilly. Or so sneered the *Mémoires secrets*.[122] In fact, Linguet had long been cultivating the Austrian authorities and would almost certainly have left anyway.

Although no new sexually salacious pamphlets sullied the reputation of the French court and monarchy for several years after Receveur's mission, a wave of other scandalous pamphlets were published from London between 1781 and 1784. Contemporaries, nineteenth-century bibliographers and Morande's only previous serious biographer, Paul Robiquet, have attributed several of these to Morande, and many subsequent scholars have treated his authorship as fact. The most plausible attributions are for *La Gazette noire, par un homme qui n'est pas blanc, ouvrage posthume du Gazetier Cuirassé* [*The Black Gazette, by a Man who is not White, a Posthumous Work by the Gazetier Cuirassé*] (1784); *Le Portefeuille de Madame Gourdan* [*Madame Gourdan's Briefcase*] (1783); and *La Vie privée ou apologie du très sérénissime prince Monseigneur le duc de Chartres* [*The Private Life or Apology of the Most Serene Prince My Lord the Duke of Chartres*] (1784), which in 1793 was translated into English as *Memoirs and Gallantries of a Prince of the Blood of Abo*. Other works that have often been attributed to him in whole or part include *Les Joueurs et M. Dusaulx* [*The Gamblers and Mr Dusaulx*] (1781); *Le Désoeuvré, ou, l'espion du boulevard du temple* [*The Idler, or the Spy in the Boulevard du Temple*] (1781); and *Le Vol plus haut, ou l'espion des principaux théâtres de la capitale* [*The Highest Flight or the Spy in the Principal Theatres of the Capital*] (1784).

All these attributions are dubious. Despite the title and some obvious similarities with Morande's early work in subject material, title and anecdotal style, *La Gazette noire*'s Rousseauist rhetoric and praise for Linguet suggest that it was probably written by Pelleport or other members of the Boissière circle. This was clearly what the police suspected when they questioned Brissot about the pamphlet's authorship.[123] The *Vie privée* – a scandalous biography of the future Duke d'Orléans – may equally have been by Pelleport, to whom it has sometimes been attributed. Computer analysis of the texts of these two pamphlets strongly suggests that they emanated from the same pen and that Pelleport is much the more probable author.[124] There is nothing specific to link Morande to the *Portefeuille de Madame Gourdan*, an epistolary exposé of the activities and clients of the ladies of the most famous Paris brothel. It could be his work, but its obscene puerilities are again more reminiscent of Pelleport's pen, particularly a scene where a client crawls around the floor with a large feather protruding from his anus, being all the while stroked on the back by a harlot who murmurs 'the beautiful peacock, the beautiful peacock.'[125] Moreover, later editions of the *Portefeuille* are almost certainly the work of several hands, for letters were added and removed each time it was republished.

Les Joueurs is a more interesting case, as it mentions Morande and several of his associates, including his former mistresses Mademoiselles Desmares and

La Cour.[126] More significantly, its main purpose is to vilify gambling dens and the crooks who ran them in collaboration with the police. This became a favourite topic in Morande's journalism, and in 1791 and 1792 he campaigned for the closure of Parisian gambling houses and castigated the municipal authorities when they failed to act.[127] However, the *Joueurs* has also been attributed to Jacquet and his collaborators Marcenay de Ghuy and the Abbé Duvernet. Indeed, a document in the Bastille archives shows it was among the works Receveur brought back from Leiden in January 1782 when he smashed Jaquet's network, and computer analysis suggests it had the same author as the most famous work of Jacquet's network, the *Historical Essay*.[128] It therefore seems unlikely that Morande, who first denounced Jacquet's activities, was involved in this pamphlet, particularly since any complicity would surely have emerged when Jacquet and his collaborators were interrogated. Likewise, Robiquet would struggle to convince modern literary historians, who are aware that intertextuality between texts (that is wholesale borrowing or what we would now call plagiarism) was standard practice in the eighteenth century, that the *Désoeuvré* and *Vol plus haut* were the work of Morande. For his argument is based solely on the premise that both texts lift passages wholesale from *La Gazette noire*, which, as we have noted, was probably not Morande's work anyway.[129]

Marion Ward has also, improbably, accused Morande of being the author of *Le Guerlichon femelle* [*The Fancywoman*], a scandalous attack on Marie-Antoinette and the Princess de Lamballe which Nathaniel Parker Forth suppressed in February 1778. Forth quickly discovered the identity of the *Guerlichon*'s author, which he never revealed, but took months to track down his residence. As Morande was well known to the British government and, almost certainly, Forth himself, his involvement can be ruled out.[130]

If the French government was little troubled by these works and believed that the queen was now safe from scandalous attacks, they were in for a rude awakening. In August 1785, a new scandal erupted which shook the monarchy to its foundations: the diamond necklace affair. In its wake it was threatened with a new set of scandalous works. Once again, Morande was on the case.

7

The Magician, the Necklace and the Poisonous Pig

The diamond necklace affair began with the fraud of the century.[1] In early 1785, the fabulously beautiful Countess de La Motte persuaded Cardinal Rohan, an aristocratic *roué* and distant cousin of the queen, to use Marie-Antoinette's forged signature to con the court jewellers out of a fabulous diamond necklace. With the contract of sale signed, the jewellers handed over the necklace. La Motte and her co-conspirators broke it up and her husband, Count Nicolas de La Motte, fenced the gems around Europe. Whether the cardinal, who was experiencing financial difficulties, was involved in the conspiracy remains uncertain. La Motte calculated that the affair would be covered up and that the Rohan clan would buy off the jewellers. Instead the jewellers approached Marie-Antoinette for payment and Louis XVI promptly ordered a trial to clear the queen's name.

This was a grave miscalculation. The case became a *cause célèbre*, pitting the Crown against the Paris *Parlement* and the Rohan faction at court against Marie-Antoinette and her allies. Worse still, the queen's name was dragged through the mud, because the cardinal claimed that he was tricked into participating in the fraud by a harlot named Nicole Guay d'Oliva who had impersonated the queen in a moonlight tryst at Versailles. To clear the cardinal – which, after a nakedly political trial, the *Parlement* of Paris did – was thus to impugn the queen's morals. It implied that it was perfectly reasonable for a high-ranking courtier to believe that she might behave in that way. The Countess de La Motte, in contrast, was found guilty, whipped, branded and gaoled for life.

The diamond necklace affair had a strikingly colourful cast of characters. Alongside the female protagonists Marie-Antoinette, Guay d'Oliva and La Motte, there were some intriguing male actors. First there was a Prince of the Church, the lecherous and (apparently) breathtakingly credulous Cardinal Rohan, whose notorious love life features prominently in the *Gazetier cuirassé*. It recounts how Rohan was caught in a brothel and, in spite of his rank, forced to sign a confession that he had known the *fille de joie* Rosalie to the point of ejaculation.[2] He is also, Morande insists gleefully, one of the prelates in whom court ladies 'place most faith' when they wish to make a little bishop.[3] However, by the time the diamond necklace scandal broke, Rohan was a benefactor to Morande's family, having granted George a bursary worth 251 *livres*.[4]

The Rohan clan and their political allies, including Vergennes, worked tirelessly to secure a not guilty verdict for Rohan. They sent police agents abroad in pursuit of Guay d'Oliva and the Countess de La Motte's lover and pet forger, Marc-Antoine Rétaux de Villette, and persuaded them to return and testify in the cardinal's favour. They may also have sponsored attempts to murder the Count de La Motte, who was safely abroad when the crime became known, either as revenge, or through fear that his testimony would inculpate the cardinal. There is certainly evidence to suggest that, while the trial was in progress, Vergennes attempted to sabotage attempts to seize the count and bring him back to France to testify.[5]

Morande was involved in the pursuit of the diamond necklace conspirators from an early stage. In September 1785, Vergennes and the Rohans sent the geologist Ramond de Carbonnières to London to trace the stolen diamonds. Carbonnières was in many ways an ideal agent. He had lived in Rohan's household for several years and knew the major protagonists in the affair. However, he was unfamiliar with London and so, on arrival, approached Morande for help. Morande provided him with useful contacts and boasted that he found 'the means to indicate several of the trails that were used to furnish the proofs used in the [diamond necklace] trial'.[6] Morande may also have assisted in attempts to apprehend and even assassinate the Count de La Motte. They certainly featured some of his closest collaborators and former agents.

La Motte claims three attempts were made on his life and liberty between his wife's arrest and her trial. The first allegedly occurred shortly after he reached London, in the late summer of 1785. A mystery assailant grabbed a handle on his carriage, smashed a window with an umbrella, thrust at him with a rapier, then fled. Fortunately, La Motte flinched and the sword missed him by inches.[7] Terrified, he consulted Linguet, an 'Irish priest' (probably Parkyns MacMahon), and the Franco-Irish Capuchin Macdermott, one-time almoner to the French ambassador. They suggested that he hide in Ireland with Macdermott's relatives, but unfortunately Macdermott betrayed his refuge to the French embassy.[8] Before long, La Motte was struck by a mystery ailment which hindered his 'performing the most natural and indispensable functions of nature'[9] and, believing himself recognized, fled to Scotland.[10]

Convinced that he had been poisoned, La Motte spent seven or eight months in Edinburgh, confined to his apartment.[11] During this time, his servant met and befriended an elderly language teacher called Costa in an Edinburgh tavern and introduced him to his master. They became friends and Costa agreed to accompany La Motte to Newcastle. In reality, however, Costa was Morande's former partner in crime, Benavent.[12] He offered to deliver the count to the French for £10,000.[13] As a result, Benavent, Vergennes, d'Adhémar and a boatload of police officers conspired to kidnap the count from South Shields. La Motte rumbled the plan and then teamed up with Benavent to wrest cash advances from the French government.

Once again Benavent proved an unreliable ally and began conspiring with French agents to drug and capture La Motte.[14] Again La Motte learned of the plan. To prevent further duplicity, La Motte met with d'Adhémar in London and announced that he was willing to go to Paris to testify at his wife's trial if given proper guarantees. On learning that La Motte's evidence would be damaging to Rohan (and hence favourable to his patron the queen), d'Adhémar wrote to Vergennes to suggest holding up the trial until La Motte could arrive.[15] His letter arrived too late and La Motte remained in London, where Morande watched him closely.

The evidence that Morande was involved in the earlier pursuit of La Motte remains circumstantial. He could have learned of the count's arrival and plans from agents in Linguet's household, including Perrine Buttet, or from his old associate Joseph Parkyns MacMahon, who served as the La Mottes' host and ghost writer.[16] This might explain the speed with which the first assassin allegedly struck after La Motte's arrival, but this is pure speculation. Nor can we be sure that Benavent, who spent the late 1770s and early 1780s in gaol for assisting an attempt to defraud the Maréchal-Duc de Richelieu, was still in contact with Morande.[17] However, his timely appearance in Edinburgh is suspicious and Morande was apparently in contact with him five years later.[18]

The most colourful character in the diamond necklace affair was the self-styled Count de Cagliostro, healer, friend and benefactor of all mankind. The greatest charlatan of the eighteenth century, Cagliostro was a mystic and prophet of the occult. He bewitched and bamboozled disciples across Europe with portentous predictions and magical, alchemical, spiritualist, magnetist and freemasonic rituals. According to judicial memoirs ghost-written by his lawyer, Jean Thilorier, Cagliostro was a dispossessed Prince of Trebizond. He claimed to have been brought up as a Christian before travelling widely in the Orient, where he had learned the mysterious rites of ancient Egyptian freemasonry among the ruins of the Nile. Styling himself the Grand Copt, he began to establish Egyptian masonic lodges wherever he went. Among other extravagant claims, he boasted of having mysterious healing powers, of discovering the philosopher's stone, and being several hundred years old. He also claimed to be able to manufacture diamonds, a boast that won him Rohan's patronage. This unfortunate combination was to be his downfall. For in her mendacious judicial memoirs, the Countess de La Motte accused Cagliostro of masterminding the fraud. In fact, he was an innocent victim of the affair and was eventually acquitted of involvement.[19]

Nevertheless, following the trial, Cagliostro and his wife were expelled from France. In June 1786 they sought refuge in England, where Cagliostro hoped to establish a masonic lodge of the Egyptian Rite. There, he was fêted by prominent masons, including the Prince of Wales and his brothers, and lionized by leading Whigs such as Sheridan and Georgiana, Duchess of Devonshire.[20] He was also introduced to Samuel Swinton who rented him a house next door to his own at number 4, Sloane Square.[21] Swinton, who dreamed of forming a business partnership with Cagliostro, welcomed the charlatan with open arms. He helped him move into his new home, recommended traders who could supply furnishings, showed him the sights of London, and introduced him to an apothecary who could manufacture Cagliostro's famous rejuvenating 'Egyptian pills'. It was through Swinton that Cagliostro met Morande.[22]

Cagliostro says that Swinton encouraged him to recruit Morande as his panegyrist. However, disdainful or ignorant of the dangers he faced, Cagliostro spurned Morande's offers. Perhaps he did not feel the need? After all, before his arrival in London, Morande's newspaper coverage of Cagliostro, although ambiguous, had verged on the generous. On 26 July 1785, the *Courier de l'Europe*'s Paris column remarked that Cagliostro's magnificent retinue and scrupulous payment of his bills suggested that he really had found the philosopher's stone. It also praised him for curing rich and poor alike free of charge and for his amusing and instructive conversation. According to the paper it hardly mattered whether his wealth came from the alchemical arts or the gifts of admirers, as 'he does not appear to be among the most dangerous class of charlatans'.[23] Morande's coverage of judicial interrogations and the diamond necklace trial was equally measured. He gave Cagliostro's history as reported during the investigation – including some of the less plausible myths – and assured readers that under questioning he had refuted all the stories fabricated against him by the Countess de La Motte. The *Courier de l'Europe* had no doubt that he was innocent.[24] It covered his arrival in London in June 1786 in similar tone:

> Letters from Boulogne have told us of the departure of the Count de Cagliostro, who several days ago arrived in this capital, where he is perfectly known owing to the various sojourns he has spent here. It is said that this extraordinary man is going to practise his talents in London. It appears that large stages appeal to him, and that it is vast projects that have made him prefer a stay in England to any other.[25]

This report was not, however, as innocent as it seemed, for Cagliostro claimed to have visited England only once before. His 'vast projects' might be a master plan to assist humanity or a huge swindle, while the statement that he was 'perfectly known' contains an implicit threat of exposure.

Cagliostro asserts that Morande and Swinton were intent on blackmail. When he ignored Swinton's blandishments, Morande visited him in person at Swinton's home. According to Cagliostro's account:

> His face did not predispose me in his favour: I found his questions inappropriate, his tone indecent, and his menaces ridiculous; and I told him so candidly, declaring that I would not be much embarrassed by anything he wrote on my account.

Having nothing to hope for from me, Mr Morande began to attack me, but with honesty and moderation, with every appearance of impartiality.[26]

Despite his claims to the contrary, Morande's own account of their first conversation appears to support Cagliostro's assertions:

[Morande]: 'You will learn, *Monsieur le Comte*, from several of your compatriots who you visit that I have asked them who you were? They gave me lots of details on your two trips to England.'

[Cagliostro]: 'Me, Sir! I have only been in England once before!'

'Excuse me, Sir, you have been here twice, and the same people who saw you under the name Balthymore [Balsamo] have also known you as *Cagliostro*. Mr. P . . . and his wife had the honour of receiving you frequently at their table during your first trip. You broke off relations with them in your second, but they have seen you nonetheless during the last few months.'

'P . . . he is a . . . [Morande says he will refrain from repeating the count's insults].'

'No, Monsieur, you are mistaken, P . . . is an honest man: moreover, he is not the only one you have seen twice in London.'

'Had I been in England twenty times, would I have harmed anyone?'

'People have said so, *Monsieur le Comte*, but it is possible that they are mistaken. They have spoken of a legal case that . . . aroused lots of interest at the time. They cite the story of a necklace, for which you were arrested, and that you returned to the person who claimed it.'

'I don't much worry about what people say about me; THE COUNT DE CAGLIOSTRO is known throughout Europe.'

'If one believed everything that is being said, you are better known in London than anywhere else.'

'I will sue everyone who talks about me.'[27]

Minutes afterwards, Morande informed Cagliostro that he had been given papers relating to his trial in London in 1772. At that, Cagliostro fell silent and waited for him to leave. Yet despite Cagliostro's assertions that Morande was trying to blackmail him, the *Courier de l'Europe* did not mention Cagliostro between announcing his arrival on 23 June and 22 August 1786, when Morande, provoked, unleashed his full arsenal.

Morande was goaded into action by Cagliostro's mistakes. Cagliostro's first error was to become the political pawn of his lawyers, the radical and ambitious *parlementaires* Thilorier and Duval d'Eprésmésnil. They had offered to defend Cagliostro in order to strike a blow against royal power. They hoped to portray Cagliostro as a victim of royal tyranny as part of a campaign against *lettres de cachet*. As soon as he was released, they persuaded him to litigate for damages against his interrogator, Chénon, and the governor of the Bastille, Launay, whom he accused of pilfering his jewels, elixirs and secret recipes.[28] On 20 June 1786, the day Cagliostro arrived in London, they filed a civil case for him at the Châtelet in Paris and published a pamphlet outlining his allegations and attacking the queen's favourite, the Baron de Breteuil.[29] Aware that Cagliostro's allegations were mere bluster, Breteuil persuaded Louis XVI to call his bluff. A commission was appointed to investigate and, in due course, Cagliostro was invited to Paris to plead his case.[30]

Cagliostro's second and fatal mistake was to take as his advisor and auxiliary Lord George Gordon, the noble firebrand whose incendiary speeches as head of the Protestant Association had literally set London ablaze in 1780. Although his rhetoric incited a week-long orgy of anti-Catholic mob violence, arson and looting, Gordon was somehow acquitted of treason for his role in the Gordon riots. His subsequent antics and espousal of unpopular causes led many Britons to conclude that he was mad. In short, he was dangerous company.

Morande and Gordon were old sparring partners. Like most men of property, Morande had been alternately amused and horrified by Gordon's actions.[31] But as a Catholic Frenchman, he had a special interest in ensuring that this maverick British nobleman should never again stoke the dying embers of popular xenophobic religious fanaticism. Thus, when Gordon petitioned against the restoration of confiscated Scottish Jacobite lands, Morande suggested that his actions were inflammatory and seditious.[32] When he led hundreds of rowdy sailors on a recruiting tour around the drinking dens of London under a Dutch flag in peacetime and demanded that they be permitted to fight alongside their Dutch co-religionists against the Austrian Emperor, Joseph II, and 'papist agitators', Morande called for him to be stopped.[33] Several days later, he called for Gordon to be incarcerated as a madman or hanged for sedition.[34] Like many British journalists, Morande also assiduously chronicled and ridiculed Gordon's growing relationship with the Jewish community, seeking to discredit him with those Protestants who still considered him anything other than a 'dangerous maniac.'[35]

By late 1785, Gordon's behaviour was so eccentric that Morande began offering regular columns of 'Gordoniana'. Pride of place went to Morande's translation of an open letter from Gordon to Joseph II.[36] It demanded that Joseph reverse his policies towards the Jews and warned that Gordon had written to Jewish populations across Europe and to the Ottoman Sultan inciting them against the Emperor and Catholicism. Gordon even advised Joseph to find sanctuary in the Dutch embassy if, as was rumoured, he believed that 'Italian priests' in his entourage were trying to poison him. Morande published Gordon's epistle under the title 'The Heights of Madness', and recommended that Gordon be committed to Bedlam asylum, as 'There is only one man in the world who can use such language to sovereigns.'[37]

The public had no need of Morande's commentaries to turn Gordon into a laughing stock, but Gordon took offence anyway. In a letter to the *Public Advertiser*, he complained bitterly that:

> Mons. Demerand [sic], the proprietor, manager, and editor of the *Courier de l'Europe*, has made a false translation of Lord George Gordon's letter to the Emperor . . . and inserted it into his paper . . . What makes this forgery . . . the more abominable is, that he has added notes and comments of the most diabolical nature, not only to mislead . . . readers . . . but also to inflame the family of Gordon against his Lordship in the most cruel manner.[38]

Ominously, Gordon attributed Morande's comments to 'the maliciousness and falsehood with which the Papists continue to persecute Lord George Gordon'.[39] The self-appointed scourge of Catholicism was attempting to incite the mob against Morande.

Undeterred, Morande continued to ridicule 'the pious evangelist' Gordon, 'who has the charity to live with Jews and treat them as brothers' and sends 'homilies' to sovereigns while wishing 'to reduce to cinders all who pronounce on his way of thinking'. Far from being an 'opinionated papist', Morande insisted that he wished Gordon 'no harm' and called on him to be 'as tolerant to all baptized people as he appears to be towards those who are circumsized'.[40] Fortunately for Morande, Gordon's influence over the plebs had now waned to the point of impotence.

Morande's mockery continued throughout late 1785 and early 1786, as farce turned inexorably to tragedy.[41] Increasingly paranoid, Gordon accused the government of spying on him; demanded official protection following hoax death threats; and claimed the American minister-plenipotentiary was a French spy.[42] In May 1786, he was even excommunicated for refusing to submit to the authority of the ecclesiastical court of Doctors' Commons.[43] Several weeks later, he took up cudgels for a Protestant woman in Nova Scotia, who complained that the local Catholic priest had turned her husband and children against her. This was, Morande mocked, a 'serious complaint' and fully worthy of Gordon's attentions.[44]

On 20 August 1786, with Morande's taunts still fresh, Gordon was present when Cagliostro was summoned to the French embassy to receive permission to return to France to plead his case. Gordon feared that this was a trap and persuaded Cagliostro not to venture alone into the lion's den. The next day, Gordon, Cagliostro and the Grand Copt's disciple Frouville, called on the French *chargé d'affaires*, François Barthélemy. The meeting was a disaster. Barthélemy received them coldly. He had not expected a delegation and found Gordon, who was armed with a claymore, particularly unsettling. He read Cagliostro Breteuil's letter of permission but refused to hand it over, offended by Gordon's frantic, intimidating gestures. Infected by his friend's paranoia, Cagliostro was guarded and suspicious. He questioned whether Breteuil had the authority to rescind a royal *lettre de cachet* and demanded a safe conduct signed by Louis XVI. Barthélemy dutifully forwarded this request, but he also cut short the meeting.[45]

The next morning, Gordon published a distorted account of events in the *Public Advertiser*. It insinuated that Breteuil's invitation was a trap, asking:

> Will any friend to liberty blame Count de Cagliostro, after ten months imprisonment ... for having his friends near him, when insidious proposals are made to him by the faction of Breteuil and the supporters of the Bastille? Men who have already sought his destruction after his innocence was declared by the Parliament of Paris, embezzled a great part of his fortune and exiled him from France?

Morande's response was swift. The same evening he reported that, in the hands of Gordon, the 'grace' which Cagliostro had been offered had become 'the basis for very injurious imputations'. He concluded by claiming prophetically that Gordon was 'the only champion who will break lances for him in this country' and insinuating that exposure would destroy Cagliostro.[46] Morande was right on both counts. Alarmed by Cagliostro's flirtation with Gordon, and hints that they would be exposed in the *Courier de l'Europe*, British royalty, high society, and Cagliostro's most distinguished freemasonic allies abandoned him.[47] Likewise, Morande's revelations concerning his origins, history and activities would shatter Cagliostro's reputation and peace of mind.

Cagliostro and Gordon disdained Morande's menaces, believing him a mere Bourbon propagandist. Two days later, Gordon struck back, wildly asserting that:

> a gang of French spies, who are linked in with Mr De Morand [sic], and the Sieurs Barthelemy, Dazimar [d'Adhémar], Combise [de Cambis] and the queen's Bastille party at Paris, are using the most insidious arts to entrap the Count and Countess [de Cagliostro], and have the effrontery and audaciousness to persecute them publicly in this free country, where these noble strangers are come to seek protection in the arms of a generous people.

He added that Cagliostro was being victimized by 'a tyrannical government' because he had warned Rohan of the queen's machinations and the secrets of a scandal which, if revealed, 'would discover too much of the base arts practised to destroy Prince Louis [i.e. Rohan] and involve in guilt persons not safe to name in an arbitrary kingdom'.[48] By publishing these words Cagliostro and Gordon crossed a Rubicon. Once again Morande found himself denounced as a Bourbon agent. Once again he resolved to destroy his accusers. In this, his success was to be complete.

Gordon's rash allegations against Morande, d'Adhémar, Barthélemy and Marie-Antoinette contained all the ammunition his enemies needed. The British government already wished to prosecute Gordon for seditious libel for distributing inflammatory pamphlets to prisoners awaiting transportation to Botany Bay. They hesitated only because they had failed to convict him once before. When the French government complained of Gordon's libels against Marie-Antoinette and d'Adhémar, the British seized a gilt-edged opportunity and began criminal proceedings. The result exceeded all expectations. In June 1787, before a packed Court of King's Bench, Gordon scandalized all present by arguing that Marie-Antoinette was already 'vilified in all the streets of Paris' and 'as great a whore as the Empress of Russia [i.e. Catherine the Great]'. She therefore lacked a reputation to libel. It was a desperate and revolting defence. He was duly convicted and sentenced to two years' imprisonment for libelling Marie-Antoinette and d'Adhémar and three more for libelling the British government.[49] However, between his trial and his sentencing hearing, Gordon slipped out of the country and took refuge in the Netherlands. He was expelled following French diplomatic pressure and returned to Britain incognito. To the guffaws of Morande and the British press, he was finally apprehended in January 1788 in Birmingham, living as a Jew, having converted to Judaism.[50] He died in prison in January 1793.

Meanwhile, from 22 August 1786 through to the spring of 1787, Morande ran a tireless vendetta against Cagliostro in the *Courier de l'Europe*. By its end, Morande had established beyond doubt that Cagliostro was really a Neapolitan adventurer named Guiseppe or Joseph Balsamo; that he was first imprisoned in France long before 1785 and had been involved in deception and petty crimes; and that he had visited Britain three times. On the first occasion, in 1771 and 1772, he lived as a painter under his real name and fought an ill-fated legal battle against a certain Benamore, self-styled representative of the King of Morocco.[51] On the second, in 1777, he masqueraded as Captain and later Colonel Cagliostro of the Prussian army while seeking admission to the masonic lodge of *Espérance*, which, Morande pointed out, was the true cradle of Egyptian freemasonry.[52] On the same trip, he was gaoled for four months for stealing a diamond necklace from Marie Fry after she lent it to him believing he could make diamonds grow.[53]

Cagliostro was released after four months, having returned the necklace, but was subsequently arrested for debts to the lawyer who represented him against Benamore. The lawyer, having recognized him in the street, swore an affidavit declaring that Cagliostro and Balsamo were one and the same.[54] Morande published this affidavit and other evidence and indicated where to find further documents in the public archives.

The speed with which Morande responded to Gordon's initial article is significant. It suggests that he wrote on his own initiative to please the French court, just as d'Adhémar claimed.[55] This impression is fortified by his source material during September and early October 1786. Many of his allegations in these early broadsides against Cagliostro were recycled from earlier pamphlet literature.[56] The fresh revelations that he offered during these months concerned Cagliostro's visits to England and drew on stories he had uncovered while hunting for the diamond necklace with Ramond de Carbonnières. During his investigations, Morande heard whispers that the Count Cagliostro imprisoned in the Bastille was the same Colonel Cagliostro who had visited London eight years earlier. When Carbonnières returned to Paris, Morande asked him to verify these rumours. Carbonnières confirmed Morande's suspicions that the colonel and the count were one and the same, but appeared well disposed to Cagliostro.[57] This was indeed the case, for while in Rohan's service, Carbonnières had served as Cagliostro's laboratory assistant.[58] Thus when Morande unearthed the truth, Carbonnières rushed to protect his old friend and colleague. He told Morande that he had heard an alternative account of the count's activities and questioned Morande's evidence.[59] This put Morande off the trail for several months, but he quickly found new informants.

Spurred on by Morande's revelations, the Paris police searched their files for intelligence on Cagliostro and his wife, which they forwarded. Soon, informants from across Europe were also coming forward to supply information and as a result Launay asked Morande to collect sworn statements against Cagliostro.[60] These led to further revelations, which culminated in June 1787 when Morande published sworn testimony from Cagliostro's uncle in Palermo about his family origins, youth and career.[61]

Cagliostro's biographers insist that Morande was paid and supplied in advance with materials for his campaign by the French police. However, a letter from the Lieutenant of Police, Louis Thiroux de Crosne, reveals that in fact his own researches were inspired by the *Courier de l'Europe*'s revelations. Crosne's findings were only forwarded to Morande by the police *commissaire* Fontaine on 16 September, almost four weeks after Morande's first article.[62] Equally, in March 1787, when Morande petitioned through d'Adhémar for a gratuity to help cover his legal and other costs, he stated 'I don't pretend to ask for reimbursement as a matter of right, but I dare to solicit with confidence.' The response of the foreign minister to d'Adhémar's request dispels any suggestion that Morande was commissioned by the French court:

> I informed the King, Monsieur, of the request that you have made in favour of Sr Morande and although this individual never had any commission from you to meddle in the affair of Sr Cagliostro, His Majesty found it pleasing that you should remit him the 100 Louis that you proposed.

This was a generous sum but nevertheless insufficient to cover the £150 Morande claimed to have spent on affidavits, legal fees, supplements to the *Courier de l'Europe* and miscellaneous expenses.[63] Yet it would have been hard to ignore Morande's request, for his quarrel with Cagliostro had caused all Europe to erupt in laughter.

It was not so much Morande's revelations that provoked such merriment. Rather it was the manner in which Cagliostro sought to refute and silence them. Cagliostro was stirred into action by the *Courier de l'Europe* of 1 September 1786, which examined his autobiographical judicial memoirs page by page, identifying living witnesses who might confirm the veracity of his account and inviting them to come forward. This was dangerous territory for Cagliostro, especially as Morande accompanied his analysis with speculation and evidence that Cagliostro's 'earliest adventures' occurred in Italy rather than Trebizond, Medina, Egypt and Malta.

Seeking to head off such speculation, Cagliostro issued Morande with perhaps the strangest challenge ever recorded: duel by sucking pig! This was a highly appropriate challenge, because Morande had ridiculed Cagliostro's claims to have fattened swine with arsenic and used their carcasses to poison wild animals in the forests [sic] around Medina.[64] Thus the challenge was designed to imply that Cagliostro had faith in his own powers. It appeared in the *Public Advertiser* and read:

> I invite you to breakfast with me on 9th of November ... You shall furnish the wine and appendages ... I shall only furnish a single dish after my own fashion – it shall be a sucking pig, fattened after my method [i.e. with arsenic]. Two hours before breakfast I shall present you the pig alive, fat, and healthy. You shall order it to be killed as you please, and prepared, and I shall not approach it until it is served ... You shall cut it in four equal parts, you shall choose that which most flatters your appetite, and I shall take that which you please. The day after that of our breakfast, one or more of four things will happen. Either both of us shall die, or we shall neither of us die, or you shall die and I survive, or I shall die and you survive. Of these four chances I give you three, and I bet you 5,000 guineas, that ... you shall die and I be perfectly well. You must either accept this challenge, or acknowledge that you are an ignorant fellow, and that you have foolishly ridiculed a thing which is totally out of your knowledge.[65]

Cagliostro finished by promising to deposit 5,000 guineas with a banker as soon as Morande accepted the challenge. Morande would have five days grace to raise a similar sum.

Whether Cagliostro was by now so ravaged by syphilis that he believed his own propaganda or calculated that Morande would act the coward or fail to raise 5,000 guineas is matter for speculation. He had, however, misjudged his adversary. Morande instead published a response which was perfectly calculated to turn the tables on the counterfeit count:

> I accept of your bet – he wrote – on *some conditions* . . . I shall not put my foot in your house, and shall not breakfast with you myself. I am neither abject enough to keep your company, nor will let it be suspected a single moment . . . You will clearly conceive that such an interview ought not, nor can be, within your doors; you would be liable to be found guilty of criminal practices in case of accident . . . As no tavern would permit such infamous scenes under its roof . . . you must . . . chuse in London a public place to make an open exhibition of your talents. This is my first condition.
>
> 2. Being unwilling . . . to submit to that degradation of assimilating myself to a *Cagliostro*, you must chuse for your guest what carnivorous animal you think proper; I will back him against you; you shall breakfast with him . . .
>
> In the mean time, as it is natural to entertain some doubts about you, I will not give myself the trouble of going further, till Mess. [sic] B. and C. to whom you have proposed your diamond watch to borrow money upon it, (which they have disdainfully refused) acquaint me that they have five thousand guineas of *yours* in their hands.[66]

Furious that Morande sought to evade his challenge, Cagliostro resorted to taunts. In a chilling response, he declared that 'in the hands of a friend of mankind' even poison 'can tend to the happiness of the human species, by preserving useful beings or destroying mischievous ones'. Thus the 5,000-guinea prize meant nothing: his wager was designed to see 'society delivered from a periodical plague'. He could not, therefore, accept Morande's offer to use a beast as his champion and denounced the proposal as a cowardly refusal.[67] This reply, as Morande pointed out, failed to refute any of his allegations. Instead, Cagliostro's response was to offer to poison his accuser and boast that this would be a public service. In short, Cagliostro was 'THE MOST DANGEROUS IMPOSTOR OF THIS OR ANY OTHER AGE'. His partisans would do well to reflect on these things.[68]

The main targets for Morande's remarks were Cagliostro's freemasonic allies, particularly would-be acolytes of the Egyptian Rite. Morande, who may have been a mason himself, found multiple ways to discredit Cagliostro with his fellow initiates.[69] One was a comic depiction of Cagliostro's initiation ceremony among the artisans and servants who comprised the distinctly plebian *Espérance* lodge in the King's Head Tavern in Gerrard Street on 12 April 1777.[70] A long, detailed account of a fake séance and the trickery it involved was another.[71] Above all, Morande is said to have invented a story of a disastrous Cagliostroan séance, a tale so legendary that it finds echoes in Mozart's *Magic Flute* and the work of William Blake. The mishap supposedly happened when a group of Cagliostro's Swedenborgian disciples gathered in their lodge intent on raising the Seven Celestial Angels. Instead, they summoned only 'a fearful horde of wild orang-utangs whose grimaces, insults, and unworthy promiscuity the chaste idealists had to endure all evening'.[72]

But Morande's most humiliating story was a comic account of Cagliostro's first visit to the English Lodge of Antiquity with several other foreigners in early November 1786. Cagliostro hoped to seize control of the lodge, but instead had to endure a burlesque impersonation by one brother Mash, whose antics mocking Cagliostro's travels, cures and other claims reduced his fellow masons to gales of laughter.[73] This publicity had its desired effect: Cagliostro had called a grand meeting on the day Morande's article appeared, but his rallying-cry was ignored. Within days the caricaturist James Gillray was satirizing the scene in a print entitled 'Extract of the Arabian Count's Memoirs' which heaped ridicule on the count's claims and supposed origins. It was accompanied by verses which begin:

> Born God knows where, supported God Knows how,
> From whom descended difficult to know;

and end:

> But fate for Brother Mash reserv'd the task
> To strip the vile impostor of his mask.
> May all true Masons his plain tale attend!
> And Satire's laugh to fraud shall put an end.[74]

Indeed, 'Satire's laugh' now turned mercilessly on 'the Arabian Count'.[75]

Exposed as an impostor, reduced to a figure of fun, and stripped of the wealthy freemasonic friends and disciples whose credulity and generosity had sustained his flamboyant lifestyle and nourished his ego, Cagliostro no longer found Britain an asylum. Once he learned that Morande was organizing his creditors to pursue him and intended bringing over to England victims he had swindled abroad, he fled to Switzerland.[76] He left behind his long-suffering wife, Seraphina, with instructions to sell their furniture before following him, but escaped with her jewels. Learning of his flight, Morande called on Seraphina and, to her surprise, offered sympathy and support. He even published an appeal for Cagliostro's former supporters to come to her aid. She was, Morande wrote, a timid and trembling victim who had married below the age of discernment and thus could not be held responsible for crimes her husband had forced her to commit.[77] Seduced by Morande's charm and insinuating manner, Seraphina opened her heart, confirming many of the journalist's suspicions, exposing Cagliostro's tricks and her own sufferings. Nevertheless, she eventually rejoined her husband in Switzerland, whence Morande continued to receive and publish reports of their activities.[78]

Before long, however, Cagliostro quarrelled with his Swiss hosts and, at his wife's promptings, returned to Italy. There, they were arrested by the Inquisition.

Hoping to save her neck, Seraphina agreed to testify against her husband. However, her tawdry revelations of how Cagliostro deceived his victims and prostituted her around Europe only incriminated her further. Following her husband's trial she was confined to a convent for life. As for Cagliostro, he ended his days in a Papal gaol in 1795, his magical powers no match for barred windows, thick walls and heavily bolted doors.[79]

While Morande was embroiled with Cagliostro, the Count de La Motte turned his hand to blackmail. In late 1786, he threatened to publish a pamphlet revealing 'the truth' behind the diamond necklace affair and its aftermath and hinted that Marie-Antoinette had plotted to ruin the cardinal.[80] At the same time, the French government began to hear whispers that La Motte possessed a compromising correspondence between the queen and Breteuil.[81]

Unfortunately for La Motte, the French government had taken to heart Morande's advice to disdain blackmailers. Vergennes and Montmorin therefore ignored La Motte and refused to deal with his associates. The French ambassador, d'Adhémar, went further still and recommended lifting the police surveillance on them, arguing that it made them feel important.[82] As a result, when La Motte finally published, in February 1787, he made little splash. D'Adhémar doubted anyone would read his absurd and disgusting publication. He believed that Marie-Antoinette – a personal friend – would be indignant at the very suggestion that it might upset her.[83] He may not have been entirely correct.

Several months later, in August 1787, the Countess de La Motte staged a spectacular escape from the Saltpetrière prison, apparently with inside help from powerful collaborators. The countess herself claims she had mysterious assistance and assumed that the queen was behind it, thus fuelling popular suspicions that Marie-Antoinette was somehow implicated in the diamond necklace fraud. A usually well-informed source adds that La Motte's escape was the fruit of a secret negotiation at Bath involving the Count de La Motte and the queen's favourites the Duchess de Polignac and Count de Vaudreuil. In return for the purported letters between Marie-Antoinette and Breteuil, the count had been promised a substantial sum of money and his wife's liberty.[84]

If the queen or her allies were behind the countess' escape, they had seriously miscalculated: no sooner had she rejoined her husband in London than she resumed her scheming. She claims she held abortive negotiations with Breteuil shortly after arriving in London, where she lodged with Morande's old associate Joseph Parkyns MacMahon.[85] Then, on 20 December 1787, the British newspapers announced her intention of publishing her memoirs, including an explosive amorous correspondence between Marie-Antoinette and Cardinal Rohan.[86] This revelation had a double purpose. It would raise public expectations to fever pitch and increase pressure on the queen to pay the countess off.

The La Mottes probably realized by now that the queen had little intention

Plate 10. Madame de La Motte. Contemporary illustration from the Countess de La Motte's *Vie de Jeanne de Saint-Rémy de Valois de La Motte* (London: John Bew, 1791). Courtesy of the British Library.

of caving in to blackmail. Instead, they had a new target: the recently disgraced French finance minister Calonne, who was in London in voluntary exile. Calonne had fallen from power after failing to persuade a specially convened Assembly of Notables of the gravity of France's financial crisis and consequent need to overhaul the entire tax system, including the fiscal exemptions of the clergy and nobility. He believed that Marie-Antoinette had played a major role in the aristocratic coup that had ousted him and saw the suppression of the countess' memoirs as an opportunity to return to royal favour. By succeeding where Breteuil had failed, he would prepare the way for his recall. It was a hope born of desperation. The La Mottes had found a willing dupe.

The La Mottes and their henchman Serres de La Tour hooked Calonne in a simple sting operation. Within hours of the publication of the countess' advertisements, La Tour called on Calonne, ostensibly to invite him to subscribe to his new periodical, *L'Azile*. Soon, their conversation turned to the La Mottes' libel. When La Tour offered to discover the nature of the correspondence in the La Mottes' hands, Calonne engaged him as his agent and loaned him £120. Within days, La Tour sent Calonne written statements from the La Mottes explaining their terms and Calonne, in turn, offered to guarantee any settlement through his bankers.[87] On 31 December 1787, Calonne sent a parcel of documents to Versailles, only to receive a firm rebuke from Louis and Marie-Antoinette, who declared 'their Majesties both believe that one should ignore all such writings'.[88]

Undeterred, Calonne decided to pay off the blackmailers himself, using the fortune of his mistress, Madame de Harvelay, to whom he was now betrothed. Her annual revenues were worth some 230,000 *livres* (almost £10,000), so an outlay of 10–12,000 *livres* per annum to pension off the La Mottes if they would retire to the United States was eminently affordable. It also appeared a good speculative investment, mere chicken feed compared to what he might earn if restored to royal favour. Thus, in May 1788, he offered to suppress the countess' memoirs.[89] The following month, on his return from honeymoon in Bath, he sent the queen the fragmentary notes that La Motte's ghost writer, MacMahon, had prepared for her autobiography.[90] In July, Marie-Antoinette replied that she held the La Mottes in complete contempt and ordered Calonne to desist in his efforts.[91]

Meanwhile, La Motte turned to Serres de La Tour to finish ghost-writing her memoirs, as MacMahon had died in January 1788. When he completed them, La Tour immediately arranged a clandestine meeting with Calonne to show him the manuscript. Amazingly, Calonne was foolish enough to use this meeting to correct La Tour's style and remove passages 'too gross and obscene' to set before a queen.[92] This was his worst error of judgement yet. It allowed La Tour and the La Mottes to allege that he had both commissioned the manuscript and spiced it up to wreak revenge upon the queen.

Calonne did much to add to the credibility of such allegations. Despite the queen's second refusal, he continued to lend La Tour money, calculating that he might yet be useful or malleable. This only fed La Tour's cupidity. Eventually, in a heated interview, Calonne refused La Tour's demands. La Tour retaliated by launching a malicious lawsuit in the Court of Chancery on 5 December 1788, claiming that Calonne had promised him large sums for his services and that his loans were a salary.[93] To pressure Calonne into settling, he and the La Mottes also launched a very public pamphlet smear campaign.[94]

Morande watched these developments with interest, seeking to turn them to his profit. The French government had ordered its diplomats to keep Calonne under surveillance, and Morande was ideally placed to help them.[95] Calonne and his brother and agent, the abbé, were close friends and political allies of Beaumarchais. Indeed, when they arrived in London in August 1787, the abbé was carrying instructions from Beaumarchais for Morande to show him around Beaumarchais' Sloane Street house and try to sell it to him.[96] By early September, Morande was claiming to be the best of friends with the abbé.[97] Moreover, during his first days living incognito in the English capital, Calonne eagerly sought Morande's advice and services. Morande supplied useful contacts and helped to secure introductions to British grandees who could arrange his presentation to George III. He even advised Calonne where to live. Calonne had been told that he would be safest living within the City of London's jurisdiction. Morande insisted that the City was no safer than elsewhere but that if Calonne chose to live there, people would conclude harshly that he had reason to be fearful.[98]

The *bonhomie* between Morande and Calonne was short-lived. During the autumn of 1787, when Calonne published an apology for his administration, the *Requête au Roi* [*Plea to the King*], Morande kept a judicious silence.[99] He knew that the *Requête* would pit Calonne against his great ministerial rival, the Swiss banker Jacques Necker, who during the American Revolutionary War had financed victory without increasing taxation. Necker had trumpeted his achievement in his best-selling *Compte rendu des finances* [*Financial Accounts*] (1781), which claimed that the war had been financed from normal revenues. Thus, when Calonne announced in August 1786 that the monarchy was effectively bankrupt, his claim was met with widespread scepticism, powerfully reinforced by wishful thinking. This made it difficult for Calonne to gather support for his subsequent financial reform package. Vitriolic political debates about responsibility for the financial crisis would poison French politics until the revolution.

Morande's silence irked Calonne.[100] He had hoped the *Requête* would win over public opinion, creating a demand for his recall, and considered Morande's actions partisan. In fact, Morande quite admired Calonne's pamphlet, at least on first reading, and recommended it to Beaumarchais. However, over time he became a convinced Neckerite.[101] Of course, Morande's choice of party was also prudent. He quickly realized the foolishness of Calonne's flirtation with the La Mottes, especially as he had placed spies in Calonne's household and favourite haunts.[102] It is also possible that Morande resented Calonne's austerity drive, which had halved his own stipend.[103] But as the campaign he unleashed against Calonne in 1788 angered his patrons Beaumarchais, Sainte-Foy and Montmorin, his rejection of Calonne's ideas was probably sincere.[104] However, he may also have had Neckerite patrons.

Morande prepared his ground in advance. In November 1787, he informed Montmorin that Calonne was sounding off about the financial policy of his successor, Archbishop Loménie de Brienne. According to Morande, Calonne had declared in the home of an English Lord and before several witnesses that:

'The Archbishop's loan will not be fully subscribed. There is neither money nor credit nor confidence in the plans of the ministry. The business of government will only be conducted by forced means, and I will be greatly avenged.'[105] Following such indiscretions, the British political elite was conversing openly and accurately on French financial affairs.

The next summer, Morande set out to engineer a quarrel between Calonne and the *parlementaire* lawyer Marc-Ferdinand Grouber de Groubentall de Linières.[106] Groubentall accused Calonne of stealing his ideas, preventing their publication and appropriating them for his own works. This alleged plagiarism became the subject of a correspondence in the *Courier de l'Europe* which Morande orchestrated to inflict maximum damage on Calonne's reputation.[107]

Morande continued to torment Calonne over the next few weeks. In September, he reported rumours that Calonne intended to make a large wager on a horse-race between London and Windsor. Morande said that he doubted this was true, because Calonne was so parsimonious that he only paid the poor priest who said mass for him on Sundays and holy days a miserly '*petit écu* and lunch'.[108] When Calonne's partisans accused Morande of trying to provoke domestic discord, he retorted that the racing story was copied from the *World* and it was only by chance that he learned about the priest the same day.[109]

Morande's hounding of Calonne was not merely satirical, for the *Courier de l'Europe* made damning comparisons between Calonne and Necker. According to Morande, Necker's latest response to Calonne, although printed in large numbers, had sold out in a single morning and totally destroyed the favourable impression created by Calonne's *Requête*. While Necker's pamphlet was full of 'loyalty, frankness, truth', Calonne's was characterized by 'flippancy, lack of candour, equivocation'. As a result, Parisian opinion was unanimously behind Necker. Those formerly seduced by Calonne now admitted that it is better to have 'a *sad* economist' at the helm of state finances than a 'trop gai' ['frivolous'] administrator who left an immense deficit.[110] Such comments apparently eroded Calonne's standing, for Morande claims that Chalmers and Evan Nepean informed him that he was no longer esteemed by the British government.[111] However, alarmed to see the dispute escalate, Montmorin now banned Morande from attacking Calonne. Unfortunately, Calonne, informed of these orders, was foolish enough to announce the prohibition in the British press. This gave Morande a pretext to ignore Montmorin's orders and continue his attacks.[112]

Calonne decided to fight fire with fire. By late September, Morande was complaining that Calonne was bribing *The Times* and Serres de La Tour's *Azile* to insult him and in December he claimed that Calonne had five newspapers in his pay.[113] He was also worried that Calonne would suborn Swinton, who had bought the *Courier de l'Europe* back from Sainte-Foy on 1 January 1788.[114]

Throughout the spring of 1789, Morande could sense his hold over the

Courier de l'Europe slipping away. Calonne was stepping up efforts to win over Swinton and had mobilized Beaumarchais, who, in March 1789, warned Eliza that Morande was bringing his paper into disrepute. Beaumarchais also wrote to Swinton, asking him to silence Morande's attacks.[115] In desperation, Morande tried to persuade Montmorin to fund him to establish a rival paper, but to no avail.[116] Finally, in late March, Morande reported that Henry Dundas, Treasurer of the Navy, had intervened with Swinton and the paper was under Calonne's control. Calonne's cash and the British government had stripped Morande of editorial control.[117]

According to Morande, Calonne was out-spending the British government on controlling the press.[118] This was truer than Morande realized, for on 17 April 1789 Calonne splashed out 2,000 guineas (£2,100) to buy a 50 per cent stake in the *Courier de l'Europe*. The purchase was made through a frontman, John Irving. The contract of sale gave Irving the right to nominate the chief editor and to place any materials he thought fit in the paper. The price was steep and seems to factor in a continued revival in French subscriptions. It therefore seems that Calonne saw the purchase as more than a means to silence Morande.[119] He also hoped to use the paper to influence opinion during elections to the Estates-General, France's ancient representative body, which had been summoned to meet in May 1789 to resolve the financial crisis.

Strangely, the final blow never fell. Although Morande complained of being sold to Calonne and grumbled that Swinton heaped up humiliations upon him and interfered continually in the editorial process, he was not dismissed. Nor did Morande resign, even when Swinton appointed a sub-editor to work in Morande's own home, thereby endangering his espionage work. Instead, Morande pleaded with Beaumarchais and Sainte-Foy to lean on Swinton to secure his position.[120] This seems to have had the desired effect. There is no documentary explanation for his continued tenure, but it is probable that Swinton was coerced. Sainte-Foy had power over Swinton because he still owed him money for the *Courier de l'Europe*, while Beaumarchais was still employing Swinton as his financial agent.[121] Presumably all three persuaded Calonne that Morande was essential to the paper's continued financial success. Morande apparently never suspected the full extent of Calonne's influence over the *Courier de l'Europe*. After April, he continued to complain about Swinton's venality but Calonne's name largely disappears from his correspondence.[122]

Morande's angriest complaints about Swinton's meddling concern his reporting of attempts to abolish the slave trade. This was one of the most explosive and controversial issues of the day, particularly in Britain, where Pitt's government was initially sympathetic to the abolitionist cause and counted evangelical Christian abolitionist MPs such as William Wilberforce among its strongest supporters. Morande's position was somewhat different. His paper denounced the brutal treatment of blacks by French planters and supported calls for the gradual amelioration of conditions in the slave trade. But it also argued that sudden and total abolition would wreck Europe's colonies.[123] Instead, Morande suggested that Britain and France should adopt a Spanish scheme that permitted slaves to buy their liberty progressively using money earned on their weekly day off. When they had earned enough, they could buy a second day of liberty per week and then a third and so on, until completely free.[124] This mix of pragmatism and horror was apparently genuine. The most graphic and disturbing paragraph Morande ever published recounts with revulsion the tale of a slave ship captain who was informed that he could not buy a comely slave without the babe at her breast. He therefore purchased both, dashed the child's brains out before the mother's eyes, then, within the hour, summoned her to his cabin to suffer his 'atrocious caresses'.[125]

Morande's opposition to outright abolition was reinforced in 1788, when his old enemy, Brissot, established a French abolitionist society, the Friends of the Blacks, with the encouragement of British abolitionists.[126] Thus, in June 1789, he was incandescent with rage when Swinton accepted 25 guineas from the slave trade abolitionists and forbade him from writing on the issue. Instead Swinton began to print abolitionist propaganda, particularly a celebrated cross-sectional diagram of a slave ship, which shows slaves lying in chains and cramped together side by side on boards below deck.[127]

This was carefully timed propaganda. In the spring of 1789 the strongest obstacle to an abolitionist triumph in Parliament was the fear that if Britain's merchant fleet withdrew from the slave trade, her portion of the trade would fall into the hands of her rivals. As her rivals expanded their merchant navies and consequently the supply of skilled seamen available for wartime service, Britain's merchant marine and pool of naval manpower would decline. The British abolitionists and their supporters in government therefore needed Britain's rivals, particularly France, to take reciprocal measures. At a Royal Session of the Estates-General on 23 June 1789 their wish was granted: the French government announced unexpectedly that it would ameliorate conditions in the slave trade. As the Friends of the Blacks had little support in France, it seems that the French government was offering an olive branch to the British. If the British would not intervene in France's internal affairs, the French would assist the British government over abolition. Ironically, Morande's newspaper and spy reports may have contributed to this development by highlighting the embarrassment of the British government.

While Morande struggled against Calonne, Swinton and the abolitionists, he was also scheming to thwart the La Mottes. In January 1789, as the countess was readying her *Memoirs* for publication, his agents called repeatedly at her house asking for copies. When none were forthcoming, he concluded that she was still counting on a suppression fee. Meanwhile, he pushed one of the La Mottes' creditors to have the count arrested and seize their assets, apparently without success. Leaving no stone unturned, he also petitioned Montmorin to let him discuss the *Memoirs* in the *Courier de l'Europe* to destroy any impressions they might make. The foreign minister remained unmoved.[128]

The countess' *Memoirs* finally appeared in February 1789. Contrary to received opinion, they were the first sexually scandalous pamphlet attack on Marie-Antoinette to appear in print, and so commanded a curious and credulous audience on both sides of the Channel.[129] A tissue of lies from start to finish, they offer a mendacious history of the diamond necklace affair in which a scheming, vindictive, duplicitous and libertine Marie-Antoinette is the chief villain. La Motte's fairy tale had no happy ending. It told how the countess had been sexually seduced by Marie-Antoinette, who used her as a pawn and go-between in her relationship with Cardinal Rohan. Step by carefully crafted step, the queen seduces Rohan, too, and together they act out her dominatrix fantasies in games of 'master and servant'. Finally, she persuades Rohan to buy her the diamond necklace on credit. This operation requires the utmost secrecy because Louis XVI has forbidden her to purchase it, saying he would rather spend the money on a battleship.

The most sinister aspect of La Motte's tale is not the queen's cupidity, dishonesty or treasonous sexual indulgence. It is her motive. Marie-Antoinette hates the cardinal. She craves sex with him only to satisfy her insatiable libido, acquire the necklace, and control him. She also hopes to advance Rohan into the Ministry, so that he might serve as an agent of her brother, the Austrian Emperor. But once he has outlived his usefulness, she intends to destroy him. This is precisely what happened when the necklace fraud was discovered. Marie-Antoinette's involvement went undetected because she had skilfully arranged for the countess to forge her signature on the contract of sale. To secure her safety, she has the countess arrested and threatened with death should she reveal the truth. Unfortunately, all the queen's calculations are undone when the countess escapes from prison and publishes her *Memoirs*, which include 32 love-letters chronicling Marie-Antoinette's liaison with the cardinal.[130]

Unfortunately for the monarchy, the countess' *Memoirs* were published in the midst of the pre-revolutionary political crisis. Many contemporaries were wise enough to see through her fabrications. However, others were credulous enough to believe them, especially once other, hitherto suppressed pamphlets describing the queen's alleged amorous exploits and duplicity emerged in July 1789 from a secret *dépôt* in the Bastille.[131] Morande found demand for the *Memoirs* unbelievable. In his expert opinion the La Mottes were inept calumniators, yet according to his reports even French travellers and persons of quality thought that La Motte's fabricated love-letters contained nothing to prove them false.[132]

His alarm was shared by Edmund Burke, who was convinced that the *Memoirs* had greatly harmed the queen's reputation, and who probably had them in mind as he penned his celebrated passage on Marie-Antoinette in his *Reflections on the Revolution in France*.[133]

Morande continued to plot against the La Mottes until he left Britain in 1791. While his courier, Menneville, cajoled and threatened sea captains and bribed dock workers to prevent the embarkation of the countess' *Memoirs*, Morande dreamt up plans to have the La Mottes transported.[134] In 1790, when the countess set about producing revised French and English language versions of her auto-biography, one of his agents infiltrated her camp to cause delays and problems. Or so the countess concluded on discovering that her translator was related to one of his employees.[135] By this time, however, she was growing increasingly paranoid. Abandoned by her husband, who returned to Paris in April 1789, and tortured by rumours of his infidelities, she began to see enemies everywhere. In June 1791, she mistook bailiffs for Royalist agents and jumped from a window to escape. She crashed into a tree, suffered terrible injuries, and died of a haemor-rhage several weeks later.[136]

Even now, Morande had not had his last word on the La Mottes. For on 4 January 1792 the count presented himself at the Conciergerie prison voluntar-ily, in order that he could apply for his sentence to be revoked and regain his confiscated goods. Various revolutionary factions had been pressing him to do this since 1789, calculating that once the sentence was overturned, Rohan, and hence the queen, would appear culpable. Then, so their logic ran, Louis would have no alternative but to renounce his wife. The temptation to overturn the sentence would be all the greater, Morande warned, now that the woman who stole the necklace was dead and Rohan, the victim of the crime, was a leader of the émigré rebels who opposed the revolution. 'However', he added:

> the death of one & the crime of the other does not mean that Monsieur La Motte did not himself sell the stolen necklace to Mr. Gray of London and that he did not consume the product with the deceased.[137]

Thus ended Morande's pursuit of the necklace. Six months later, on 20 July 1792, the verdict against the count and countess was quashed, not on the grounds of evidence, but a technical irregularity.[138]

None of this prevented the posthumous publication of La Motte's *Life of Jane de Saint-Rémy de Valois, heretofore Countess de La Motte*. Her publisher, John Bew, and friend, the perfumier Richard Warren, had invested heavily in the countess' new book and wanted a return on their money. They therefore published the British edition and approached Marie-Antoinette, offering to sell her the entire French edition. She refused their blackmail, but in May 1792 her beleaguered husband was not so resilient. Louis XVI suppressed the work, fearing for his wife's safety, particularly as France was by then at war with Austria. He ordered the books burned in a kiln at the Sevrès porcelain works, but unfortunately the revolutionary Legislative Assembly learned of the *auto da fé* and ordered an investigation.[139] The book-burning – which by a curious coincidence was reported in Morande's last ever newspaper edition – thus succeeded only in 'creating suspicions of a greater secret'.[140] Eleven weeks later, on 10 August 1792, the monarchy was overthrown.

With the monarchy sidelined, the sexual slander pioneered by Morande's *Gazetier cuirassé* and turned against the queen by his successors bore its poisoned fruit. In September 1792, angry mobs burst into the city's prisons and butchered royalist sympathizers. There they found the queen's favourite, the Princess de Lamballe, who, according to the pamphleteers, had been the queen's lover and chief associate in her wild sexual orgies. She was thus singled out for special treatment. According to some reports she was gang-raped before being decapitated. Then her head was taken to the Temple prison 'so that the queen might kiss it one last time', while some accounts say that her sexual organs and breasts were hacked out and paraded around the city on pikes.[141] Shortly thereafter, the revolutionary government published a new edition of La Motte's *Life*, based on a copy that had escaped the flames. It contained a preface explaining that 'the lengths to which the court has gone to prevent publication of this work clearly prove how greatly the monarchy feared its publication' and that the 'facts' it contained would become public knowledge.[142] The revolutionaries clearly believed their own propaganda, because at Marie-Antoinette's trial, in October 1793, they repeatedly described the queen as a new Messalina or Agrippina. They even charged her with having an incestuous relationship with her son. Although she refuted this allegation with virtuous indignation, provoking supportive murmurs among the women present when she asked whether any mother could behave thus, it made no difference to the outcome.[143] She was condemned and executed as an enemy of the people and an unnatural woman. A process begun by Morande's sexually slanderous satires against Madame du Barry had ended in the grotesque, murderous carnival of revolution.

8

The First Revolutionary Journalist

Morande never intended nor approved the violence meted out to Lamballe and Marie-Antoinette.[1] Nor did he support the republican drift of the revolution. He was first and foremost a creature of the old regime. His consistent political goal, from the *Gazetier cuirassé* in 1771 until the end of his journalistic career in 1792, was the establishment of a liberal constitutional monarchy. Although this was by 1792 a rather conservative position, Morande nevertheless deserves to be considered one of the founding fathers of revolutionary journalism. This, ironically, is a distinction he shares with his enemies, Linguet, Mirabeau, and Brissot. In effect, Morande fused British editorial practices with the impassioned, socially radical, sometimes paranoid, campaigning essay-style of Linguet's *Annales*. This style was then appropriated by Brissot's influential *Patriote françois* and adopted by dozens of the revolutionary newspapers that appeared in its wake. Thus Morande's *Courier de l'Europe* forms an evolutionary link between the popular pre-revolutionary periodical journalism of Linguet and the revolutionary newspaper press, which did so much to 'script the revolution'.[2]

On 20 January 1784, when Morande took over the editorship of the *Courier de l'Europe*, the paper's fortunes were at low ebb, and for a simple reason. Between 1776 and 1783, while the American Revolutionary War was the great European news story, the *Courier de l'Europe*, offering fresher coverage of both Britain and America than rival international gazettes, was uniquely attractive. Once the war ended, francophone readers across Europe had much less reason to buy the paper and subscriptions collapsed from 6–7,000 to under 1,200.[3]

Within three months, Morande had arrested this decline and slowly begun to rebuild the paper's subscriber base, much to Swinton's delight. By April 1787, there were over 1,500 subscribers, of whom 1,300 were in France, and their number continued to rise as the revolution approached.[4] These figures, though small, were significant. They account for around one tenth of international gazettes sold in France and one in 30 of all French newspaper subscriptions. Even at the height of the war, in 1781, there were only 45,000 newspaper subscribers in the entire country. According to contemporary estimates of ten readers per copy, this implies a readership of 450,000 in a population of around 28,000,000. However, Morande's paper, like other international gazettes, provided high quality political information to an elite readership, so had a potential influence greater than raw numbers suggest. He was read by politicians, policy-makers and aristocrats, the people who mattered in the small, enclosed world of old regime politics.

Traditionally, international gazettes followed certain conventions. They tended to be printed twice weekly in tightly cramped eight-page octavo instalments scarcely bigger than a book. They reported little but high politics. News from faraway lands was reported first, and 'local' political news, if not omitted due to censorship, was saved until last. Reports were structured in paragraphs, supplied without editorial comment, under a putative place of origin and dateline, and conflicting news might be reported from several places. In the absence of headlines or contextual information, readers had to make sense of stories for themselves. The gazetteer's role was to compile rather than to interpret the news.

In large part, this approach was pragmatic. The absolute rulers of Europe had little desire to open their actions to scrutiny and possible censure. Yet increasingly they found that they needed the international gazettes to represent their actions and publish their manifestos, in order to influence the cosmopolitan financial and political elites who sustained their authority, invested in government stock, and helped shape the policies of foreign courts. Thus, while they attempted to control negative reporting using interdictions, censorship and diplomatic pressure, they also needed journalists to appear to endorse their policies freely. The result was a perpetual game of cat-and-mouse between European monarchs and the gazetteers, who needed the permission of foreign rulers to sell their products, but had to appear independent in order to attract readers. From these tensions, international journalists gradually carved themselves a narrow and precarious freedom. From the 1760s, the boldest of the international gazettes, notably the *Gazette de Leyde* and its arch-rival, the *Courier du Bas-Rhin*, began to inject clearly demarcated paragraphs of editorial comment into news stories. A decade later, the *Courier de l'Europe* proved much more adventurous.[5]

Under its first editor, Serres de La Tour, the *Courier de l'Europe* adopted an innovative eight-page quarto format, carrying more extensive and varied copy and advertising than its continental counterparts in less constricted columns. As a result, it looked more like an eighteenth-century English newspaper than a traditional gazette, offering a miscellaneous assortment of book and theatre reviews, poetry, financial news and essays as well as political reports and views. Morande continued this policy. On 6 February 1784, he advised readers that with peace restored, his paper would offer less military and diplomatic news and concentrate instead on giving foreigners an idea of English manners, customs, arts, sciences, finances, maritime discoveries, public institutions and domestic politics. Nevertheless, the paper still lacked designated editorial space. This was to be Morande's next initiative.

Morande's first editorial innovation, his regular *Bulletin de Londres* column, introduced on 21 May 1784, was clearly modelled on the British press. It offered a miscellaneous mix of stories and editorial opinion, just as in the London newspapers. In any given issue it might report briefly on parliamentary affairs, comment on international developments, review the latest theatrical productions, and offer human interest or true crime stories. Although it bore little resemblance to a modern editorial column, the *Bulletin de Londres* was nevertheless an evolution in that direction. Uniquely among the international gazettes, the *Courier de l'Europe* now had a regular designated space for editorial material.

The chief obstacle to further editorial innovation was the French censorship regime and, in particular, the *Courier de l'Europe*'s notorious censor, the Abbé Aubert, who ordered that the paper be reprinted on 17 occasions in a single year.[6] Morande's letters to Beaumarchais contain numerous complaints about this 'acolyte of Satan',[7] but his attempts to escape Aubert's yoke proved fruitless until late 1787, when the French censorship apparatus broke down. Fortunately, from December 1786, Aubert 'fell asleep on the scaffold', allowing Morande to spread 'the sacred principles of a constitutional liberty' in a series of essays and letters signed 'un voyageur'.[8] Writing in 1791, Morande recollected that:

> He [Aubert] let pass, among other articles, denunciations of the venality of offices and of the nobility, *which paralysed so many useful citizens.* I profited from his lethargy to attack the notorious solicitations of judges, while the *parlements* were still in full possession of their powers. I proved, before the convocation of the Estates-General, the advantages of a Constitution to assure the strength of the government and the happiness of the governed. I can and dare say, *because it is the truth,* that a great number of abuses which have been reformed by the [revolutionary] National Assembly, had been denounced in these letters, before the reform in question was made.[9]

These claims were essentially true. Moreover, in his *Lettres d'un voyageur*, Morande developed a radical new style of newspaper essay journalism, comprising partisan editorial articles on French policy matters.

The earliest *Lettres d'un voyageur* address British commerce and trade, seeking lessons for France. Morande attributes Britain's economic success to the British workman's pride in his products; the ubiquity and quality of machinery in British factories; the role of financial institutions, insurance companies, and public credit; and the respect and harmony that unite men of wealth, regardless of the origins of their fortune. He therefore proposes a radical reorganization of French society and culture along British-style commercial lines. This involves a full-frontal assault on the laws and social customs which underpinned noble exclusiveness, notably the law of *dérogeance,* which stripped nobles who engaged in trade of their status and privileges, but also the aspiration of successful merchants and manufacturers to abandon their professions and purchase ennobling offices. Likewise, he attacks the French system of granting royal *privilèges* [monopolies], which he sees as arbitrary. He prefers the British system of legal patents, which creates a far better incentive to innovation, being independent of political favour, transparent and uniform in its application.[10]

Morande was an early and enthusiastic proponent of an Anglo-French commercial agreement.[11] However, he disliked the way the Eden free trade treaty of 1786 was implemented. A second series of *Lettres d'un voyageur*, published between 4 December 1787 and 18 January 1788, reports systematic attempts by the British to evade or manipulate the treaty and exposes the predatory practices and corruption of customs officers. According to Morande, obscure, incomprehensible and ancient laws, with which compliance was virtually impossible, were being dusted off to persecute French merchants, and applied by officials who had a personal interest in the goods that they confiscated. Morande repeated and extended these allegations four years later, when he republished several of these articles and asked merchants with complaints to come forward so that he could list their grievances in an address to the British people.[12] These patriotic crusades attracted attention on both sides of the Channel. In Britain, Morande claims he was threatened with legal action, which he quashed by tendering proof of his allegations. In France, in both 1792 and 1797, revolutionary governments consulted his writings as they contemplated a new commercial treaty with Britain. In 1797 it is possible that he was even consulted in person.[13]

Once freed from the shackles of Aubert's censorship, Morande's *Voyageur* columns began to address French high politics. The first such article, a summary of the political state of France, was published on 1 January 1788. It denounced the *parlements'* opposition to royal reforms and, in particular, to the establishment of provincial assemblies, which they feared would undermine their own moral authority. No longer able to applaud them as bulwarks against despotism, Morande now saw the *parlements* as obstacles to reform. He wished for genuine and regular representation through the provincial assemblies and the Estates-General. Morande accused the *parlements* of risking anarchy in the reckless pursuit of self-interest. Their actions sapped the authority of the king, which guaranteed 'the strength and the grandeur of the kingdom'.[14]

This essay raised many of the themes that characterize Morande's journalism during the prerevolutionary crisis of 1787–1789. He would continue to champion a strong royal executive and oppose the *parlements'* political pretensions, condemning their opposition as dangerous, disloyal and culpable.[15] In Morande's eyes, the *parlementaires* were merely the upper rung of an invidious judicial system and bloated, parasitic legal profession comprising '3,000 judges' and '300,000 men of law'.[16] From 1788, he campaigned for a reduction of France's legal establishment and the dismantling of her litigious culture, noting that through judicious use of juries and quarterly assizes, England needed only 12 judges for the whole country.[17] He also applauded the abolition of judicial

torture, although surprisingly he argued in favour of *lettres de cachet* as a means
of maintaining family honour, patriarchal authority and, on rare but necessary
occasions, state security. It was only their despotic abuse by ministers that he
found abhorrent.[18]

What Morande was attempting in his *Lettres d'un voyageur* was innovative
and original. Admittedly, some gazette editors had produced annual opinion
pieces on the political state of Europe,[19] but editorial essays concerning domestic
policy were a novelty. Nothing like them had been seen in the French-language
newspaper press before. However, once the French domestic press slipped the
censor's leash in mid 1789 and began their massive revolutionary proliferation,
they were rapidly imitated, first and foremost by Brissot's path-breaking *Patriote
françois*. Nor did the English newspaper press have anything equivalent: its leader
columns only evolved slowly across the next few decades. Thus, by the end of
1788, Morande's *Courier de l'Europe* had emerged as a leader in the provision of
editorial comment and the interpretation of politics.

Morande knew that many of his observations might irritate his paymasters
in Paris. This is nowhere more apparent than in a justificatory letter he sent to
Montmorin on 18 June 1788 to try to forestall criticisms from the ministry:

> I will continue the observations . . . in the *Courier de l'Europe* on the affairs of the
> time. I have seized this occasion to show my zeal for my country . . . If, among these
> observations, there are some that are not perfectly in conformity with the views of the
> government, these are haphazard inconsequential ideas, which prove that these observa-
> tions have not been dictated to me. I have conferred about them with the ambassador . . .
> who found nothing wrong with them. I have often substituted the words *nation – peuple*
> for government – because each reader will be drawn to the word he believes applies to
> him. The fashion of the day is to speak politically, [and] I believe I have a duty to give the
> favoured kind of text for all those who meddle in politics. I have succeeded in demon-
> strating that the *parlements* are not the people's representatives and that the power they
> have arrogated to themselves is not given to them by the [ancient, unwritten] constitution
> of France. I dare . . . to believe that I have succeeded in persuading Frenchmen who love
> their country of the same thing.[20]

Yet by late 1788, the most pressing political question agitating France was not
the role of the *parlements*, but how the Estates-General should be constituted.
According to the traditional forms adopted at their last meeting in 1614, the
Estates-General was divided into three separate and roughly equal sized 'Estates'
or 'Orders', one each for the clergy, nobility, and Third Estate or commoners. Each
Estate deliberated and voted separately and a majority in any one Estate could
veto the other two. However, as the Third Estate represented over 95 per cent
of the population, there were widespread demands that their numbers should

be doubled and that voting should be conducted by majority decision and not by order. This would give the Third Estate a dominant voice. The proposal was vociferously opposed by the First and Second Estates and the Paris *Parlement*, which on 25 September 1788 decreed that the Estates-General should meet according to the 'forms of 1614'.

This decision exposed the *parlements'* claims to represent the whole nation as a sham and stripped away their popular support: in 1790 they would be abolished with barely a whimper of opposition. However, the decision of the Paris *Parlement* did not decide the matter, for the initiative remained with the king and his Council, which on 27 December 1788 announced a characteristic fudge. Instead of backing the Third Estate wholeheartedly to outflank the privileged orders, Louis XVI consented to double their representation but left the final decision on voting to the Estates-General. The results were predictable: a flurry of pamphleteering and, when the Estates-General met, a shambolic political *impasse*. The kindest interpretation of Louis XVI's actions is that they were a blundering attempt at divide and rule. Their effect was to set the Third Estate on a collision course with the other two Orders and unleash an explosive class-based political rhetoric.

Morande took an early stand in favour of the doubling of the Third Estate and unification of Orders. 'When' – he asks in August 1788 – 'will we see prejudice give way to reflection, to make only one corps of the French nation?'[21] On 6 December 1788, he was still more explicit in pressing the claims of the Third Estate:

> Is not that order [the Third Estate] distinguished by the services, the wisdom and the riches of those who compose it? Have not commerce and the arts experienced an expansion, unknown in the century to which we are referring back, which has quadrupled the number of men in the informed classses? Do not the lower clergy, the municipalities, the whole body of manufacturers and merchants, the bourgeoisie, contain an infinity of citizens worthy to be admitted into the national assembly? Are not the liberal professions multiplied and has there not been a considerable growth in the numbers of subjects practising each of them since that time? . . . The King's subjects cannot all be born gentlemen, nor become members of the upper clergy . . . but they are all Frenchmen and must all be citizens.[22]

Such statements accompanied Morande's regular denunciations of the self-interest of the magistrates in the *parlements* and the reactionary parts of the nobility and clergy.

As we might expect, Morande developed this language of denunciation and invective, his stock in trade since the *Gazetier cuirassé*, further. The revolution provided him with new targets, but it also brought old adversaries, including Mirabeau, to prominence. Beaumarchais and Morande had crossed swords with Mirabeau in 1785 over shares in the company supplying water to Paris. The issue of new shares in the company had unleashed a wave of speculation, during which pamphleteers working for the Genevan financial speculator Etienne Clavière, notably Mirabeau, argued that the shares were overpriced.[23] The battle was explosive because it had a political dimension. Clavière and his minions, who also included Brissot and Jean-Louis Carra, habitually attacked the share prices of companies closely associated with the government, simultaneously undermining confidence and manipulating the market.[24] However, in this particular dispute, Morande pulled his punches, deleting some of the most pointed phrases when he republished Beaumarchais' riposte to Mirabeau in the *Courier de l'Europe*.[25] He was hoping, so he told Beaumarchais, to goad Mirabeau just far enough to appear justified in raking over the coals of the Hardy case once more.[26]

The clashes of Beaumarchais and Morande with Mirabeau and his allies intensified in 1787. This time the pretext was an acrimonious divorce case between a Strasbourg banker named Guillaume Kornmann and his much younger wife, Catherine. The case revolved around Catherine's affair with a wealthy, well-connected local official, Daudet de Jossan, a liaison that her husband initially encouraged, hoping to profit from Daudet's political connections, including Lenoir. Originally a dispute between spouses, the case was turned into a *cause célèbre* by Kornmann's friend and lawyer, the radical reformer Nicolas Bergasse and his political backers. These included the Duke d'Orléans; Necker; the Marquis de Lafayette, hero of the American revolution; and Clavière and his stable of pamphleteers. They hoped to use the case to topple Calonne, propel Necker back into government, and promote a radical reform agenda. Their mud-slinging tactics included insinuating that Daudet had shared Madame Kornmann's favours with Lenoir, whom they portrayed as Calonne's right-hand man.[27]

Beaumarchais, a close friend of Daudet, entered the lists as Catherine's defender. Morande, who also considered Daudet a friend, soon followed, republishing and praising Beaumarchais' pamphlets and attacking Kornmann's advocates.[28] His partisanship so irritated Kornmann that he complained to Montmorin, who promised to punish Morande if he did not moderate his tone. This gave Morande pause for thought, especially as Aubert had just banned two editions of the *Courier de l'Europe* over the issue.[29]

Kornmann's complaints found an echo in a forged, spurious letter purportedly to Beaumarchais from Morande, dated 6 July 1787, which was doubtless penned by one of Kornmann's allies. It suggested that Morande had received a guinea per line to publish his attacks on Cagliostro and Beaumarchais' articles against Kornmann. The false Morande also worried that the *Courier de l'Europe* might be banned in France as a result of Kornmann's complaints.[30]

Naturally, Morande hastened to respond to this attack, castigating Kornmann's advocates for resorting to such impostures. He denied that he had been paid to attack Cagliostro or that the articles on the Kornmann affair in the *Courier de l'Europe* were sent to him by Beaumarchais. This seems to have been true.[31] He claimed that they were copied from manuscript newsletters, although he admitted to spicing them up. However, as the case was a matter for the courts, he denounced Kornmann's propagandists as perturbers of the public peace.[32] After that, Morande fell silent. However, a year later, when Bergasse visited London, Morande savaged him for his faith in Mesmer and animal magnetism. According to Morande, Mesmer had turned Bergasse from 'an enthusiast', to a 'maniac' and finally into 'a hydrophobe'.[33]

In April 1789, the final judgment in the Kornmann case awarded damages to both Madame Kornmann and Beaumarchais. By then, however, Kornmann's allies had seen many of their political wishes granted. Necker was back in government, applauded by most of the political classes, including Morande, and they had high hopes of the Estates-General. Indeed, in the spring of 1789, several of Kornmann's spokesmen were campaigning for seats. Among them were Mirabeau and Bergasse. The stage was set for another clash.

In March 1789, Mirabeau published a letter denying that he wrote a scandalous pamphlet entitled *Histoire secrète de la cour de Berlin*. Morande, delighted, wrote at once to Beaumarchais, promising to contradict Mirabeau, publish documentary evidence of his 'insanity and wickedness', and implicate him in the theft of a watch.[34] Morande's article, entitled 'Disaveu mal fait' ['A Disavowal Badly Made'] lived up to its promise, castigating Mirabeau and proclaiming him unfit to sit in the Estates-General.[35] His claims that Mirabeau was the pamphlet's author – claims which are generally accepted – carry all the more authority because his informant was Henriette de Nehra, who had dumped Mirabeau in Berlin and fled to London to escape his clutches.[36] The *Parlement* of Paris condemned the work to be burned.[37] Mirabeau was elected anyway.

After Mirabeau was elected, Morande returned to the fray, possibly at the bidding of Montmorin, who was incensed by Mirabeau's pamphlet.[38] He claimed that the attorney-general had received compelling evidence that Mirabeau was the author of the *Histoire secrète*, including – wrongly as it happens – proofs corrected in Mirabeau's own hand.[39] Timed to appear as the Estates-General convened, Morande clearly hoped to discredit Mirabeau with his fellow deputies. A month later, Morande attacked Mirabeau again, this time for abusing his position as a deputy by publishing a journal of proceedings in the Estates-General.[40] However, events soon overtook Morande's campaign. After the Royal Session of the Estates-General on 23 June 1789, Mirabeau led the Third Estate in refusing to disperse, informing the king's Master of Ceremonies 'Go and tell those who sent you that we are here by the will of the people, and that we shall not leave except by force of bayonets'.[41] The revolution had found a voice, and it belonged to Mirabeau. Thereafter, Morande fell silent. Two years later he described Mirabeau's death as 'a public calamity'.[42]

Morande's denunciations were not limited to individuals. They frequently covered whole social groups, notably the *parlementaires*, nobility and clergy. But from July 1788, in a chilling new development, Morande's *Courier de l'Europe* also began denouncing political opinions, declaring that anyone claiming that the Estates-General was not the best means to end political unrest and 'assure the principles of the French constitution' was 'the enemy of his country'.[43] Likewise, when the Breton nobility decided to boycott the Estates-General, Morande denounced their particularism and adopted the exclusionist language of the patriot leader Siéyès, arguing 'in France the only thing which exists is the French nation.' By implication, the Breton nobles were no longer true Frenchmen.[44]

Thus, by the time the Bastille fell in July 1789, Morande's attempts at regenerating French society had led him to develop a radical new form of newspaper journalism. On the one hand his pioneering *Lettres d'un voyageur* had reached their mature form, each now characteristically addressing a single, discreet theme. On the other, his paper had already been infected by the polarizing denunciatory language that would characterize revolutionary journalism and rhetoric, stigmatizing both individuals and opinions. Morande was thus a forerunnner of the self-styled revolutionary 'tribunes of the people', demagogic journalists who claimed to speak for the populace and to police, judge and pass sentence on the acts of authority.[45] Unsurprisingly, such 'tribunes of the people' – including both Brissot and Marat – became key promoters of political instability and revolutionary violence.

This was ironic, because Morande's political goal was to reconcile patriotic revolutionary reform with royalism and establish a stable constitutional monarchy. He expressed his support for revolutionary reform through a crippling and familiar indictment of the abuses of the old regime. He denounced the world of the court, where grasping favourites sought pensions and sinecures with callous disregard for the indebtedness of the state. He castigated the legions of worldly abbés who sought preferment above Christ-like poverty. And he condemned the partisan *esprit de corps* of the nobility, army, clergy and legal fraternity, who placed corporate interests before those of the entire nation.[46] Morande rejected the sycophantic, self-interested, calculated royalism of courtiers and timeservers, but argued that the revolution made possible a new kind of patriotic royalism. The new *patriote royaliste* loved the constitution above even the king, promoted public order, and recognized that the interests of a constitutional king coincided with those of his subjects.[47]

Morande exalted in the fall of the Bastille on 14 July 1789, which assured the triumph of the Third Estate and recognition of the Estates-General's metamorphosis into a unitary National Assembly.[48] He described the Bastille as 'the most horrifying . . . of all abuses of ministerial power' but argued that the violence of July 1789 was not caused by the king's personal unpopularity. Instead it stemmed from abuses accumulated over three centuries and 'the yoke of a disguised aristocracy' imposed under Louis XIV and Louis XV. He even argued that Louis XVI was the most popular king since Henri IV, who died in 1610. He had led the struggle to abolish abuses and overcome the entrenched privileges of the clergy and nobility. His reform initiatives led to revolution only due to centuries-old injustices and fears of an aristocratic counter-coup, but Louis himself had never endorsed plans to repress Paris and the National Assembly by force.[49] In Morande's schema, Louis was above reproach, a patriotic and enlightened king who loved liberty and wanted nothing more than the happiness of his people and the political, financial and moral regeneration of France.[50]

Morande's rhetoric and faith in the king mirrored that of the National Assembly and the population of Paris, who *fêted* Louis XVI as the restorer of French liberties when he visited his capital on 16 July. Nor was Morande's support for the monarch mere sycophancy, for his reform programme – which paralleled that of the patriotic reformers – was more radical than anything Louis was prepared to concede. The *Courier de l'Europe* preached civic equality, equality of opportunity, the abolition of the vestiges of feudalism and the tithe, ministerial responsibility, and freedom of the grain trade, the press and the individual.[51] It even advocated resolving the financial crisis by nationalizing Church lands, fully two weeks before Talleyrand announced a similar scheme that would be adopted by the National Assembly on 2 November.[52]

Yet, although he called for sweeping reforms, Morande insisted that the king should maintain a dominant voice.[53] Morande espoused Montesquieu's argument that France was necessarily a monarchy because of her size, and hence that 'the liberty of the French people' must be 'founded' on 'the necessary prerogatives of the throne as well as the imprescriptible rights of the nation and her love for her sovereign'.[54] Those rights included key safeguards against ministerial or royal despotism: the establishment of liberty, security of property and ministerial responsibility. These should be the limit of the people's aspirations, 'if they did not wish to undermine the foundations of governmental strength' and risk France's international security.[55] At heart, Morande's programme was statist: revolutionary regeneration would liberate the resources of the nation.

Morande's politics were undoubtedly influenced by his long stay in Britain. Nevertheless, he was ambiguous about the British constitution, which he compared to a once-beautiful woman showing the blemishes of age.[56] He thus set out to educate his readers about 'the useful institutions of Great Britain, as well as the abuses attached to her constitution, and the vices of some of her laws'.[57] Like many of his contemporaries, Morande admired the representative nature of the British constitution and the checks and balances inherent in the principle of ministerial responsibility.[58] However, he also saw British politics as tumultuous and mired in corruption. He was horrified by the violence, malpractice and huge costs that often accompanied contested elections, and appalled by electoral corruption in the smaller 'pocket boroughs', where great landlords effectively nominated two members of Parliament. As a result, he sided with reformers who called for shorter Parliaments and a wider, more uniform franchise.[59] This drew him into the ambit of British radicals, including John Horne Tooke, about whom, in a rare effusive moment, he reminisced:

> It is not without emotion that I recall the delicious moments that I passed in the company of [Tooke] . . . I never left his home without having learned things that books do not teach, without being filled with a most profound esteem for him.[60]

Nevertheless, prior to the French Revolution, Morande argued that 'of all popular governments [the British] is the least imperfect',[61] not least because it could survive the internecine disputes of the regency crisis.[62] He contended that British stability stemmed from institutional and conceptual frameworks that guaranteed personal liberty and the security of the state, above all the notion of a loyal opposition.[63] This was a concept that old regime politicians and diplomats struggled to grasp. The revolutionaries, too, failed to accept that opposition could be legitimate. This was largely due to a fixation with Rousseau, who insisted that a free state should be governed according to an infallible 'general will' to which all men of good faith and patriotism would naturally subscribe. The price of this tragic error would eventually be blood and Terror.

With his statist, mildly anglophile prejudices, Morande's political sympathies in late 1789 lay with the *monarchien* grouping in the National Assembly.[64] Like him, the *monarchiens* hoped to establish a strong royal executive within the framework of representative constitutional government. Taking their cue from Britain, they called for a two chamber legislature and an absolute legislative veto for the king. By the autumn of 1789, the leaders of this group, including Mounier, Malouet, Lally-Tollendal and Morande's old enemy Bergasse, were prominent in the National Assembly.[65] However, in the constitutional debates of September, their proposals were decisively rejected, not least because many deputies were suspicious of the king. The revolution was growing more radical than Morande.

Despite the defeat of the *monarchien* proposals, the broader outline of Morande's reform programme had been accomplished by December 1789. Abuses had been abolished; a representative National Assembly established; the principles of a liberal constitution laid down in the newly promulgated Declaration of the Rights of Man and Citizen; and meritocracy proclaimed in place of feudalism and noble privilege following the celebrated August decrees. The Bastille was demolished, torture and *lettres de cachet* abolished; freedom of conscience and press liberty proclaimed. Finally, the Church had been stripped of its wealth and subordinated to the state. All that remained was to restore order.

Morande's call for order was long-standing. Scarred by the Gordon riots, he had reservations about mob violence from the beginning. When rioters pelted royal troops with missiles from the rooftops of Grenoble on 7 June 1788, Morande insisted that the soldiers had been attacked 'not by citizens', but 'by a troop of brigands & robbers who sought to pillage the inhabitants of Grenoble'. He drew direct parallels with events in London in 1780, when he had witnessed:

> all prisons of this capital alight on same day, & 100 houses burned by . . . disciples of a maniac . . . wretches . . . recruited in prisons by Gordon [who] ran through all the streets . . . for 4 days torches in hand to preach Protestantism to the Catholic inhabitants of London by pillaging all that they owned before setting light to their homes.

Morande recommended that the French authorities should respond like the British by hanging several dozen rioters, arguing that severity at the outset is always the cheapest and most effective way to prevent disorders exploding into revolt.[66] Similarly, even while celebrating the symbolic and political implications of the fall of the Bastille, Morande condemned the excesses that accompanied it, including the murders of both his handler, the fortress' governor, Launay, and his old enemy, Flesselles. He was equally horrified by the violence at Versailles on 5 and 6 October 1789, during which a mob led by women compelled Louis XVI to move to Paris and become a virtual prisoner in his own capital.[67]

Morande's position on disorder was consistent and sincere. As the revolution progressed, he increasingly called for unity and respect for the constitution, castigating those who espoused violence and unconstitutional means whether from the royalist right or, on the political left, from members of the Jacobin club, the so-called 'Friends of the Constitution'. Among the first to condemn the radical Jean-Paul Marat for inciting popular violence, Morande was also the first to suggest that he had been convicted of robbing the Ashmolean Museum in Oxford. In a characteristic piece of defamation, Morande called on members of the University to confirm that Marat was the robber in question, but then fell tactically silent. Presumably he had learned the truth: it was a case of mistaken identity. Or perhaps he knew all along. Whatever the case, his allegation was taken seriously for almost 200 years.[68]

If Morande called for action against Brissot, Robespierre and the Commune, he also attacked the so-called 'friends of the king'. These included the court-sponsored editor of *Les Actes des Apôtres*, Jean-Gabriel Peltier and the royalist conspirator Favras, whose activities on a trip to London in late 1789 and apparent links to the king's brother, Provence, Morande denounced vociferously.[69] In February 1790, Morande pronounced Favras justly executed. For dramatic effect, he added that the noble and clerical privileges Favras wished to restore were maintained by 'rivers of blood' and shouts of 'treason' and 'impiety' whenever they came under attack.[70] Only once royalist or Jacobin extremists accepted the new constitution and abandoned attempts to change it by violence would order be restored and constitutional monarchy secure. Morande was still repeating this increasingly urgent message in May 1791 when he took an unexpected step. He withdrew his daughters from their school in Hampstead and moved his family to Paris.[71]

Morande left London in secrecy and haste. Probably he feared Swinton or his creditors would try to prevent his leaving. In the event, Swinton only learned of his departure when he received a letter Morande sent him from Boulogne.[72] By then, Morande was safely in Paris, where he rented a modest fourth-floor apartment on the *rue Taitbout* and established a new newspaper, the *Argus patriote*.[73]

In the *Argus patriote*'s prospectus, Morande informs his readers of his reasons:

> Having witnessed the death of the liberty of the press in Britain [which Morande claimed was being destroyed by the Pitt government], I saw it reborn in France, and I abandoned the cadaver to the worms devouring it in order to approach a healthy and vigorous wetnurse, who enjoyed the most robust health.

Faced with growing abuses in the British constitution, he favoured France as 'the freeest country in the universe.'[74] However, his real motives were probably much more complex.

Cash was doubtless an important consideration. With turmoil in state finances, it is probable that he was no longer receiving his stipend from the French government.[75] With sales of the *Courier de l'Europe* in steep decline, too, his livelihood looked insecure.

Perhaps, too, Morande was forewarned of the content of Pierre-Louis Manuel's sensational *La Police de Paris dévoilée* [*The Paris Police Unveiled*], which drew on police archives and offered genuine documentary evidence of his police activities. If so, he may have feared for his safety if he remained in London. Certainly he was aware of Manuel's revelations within days of returning to Paris, while his book was still in press.[76]

His revolutionary enemies insist that Morande was brought over by the court to spearhead the fight against Jacobin radicals, especially Brissot.[77] However, there is no hard evidence that the Crown subsidized the *Argus patriote*, and Morande's brand of royalism was little to the king's taste. Indeed, even Manuel had to admit that Morande wrote almost like a revolutionary patriot.[78] Besides, Morande did not begin campaigning against Brissot in earnest until three months after his arrival. It is also possible that Mirabeau's death influenced his thinking, as Morande might expect a lukewarm welcome from constitutional monarchists while Mirabeau was their chief powerbroker.

Finally, there were family reasons. Morande's mother's health was failing and he dreamed that they might be reconciled before she died. Doubtless he also wished to protect his inheritance against grasping relatives. By 16 February 1792, when Morande recounts a recent visit to Arnay to perform his 'sacred duty' to his 'dangerously ill' mother, she was on her deathbed. Morande tells his readers, with a filial tenderness perhaps more feigned than real, that:

> I saw her. I pressed her on my heart. She locked me in her arms. And although I could only be parted from her with sadness . . . I resisted the desire which overcame me. I embraced the relatives that I love, the friends who showered me with marks of their affection. I tore myself from their company, and returned to take up my task once more in order to devote all my time to my homeland.[79]

Nine days later Philiberte Belin was dead.[80] Within weeks her family were quarrelling about her last wishes and the validity of her will.[81]

Nevertheless, Morande's assertions that he returned for patriotic reasons ring true. In the *Argus patriote* he continued his campaign to cement the 'sacred principles of constitutional liberty' and thwart its enemies, whatever their political hue.[82] He began his first number with a scathing attack on the émigrés, appealing to those who loved their country to return home and condemning the rest as 'criminals who forget that they are Frenchmen and wish to overthrow the state'.[83] To entice the émigrés back, Morande sketched a tableau of a France in the process of regeneration and with every prospect of political harmony, if only patriotic writers would all rally to defend and propagate the principles of the constitution.[84]

Morande's optimism was quickly overtaken by events. On the night of 20 June 1791, the king and royal family fled Paris. Unfortunately, they were recognized at Varennes, arrested, and returned to Paris in disgrace. Worse still, a declaration of the king's motives for his flight, explaining his opposition to most of the measures taken by the Assembly since 23 June 1789, was found in the royal apartments. In the long term, this was to prove perhaps the most decisive event of the revolution. It persuaded many French citizens that Louis XVI could not be trusted. In the short term, however, most members of the National Assembly were so politically, emotionally and ideologically committed to their draft constitution that they could not let it fail. Although they suspended Louis from office, they agreed to reinstate him once he accepted the completed constitution. Radical politicians protested and organized a popular petition calling for Louis to be deposed but were brutally suppressed following a bloody confrontation in which trigger-happy national guardsmen massacred unarmed petitioners at a rally on the Champ de Mars. The incident was an indelible stain on the reputation of the commander of the National Guard, Lafayette, and the moderate leaders, known as Feuillants, who had broken with the Jacobins and formed their own political club after Louis' flight to Varennes.

Over the following months, Morande aligned himself with Lafayette and the Feuillants, whom he styled 'the true friends of the constitution'.[85] Though he never formally joined their club, he championed the Feuillant cause and chronicled the club's rise, decline, revival and final closure following attacks by riotous Jacobin agitators.[86] Yet despite their apparent solidarity with Louis XVI, in private constitutional monarchists found their faith severely tested by the king's flight and hence Feuillant support proved fickle. In the autumn of 1791, more newly elected deputies gravitated towards the Feuillants than the Jacobin Club, but the more ambitious of them rapidly deserted to the Jacobins, where proceedings were more public and reputations made more quickly. Likewise, in the press, 'after 21 June it was difficult to find a single newspaper – aside from those of the most reactionary royalists – with anything positive to say about the monarch'.[87] Morande's *Argus patriote* was an exception.

Nevertheless, the flight to Varennes also provoked a crisis of faith in Morande. Initially, he swallowed the official line that the king had been kidnapped or misled by evil advisers. However, the *Argus patriote* of 26 June hints at considerable misgivings, which he works through as he writes. He admits that the king's declaration and orders suggest a 'profoundly meditated escape', but declares himself reluctant to pronounce on Louis' motives. Several pages later, he concludes that the king's declaration cannot be considered his own work, and optimistically suggests that Louis must now realize he has been deceived. He hopes for a rapprochement between king and people and questions the assumption that Louis intended to return at the head of foreign armies.[88] On 30 June, he insisted once more that France must remain a kingdom on account of her size and argued pragmatically for reinstating the king if he would accept the constitution. If he refused, Morande insisted that the sceptre should pass to his six-year-old son under a regency. Either way, the challenge would be to restore confidence between king and nation.[89]

Morande maintained that the best solution to the crisis lay in cabinet government and ministerial responsibility along English lines, contending that this was precisely what the the new constitution envisaged. As in England, the king's preponderance would only be apparent – all would be done in his name, but rarely would it be his will. In effect, Morande was advocating a very limited monarchy. This seems inconsistent with claims that he was a puppet of the court.

Once the Constitution was completed and accepted by the king, the work of the National Assembly came to an end and a new legislature was elected. The elections were fought against the background of the flight to Varennes and uncertainty about the king's intentions. The radicals, keen to make political capital from fears of conspiracy and royal treachery, believed that circumstances would ensure victory for their favoured candidates, above all Brissot. Brissot, whose quest for national office had previously been fruitless, believed his moment had arrived. Morande had other ideas.

By the time Morande and Brissot crossed swords in Paris, each had new reasons to hate the other. Morande believed that Brissot was complicit in the production of Manuel's *Police dévoilée*, particularly the savage biographical passage accusing Morande of betraying Henri de La Motte, selling secrets to the British, and killing his own father through chagrin.[90] Likewise, Brissot now knew for certain that Morande had been behind his arrest and imprisonment, for Manuel had passed him the originals of Morande's letters denouncing him to the police.[91]

In the early numbers of the *Argus patriote*, Brissot is attacked more than any other individual. In his second number, Morande describes him as a 'false French Patriot' who feigns respect for the Constitution.[92] However, he also drew attention to Brissot's links with the British abolitionist Clarkson, accusing them both of kindling the flames of racial discord in France's colonies.[93] By mid July he was suggesting that Brissot had become 'the chief of the *republicomanes*' and 'chief clerk of all the traitors to the motherland', 'interpreter of all the foreign emissaries' and 'general agent of all the enemies of the public interest'. According to Morande, Brissot's paper was open to all enemies of the Constitution, including counter-revolutionary puppeteers who were using extreme republicans to pursue their anarchic ends.[94] Such allegations were buttressed by frequent denunciations of foreign-born revolutionary activists as *agents-provocateurs* and enemy agents.[95]

With elections looming, Morande's abuse intensified until Brissot could no longer ignore it.[96] He accused Morande and the royal court of orchestrating a mud-slinging pamphleteering and poster campaign against him and began writing a pamphlet in his defence.[97] According to Brissot, the campaign was managed by the deputy and journalist Duquesnoy, who hired the authors of pamphlets such as *Le Babillard* [*The Babbler*] and defamatory placards such as the *Second Chant du coq*. The latter, widely rumoured to be Morande's work, accused Brissot of embezzling 580 *livres* while President of the Parisian district of Filles Saint-Thomas in 1789.[98] Brissot's allegations cannot be verified, but it seems certain that his enemies were co-ordinating their attacks: when Morande denied producing the *Second Chant du coq*, he also revealed that he knew its authors' identities.[99]

Brissot's justificatory pamphlet tackled Morande's charges head on, noting that he had been accused of 'leading an odious life' and being 'paid by foreign powers'; of having had 'intelligence with Clarkson'; and of 'making dupes of and seizing the fortune of his business associates'. Brissot challenged Morande to provide credible evidence and noted that Desforges had refused to bring the swindling charge to trial. He also offered to discuss such evidence if it was genuine and deposited with a public official. Otherwise, Morande's testimony must be considered as false, since he was a known perjurer and had made false allegations against Brissot in the past. To reinforce this point, Brissot republished damning descriptions of Morande from the works of Voltaire, Lauraguais, Villette, Mirabeau, Linguet, Manuel and Mairobert's *Espion anglois* [*English Spy*], before adding the devastating judgement 'when a whole generation raises its voice to testify against an individual, it is hard to believe that person is not guilty. If there is anyone who knows Morande and does not despise him, let him stand up!'[100]

On 18 August, Morande retaliated with his *Réplique à Brissot*, probably the most destructive pamphlet he ever wrote. It opened with a detailed autobiographical account, answering and mocking the charges brought against him. *Inter alia*, it pointed out that the history of Henri de La Motte's betrayal and trial was public and made no mention of him.[101] It also claimed that his links to the police were limited to meeting Receveur at the French embassy and a couple of letters to the Lieutenants of Police. Morande even pretended that Buard alone was responsible for betraying Pelleport. Yet he also asserted that there was nothing reprehensible about helping the authorities to prevent scandalous pamphlets. If that made him a 'barbarian', as Manuel and Brissot asserted, he was happy to accept the label.[102] Finally, he playfully ridiculed Manuel's charge that he 'was a thief BEFORE BEING A LIBERTINE' because he first visited a brothel 'to steal a gold box'. For, as Morande remarked, 'to go to a house of debauchery, it is necessary first to be a little libertine'.[103]

Having offered his autobiographical justification, Morande shifted to the attack, repeating the main charges against Brissot. He was an agent of Clarkson who wished to see France's colonies in flames; mixed-up in the production of *libelles*, especially the *Diable dans un bénitier*; and a 'fugitive bankrupt accused of theft' for having swindled Desforges. Morande backed his account with 42 pages of documentary appendices concerning Brissot's relations with Desforges, the *Lycée de Londres* and the *Diable dans un bénitier*. There is little doubt they are genuine. Most came from a cache of 80 letters that Brissot foolishly left with Desforges in May 1784 so that Desforges could verify their accounts. They were never returned.[104] Instead, Desforges handed them to Morande so that he could prepare a legal brief against Brissot.[105] Brissot never denied their authenticity and much of the information they contain tallies with other sources.[106]

According to Morande, these documents proved that the *Lycée de Londres* was a chimera devised to fleece Desforges. Brissot never intended to hold the weekly assembly promised in his prospectus. The house he rented was too small and he made no serious efforts to find other premises. Effectively, Brissot had used

15,000 *livres* of Desforges' money to fund his rent and buy books and furniture. But was this true?[107]

Although the documents themselves were genuine, the inferences Morande drew from them were malicious and false. Brissot's surviving correspondence proves his enthusiasm for the *Lycée* project and shows that he made extensive efforts to set up connections with Britain's intellectual elite.[108] He had every reason to hope for its success. Moreover, in the course of his career, Brissot founded several associations, most notably the Friends of the Blacks, to advance himself and his political goals. There is no reason to believe the *Lycée de Londres* was any different. He was, however, guilty of naivety and ignorance. Brissot had expected to meet rental costs on meeting rooms from subscriptions. However, the British expected payment in advance, and Brissot's negotiations to hire premises jointly with the British philosopher David Williams failed for precisely this reason. Cash flow, rather than fraud, appears to explain why the *Lycée* never met.[109]

This made little difference to Morande's readers, few of whom had the time and patience to get to the bottom of his charges. Despite Brissot's rhetorical plea 'Who will believe Morande?'[110] the muck Morande threw in the *Réplique* and two subsequent pamphlets stuck. It was also raked far and wide, for copies of all three pamphlets were sent to every subscriber to the *Argus patriote* and anyone else who requested them.[111] Sadly, we do not know who financed this giveaway. It could have been the court, as Brissot alleged. But it could equally have been rival candidates, Feuillant leaders, Morande himself, or any other of Brissot's revolutionary enemies.

The Parisian election results bear testimony to the success of Morande's campaign. The elections were conducted as a series of head-to-head run-offs over several days until all 24 Parisian deputies were chosen. Brissot was the radical Jacobins' most favoured and, thanks to his journalism, most high profile candidate. They expected him to be a shoo-in. Morande's mudslinging changed that. As the elections began, Brissot's ally François-Xavier Lanthénas remarked presciently: 'Morande spreads his poisons in still greater abundance. The electoral assembly here shows itself ill-disposed.'[112] In the event, the elections turned into a nerve-wracking ordeal. Ballot after ballot, Brissot was selected as the Jacobin candidate. Time after time he was defeated, often decisively. Finally, in the eleventh ballot, he scraped home narrowly, the fourth of eight radicals returned. His election led to bitter recriminations and caused the electoral Assembly to split into two rival bodies.[113]

Brissot's election was pregnant with significance. The Legislative Assembly was elected in an atmosphere of intense political insecurity and suspicion, and the deputies chosen reflect this. Due to a self-denying ordinance passed by the National Assembly, existing deputies could not stand for re-election. Hence the men elected to the new legislature were all new to national government, but most were experienced and reliable supporters of the revolution. They had cut their political teeth in the new revolutionary local authorities, so knew who the revolution's enemies were. Top of the hit-list internally were the non-juring clergy, the numerous priests who rejected the revolutionary religious settlement and refused to swear an oath of civic allegiance. The main external threat came from the émigré armies gathering in the German Rhineland under the leadership of Louis XVI's brothers and the Prince de Condé. Thus the first priorities of the new legislature included the passage of punitive laws against the émigrés and non-juring priests and bellicose calls for action against the German princes who hosted the émigré armies and their Austrian and Prussian protectors. The most vociferous proponent of direct action was Brissot.

The Legislature's actions were problematic for the king. He was unwilling to outlaw his own brothers, genuine refugees, or any nobleman who believed that he was serving Louis by joining the émigré army. Nor would he persecute the non-jurors, not least because he, too, deplored the religious settlement. He therefore used his veto to delay both decrees. This was completely within his constitutional rights, but for many revolutionaries it merely proved that he was siding with their enemies. Consequently, the vetos fuelled republicanism and calls for his overthrow.[114]

Ironically, Louis XVI was not averse to war, which appeared to offer him a route out of his predicament. If the French army performed well, he would emerge a victorious patriotic hero. If they performed badly, he might hope to seize emergency powers or find his authority restored by the victorious invaders. The latter outcome seemed more likely, because over half the French officer corps had gone over to the émigrés. Thus the king adopted a hawkish position, backing the Legislative Assembly's bellicose posturing even though the Austrians made conciliatory gestures, until finally, on 20 April 1792, France declared war. For Louis, it was the last throw of the dice.

Morande chronicled these developments with prescience, acuity and concern. He was supportive of Louis XVI's use of the veto, but not through any sympathy for émigrés or non-jurors, whom he styled respectively supporters of 'Byzantine despotism' and the 'iniquities of the inquisition'. He considered the wealth of the clergy essentially unChristian: 'The Christian religion preaches poverty, pure morals & humility, but the Ecclesiastical Hierarchy was founded on pride and wealth: and the conduct of the majority of priests and *abbés de cour* scandalized the faithful.' The pretensions of the nobility were no better founded, while the feudal abuses the émigrés wished to restore were vicious. He was, moreover, acutely concerned about the flight of émigré capital.[115] Hence he announced himself favourable to any law that would help bring the émigrés back. However, the actual émigré legislation was too late, unconstitutional and despotic. It sought to extend the authority of the French state beyond her borders and to condemn citizens to death in absentia on the uncertain evidence of a denunciator.[116] Thus Morande applauded the royal veto both because the law was unjust and because it disproved the claims of émigrés, royalists and foreign governments that Louis XVI was no longer a free agent.[117] Likewise, he opposed the decree on non-juring priests, advocating toleration and warning against violating the constitutional principle of freedom of conscience, for he rightly foresaw that religious schism would fuel civil war. Nevertheless, he condemned non-jurors for their obstinate opposition to the national will and recognizing 'an authority foreign to the laws of the nation' [i.e. the Pope].[118] A child of the Enlightenment, he prescribed Church disestablishment, political equality between ministers of all faiths, and the abolition of the clerical oath as the best antidote to religious violence.[119]

Morande's analysis of the darkening international situation was also generally acute. In particular, he stressed that the Eastern powers (Prussia, Russia and Austria) were far more concerned to carve up Poland, where a royal-led revolution threatened to end centuries of foreign domination, than to intervene in France. He therefore recognized the Austro-Prussian declaration of Pillnitz of August 1791, which promised military action against France if the other powers gave their unanimous backing, as hollow bluster. Unlike many revolutionary commentators, who portrayed the declaration as proof of hostile intentions, Morande rightly saw it as a hollow attempt at intimidation. The Austrians and Prussians were confident that the other powers would never back them unanimously.[120] Two months later, when Austria, Prussia, Britain and Holland recognized the new constitutional monarchy, Morande denounced Brissot's assertions that their public dispositions masked sinister designs. In Morande's view, France had no need to fear her neighbours. A counter-revolution was now impossible.[121]

Nevertheless, Morande shared Brissot's conviction that, in the event of war, the patriotism of French citizen volunteers would overcome mercenary and serf armies. So did the revolutionary legislators, whose support for the declaration of war was almost unanimous. By early winter, Morande, too, was swept up in the bellicose tide, calling for strong action against German princes who permitted émigré armies to assemble on their territory and applauding when the king issued one of them, the elector of Trier, with an ultimatum.[122] However, when Trier, pressured by Austria, gave way, Morande again argued that the Powers had no interest in war with France. He now warned against provocation and insinuated that the leaders of the war party were foreign agents.[123]

Although Morande repeatedly denounced the rulers of Europe, he was opposed to France's exporting her revolution.[124] If every European people were left to win their own liberty, he was confident that they would do so. Hence, when the reactionary Gustav III of Sweden was assassinated, Morande predicted universal and successful revolution: 'The Centuries of despotism are past and, if those who govern them leave them under any other yoke than that of justice, the year 1800 will see all the peoples of Europe free and masters of their countries.'[125] He probably believed this rhetoric, for from 1789, with the exception of the conservative and priest-ridden Belgian revolt, he consistently applauded popular disturbances across Europe as symptoms of the advance of liberty against despotism.[126]

In early 1792, Morande began portraying the British Prime Minister, William Pitt, as the *deus ex machina* behind the growing hostility of the European powers towards France.[127] Perhaps he was preparing for a *volte face* about the need for war, driven by Louis XVI's increasingly bellicose stance? Or perhaps he hoped to further discredit Brissot's links to Britain? Nevertheless, his campaign is consistent with earlier comments about Pitt, whom he blamed for British infringements of the Eden treaty and riotous attacks on British radicals, most notably Joseph Priestley.[128] Driven by this belief, by early April 1792, Morande was ready to welcome war and its potentially unifying effects.[129] When Louis went to the Assembly to request support for war, Morande declared:

> At last the die is cast. The French nation has been forced to purchase her liberty at the price of blood; the sad sacrifice that has been imposed upon her is about to be consummated, and her enemies will learn . . . that a free people which has crushed the despotism in her breast, knows [how] to defend her independence against the league of tyrants.[130]

A few days later, he followed this rallying call with an extraordinary profession of faith in royal leadership:

> Let us enjoy the benefit that the Supreme Master of the Earth has accorded us, in giving us a monarch who . . . always sought . . . to make his people happy. He long groped along, misled by unfaithful ministers . . . but he has at last seen the light and followed its flame, and the Nation which is most worthy to have a great King can today boast the first Monarch in the Universe.[131]

Unfortunately, fewer and fewer Frenchmen shared Morande's sentiments. The declaration of war temporarily rallied opinion behind the king but only bought him a little time. As French armies retreated, he was viewed with growing suspicion and hostility.

By late 1791, as the king's authority slipped, Morande was becoming increasingly strident against Jacobin agitators, particularly Brissot, Carra and their allies. Then, at the end of November, news began to trickle through of a massive slave insurrection in Saint-Domingue (Haiti). Like many Europeans, Morande's first reaction was disbelief. However, as the hitherto unthinkable scale, violence, destructiveness and success of the revolt grew clear, Morande seized every opportunity to fulminate against Brissot, Clarkson and other 'Friends of the Blacks', whose abolitionist propaganda he blamed for everything from rebel atrocities to sugar riots in Paris.[132] In the long run, such charges would damage Brissot, but for now the tide was flowing too fast in his direction.

At the end of May 1792, with France's military situation and the king's position looking increasingly desperate, Morande abandoned the *Argus patriote*. It had lasted for just under a year. He gave subscribers no warning of the paper's imminent demise: indeed his final number reminds them to renew their subscriptions. Those who responded probably never saw their cash again. Unable to sustain himself on the paper's revenues, Morande probably took their money and ran. By late 1792, he had run up new debts of 14,000 *livres*. Much of this was owed to his publisher, Jacques-François Froullé, who was still waiting for Morande and Eliza to pay him 4,726 *livres* when he was guillotined in 1794.[133] It is unlikely, however, that Morande's subscribers chased him for refunds, as revolutionary newspapers folded all the time. Few would have suspected deliberate fraud: a publication that lasted a year was considered relatively successful.

Morande probably feared to persist in his futile public support of constitutional monarchy. Harassment of royalist journalists by revolutionary 'delegations', mobs and the authorities had been common since 1790, but in May 1792 the risks were intensifying. War made opposition to the government appear suspect and the authorities and revolutionary mobs wanted scapegoats for military defeat. Thus Royou's counter-revolutionary *Ami du Roi* [*Friend of the King*] was forcibly closed down by the government on 3 May 1792. Three weeks later, the veteran Genevan journalist Mallet Du Pan, by no means a counter-revolutionary extremist, slipped out of France on a clandestine one-way mission for Louis XVI.[134] With the disappearance of journalists on the extreme and moderate right, Morande's own brand of constitutional royalism looked dangerously exposed. His decision to stop the presses was in part an act of self-preservation.

In the weeks that follow, Morande's decision looks increasingly prescient. On 20 June, the anniversary of the flight to Varennes, a sombre-faced revolutionary crowd invade the Tuileries palace and force the king to don the cap of liberty and drink to the health of the nation. On 10 August 1792, after a bloody pitched battle, they invade the Tuileries again forcing the king's abdication. The Legislative Assembly dissolves itself and appoints in its place a Provisional Executive Committee, until a new legislature, the Convention, can be elected. One thousand years of monarchy has come to an end.

After the king's overthrow, the Jacobins shut down the remaining right-wing newspapers and conduct house-to-house searches for non-juring priests and royalist sympathizers. As arrests run into the thousands, former religious buildings are converted into makeshift prisons. Throughout the late, hot summer, as allied armies close in on Paris, political tension on the streets mounts.

The allied commander, the Duke of Brunswick, has threatened to take an exemplary revenge on the capital if the royal family are harmed. As Danton rallies Parisians for a last-ditch defence, this ultimatum and fears that royalist prisoners might escape and form a fifth column cause panic in the capital. Finally, on 2 September, armed mobs break into the prisons. After kangaroo-court trials which cover murder with a fig leaf of justice, they butcher those they find 'guilty'. Montmorin is among the victims. Radical Jacobin politicians, including Danton and Robespierre, are probably complicit in the massacres, which were evidently planned in advance and last for several days. The revolutionary authorities do little to prevent them.

Morande spends August and early September 1792 in a state of perpetual fear. He is incapacitated by a severe attack of gout and is unable, or too afraid, to show himself in public. On 16 August, he sends George to try to beg a loan from Beaumarchais, who refuses him, having enough financial headaches and worries of his own.[135] His enemies are circling and within days he is arrested, accused of embezzling money intended for the American cause. Fortunately, his luck holds. On 30 August, Beaumarchais is released with a certificate from the municipality attesting his innocence. Three days later the massacres begin.

Morande's enemies scent blood. Brissot, agitated, asks eagerly whether Morande is among the dead. Learning that he is not, he goes to the Provisional Executive Committee on 3 September and declares 'They have forgotten Morande'. A warrant is issued for Morande's arrest.[136]

Morande is picked up on 7 September 1792. In Paris, the massacres have subsided, but the blood spilt is barely dry when he is taken to Saint-Pélagie prison. Elsewhere, copycat prison murders continue unabated. Tormented by gout and nightmares that the killing may resume, Morande's health deteriorates rapidly.

In desperation, Morande writes to the authorities of the Section of Montblanc, the Parisian municipal district in which he lives. His letter protests that he has been imprisoned without being interrogated or told of the charge against him. He demands his release and the lifting of seals on his property. The Section considers his plea and, in the light of his 'deplorable state' and the 'alarm of his wife and children', demands his release into the Section's custody and safekeeping.

On 10 September, Morande is subjected to a cursory interrogation by representatives of the Commune. They accept his statements that he was laid up at home suffering from gout during the 10 August insurrection and that he does not mix with suspect persons. In consequence, they order that he be handed over to his Section and that, subject to a satisfactory search, the seals be lifted from his apartment.

Nine days later, Morande accompanies several officers to the *rue Taitbout*. For two days they inspect his apartment, papers, books and newspapers. On

21 September 1792, nothing suspect having been found, the seals are lifted and the General Council of the Paris Commune orders Morande's release.[137]

Morande's release bears the hallmarks of factional politics, for the Paris Commune was dominated by Jacobin extremist supporters of Robespierre. Robespierre detested Brissot and his fellow Girondins, whom he suspected of prevaricating over the fate of the king. On 2 September 1792, Robespierre denounced Brissot and his associates to the Commune as foreign agents. The Commune immediately issued arrest warrants, but they were never enforced, probably due to the intervention of Danton.[138] It would have been natural for the Commune to wish to preserve Morande as a potential weapon against Brissot. Indeed, Robespierre's close ally, Camille Desmoulins, almost admits as much, asserting that Morande 'has almost deserved from the nation his pardon for his numerous slanders, for having told so many truths of Brissot'.[139]

Morande is freed as the revolution is saved. At Valmy, on 20 September, the cannons of the Republic cow the enemy into retreat. Yet Morande's ordeal is not over. In Paris, he is dangerously exposed. He wishes to retire to Burgundy, but to do so he needs passports for his family, which in turn requires certificates of *civisme* [good citizenship] from the authorities. He and Eliza soon learn just how hard it will be to acquire them through labyrinthine revolutionary structures filled with their enemies.

Eliza is desperate to return to Britain to receive a legacy. In December, she requests a passport via the General Assembly of the Montblanc Section. They support her request and refer her to the Directory of the *département* of Paris. However, the *département* passes it to the General Council of the Commune, where, despite the Robespierrist majority, Manuel is *Procureur-général*. This may explain the outcome. Her request is refused on the grounds that she 'is allied to a man known to be the author of the *Gazetier cuirassé*, the *Courier de l'Europe* and several other *libelles* of this type'. Eliza persists and petitions the newly elected Convention, which refers the matter to its Committee of General Security.[140] They presumably grant her request, for by 30 December she has reached London, only to be denounced as a probable émigré agent by the radical Jacobin and spy Pereyra, who had once worked for her husband. As Pereyra's denunciation noted that Eliza had been 'refused a passport at Paris', he was clearly in contact with Morande's enemies inside France.[141]

Within weeks of her return, Morande, Eliza and their children finally manage to retire to Arnay-sur-Arroux, as the revolutionaries have renamed his home town. There, their alien appearance and foreign habits attract widespread curiosity. Decades later, César Lavirotte would attest that:

People ... still recall ... the arrival ... of this Anglo-French family, composed of M. de Morande who attracted attention by his large size, his foreign appearance and his short, round, unpowdered wig, his wife . . . his slightly deformed son . . . who brought from his native land only some romantic ideas which were soon put into action by carrying off his young cousin Manette Villedey to make her his wife, and a propensity for drunkenness which soon carried him to his grave, and finally two distinguished-looking, very pale, very blond, young ladies, the one, Betsey [Elizabeth], a large person of English character . . . and Henriette, a small and lively girl who, despite turning this way and that in a thousand ways to make herself seem more agreeable finished up unmarried.[142]

In Arnay, the family enjoy the protection of Morande's brother Louis, now a local revolutionary and magistrate, who defends them during the political Terror that engulfs France in 1793 and 1794 under the reign of Committee of Public Safety and Robespierre. When the authorities at Arnay are ordered to draw up lists of 'suspects' in April 1793, Louis ensures that Morande's name appears among the third and lowest category of persons. As his enemies Brissot, Linguet, Clavière, Manuel, Carra, Pereyra, d'Orléans and, scratching and screaming like a cornered animal, Madame du Barry, are delivered to the guillotine, Morande is merely kept under low-level surveillance.[143]

Morande was complicit in at least one of these deaths, for he was mentioned in the courtroom and apparently even sought to testify at the trial of Brissot and the Girondins, who were arrested following violent demonstrations at the end of May 1793 and accused, falsely, of conspiring against the republic. Among the papers relating to the trial is a letter from a certain Siessel, *fils*, to the notorious public prosecutor for the revolutionary tribunal, Fouquier-Tinville, which recommends that Morande be summoned from Burgundy as a witness. It notes that 'in all his newspapers he [Morande] has said that that rascal [Brissot] was the agent of the Court of London'. 'Morande knew all the intrigues of the British cabinet in depth' and might thus 'greatly contribute to uncovering the threads of this great conspiracy'. Siessel's knowledge of Morande and his whereabouts strongly suggests that Morande was no stranger to this letter, which Fouquier-Tinville ignored.[144]

Although Morande was not invited to testify, he was present in the courtroom in spirit, for the charge sheet mentioned that Brissot had sought his death during the September massacres and the judgment of the revolutionary tribunal reflects many of Morande's allegations. It describes Brissot as 'dishonoured, even under the *ancien régime* by base intrigues', dwells on his stay in London, and declares that he and his accomplices were 'the agents of the English faction' who set out to destroy France's colonies 'under guise of philanthropy.'[145]

After the Terror, Morande may have returned briefly to Paris, for the author of a British biographical dictionary of the French Revolution published in 1797 claims that he 'repairs daily' on crutches to the Palais Royal to 'entertain' passers-by with 'his opinion of the events of the time and the great men of the day.'[146] However, he spent most of his time in Arnay: between 1795 and 1798 his name appears on every list of electors drawn up for the annual elections to the legislative Councils that shared power with the five-man Executive Directory.[147] According to Lavirotte, he lived in quiet retirement, shunning cafés and keeping his own counsel on political matters, 'perhaps regarding it as beneath his dignity to join in with our poor Arnetois politicians'. Instead, he spent his time walking or reading in his library, dining, entertaining and, above all, 'drinking heavily in the English manner'.[148]

When Lavirotte was on leave from the revolutionary army, he would call on Morande and listen avidly to tales of England and his adventures. Sometimes, too, Morande would spice up his conversation with libertine anecdotes, tales of his sexual escapades, or advice for the younger man on how to treat the fair sex. 'It was then', Lavirotte remarks prudishly, 'that I recognized that unfortunately all that had been written on the shamelessness of his thoughts, his cynicism and his immorality was all too accurate'.[149]

Morande's greatest pleasure in retirement was to await the arrival of the mail-coach with the latest news from Paris. He was probably one of the first townsfolk to learn of the momentous overthrow of Robespierre at the end of July 1794; the various *coups d'état* that punctuated the rule of the Directory between 1795 and 1799; the victories and tribulations of the revolutionary armies in Germany, Italy and Egypt; and finally the climactic seizure of power by Napoleon Bonaparte in November 1799.

Sadly, there is no record of how Morande received such news, though, like his former *monarchien* allies, he probably approved the Napoleonic consular regime, which concentrated power in a one-man executive while preserving parliamentary forms. What is clear is that Morande's thirst for news was as impatient as ever. Lavirotte recounts how one young traveller, taking Morande for a provincial hick, tried to bamboozle him with tall tales. Morande, who did not appreciate the joke, boxed him around the ears and sent him on his way, to the applause of bystanders. The townsfolk made no such mistake. They regarded Morande with a mixture of awe and affection, treating him as the local muse. In this capacity, they frequently called on him to compose impromptu verses for public ceremonies and the endless revolutionary festivals that had replaced Saints' days and religious celebrations.[150]

In financial matters, Morande remained incorrigible to the end. Between 15 December 1791 and 20 August 1792 he borrowed 8,300 *livres* from Beaumarchais. In 1798, his benefactor, ruined by revolutionary sequestrations, begged him to return the money. Morande ignored him. Beaumarchais' heirs and executors were still trying to reclaim the money six years later. He was similarly hard-hearted when Swinton, who faced ruin as the *Courier de l'Europe* was progressively banned from most of Europe, pleaded for him to return money he had advanced at Beaumarchais' request.[151]

Morande fended off these requests by claiming that he faced hardship himself. If this was true, it did not prevent Betsey from contracting an advantageous marriage in July 1802 to Antoine Guiot, whose father was a lawyer and deputy at the Estates-General. It does seem, however, that Morande gradually consumed his way through the estate left by his mother. By 1803, he was living from the income of two small parcels of land; Eliza was increasingly infirm; and he was incapacitated by gout and – as Lavirotte delicately puts it – the other 'diseases which were the result of his intemperances'. When he died in 1805, his debts, including funeral costs, exceeded the value of his portable goods.[152]

Morande died one of history's great survivors. He had provoked the wrath of Louis XV, his mistress and all-powerful ministers yet lived to tell the tale. He had preserved his life and liberty in England while working for Beaumarchais and American independence. He had survived, suffered, or avoided challenges, assaults and beatings from Bate, Fontaine, d'Eon, O'Gorman, Lauraguais and Horneck. He had got away with perjury more than once and, for the most part, evaded imprisonment for debt. He had spied under the noses of the British for over a decade unmolested and served almost as long as a French police agent without being run out of town. He had pleaded the cause of a dying monarchy and braved the fury of the Girondins and Jacobins. He had witnessed the wrath of the British, the September massacres and the guillotine. Yet in the end Thanatos took him peacefully in his bed. It was a remarkable achievement.

Morande's family line did not prove so resilient. His faithful, long-suffering Eliza remained in Arnay and followed him to the grave on 28 November 1807. His brother, Louis, expired, childless, the following year. His son, George, died comparatively young, a French landed gentleman and drunkard, on 31 October 1815, just four months after the battle of Waterloo. With him, Morande's male line was extinguished. George's five children were all daughters, of whom three died in childhood, one became a nun and the other never married. Thus Morande's only legitimate great-grandchildren were the descendants of Betsey and Antoine Guiot.

And yet, mysteriously, the name Théveneau de Morande lived on. Among the prisoners arrested following the Parisian insurrection of June 1848 was a printer named Adolphe-Charles Théveneau de Morande. Was he Morande's descendant, perhaps through one of his mistresses? All we know of him, from his use of the family names Charles and (the comparatively rare) Adolphe to his employment in the print trades and, above all, his character, suggests as much. For in 1853, the prison authorities reported that he was highly 'dangerous', a 'man of bad conduct', notable for his 'insinuating character' and 'the most evil instincts' which he hid 'under an honest facade' and used to 'exercise a great influence over his comrades'. Such phrases could have been plucked directly from police reports written eight decades earlier on his more illustrious namesake.[153]

9

Afterlife: Morande in Fiction, Myth and History

Myth surrounds Morande even in death. According to Lavirotte, the ground was so deeply frozen when he died that it refused for several days to accept his 'sad remains'. This is surely untrue. For Morande died on 17 messidor of the year XIII by the revolutionary calendar, that is 5 July 1805. The ground may have been baked hard, making the gravedigger's task tougher than usual, but it was certainly not frozen. The tale is clearly a fictional parable, intended to emphasize Morande's demonic qualities.[1]

This process of demonizing Morande, transforming him from a notorious rogue into a mythical symbol of the despotism, corruption and degradation of the old regime, began in his lifetime. As we have seen, Brissot, Manuel and Pelleport all produced quasi-factual exposés portraying him as a base and cynical criminal who, having thoroughly besmirched the monarchy, thought nothing of being born again as its most dastardly agent or ruthlessly betraying rival agents. In this endeavour, they found support in the writings of Voltaire, Lauraguais, Mirabeau, d'Eon and Villette. Had they wished, they could have called on the more tainted testimony of Cagliostro and his defenders. Most damning of all, they recalled Morande's own boasts that he could 'destroy in an hour the reputation of 50 years standing'.[2]

In addition, Morande appears in his enemies' fictional works. He is one of the chief villains of the Jacobin novel *Julie philosophe*, and as we have noted, both seduces and despoils its heroine before she learns, belatedly, that he is a scoundrel of legendary proportions. Finally, Morande was also the sexually voracious villain of the allegorical novel *Les Bohémiens*, which Pelleport wrote while in the Bastille but only published in 1790.

Pelleport's story depicts Mordanes [Morande] and several other French refugees (whose identities are all thinly disguised) as a band of brigands crossing Northern France. It satirizes Morande as the chief of the '*communico-luxurico-friponiste* philosophers' who teach that 'goods, wives, fathers, mothers, sisters, brothers and especially purses are common property in this world'.[3] This is a philosophy he lives out by stealing chickens, which he sadistically tortures to death before feeding them to his criminal band, and through his monstrous libertinism. As we have noted, Mordanes rapes and sodomizes the not entirely reluctant 'Félicité Bissot' [i.e. Félicité Brissot], but he also has an on-going liaison with her mother, the insatiable Voragine. Their relationship indirectly inspires the most obscene pornographic scenario in Pelleport's entire *oeuvre*. It occurs one dark night, when a libidinous Mordanes goes searching Voragine among his sleeping band and a group of travelling monks who are sharing their bivouac. Instead, he encounters the sleeping father superior and, mistaking his beard for his lover's pudenda, parts the folds of the monk's hood and has his way with the hapless Capuchin, almost choking him in the process.[4]

If the Mordanes described here is a genuinely Sadian fiend, his monstrousness mitigated only by Pelleport's dark, slapstick humour, it is perhaps not surprising. Pelleport and the Marquis de Sade were fellow prisoners in the Bastille and probably swapped notes and incited one another's warped imaginations. Yet Pelleport's novel was ignored or reviled by his contemporaries, fell dead from the presses, and had little influence on subsequent literary and cinematic allusions to Morande.[5] These include Edouard Molinaro's *Beaumarchais* (1996), in which Morande appears briefly as the stereotypical blackmailing *libelliste*, peddling, ironically, a pamphlet treating Louis XVI's alleged impotence and, implicitly, the supposed infidelities of Marie-Antoinette. More intriguingly, a character suggestively named Théveneau de Morande 'after the traitor of the rococo impostor Cagliostro' appears in Aka Morchiladze's allegorical novel *Santa Esperanza*, which offers a parable of recent Georgian history set in a mythical Black Sea archipelago.[6]

Morande's enemies' attempts to demonize him run aground on interesting moral reefs and hypocrisy, as Morande's self-justifications reveal. As he pointed out, 'if Manuel [who was embastilled for peddling scandalous pamphlets], if Brissot had written the *Gazetier cuirassé*, the wretches, instead of saying loyally, as I do, that it was a child of anger, would extol it as the precursor of the revolution, and make it a claim to glory', rather than describing it as a 'horrendous work'.[7] Moreover, whatever Morande's crimes under the *ancien régime*, during the revolution he could present himself as more innocent than many of his enemies:

> I am guilty of a great sin, in the eyes of five or six writers, for never having dipped my pen in the blood of the victims of the revolution, in order to soil my paper . . . As it is not guided by that type of patriotism, I have always despised their opinion of me.[8]

Nor, Morande might add, was he guilty of inciting murderous (if to modern eyes heroic) slave insurrections in Guadeloupe and Saint-Domingue.

His enemies were on equally shaky ground in portraying him as 'a devil in holy water' for serving the police. If his *Gazetier cuirassé* was reprehensible, so, too, were the scandalous or pornographic pamphlet attacks on the monarchy that he pursued, and that Pelleport, Manuel and Brissot helped to distribute. Moreover, his enemies may well have been hypocritical in denouncing his espionage links with the police. There is compelling evidence to suggest, for example, that Brissot and Mirabeau worked for the police in the mid 1780s, although probably not as 'police spies' in the accepted sense.[9] Nor were they the only revolutionaries who served the monarchy before it became an embarrassment to do so. After all, under the old regime, government service was the only way to influence policy and help remodel society.

Of course, none of this absolves Morande of his blackmail, extortion, perjuries, forging of evidence, wilful slanders, nor, particularly to modern eyes, his measured opposition to the slave trade abolitionists, pimping, or brutality, particularly towards women. It does, however, muddy the waters and suggest that his moral turpitude can be overstated, or at least viewed from a variety of perspectives. Indeed, it is probable that Morande and his fellow blackmailing pamphleteers saw their own actions as little different from those of courtiers, aristocrats, ministers and financiers who pillaged the state or, by making their support contingent on favours, effectively held it to ransom. Though we should beware of embracing such moral relativism, Morande's self-justification does highlight the fact that the French Revolution threw up far worse demons than he, and frequently abetted their crimes with the full weight of state power. Perhaps it is not surprising, therefore, that for much of the nineteenth century he was best remembered as the *libelliste* who successfully blackmailed Louis XV and Madame du Barry.

Morande's reputation as a *libelliste* dominated early nineteenth-century accounts of his life. The first biographical articles are unanimous in their condemnation: while they do not portray him as the depraved monster of Girondin myth or Pelleport's graphic allegorical fantasies, they were hardly generous. Writing in the *Biographie universelle* in 1821, at the height of the Bourbon restoration, M. Foisset concluded an error-strewn article:

His audacity . . . was no longer a reason to be noticed once the press became free [i.e. from 1789]. Floating between parties, he ended by making himself suspect in the eyes of that which dominated. The *Argus patriote*, which he published from June 1791 until 10 August 1792 [sic], was denounced as a paper indirectly favourable to the court, and its author perished in the September massacres [sic]. We hasten to add that he did not merit this honour.[10]

Alfred Franklin, writing in 1865 in the *Nouvelle biographie générale*, felt that this judgement was a little too harsh, particularly in the light of Louis de Loménie's recently published *Beaumarchais et son temps* (1856). As Franklin noted, Loménie had revealed 'all the influence that advice and contact from Beaumarchais exercised on the second half of the pamphleteer's life' and that in the '*Argus patriotique*' [sic] Morande 'defended the monarchic party with courage and talent'. Franklin therefore concluded ambiguously:

> Morande has so far been treated too severely: the just contempt excited by his early years
> has fallen on his entire life, and his name, become one of the most denounced *libellistes*
> of the eighteenth century, has not yet encountered an impartial judge.[11]

Franklin's ambiguity was carried over into the first full-length biography of
Morande, Paul Robiquet's *Théveneau de Morande: Étude au Dix-huitième Siècle*,
[*Théveneau de Morande: A Study in the Eighteenth Century*] published in 1882.
As the sub-title suggests, Robiquet wished to suggest that Morande was in many
ways emblematic of his era and, on this score, his concluding remarks did not
disappoint. For Robiquet, Morande was:

> A hybrid and complex figure, who personifies simultaneously the superficial and brilliant
> understanding of the eighteenth century, the corruption of the society whose era was
> coming to a close, and the tumultuous aspirations of the [new] society which was arising
> . . . a flesh and blood Figaro, so devious that he exploited Beaumarchais himself.[12]

Robiquet's biography was, in many ways, a remarkable achievement, but it was
limited by its dependence on printed sources. Thus, although he exploited the
letters concerning Morande's imprisonment in Ravaisson's *Archives de la Bastille*,
he ignored the rest of the rich documentation in Morande's prison dossiers.
Likewise, he was reliant on the hostile reports concerning Morande's liaisons
with the police in Pelleport's *Diable dans un bénitier*, Manuel's *Police dévoilée*
and the *Mémoires secrets*, but was unaware of his extensive espionage and police
correspondence in the French foreign ministry archives. Nor did he have access
to British newspaper sources, Beaumarchais' unpublished correspondence with
Morande, or most of the archival materials on Morande's relations with d'Eon.
His treatment of Morande's journalism depended almost exclusively on the *Argus
patriote*. Thus, Robiquet's biography contains major gaps, as well as attributing
several works to Morande erroneously.

Ironically, these mistaken attributions helped keep Morande alive in public
memory from the 1880s to 1914. For, inspired by the Goncourt brothers, whose
voluminous writings included several books dedicated to the most celebrated
actresses, courtesans and royal mistresses, the late nineteenth century witnessed
a rediscovery of the libertine literature and sub-culture of the old regime. As
a result, the decades prior to World War One witnessed the republication of
numerous late-eighteenth-century scandalous works, usually with short pseudo-
scholarly introductions. Among them were the *Gazetier cuirassé*, the *Portefeuille
de Madame Gourdan*, and Mairobert's *Anecdotes sur Madame du Barry*, which
was not infrequently erroneously attributed to Morande. These new editions
were probably aimed as much at Third Republic libertines as true bibliophiles,
but they nevertheless kept Morande's name and notoriety alive among literary

historians and the cognoscenti. However, by the 1960s, he and his works were almost universally forgotten, particularly outside France. This obscurity was not to last.

In 1971 Morande was propelled to the centre of the historical stage by the iconoclastic young American historian Robert Darnton. His pathbreaking essay 'The High Enlightenment and the Low-Life of Literature', suggests that Morande was the archetype of those Grub Street literary hacks who, according to Darnton, desacralized the Bourbon monarchy, stripping it of its sacred aura, thereby preparing the revolution. Ironically, this was a distinction Morande shared with Brissot and Brissot's allies, Carra, Manuel and Gorsas, as well as other writers who failed to make it into the high-brow, feather-bedded literary *monde* of the enlightenment and so did not benefit from the state's literary patronage. Yet it was Morande who furnished his prime example. According to Darnton, works such as the *Gazetier cuirassé* 'expressed the passion of men who hated the old regime in their guts, who ached with hatred . . . [and] . . . began the political education' of the common people, who, unable to understand the high-brow political philosophy of Rousseau, 'would soon be reading *Le Père Duchesne* [Jacque-René Hébert's influential, obscene and extreme revolutionary political paper]'.[13] Such men, Darnton claimed, were nihilistic in outlook and expression:

> Morande . . . and his fellow hacks had no interest in reform. They hated the system in itself: and they expressed that hatred by desanctifying its symbols, destroying the myths that gave it legitimacy in the eyes of the public, and perpetrating the countermyth of degenerate despotism.[14]

Darnton's essay is one of the richest and most influential historical articles ever written. At a moment when literary scholars were beginning to look beyond the traditional canon of 'great literature', Darnton suggested that historians needed to do the same thing. For Darnton, texts like the *Gazetier cuirassé* were more important than high enlightenment texts for communicating subversive messages to the French people.[15]

This biography suggests that in many ways Morande does not fit Darnton's model.[16] He was no nihilist or radical revolutionary, either before 1789 or thereafter. While he detested the old regime hierarchy and wished for sweeping constitutional reforms in Church and State, he remained a committed constitutional monarchist throughout his career and was an advocate of strong executive power. Within this framework, he was strongly committed to order and the rule of law. Nor can he be dismissed, in Iain McCalman's words, as 'Europe's most dangerous pen for hire', for he argued his views with such consistency that he cannot be suspected of cynicism.[17] His views were sincerely held and forcefully argued, even when the revolution's lurch to the left made that risky. His political interventions in the *Gazetier cuirassé* must thus be understood within the context of the old regime as a rejection of the despotism and corruption associated with a single ministry and a specific royal mistress. His points, exaggerated for satirical and rhetorical effect, indict individuals and widespread abuses, but they do not reject monarchy *per se*, still less call for a radical or republican revolution. Abuses and ministerial despotism are equally castigated in the editorial columns of the *Courier de l'Europe* and their passing is applauded in the *Argus patriote*. Such conclusions are supported by the work of Gunnar and Mavis von Proschwitz, who noted as long ago as 1990 that 'in the role of pedagogue in political matters [between 1787 and 1792], Morande played the most important role of his life' by attempting to educate Frenchmen in the principles of constitutional monarchy and the rule of law.[18] Thus, beyond the scurrility and venality of the blackmailer lurks a previously unsuspected political ideology of patriotic reform and commitment to the principles of constitutional monarchy. This was, intriguingly, a position that he appears to have shared with some of London's other blackmailer-pamphleteers. These masterless men and women were would-be reformers of the old regime rather than harbingers of the new.[19]

This is not to deny Morande's writings an important destabilizing or revolutionary effect. For building on the example set by the *Gazetier cuirassé*, the violence of subsequent scandalous texts intensified, particularly from 1789. This was true both of content and rhetoric. Morande played a major role in developing discourses which portrayed France as a despotic state, while revolutionary political pornography drew heavily upon anti-Marie-Antoinette blackmail pamphlets whose authors had been inspired by Morande's example. Likewise, revolutionary political essay journalism drew upon the declamatory style and single issue focus that Morande had helped to pioneer before the revolution. As a result, Morande is heavily implicated in some of the most subversive literary developments of the entire period.

Morande is thus a character of extraordinary complexity, unsuspected loyalties, often treacherous and full of unexpected paradoxes. If we take him as merely a representative figure, whether as the incarnation of evil, epitome of an eighteenth-century 'rogue', 'prince of blackmailers', muckraking pamphleteer, archetypical Grub-Street hack, constitutional monarchist, journalist, anglophile, French patriot or spy, we will surely fail to understand him. His multi-faceted career and influence embraced all these roles.

A tale of intrigue, blackmail, espionage, kidnap, murder, politics, conspiracy and crime, Morande's life story has all the ingredients of a suspense thriller. At the same time, it sheds light on many of the most important issues for historians of the revolutionary period. These include the role of scandal and scandalous pamphleteering in the origins of the revolution and how the French government came to be seen increasingly as despotic, both through the printed word and its own actions; the political and cultural influence of London's exile community; and the practice and significance of journalism and espionage in the age of the American and French Revolutions. It also sheds new – and often unflattering – light on the biographies and reputations of numerous prominent literary and political figures, among them Louis XV, Beaumarchais, Mirabeau and Brissot.

Yet, Morande was more than a bit-part actor in the lives and events that he manipulated and described. He was also a phenomenon in his own right: a notorious anti-hero of his day, yet also a reformist Cassandra who warned of the dangers of revolutionary excess.[20] His career and success reveal the possibilities inherent in the expansive, globally focused age in which he lived. It was a moment when information was increasingly available but also an increasingly valuable commodity, and most of Morande's careers were based upon this insight. Whether acting as a scandalous pamphleteer, journalist, financial speculator, blackmailer, spy, political analyst, or advisor to governments, Morande depended on acquiring, presenting and manipulating information. It is tempting to speculate what might become of a man of Morande's talents in a contemporary egalitarian, democratic, consumerist Western society. Would he become a tabloid journalist or popular blogger? A political commentator or celebrity satirist? An intelligence analyst or a spook? A politician or diplomat? An investment guru, speculator, big businessman or insider dealer? Or would the stain of a youthful criminal record forever close such careers to him and drive him into a life of pimping or crime? Viewed in this light, his biography perhaps has more relevance to the citizens of a postmodern 'information society' than to our nineteenth and twentieth-century forebears. If it is a parable, it is one for our own times.

Glossary

abbé	abbot. Abbés were usually absentee sinecure holders
antiphysique	homosexual
bardache	passive male partner in sodomy
bona fide	genuine; a reference proving credentials
chez	[at/in] the home of
cour	court
dauphin	the heir to the throne
département	largest geographic unit of revolutionary local government
écu	unit of currency worth 3 *livres*
femmes galantes	women of loose sexual morals
Feuillants	French constitutional monarchist party in 1791–1792
fille de joie	prostitute
fils	son
galanteries	amorous liaisons / amorous adventures
grande dame	great/high ranking lady
greluchon	favoured lover of a woman who sells sex to others
guerluchonnage	lifestyle associated with having a *greluchon*
Jacobin	member of Jacobin club, committed left-wing revolutionary
Jansenism	quasi-Protestant movement within French Catholicism
Jesuits	members of hard-line pro-Papal Catholic religious order
lettre de cachet	arbitrary arrest order (literally, sealed letter)
libelle	scandalous pamphlet (also a lampoon or any pamphlet)
libelliste	writer of scandalous pamphlets
livre	unit of currency
Louis	unit of currency worth 20 *livres*
marchande de modes	seller of fashionable accessories, trinkets, ribbons, etc.

monarchiens	moderate constitutional monarchist grouping in 1789
nouvelles à la main	manuscript newsletters
nouvellistes	writers of *nouvelles à la main*
old regime	social and political structure of pre-revolutionary France
parlements	sovereign law courts of France (see chapter 2)
parlementaires	magistrate sitting in, or supporters of, the *parlements*
patriote	supporter of reform in 1770s, and later of revolution
philosophe(s)	French enlightenment philosopher
politiques	men active in the world of high politics
roi	king
Sieur	squire, as in Monsieur

Abbreviations

AB	François Ravaisson, *Archives de la Bastille*, 19 vols (Paris: Durand et Pedone-Lauriel, 1866–1904)
ADCO	Archives départementales de la Côte d'Or, Dijon
Add. MS.	Additional Manuscripts (in BL)
AFB	Archives de la famille Beaumarchais, Morande-Beaumarchais correspondence
AN	Archives nationales, Paris
AP	*L'Argus patriote ou le surveillant*
Arsenal	Bibliothèque de l'Arsenal, Paris
BCE	Gunnar and Mavis von Proschwitz, *Beaumarchais et le Courier de l'Europe: documents inédits ou peu connus*, 2 vols, *SVEC* 273–4 (Oxford: Voltaire Foundation, 1990)
BL	British Library
BMT	Bibliothèque municipale de Tonnerre
BN	Bibliothèque nationale, Paris
CE	*Courier de l'Europe*
CL	*Courier de Londres* (this was the London edition of the *CE* and is dated one day after the continental edition)
CPA	Correspondance politique, Angleterre (this series is in the MAE)
CSB	Didier Ozanam and Michel Antoine (eds), *Correspondance secrète du comte de Broglie avec Louis XV*, 2 vols (Paris: Klincksieck, 1956–1961)
CSCV	M. de Lescure (ed.), *Correspondance secrète inédite sur Louis XVI, Marie-Antoinette, la cour et la ville de 1777–1792*, 2 vols (Paris: Plon, 1866)
CSI	M. E. Boutaric (ed.), *Correspondance secrète inédite de Louis XV*, 2 vols (Paris: Plon, 1866)
CSMT	*Correspondance secrète entre Marie-Thérèse et le comte Mercy-d'Argenteau*, ed. A. von Arneth and M. Geoffroy, 2nd edition, 3 vols (Paris: Firmin-Didot: 1874–1875)

CSP	*Correspondance secrète, politique et littéraire, ou mémoires pour servir à l'histoire des cours, des sociétés et de la littérature en France, depuis la mort de Louis XV*, 18 vols (London: John Adamson, 1787–1790)
LMA	London Metropolitan Archives
MAE	Archives du Ministère des affaires étrangères, Paris
MD	Mémoires et documents series (in the MAE)
MSB	Bachaumont, Louis Petit de, (attrib.), *Mémoires secrets pour servir à l'histoire de la république de lettres en France, depuis 1762 jusqu'à nos jours*, 36 vols (London: John Adamson, 1777–1787)
MO	Médiathèque d'Orléans, Lenoir papers
NA	National Archives, Kew (formerly known as the Public Records Office)
SHD	Service historique de la défense, Château de Vincennes, Paris
SVEC	*Studies on Voltaire and the Eighteenth Century*
ULBC	University of Leeds, Brotherton Library, Brotherton Collection, papers of the Chevalier d'Eon

Notes

Notes to prologue: Auto da fé

1   On the *auto da fé* and manoeuvres that preceded it, see above, pp. 57–70.
2   It is not certain that d'Eon was personally present at the burning, though he suggested the venue. Both Beaumarchais and d'Eon claim that they first met the following year, though they offer contradictory accounts of their meeting. See Donald Spinelli, 'Beaumarchais and d'Eon: what an affair' in Simon Burrows, Jonathan Conlin, Russell Goulbourne and Valerie Mainz, eds, *The Chevalier d'Eon and His Worlds: Gender, Espionage and Politics in the Eighteenth Century* (London: Continuum, 2010), pp. 57–71, at pp. 60–1.
3   See, for example, *MSB*, I, 1 January 1762; VII, 13 February 1774.
4   *MSB*, VII, entry for 7 June 1773.
5   The only previous biography of Morande is Paul Robiquet, *Théveneau de Morande: étude sur le XVIIIe siècle* (Paris: Quantin, 1882). This can be supplemented by *BCE*, which contains over 600 documents, many of which relate to Morande, and my own works, notably, 'A literary low-life reassessed: Charles Théveneau de Morande in London, 1769–1791', *Eighteenth-Century Life* 22:1 (1998), 76–94, and *Blackmail, Scandal, and Revolution: London's French Libellistes, 1758–1791* (Manchester University Press, 2006).
6   These rumours – repeated in several nineteenth-century sources – are probably a case of mistaken identity, as one of Louis XV's servants and procurers was named Morand.
7   The satirist Pietro Aretino [Aretin] (1492–1556), the inventor of modern literary pornography, famed for the depictions of sexual positions that accompanied his works.
8   Beaumarchais to unknown correspondent, Paris, 24 January 1781, in *BCE*, I, 112–15, at p. 113; CPA 517 fo 242, d'Eon's second 'billet' to Morande, 8 August 1776 (the original French text appears in CPA 517 fos 239–40 and CPA supplément 17 fos 11–12); Pierre-Louis Manuel, *La Police de Paris dévoilée*, 2 vols (Paris: Garnery, l'an II de la liberté [1791]), II, 265. Manuel's statement was republished by Jacques-Pierre Brissot in *Patriote françois* no. 740, 19 August 1791, p. 212, in an article entitled *Réponse de Jacques-Pierre Brissot à tous les libellistes qui ont attaqué et attaquent sa vie passée*, which had appeared as a pamphlet several days earlier.
9   Gary Kates, *Monsieur d'Eon is a Woman: A Tale of Political Intrigue and Sexual Masquerade* (New York: Basic Books, 1995), p. 214; Peter Wagner, *Eros Revived: Erotica of the Enlightenment in England and America* (London: Paladin, 1988), p. 91; Robiquet, *Théveneau de Morande*, p. 307.
10   Robert Darnton, 'The high enlightenment and the low-life of literature in prerevolutionary France', *Past and Present* no. 51 (1971), 81–115.
11   Robert Darnton, *Forbidden Best-Sellers of Pre-Revolutionary France* (London: Harper Collins, 1996), p. 65. Unfortunately Darnton's figures, which come from orders to a single publishing house, attribute to Morande several works that were almost certainly produced by other writers.

Notes to Chapter 1: The Sins of his Youth

1   Morande's uncle's full name was also Charles-Claude but he was apparently known as Claude.
2   Andrea de Nerciat, André-Robert (attrib.), *Julie philosophe, ou le bon patriote*, 2 vols (Paris: Le Coffret des Bibliophiles, 1910 [original edition, 1791]), II, 10.

3   Genealogical and professional information on the Théveneau family is taken from the État Civil d'Arnay-le-Duc in the Mairie of Arnay-le-Duc (which is indexed) and the unindexed copies in ADCO, 2E26/4–24. I have also consulted miscellaneous articles from the *Pays d'Arnay* (the bulletin of the Association des Amis du Pays d'Arnay) supplied by its editor, Bernard Leblanc. See also the brief article by A. Albrier, 'Charles Théveneau de Morande', *Bulletin du Bouquiniste*, 15 December 1875, 1–4.

4   His first documented use of the name 'Théveneau de Morande' is in Arsenal, MS 12,345 fos 198–9, Morande to Sartine, 4 August 1769. For rental contracts on his family's small holdings see ADCO, 4E64/261.

5   The information in this and the preceding paragraph is from E. Badin and M. Quantin, *Géographie départementale, classique et administrative de la France. Département de La Côte d'Or* (Paris: J. Debochet, Le Chevalier et cie, 1847) and the 1793 census of the district of Arnay-sur-Arroux (the revolutionary name for Arnay-le-Duc): ADCO, L 1274. In 1793, the canton of Arnay had a population of 2,550. No other settlement in the district (total population 6,804) had a fair.

6   Both Morande's son and his brother Lazare would marry first cousins. Others who signed Morande's parents' wedding register included Philiberte's parents, Antoine Belin and Marie Hoüard; her brother Gabriel Belin; her maternal cousin Claude Bauzon; the groom's parents Charles Théveneau and Rose Despres; his uncle Guy Théveneau; and his first cousin Pierre Guichot.

7   See p. 192.

8   Morande's grandparents, Charles Théveneau and Rose Despres, lost 10 children in early infancy.

9   The best source of information on Philiberte Belin and Morande's siblings is the Morande-Beaumarchais correspondence in the Archives de la Famille Beaumarchais [AFB], which remain in private hands. A significant portion of this correspondence is published in *BCE*, but letters concerning Morande's family are mostly omitted or abridged. For example, the quotes in this and the previous paragraph are from AFB fos 22–5, Morande to Beaumarchais, 24 January 1786, but do not appear in the published version, *BCE*, document 460.

10 The tales of Morande's youthful escapades come from César Lavirotte, 'Notice sur M. de Morande', unpublished manuscript. I thank M. Bernard Leblanc for supplying a transcribed copy of this manuscript, which was uncovered by Claude Guyot (1890–1965), mayor of Arnay-le-Duc, among Lavirotte's papers. Lavirotte's sources included local folk memory; his own recollections; conversations with Morande; and published materials. Many episodes Lavirotte recounts can be verified, often only from sources unavailable to its author. Where Lavirotte makes verifiable errors it is usually due to reliance on published sources. The stories recounted here probably came from village legend or Morande himself.

11 Morande, *Réplique de Charles Théveneau Morande à Jacques-Pierre Brissot: sur les erreurs, les infidélités et les calomnies de sa Réponse* (Paris: Froullé, 1791), p. 7, says he continued his studies until 17 years old. This implies he attended university.

12 SHD, 4YC[11], Contrôle des troupes, dragons de Bauffremont, 1748–1760: 6e Etat, Compagnie d'Aigremont; YB[605], Contrôle des officiers: Bauffremont, fo 22. The former document appears to refute Morande's statement that his father's friend took him to join up in late 1759.

13 The table of the social backgrounds of over 16,000 soldiers recruited between 1753 and 1763 in André Corvisart, *L'Armée française de la fin du XVIIe siècle au ministère de Choiseul. Le Soldat*, 2 vols (Paris, 1964), I, 467, suggests that less than 1 per cent came from bourgeois families. Corvisart also reveals (I, 533–4) that in a sample of 138 soldiers in Morande's regiment, over 70 per cent could sign their name and almost 38 per cent held a pen well.

14 Morande's critical comments are found in *Le Gazetier cuirassé ou anecdotes scandaleuses de la cour de France* (n. p. [London], 1771), pt I, 'Le Gazetier cuirassé', pp. 37–8, 59–60, 66, 151–2; pt II, *Mélanges confus sur des matières forts claires*, pp. 3–5. The *Gazetier* also contains a third part, *Le Philosophe cynique*. As each part resembles a separate pamphlet and is paginated separately, henceforth they are referred to as Parts I, II and III respectively.

15 This account of Morande's military career is taken from Morande, *Réplique à Brissot*, p. 7. Lavirotte's 'Notice sur Morande' says his father bought him out.

16 There appears to be some poetic licence in Morande's description of his 'comrades' lying dead, since SHD, 4YC[11], Contrôle des troupes, dragons de Bauffremont, reveals that no one in his regiment was killed in July 1761.

17 BL, Add. MS 11, 340, fo 21, cutting from *Public Advertiser*, 5 September 1776 and *passim*.
18 SHD, 4YC[11]: Contrôle des troupes, dragons de Bauffremont, 1748–1760; 7YC[3]: Contrôle des troupes, dragons Bauffremont, Lorraine 1763–1776.
19 For the regimental records see SHD, 4YC[11]; 6YC73; 7YC[3]; YB[104]; YB[605]; YB[839]. For other documents concerning Morande's claims, see BL, Add. MS 11, 340, fos 24 and 34, *Westminster Gazette*, 3–7 and 10–14 September 1776; Morande, *Réplique à Brissot*, p. 18; Arsenal MS 12,345, fos 132–3, Marais to Sartine, 17 May 1768; *Morning Chronicle*, 12 October 1776. Poyane's letter read: 'In the corps of Carabiniers, Sir, there has been no such officer as Demorande, and no Field Officer, nor even any other Officer of that corps has been in England.' Thus Morande's counter-assertion (*Morning Chronicle*, 14 October 1776) that he had claimed only to be in the 'suite' of the Carabiniers [i.e. a staff officer] and not a 'Field Officer' was specious. An accompanying letter from the (conveniently deceased) Marquis de Chauvelin, which turned down Poyane's recommendation of Morande to serve as Chauvelin's aide-de-camp in Corsica in 1768, was also irrelevant to the discussion, and perhaps a forgery. When Morande was arrested in 1765, he seems only to have mentioned his service in the Bauffremont regiment. His narrative of his military service in the *Réplique à Brissot* leaves little time for his promotion to an elite unit. The story is also improbable because neither side suffered cavalry losses at Vellinghausen.
20 Morande, *Réplique à Brissot*, p. 8.
21 Lavirotte, 'Notice sur Morande'.
22 The indexes to the Etat Civil at Arnay-le-Duc reveal that there was indeed a widow Finel or Finelle in Arnay. Her maiden name was Anne Follot, and between May 1723 and April 1747 she had 15 children by three different husbands. Her final spouse was Etienne Finelle, a merchant, who originally came from Précy-sous-Thil, 30 kilometres from Arnay. Ten of her children were buried at Arnay, but all died either in childhood or after 1805. Of the remaining five, only one, Jacques Noirot, was male. He was 38 or 39 at the time of the alleged duel and so, quite apart from the burial evidence, seems an unlikely candidate for fighting a man almost 20 years his junior. Nor is it likely that Lavirotte was merely confused about Morande's rival's identity. Only four men aged between 14 and 35 were buried in Arnay between 1762 and 1764 (the years when the duel could have occurred). They comprised a saddler, a tailor, a gardener who died of an infection, and a passing soldier, who was found dead in his lodgings. None seems a likely challenger for Morande, and none shared a surname or next of kin (where listed) with any woman who died in the same time period. Moreover, the Follot and Théveneau clans remained tied by blood and friendship. Anne Follot was related to the Théveneaus through her first husband, Jean Noirot, and in 1841 a Dr Jean-Jacques Follot married Morande's granddaughter, Louise Guiot. Louis, Claude and Charles Théveneau were witnesses at Anne Follot's wedding to Etienne Finelle.
23 This account of Morande's adventures follows Morande, *Réplique à Brissot*, pp. 8–12.
24 Arsenal, MS 12,345 fo 136, Juliot to Sartine, undated letter [c. May 1768].
25 Morande, *Réplique à Brissot*, p. 12. Morande cited as a witness for his life history up until 1764, M. Buillote, curate at Arnay-le-Duc, who at the time that Morande wrote (1791) was a deputy in the National Assembly.
26 Pamela Cheek, 'Prostitutes of "political institution"', *Eighteenth-Century Studies*, 28 (2) (1994–5), pp. 193–219.
27 Arsenal, MS 12,247 fos 315–16, La Saule to Sartine, rue du Battoir, 3 March 1765. La Saule claims this money was given to Morande by his family and that they sent further sums subsequently. His father's testimony that Morande had slipped away contradicts this. It is not clear whether La Saule was aware of the truth.
28 His victims probably included Monsieur de Seguenot, a Burgundian gentleman; Monsieur Faillers [?], doctor to the King of Poland; and Monsieur de La Chaise, whose watches had all been pawned by Morande. All are named in an explanatory letter to La Janière, who was suspicious about the watches. Morande claimed that all been lent to help him raise funds following gambling losses, and that he had repaid their owners. He added that La Saule could confirm these facts. See Arsenal, MS 12,247 fos 311–12, Morande to La Janière, 22 February 1765.
29 Arsenal MS 12,345, fos 132–3, Marais to Sartine, 17 May 1768. Marais repeated his assertion that Morande was strongly 'suspected of pederasty' in an annotation on MS 12,345, fo 196–7, Morande to Sartine, 26 July 1769.
30 This discussion of eighteenth-century French homosexual sub-cultures is drawn primarily from Olivier Blanc, 'The Italian taste in the time of Louis XVI' in Jeffrey Merrick and Michael

Sibalis, eds, *Homosexuality in French Culture and History* (Binghampton, NY: Haworth Press, 2001), pp. 69–84; Jeffrey Merrick, 'The Marquis de Villette and Mademoiselle de Raucourt: representations of male and female sexual deviance in late eighteenth-century France' in Jeffrey Merrick and Bryant T. Ragan Jr., eds, *Homosexuality in Modern France* (Oxford University Press, 1996), pp. 30–53.

31   Arsenal, MS 12,247 fos 303–4, La Janière to Sartine, 17 February 1765. (This letter is reproduced in *AB*, XII, 475).

32   Ibid.

33   Arsenal, MS 12,247 fos 315–16, La Saule to Sartine, 3 March 1765.

34   Ibid., fo 320, Sartine to Saint-Florentin [undated]. Annotated by Saint-Florentin 'bon pour ordre', 14 March 1765.

35   Ibid., fos 315–16, La Saule to Sartine, 3 March 1765; MS 12,345 fos 198–9, Morande to Sartine, 4 August 1769.

36   Arsenal, Bastille MS 12,345 fo 164, Antoine Durand, lace merchant, to Sartine, rue de Grenelle, Faubourg St Germain, undated letter received 15 July 1768. Of the three ducal branches of the family, Durand probably meant to indicate the Duke de Sully-Bethune: members of that branch are mentioned in Morande, *Réplique à Brissot*, p. 18.

37   Arsenal, MS 12,345 fos 198–9, Morande to Sartine, 4 August 1769; fos 132–3, Marais to Sartine, 17 May 1768. (The latter letter is reproduced in *AB*, XII, 481–2.)

38   Ibid., fos 160–1, Jumeau (tailor) to Sartine, undated letter received 14 July 1768.

39   Ibid., fos 132–3, Marais to Sartine, 17 May 1768 (reproduced in *AB*, XII, 481–2); fo 162–3, Sébastien Frelle to Sartine, undated letter received 15 July 1768; fo 165, Lasagne dit La Forest to Sartine, undated letter received 16 July 1765.

40   Arsenal, Bastille MS 12,345 fo 164, Antoine Durand to Sartine, rue de Grenelle, Faubourg St Germain, undated letter received 15 July 1768; fo 159, Ketteng (jeweller) to Sartine, 14 July 1768; fos 160–1, Jumeau (tailor) to Sartine, undated letter received 14 July 1768.

41   Save where indicated, the detail in this and the next three paragraphs is taken from Arsenal, MS 12,345 fos 132–3, Marais to Sartine, 17 May 1768, (*AB*, XII, 481–2). Intriguingly, two of the women this letter mentions, Mesdemoiselles La Cour and Desmares are also mistreated in an anonymous pamphlet sometimes attributed to Morande, *Les Joueurs et M. Dusaulx* (Agripinae [London]: N. Lescot, 1781 [first edition, 1780]). The attribution is nevertheless almost certainly wrong: see pp. 152–3.

42   Quote in Anon., *Joueurs*, p. 9. Bicêtre is mentioned only in Anne-Gédeon de Lafite de Pelleport (attrib.), *Le Diable dans un bénitier et le Gazetier Cuirassé transformé en mouche* (London, 1783), p. 34 and CPA 516 fos 211–18, d'Eon to Vergennes, London, 27 May 1776 [also at BMT, R20]. The rest of the incident is mentioned by Marais. On Charlotte Desmares and Angélique Delavaux, a.k.a. *la Beauchamp*, see also Camille Piton, ed., *Paris sous Louis XV: rapports des Inspecteurs de police au roi*, 5 vols (Paris: Mercure de France, 1906–1914), I, 353; II, 135; IV, 78–106. I have been unable to verify *la Beauchamp's* relationship with Casanova from his *Memoirs*.

43   *Guerluchonnage* was a contemporary term and is used by Marais, although it does not appear in any modern or historical dictionary I have consulted. It signifies the practice of having more than one lover while supposedly a kept woman and presumably derived from the term *greluchon*, which means the favoured, secret lover of a woman who makes other men pay for her favours. Morande himself provides a brief definition of *greluchon* in his *Gazetier cuirassé* (pt. III, *clef des nouvelles*, p. vii), where he says that custom allows theatre girls three lovers: 'un entreteneur, un bon ami, et un troisième amant domestique, qui s'apelle [sic] un greluchon'.

44   On La Cour see Piton, ed., *Paris sous Louis XV*, II, 253, 258; *MSB*, XVIII, entry of 7 April 1768 (this entry is out of chronological sequence: 7 January 1768 is probably intended). On Sonville or Souville, also known as Frédérique, see Piton, op. cit., I, 335, 339; II, 212; III, 188, 202, 261–2.

45   Manuel, *Police dévoilée*, I, 265 affirms that Morande took La Cour away from Lamballe. If true, she must have returned to Lamballe, as she refused to leave his deathbed until offered a large sum of money. Lamballe died after falling from a horse: see Alain Vircondelet, *La Princesse de Lamballe: l'ange de Marie-Antoinette* (Paris: Flammarion, 2005).

46   [Morande], *Gazetier cuirassé*, pt III, p. 87.

47   On the d'Oppy case see Mathieu-François Pidansat de Mairobert (attrib.), *L'Espion anglois, ou correspondance secrète entre Milord All'Eye et Milord All'Ear*, nouvelle édition, 10 vols (London: John Adamson, 1779–1785), II, 50–64 (which is sceptical of d'Oppy's defence); and *MSB*, IX,

entries for 19, 20 and 23 June 1776. The link to Morande is made in Arsenal, MS 12,345 fos 132-3, Marais to Sartine, 17 May 1768. Although Marais refers to d'Oppy as 'demoiselle', a term usually reserved for unmarried women, he also says her papers are 'under seals'. This seems to confirm that Morande's d'Oppy is indeed the gentlewoman arrested a month earlier *chez la Gourdan*. A letter from Morande was found among her papers.

48 Morande, *Réplique à Brissot*, p. 13; Arsenal, MS 12,345 fo 136, Juliot to Sartine, [undated]; fos 137-8, copy of the power of attorney of Louis Théveneau; fo 152, certified true copy of letter of Claude Théveneau to [Juliot]; fo 153, certificate of Juliot and (on the reverse) the original of the power of attorney of Louis Théveneau, dated Arnay-le-Duc, 27 January 1768.

49 For Danezy's history see Arsenal, MS 12,345 fos 132-3, Marais to Sartine, 17 May 1768 at fo 133 (*AB*, XII, 482). Delamotte is no relation of Henri de La Motte or the Count and Countess de La Motte who feature later in this book.

50 Ibid., fos 126-7, Desmoulins, huissier à cheval to [Sartine], 8 April 1768.

51 Ibid., fos 124-5 Morande to Sartine, 5 May 1768. (This letter is reproduced in *AB*, XII, 479-81).

52 Ibid., fos 130-1, Clermont-Arnoul to Sartine, 17 May 1768.

53 Manuel, *Police dévoilée*, I, 265.

54 Arsenal, MS 12,345 fos 128-9, Flesselles to Sartine, undated letter, [c. 11 May 1768]; fos 131-2, Marais to Sartine, 17 May 1768 (*AB*, XII, 481-2); Morande, *Réplique à Brissot*, p. 13.

55 Arsenal, MS 12,345 fos 134-5, Danezy to Sartine, 24 May 1768; Sartine's annotations on the same, dated 25 May 1768; Morande, *Réplique à Brissot*, p. 13. Saint-Florentin signed an order for Morande's arrest on 27 May.

56 Arsenal, MS 12,345 fos 141-2, Marais to Sartine, 25 June 1768; fos 139-40, Saint-Florentin to Sartine, 27 May 1768.

57 Ibid., fos 148-9, Duvergé to Sartine, Fort l'Évêque, 6 July 1768. (This letter is reproduced in *AB*, XII, 483-4).

58 Ibid., fos 143-4, Bethune to Sartine, 2 July 1768. Bethune, a member of one of France's leading noble families, claimed Morande's family had asked him to look out for him. One can only imagine the reply that Sartine sent him five days later!

59 Ibid., fos 150-1, Juliot to Sartine, 10 July 1768; fo 154, Louis Théveneau to Sartine, 9 July 1768; fos 168-9, Marais to Sartine, 22 July 1768 (*AB*, XII, 486).

60 Arsenal, MS 12,345 fos 175-6, Morande to Sartine, Armentières, 27 July 1768; fos 177-8, Morande to Sartine, Armentières, 10 August 1768. The letters of Morande's creditors are filed in MS 12,345. Several are cited above.

61 Arsenal, MS 12,345 fos 183-4 Croquison to Sartine, Armentières, 4 May 1769 (this letter is reproduced in *AB*, XII, 485); fos 185-6, Morande to Sartine, Armentières, 4 May 1769; fos 187-8, Juliot to Sartine, undated letter; fo 189, procuration of Louis Théveneau, Arnay-le-Duc, 30 May 1769.

62 Arsenal, MS 12,345, Croquison to La Saule, Armentières, undated letter, annotated 1 June 1769; fo 192, Sartine to Saint Florentin, 7 June 1769; fos 194-5, Croquison to Sartine, Armentières, 17 July 1769 (this letter is reproduced in *AB*, XII, 485).

63 Ibid., fos 196-7, Morande to Sartine, 26 July 1769, including annotations; fos 198-9, Morande to Sartine, 4 August 1769 and annotations; fos 202-3, Morande to Sartine, 13 August 1769.

64 Ibid., fos 200-1, Morande to Bignicourt, undated letter; fos 204-5, Commissaire Chénu to Sartine, Amiens, 8 December 1768.

65 Ibid., fos 210-11, Narbens to Sartine, 13 May 1769, and Sartine's annotations on the same.

66 Morande, *Réplique à Brissot*, p. 17.

67 Ibid., pp. 17-18.

Notes to Chapter 2: The Armour-Plated Gazetteer

1 AN, 277AP/1, dossier Morande, fos 347-8, Morande to d'Eon [1773].

2 Ibid., fo 377, Morande to d'Eon, undated letter [1770 or 1771].

3 [Morande], *Gazetier cuirassé*, pt I, p. vi.

4 CPA 502 fos 177-9, d'Eon to Broglie, London, 13 July 1773, implies that Morande had told d'Eon

that La Vrillière (rather than Sartine) was behind his flight. For Morande's mendacious tale and the ode, see Morande, *Réplique à Brissot*, pp. 15–17.

5 Jeremy Boosey and Ernst Roth, *Boosey and Hawkes 150th Anniversary* (London: Boosey and Hawkes, 1966), p. 1.

6 *The Register Book of Marriages of the Parish of Saint-George Hanover Square in the County of Middlesex* (Harleain Society, 1886), I, 208. Morande's address appears in Morande to d'Eon, 15 July 1771, AN, 277AP/1, dossier Morande, fos 321–2.

7 In November 1773, d'Eon refers to Morande having three infant children, which implies that two children – possibly twins – were born within 22 months of George. These included a daughter baptized on 11 July 1773: Morande invited d'Eon to be her 'godmother' (see CPA 502 fos 177–9, d'Eon to Broglie, London, 13 July 1773). Undated cuttings from the *Lloyds Evening Post* and the *Universal Magazine* from 1777 preserved in the Brotherton Library, Leeds, in their extra-illustrated edition of Ernest Alfred Vizetelly, *The True Story of the Chevalier d'Eon* (London: Tylston and Edwards and A. P. Marsden, 1895), compiled by A.M. Broadley and bound in seven folio volumes, suggest Morande made another such request on 3 July 1774. Or perhaps the newspapers confused the dates? In an undated letter from 1773 (CPA 503 fo 378), Morande refers to having 'the posterity of Jacob'. D'Eon refers to a further child, born in December 1775 and in August 1776 Eliza was seven months pregnant. Nothing more is known about the children who died in infancy.

8 Lavirotte, 'Notice sur Morande'.

9 AFB fos 34–5 Eliza to Beaumarchais, Cachan, 16 August 1782 (published abridged in *BCE*, II, 713n. 4); fos 20–1, Morande to Philiberte Belin, 23 March 1786.

10 Francy to Beaumarchais, 8 February 1784, cited in *BCE*, I, 119.

11 CPA 502 fos 182–3, Eon to Broglie, London, 15 July 1773; Anne Latouche de Gotteville, *Voyage d'une françoise à Londres ou la calomnie détruite par la vérité des faits* (London: Mesplet, 1774), pp. 63–4.

12 CPA 503 fos 380–1, Morande to d'Eon, undated letter [probably dating from early 1774]; 277AP/1, dossier Morande fo 196, Morande to d'Eon, undated letter [1774]; CPA 517 fos 228–9, d'Eon to Morande, 3 August 1776, copy [translated] of d'Eon's first billet.

13 CPA 516 fos 211–18, d'Eon to Vergennes, London, 27 May 1776 [or copy at BMT, R20]; BMT, R22, d'Eon to Vergennes, 'Campagnes du Sr Caron de Beaumarchais en Angleterre, années 1774–1776'.

14 Spinelli, 'Beaumarchais and d'Eon', p. 61, notes that Morande wrote that Beaumarchais 'never stepped out of his slippers, loved working, and was too lazy to go out on the town.' He adds (p. 70n.14) that Beaumarchais was often accompanied to London by his mistress and future wife. Spinelli's sources are *BCE*, I, 222 and 293n.18.

15 Pelleport, *Diable*, pp. 101–2.

16 Andrea de Nerciat, *Julie philosophe*, II, 8–10.

17 Anne-Gédeon La Fite de Pelleport, *Les Bohémiens*, 2 vols (Paris: Rue des Poitevins, hôtel Bouthillier, 1790), II, 114–17. For further discussion of this work, see Robert Darnton, *Bohemians before Bohemianism* (Wassenaar: NIAS, 2006), esp. p. 37.

18 AFB fo 6 bis, Eliza to Beaumarchais, [Mantes], 23 November 1783, *BCE* document 349.

19 Francy to Beaumarchais, 8 February 1784, cited in *BCE*, I, 119.

20 Ibid.

21 AFB fos 40–1, Morande to Beaumarchais, 16 April 1784, (published abridged in *BCE*, document 375).

22 Beaumarchais to Morande, 7 August 1788, *BCE*, document 523.

23 Morande, *Réplique à Brissot*, p. 19.

24 Pelleport, *Diable*, p. 29. On homosexuality and the law, see Netta Murray Goldsmith, *The Worst of Crimes. Homosexuality and the Law in Eighteenth-Century London* (Aldershot: Ashgate, 1998).

25 Except where indicated, the narrative of d'Eon's life in this and the following paragraphs is taken from Kates, *Monsieur d'Eon*. For supplementary details concerning the Guerchy affair see Burrows, *Blackmail*, pp. 91–5.

26 See ULBC, file 58 fos 53, 53 bis, and 59–60 (insert), cuttings from the *Gazette britannique*, 8 March 1765; *London Chronicle*, 29 September–1 October 1767; *Political Register*, September 1767.

27   ULBC, file 65 fo 157, account book entry, 22 March 1776; file 58 fo 57, *London Evening Post*, 15 to 18 June 1765. Serious biographers have tended to doubt tales of d'Eon's dressing as a woman before his return to France in 1777. However, the fact that his private account book states that he did so while in hiding appears to establish the fact beyond reasonable doubt.

28   On the Wilkes-d'Eon parallel see: Jonathan Conlin, 'Wilkes, the Chevalier d'Eon and the dregs of liberty: an Anglo-French perspective on ministerial despotism, 1762–1771', *English Historical Review* 120:5 (2005), 1251–88.

29   BL, Add. Ms. 11,341 fos 193–4, account of policies on d'Eon's sex, 28 March to 19 June 1770. This document records the purchase of policies on d'Eon's being a woman at long odds and their subsequent sale at much shorter odds. A quarter share of the profit marked 'your share' was passed to an unnamed individual. The presence of this document in d'Eon's papers suggests that he was paid a commission to manipulate rumours on his sex, but did not technically lie when he denied trafficking in the policies. For further evidence that d'Eon at least considered profiting from the policies see below Chapter 4 note 74.

30   CPA 502 fos 182–3, d'Eon to Broglie, London, 15 January 1773, asserts 'he [Morande] would come every day . . . if I was inclined to receive him . . . every time he comes to knock at my door'. AN, 277AP/1, dossier Morande, contains 82 letters from Morande to d'Eon dating from 1771–1776, 1786 and 1789–1791. The earliest dated letter was written on 2 March 1771, but an earlier but undated letter expresses regret that Morande's 'trip' to England will pass without seeing d'Eon, save briefly.

31   CPA 502 fos 177–9, d'Eon to Broglie, London, 13 July 1773, at fo 177. This quote has been edited for readability.

32   Ibid., at fo 179.

33   AN, 277AP/1, dossier Morande, fos 328–30, Morande to d'Eon, undated, [filed with letters from 1771]. As Gary Kates has noted, there is no evidence that d'Eon ever had a sexual relationship. Frédéric Gaillardet, d'Eon's otherwise scholarly nineteenth-century biographer, suggested that d'Eon dressed as a woman to gain sexual access to the wives of other men, including Morande and George III. Gaillardet later admitted that he fabricated his evidence concerning such encounters. His fabrications were perhaps inspired by the memoirs of an earlier French cross-dresser, the Abbé de Choisy, who tells of several sexual encounters while dressed as a woman.

34   CPA 502 fos 177–9, d'Eon to Broglie, London, 13 July 1773, at fo 177. Several dates given in this letter relating to the compilation and publication of the *Gazetier cuirassé* are erroneous.

35   Ibid and AN, 277AP/1, dossier Morande, fo 333, d'Eon to Morande 16 July 1771.

36   Vizetelly, *The True Story of d'Eon*, p. 273; BMT, J. 166, Madame de Courcelle to d'Eon, Paris, 1 January 1776. This letter, occasioned by rumours that Beaumarchais intended to marry d'Eon, berates d'Eon for inconstancy towards Constance, and expresses surprise that he is considered a woman. If genuine and not intended as a joke (which seems unlikely), this letter is the only evidence that d'Eon ever had an emotional relationship.

37   CPA 507, fos 301–11, Tort to Louis XVI, 15 December 1774, mentions Courcelle in relation to the case.

38   Morande, *Réplique à Brissot*, p. 19. The 17 day claim may well be correct, as the *Gazetier cuirassé* was published by 15 July 1771 and refers to d'Aiguillon's promotion to foreign minister, which occured in early June.

39   CPA 542 fos 402–3, d'Adhémar to Vergennes, 15 June 1783.

40   Ibid., fos 201–2, Moustier to Vergennes, London, 6 May 1783.

41   CPA 502 fos 177–9, d'Eon to Broglie, London, 13 July 1773, at fo 177.

42   Pelleport, *Diable*, pp. 29, 62.

43   CPA 497 fos 111–13, Marin to d'Aiguillon, Paris, 3 August 1771; CPA 502 fos 182–3, d'Eon to Broglie, 15 July 1773. *MSB*, XXI, 1 September 1771, puts the figure at £1,000. Robert Darnton, *The Corpus of Clandestine Literature in France 1769–1789* (New York: Norton, 1995) places the *Gazetier cuirassé* 53rd on his list of illegal bestsellers.

44   On the international gazettes see esp. Simon Burrows, 'The cosmopolitan press' in Hannah Barker and Simon Burrows (eds), *Press, Politics and the Public Sphere in Europe and North America 1760–1820* (Cambridge: CUP, 2002), pp. 23–47.

45   Voltaire, *Questions sur l'Encyclopédie par des amateurs*, nouvelle édition soigneusement revue, corrigée et augmentée, 9 vols (1771–2), IX, 226.

46   *MSB*, V, 15 August 1771; AN, 277AP/1, dossier Morande fo 333, d'Eon to Morande, 16 July 1771.

47 This refers to the division of the pamphlet into three parts as described above, Chapter 1 note 14. Although each part had separate title page, prefatory materials and pagination, there is no evidence that they were ever published separately, particularly in the light of Marin's description here.

48 CPA 497 fos 111–13, Marin to d'Aiguillon, 3 August 1771.

49 See Darnton, *Corpus*, pp. 253, 260.

50 Michel Schlup, 'La Société Typographique de Neuchâtel (1769–1789): Points de Repère' in Michel Schlup (ed.), *L'Edition neuchâteloise au siècle de lumières: la Société typographique de Neuchâtel (1769-1789)* (Neuchâtel: Bibliothèque publique et universitaire de Neuchâtel, 2002), pp. 61–105, at pp. 76–8.

51 CPA 513 fos 439–43. Since Morande often concealed identities behind initials, abbreviated names, or enigmas, d'Eon's list is an invaluable guide to Morande's text. However, it is not comprehensive nor entirely accurate: a few names listed were mentioned only incidentally and in passing.

52 *Gazetier cuirassé*, pt I, pp. 93 (Bishop of Saint Brieux); 94 ('Fecundity'); 94–5 (clergy incest); 116–17 (Port Royal convent); pt. III, pp. 87–8 (Abbé Grizel).

53 Ibid., pt II, pp. 27–8 (charlatanism); pt III, pp. 78–9 (Cardinal Bernis). In the Bernis quote, it is unclear whether '*enfant de coeur*' (rather than *choeur*) is a misprint or deliberate *double-entendre*. I have assumed *choeur* was intended.

54 Ibid., pt I, pp. 84–5 (Louis XV's confessor); pt I, 109 (confessors as informants); pt II, p. 47 (God's contract).

55 Ibid., pt II, pp. 1, 74.

56 Ibid., pt I, pp. 92 (robust fellows); 114 (Savoyard Sweeps); pt II, pp. 2 (aristocratic incest); 21 (system of Rousseau); 39–40 (insurance premiums).

57 Ibid., pt I, pp. 26 (contemplative monks); 59–60 (Minden and Rossbach); pt II, pp. 3–4 (colonels); 4–5 (rank and talent); 16 (monks, dervishes and Brahmins); 35 (Minden and Rossbach, again).

58 Ibid., pt I pp. 57–8 (Order of Saint-Nicole); 89–90 (barrel; du Barry's ascendancy), pt II, pp. 43–4 (sceptre).

59 See Burrows, *Blackmail*, especially chs 2 and 5.

60 On the kidnaps see ibid., pp. 193–5. Morande refers to Fratteaux and d'Eon in the *Gazetier cuirassé*, pt II, p.16.

61 *Gazetier cuirassé*, pt II, p. 33.

62 Ibid., pt I, unpaginated page entitled 'Explication du frontispice'.

63 Ibid., pt I, pp. ix–xii.

64 Ibid., pt II, pp. v–viii contains a letter to Morande's 'Mentor' [clearly d'Eon] which announces that Morande wishes to demonstrate that he is 'without fear of the vicious men whom I detest'.

65 Ibid., pt I, p. 101 (Gourdan and Brissac); pt II, pp. 1–2 (venereal disease); pt III, pp. 53–4 (grenadier's compliment); 64 (countesses and marchionesses); 74–93 (*Transparent News*).

66 Ibid., pt III, pp. xi–xii.

67 Ibid., pt III, p. xvi.

68 Ibid., pt III, pp. viii–ix.

69 Ibid., pt III, pp. 86–7.

70 Ibid., pt III, p. 82.

71 Ibid., pt I, p. 50 (Louis XV's liberties); pt II, pp. 2 (Maupeou's definition); 37–8 (hanging machine).

72 Ibid., pt I, pp. 27 (Choiseul's plans); 39–40 (holy anuses); 68–9 (Maupeou and Jesuits); 112 (reintroducing Jesuits). Not everyone spotted the joke concerning the holy anuses – a 1777 pirate edition of the *Gazetier* amended the passage in line with the errata to read 'agnus'. This must have left readers perplexed.

73 Ibid., pt I, pp. 51 (venereal disease); 118 (La Vrillière gaols fathers); 133 (policing ban); 135 (gaoling lover's husband).

74 Ibid., pt I, pp. 35–6 (paying judges); 45 (Praslin). Pt III, pp. 47–8 and 71–2 suggest judges' decisions, even in capital cases, are swayed by the ability of one side to pay.

Notes to Chapter 3: A King's Ransom

1 'Quisquis' in Voltaire, *Questions sur l'Encyclopédie*, IX, 224–5.

2 Some bibliographers attribute the *Rémarques historiques* to Brossais du Perray. Only three nineteenth-century scholars (M. Foisset, Alfred Franklin and A. Albrier) have previously linked it to Morande, apparently because the 1777 edition of the *Gazetier cuirassé* contains the *Rémarques historiques*. The attribution to Morande is reinforced by the pamphlet's timing, the lack of any other contemporaneous Bastille pamphlets, its defamation of Voltaire, and its political stance. The presentational features and use of language are also distinctly Morandian. Claims in the text that the work was published posthumously and that the author spent time in the Bastille thus appear to be red herrings. As Howard's translation is generally close to the original, I have quoted the English text throughout. On the sale by subscription, see CPA 502 fos 177–9, d'Eon to Broglie, 13 July 1773.

3 Hans-Jürgen Lüsebrink and Rolf Reichardt, *The Bastille. A History of a Symbol of Despotism and Freedom* (Durham NC and London: Duke University Press, 1997), p. 18. Howard's translation was published in London by T. Cadell and N. Conant in 1780. In 1792, it was republished in *The Works of John Howard*.

4 Morande (attrib.), *Historical Remarks*, preface, first unpaginated page. This preface is missing from the 1777 French edition.

5 Ibid., second unpaginated page.

6 Ibid., pp. 6n., 17. Quote at p. 17

7 Ibid., p. 12.

8 Ibid., p. 13.

9 The case studies are in ibid., pp. 21–9. The passage concerning Jesuit confessors was omitted from Howard's English translation, but appears in the *Rémarques historiques* (1777 edition) at p. 52.

10 This account of the Lally case draws on Roger Pearson, *Voltaire Almighty. A Life in Pursuit of Freedom* (London: Bloomsbury, 2005), pp. 356–8.

11 Morande (attrib.), *Historical Remarks*, pp. 28–9.

12 Lüsebrink and Reichardt, *The Bastille*, p. 19.

13 CPA 502 fos 177–9, d'Eon to Broglie, London, 13 July 1773.

14 On Courcelle's flight and the jewellery, see BMT, J. 154 to J. 164. Quote from BL, Add. MS 11,339, fos 347–55, Joseph Lautens to d'Eon, undated [October or November 1784?] at fo 352.

15 BL, Add. MS 11,339, fos 347–55, Lautens to d'Eon, undated [October or November 1784?].

16 BMT, J. 153, Declaration of Morande, 15 September 1771; J. 160, d'Eon to Mme. de Courcelle, 22 September 1771.

17 CPA 503 fos 308–10, Morande to d'Eon, undated letter [received by d'Eon at Stanton-Harold, 21 December 1773], [copy], at fo 310.

18 BMT, J. 166, Mme. de Courcelle to d'Eon, Paris, 1 January 1776.

19 AN, 277AP/1, dossier Morande fos 148–9, Morande to d'Eon 17 November 1773.

20 Ibid., fos 218–20, Morande to d'Eon, undated letter (in file for 1775); ULBC, file 65 fo 155, entry for 4 March 1776; Pelleport, *Diable*, p. 29.

21 See NA, C12/2114/28, de Morande versus Simond, 1778.

22 For Louis Théveneau's will, dated 22 September 1772, see ADCO, 4E64/261, 'Testament de Louis Théveneau'. See also ADCO, C7836, Contrôle des Actes, Arnay-le-Duc, fos 15–16. His death is recorded in the Etat Civil for Arnay-le-Duc in the mairie in Arnay and ADCO, 2E26/7. The house at 40 Duke Street is first mentioned in contracts suppressing the *Secret Memoirs of a Woman of Pleasure*, which date from 1774.

23 CPA 518 fos 78–90, [d'Eon?], 'Anecdotes du Gazetier cuirassé ou du Mandrin Littéraire, extrait d'une lettre du Marquis de *** actuellement à Londres au Chevalier de *** à Paris', 12 September 1776', at fo 79. Although no printed copies of the *Mandrin littéraire* are known, it was definitely published. It appears in a catalogue of the Philadelphia booksellers Boinot and Gaillard from 1784. I thank Dr Mark Curran for this reference. The manuscript copy of the *Mandrin Littéraire* in the MAE is in d'Eon's hand, but a short, very similar passage appears in Mathieu-François Pidansat de Mairobert (attrib.), *Anecdotes sur Madame la comtesse Du Barry* (London, 1775), p. 314. There is reason to believe that d'Eon and Mairobert were in contact.

24 CPA 502 fos 177–9, d'Eon to Broglie, London, 13 July 1773; *BCE* I, 112–15, Beaumarchais to unknown correspondent, Paris, 24 January 1781.

25 See Burrows, *Blackmail*, pp. 26, 90.

26 See especially Pelleport, *Diable*, p. 62.

27 *CSCV*, I, 179; Piton, ed., *Paris sous Louis XV*, I, 342.

28 [Morande], *Gazetier cuirassé*, pt III, p. 79.

29 Broglie to Louis XV, Ruffec, 18 November 1773, published in *CSB*, II, 464–6. The pamphlet was entitled *Le Pétangueule*.

30 CPA 518 fo 78–90, 'Le Mandrin littéraire' at fo 79; Pelleport, *Diable*, p. 62; BL Add. MS 11,340 fos 18–19, *Public Ledger*, 3 and 4 September 1776; BMT, L. 102, d'Eon to Sir John Fielding, 28 August 1776.

31 [Morande] *Gazetier cuirassé*, pt I, p. 40 (anuses); pt II, pp. 10 (coward), 42 (coach); pt III, p. 75 (facial hairs). In Plato's *Symposium*, it is hinted that Socrates' pupil Alcibiades was also his lover.

32 [Morande], *Gazetier cuirassé*, pt III, pp. 78 (Mlle Clairon), 86 (mistress). On Villette see Merrick, 'Villette and Raucourt'.

33 Villette, *Oeuvres*, preface, cited in Brissot's *Patriot François*, no. 740 (19 August 1791), p. 211. Morande, *Réplique à Brissot*, pp. 34–5, denies, improbably, that he wrote the letter in question.

34 Voltaire is named as a victim in Manuel, *Police dévoilée*, II, 252. Foisset (*Biographie universelle*) and Franklin (*Nouvelle biographie générale*) say that he published Morande's letter, but neither gives a source. Likewise Wagner, *Eros Revived*, p. 91. I have found nothing in Voltaire's correspondence to substantiate the story. The Fréron reference is in *Gazetier cuirassé*, pt III, p. 81.

35 Morande, *Réplique à Brissot*, p. 33. The reference to the noose is probably an allusion to Voltaire's comments in *Questions sur l'Encyclopédie*, IX, 224–5, cited at the start of this chapter.

36 For the *Mandement du Muphti* see *Le Tocsin des Rois Par M. de VOLT**** suivi d'un Mandement du Muphti, ordonnant la SUPPRESSION de cet Ouvrage; et d'un Decret du DIVAN, qui condamne l'Auteur à être empalé* (Imprimé à Constantinople [i.e. London]: L'An de l'Égire 1168. Se trouve à LONDRES, chez BOISSIÈRE, Marchand-libraire, Ruë de St. James, près le caffé de Smyrne). The actual date of publication was probably 1772, making it the earliest known edition published by Boissière. No known bibliographical work or catalogue attributes the *Mandement* to Morande, which has thus escaped the attention of previous scholars: even Robiquet fails to mention it. Morande is also named as the author of the *Mandement* in CPA 518 fos 78–90, [d'Eon], 'Le Mandrin littéraire' [1776], at fo 82. Nicholas Cronk raised the possibility (private conversation with author) that perhaps Voltaire wrote the *Mandement* himself. However, although computer analysis using *Signature* author recognition software (see below Chapter 6 note 124) drew strong correlations between the *Mandement* and one sample Voltaire text, the other Voltaire texts scattered widely, making any conclusion based on the computer analysis tenuous. There are, in contrast, multiple forms of evidence linking it to Morande.

37 [Morande], *Mandement*, pp. 16–18.

38 Ibid., pp. 50–1.

39 Ibid., p. 18.

40 *MSB*, XXI, additions for 2 July 1771, 6 July 1771, 8 July 1771.

41 See Louis-Léon de Brancas, Count de Lauraguais, *Mémoire pour moi, par moi* (London, 1773); *MSB*, VII, 7 June 1773. Several documents detailing Drogard's complaints survive in CPA 498. Brancas' pamphlet is dated 12 February 1773.

42 Lauraguais, *Mémoire pour moi*, p. xvii.

43 [Morande], *Gazetier cuirassé*, pt III, p. 73 and *cléf* to pt III, p. xvi.

44 Morande, *Réplique à Brissot*, p. 23. The rumours are contradicted in *MSB*, XXI, addition for 1 September 1771; Mairobert, *Anecdotes*, p. 185.

45 CPA 502 fos 177–9, d'Eon to Broglie, London, 13 July 1773. The abridged version of this letter in *CSI*, I, 356–8 gives only a brief and partial view of the affair.

46 CPA 502, fos 177–9, d'Eon to Broglie, London, 13 July 1773, at fo 178.

47 Morande, *Réplique à Brissot*, p. 22.

48 The letter to the *Morning Post* is known to me only through the letter to the *Morning Chronicle*. Morande is accused of denouncing himself in CPA 517 fos 239–40, d'Eon's 'Second billet' of 8 August 1776 (which challenges Morande) and CPA 518 fos 78–90, 'Le Mandrin littéraire', which is dated 12 September 1776 and probably emanated from d'Eon's camp. The allegation resurfaces in Manuel, *Police dévoilée*, II, 252.

49 CPA 502 fos 177–9, d'Eon to Broglie, London, 13 July 1773.
50 Morande, *Réplique à Brissot*, pp. 21–2. Morande called Lauraguais to witness these facts.
51 CPA 502 fos 177–9, d'Eon to Broglie, London, 13 July 1773. Quote at fo 178. Lauraguais was presented to George III by the French ambassador in late 1772: see CPA 500 fos 328–31, Guines to d'Aiguillon, 27 December 1772.
52 Morande, *Réplique à Brissot*, p. 22.
53 CPA 518 fos 78–90, 'Le Mandrin littéraire', at fo 84.
54 Morande, *Réplique à Brissot*, p. 22.
55 CPA 518 fos 78–90, 'Le Mandrin littéraire', at fo 84.
56 AN, 277AP/1, dossier Morande fos 148–9, Morande to d'Eon, undated letter, (received 17 November 1773); BL, Add. MS 11,339 fos 208–9, d'Eon to Joseph Lautens, 21 December 1773.
57 Manuel, *Police dévoilée*, I, 267. Morande, *Réplique à Brissot*, p. 34, denies both details. See also Joseph Balsamo, *Lettre du Comte de Cagliostro au peuple anglois* (1786), p. 87.
58 *Morning Chronicle*, 29 November 1773. See also *London Evening Post*, 26 November 1773.
59 BL, Add. MS 11,339 fos 208–9, d'Eon to Joseph Lautens, 21 December 1773.
60 Mathieu-François de Pidansat de Mairobert (attrib.), *Letters to and from the Countess Du Barry, the Last Mistress of Lewis XV of France*, translated from the French (Dublin: P. Higly, 1780), pp. 217–20. In the contracts suppressing Morande's libel in CPA 507, the title is given as *Mémoires secrets d'une femme publique, ou recherches sur les aventures de Madame la comtesse du B**** depuis sa berceau jusqu'au lit d'honneur, enrichis d'anecdotes et d'incidens relatifs à la cabale qui l'a levée au Ministère et à l'exil du Duc de Chois*** aux belles actions du Ducs d'Aiguillon &c. &c.*
61 [Morande], *Gazetier cuirassé*, I, pp. 137–40. Emphases as in original.
62 Mairobert, *Anecdotes*, p. 239.
63 Mairobert, *Letters to and from Du Barry*, pp. 220–1. The full title of Morande's *Secret Memoirs* (see above note 60) supports Mairobert's suggestion that Morande intended to insinuate that d'Aiguillon was du Barry's lover.
64 Mairobert, *Espion anglois*, II, 16.
65 NA, SP78/285, fos 210–11, Morande to Benavent, undated letter [May 1772]; fo 212, Sartine [?] to d'Aiguillon, undated note [May 1772].
66 NA, SP78/285 fos 205–6, Harcourt to Lord Rochford, 20 May 1772. Emphasis as in original. Rochford was head of the Northern department, one of two bureaux that handled British foreign policy prior to the establishment of a unitary Foreign Office in 1782.
67 Mairobert, *Anecdotes*, pp. 314–15.
68 NA, SP78/285 fos 293–4, Harcourt to Lord Rochford, Compiègne, 16 July 1772. Mairobert, *Anecdotes*, p. 236, describes the Count's stormy relationship with Mme Murat.
69 On Boissière's circle and business see Burrows, *Blackmail*, pp. 63–4, 68–9; Manuel, *Police dévoilée*, II, 231–69 passim.
70 On the kidnap attempt see Lavirotte, 'Notice sur Morande'. Lavirotte claimed to have the tale from Morande himself. As it is incompatible with accounts of the later police mission of Béranger, it seems plausible to link this attempt to Fontaine. That said, Lavirotte seems to conflate Béranger and Fontaine. CPA 541 fos 346–9, Goëzman to Vergennes, 4 April 1783, attests Boissière's role. Further circumstantial evidence of Fontaine's intentions appears in Morande's reference to later kidnappers 'who seemed as artless as dear Fontaine, though without the same massive bulk': CPA 503 fos 374–5, Morande to d'Eon, [undated letter, probably written 4 January 1774].
71 CPA 498 fos 378–9, Sartine to d'Aiguillon, Paris, 31 August 1772, encloses a kidnap plan submitted by the Chevalier Saby. D'Aiguillon's annotations show he returned the plan on 4 September, implying that the response was negative.
72 Broglie's letter to d'Eon dated 6 July 1773, which asked for intelligence about the Spanish ambassador's secretary, has been removed from CPA 517 fo 26. I have been unable to locate a copy.
73 CPA 502 fos 182–3, d'Eon to Broglie, London, 15 July 1773.
74 AN, K 157, Broglie to Louis XV, Compiègne, 29 July 1773, including Louis XV's annotations; CPA 502 fos 416–17, [Eon] to [Broglie], 29 September 1773 [copy]; MD France, 540 bis fos 168–9, Broglie to Louis XV, Ruffec, 18 November 1773, published in *CSB*, II, 464–6.

75   MD France 1398, fos 176–81, Lormoy to Louis XVI, 1 July 1784. Lormoy's model for an agree-
     ment with Morande can be found in the Bayerisches Hauptstaatsarchiv, Munich, Politische
     Korrespondenz des Herzogs von Pfalz-Zweibrücken, Kasten blau 405/34.
76   AN, 277AP/1, dossier Morande fos 148–9, Morande to d'Eon, undated letter [received by d'Eon
     at Staunton Harold, 17 November 1773].
77   CPA 503 fos 258–62, 12 December 1773. D'Eon alleged such rumours originated with Lormoy
     and were patently false, since d'Eon had been away from London for seven weeks.
78   Manuel, Police dévoilée, I, 266; CPA 503 fo 289, [Béranger], 'Soumission de S. (inconnu)',
     18 December 1773. Béranger's rival, La Roche de Champreux, demanded 96,000 livres to kidnap
     Morande.
79   CPA 505 fo 127, Gotteville to Finet, [undated letter from London, received in Paris 6 April 1773].
     Gotteville's lovers included the Count de Morangiés and Beaumarchais, who wrote that she 'had
     the most beautiful body in the world' and was 'one of the most seductive women I have known'.
80   Mairobert, Anecdotes, p. 315. Gotteville, Voyage d'une françoise, denies any contact with Morande,
     but Morande's knowledge of what happened at Dover (above, p. 66) makes this improbable.
81   MD France 1398, fos 176–81, Lormoy to Louis XVI, 1 July 1784
82   Andrea de Nerciat, Julie philosophe, II, 11. The original text reads 'Louis', which I have taken to
     indicate a sovereign.
83   CPA 503 fos 374–5, Morande to d'Eon [3 or 4 January 1774].
84   AN, 277AP/1, dossier Morande fo 145, Morande to d'Eon, 4 January 1774 at 11 p.m. There is a
     copy at CPA 504 fo 20.
85   CPA 504 fos 20–1, note of d'Eon [January 1774].
86   Ibid., fos 31–2, annotation of d'Eon on Morande to d'Eon, 8 January 1774.
87   See also Woodfall's Morning Chronicle of 5 January 1774.
88   CPA 504 fos 31–2, annotation of d'Eon on Morande to d'Eon, 8 January 1774.
89   Ibid; MD France 1398 fos 176–81, Lormoy to Louis XVI, 1 July 1784 at fo 180; Morande, Réplique
     à Brissot, p. 21. I have not located a copy of the Morning Post of 11 January 1774. Pelleport,
     Diable, pp. 30–1, claims that Morande bribed his valet to swear a false oath against the agents.
     This contradicts earlier sources.
90   Siméon-Prosper Hardy, Mes Loisirs, ed. Maurice Tourneux and Maurice Vitrac, 2 vols (Paris,
     1912), II, 91; MSB, VII, 5 February 1774. Morande, Réplique à Brissot, p. 21, says it was his
     recourse to the law that put the officers to flight, while Mairobert, Anecdotes, pp. 314–15, denies
     the lynchings, but says the officers hid until they could escape. He adds that Receveur lost his
     wits. The mention in Gotteville, Voyage d'une françoise, p. 62, of 'tall stories of six Frenchmen
     hanged at London', also contradicts tales of lynchings.
91   CPA 505 fos 31–2, Lauraguais to the Count [du Barry?], 9 March 1774; fo 168, d'Eon to Broglie,
     London, 18 April 1774; CPA 518 fos 78–90, 'Le Mandrin littéraire', at fo 90; Mathieu-François
     Pidansat de Mairobert (attrib.), Journal historique de la révolution opérée dans la constitution de la
     monarchie française par M. de Maupoeu (London, 1775), p. 292; Mairobert, Anecdotes, p. 315.
92   Sarah Maza, Private Lives and Public Affairs: The Causes Célèbres of Pre-Revolutionary France
     (Berkeley and London: University of California Press, 1993), pp. 130–4; Maurice Lever, Pierre-
     Augustin Caron de Beaumarchais, 3 vols (Paris: Fayard, 1999–2004), I, 460–3.
93   AN, 277AP/1, dossier Morande fos 198–9, Morande to d'Eon, undated letter [received 9 March
     1774]. This letter is misfiled in the folder of correspondence for 1776.
94   AN, 277AP/1, dossier Morande fo 212, Morande to d'Eon, undated letter [late March or early
     April 1774].
95   Memoir of Beaumarchais to Louis XVI [June 1774], published in Jacques Donvez, La Politique de
     Beaumarchais (Leiden: IDC, 1980), pp. 242–3; Morande, Réplique à Brissot, p. 21. AN, 277AP/1,
     dossier Morande fos 202–5, Morande to d'Eon, 24 March 1774, says that the books would all be
     assembled by the following Sunday (27 March). Mairobert, Anecdotes, p. 316, reports that on
     12 March 1774, after French diplomatic pressure, the Dutch government banned booksellers
     from distributing or reprinting Morande's work.
96   Lever, Beaumarchais, I, 475.
97   CPA 505 fo 72, Garnier to d'Aiguillon, 25 March 1774; fo 113, d'Aiguillon to Garnier, 3 April
     1774; fos 154–8, Garnier to d'Aiguillon, London, 12 April 1774.
98   CPA supplément 18 fo 32, d'Aiguillon to Beaujon, 18 April 1774; CPA 505 fos 31–3, Lauraguais
     to the Count [du Barry?], 9 March 1774.

99 See CPA 503 fos 308-10, Morande to d'Eon, 21 December 1773. D'Eon also claimed to have suggested the venue for burning the books.

100 CPA 517 fos 239-43, d'Eon to Morande, 8 April 1776. Barbier and some later bibliographers assume that Mairobert's *Anecdotes sur Madame Du Barry* were really the *Secret Memoirs of a Woman of Pleasure*. However, Louis Dutens, *Mémoires d'un voyageur qui se repose*, 3 vols (London: Dulau, 1806), II, 40, reports that Beaumarchais assured him that the two works were very different. Contemporaries (eg. *CSP*, II, 314) also noted that the *Anecdotes* were gentler than the *Gazetier cuirassé*, which according to the *Anecdotes* (p. 326) was 'rosewater' in comparison to the *Secret Memoirs of a Woman of Pleasure*. Moreover, in his *Réplique à Brissot* (1791), Morande himself lamented that had a copy survived, he could cite it as proof of his 'patriotism'. On the question of whether d'Eon was present see above, notes to the prologue, note 2.

101 For French translations of the contract with Van Neck, see CPA 504 fos 197-200 and CPA 505 fos 208-11. An English original is at CPA 505 fo 207. The contract with Lauraguais is at CPA 505 fos 205-6. For Morande's comment on assassination see CPA 503 fos 308-10, Morande to d'Eon, undated, received 21 December 1773, at fo 308. The destruction of printed illustrations (estampes) and the manuscripts of further works is mentioned in a memoir of Beaumarchais to Louis XVI partially reproduced (after Lintilhac) in Lever, *Beaumarchais*, II, 420, note 13. AN, 277AP/1, dossier Morande fos 202-5, Morande to d'Eon, 24 March 1774, records that Morande has just paid his designer and engraver and hence confirms that the work included illustrations.

102 *MSB*, VIII, 25 August 1775; Mairobert, *Anecdotes*, pp. 327-8; Mairobert, *Letters to and from du Barry*, pp. 221-3; Mairobert, *Espion anglois*, II, 15-17; Pelleport, *Diable*, p. 30; and Manuel's *Police dévoilée*, II, 251. See also Guillaume Imbert, *La Chronique Scandaleuse*, 3rd edition, 4 vols (Paris, 1788), I, 33.

103 Lever, *Beaumarchais*, II, 23.

104 Unpaginated letter dated 20 May 1774 at back of [Morande], *Gazetier cuirassé*, 1777 edition. It is possible that Morande was the author of this letter.

Notes to Chapter 4: Figaro's Nemesis

1 Beaumarchais to unknown correspondent, Paris, 24 January 1781, BCE, I, 112-15.

2 Beaumarchais to Sartine, 11 June 1775, *BCE* document 5.

3 Vergennes to Beaumarchais, 21 June 1775, *BCE* document 6.

4 All these topics feature in Morande's published correspondence with Beaumarchais in *BCE* and unpublished documents in AFB. *BCE* Chapter 22 discusses *Tarare*.

5 For Beaumarchais' amorous correspondence with Mme. Gotteville (whose name he spelt Godeville), see Beaumarchais, *Lettres à Madame de Godeville, 1777-1779*, edited by Maxime Formont (Paris: Lemerre, 1928); Beaumarchais, *Les Lettres galantes de Beaumarchais à Madame de Godeville*, ed. Maurice Lever (Paris: Fayard, 2004).

6 Beaumarchais to Sartine and Louis XVI, 20 June 1774, in Pierre-Augustin Caron de Beaumarchais, *Correspondance*, edited by Brian Morton and D. Spinelli, 4 vols (Paris: Nizet, 1969-78), II, 49-51; Paul Huot, *Beaumarchais en Allemagne, révélations tirées des archives de l'Autriche* (Paris: Librairie internationale, 1869), p. 182; and René Pomeau, *Beaumarchais ou la bizarre destinée* (Paris: PUF, 1987), p. 87. Extensive extracts of the *Avis à la branche espagnole* appear in Lever, *Beaumarchais*, II, 421-4n. and Donvez, *Politique de Beaumarchais*, pp. 257-72. The original manuscript survives in the Austrian State Archives. A printed copy given to Sartine by Beaumarchais has disappeared.

7 This account of the Angelucci affair is adapted from Burrows, *Blackmail*, pp. 99-103, which gives full references. My main sources are Paul-Philippe Gudin de La Brenellerie, *Histoire de Beaumarchais* (ed.) Maurice Tourneux (Paris: Plon, 1888), pp. 125-41; and the documents in Louis de Loménie, *Beaumarchais et son temps*, 2 vols (Paris: Michel Levy frères, 1856), I, 389-403; Beaumarchais, *Correspondance*, II, 54-118, passim; Alfred von Arneth, *Beaumarchais und Sonnenfels* (Vienna: Wilhelm Braumüller, 1868), pp. 65-107; Huot, *Beaumarchais en Allemagne*; Donvez, *Politique de Beaumarchais*, pp. 274-387; and Lever, *Beaumarchais*, II, 24-58, 420-34.

8   Agreements between Beaumarchais and 'Hatkinson'/'Angelucci' suppressing the *Avis*, dated London, 22–23 July, and Amsterdam, 4 August 1774, are reproduced by Donvez (*Politique de Beaumarchais*, pp. 274–9, 284–5) and Lever (*Beaumarchais*, II, 425–7n.). Several commentators believe Beaumarchais forged these documents.

9   For Dratz's statement, dated Neustadt, 14 August 1774, see Arneth, *Beaumarchais und Sonnenfels*, pp. 65–8, and Beaumarchais, *Correspondance*, II, 75–7. For French translations see Donvez, *Politique de Beaumarchais*, pp. 296–300); Huot, *Beaumarchais en Allemagne*, pp. 69–75; Lever, *Beaumarchais*, II, 430–31n.

10 In one account, Beaumarchais' assailants call one another 'Hatkinson' and 'Angelucci', suggesting that Hatkinson and Angelucci were separate people (Huot, *Beaumarchais en Allemagne*, pp. 60–4). Beaumarchais to 'M. R.', 15 August 1774 (Beaumarchais, *Correspondance*, II, 66–74), identifies the robbers as German highwaymen.

11 *CSMT*, II, 224–7, 230–5, 239, 244, 254, gives correspondence between Maria-Theresia, Mercy-Argenteau, and Marie-Antoinette concerning Beaumarchais and the *Avis*. For changes to his story, see Beaumarchais' letters to Maria-Theresia, Vienna, 23 August 1774, and Seilern, Vienna, 24 August 1774, (Beaumarchais, *Correspondance*, II, 92–7, 98–9).

12 For a run-down of biographers' views, see Burrows, *Blackmail*, p. 118n.111. The most credible defence is that Beaumarchais dreamed up his Vienna jaunt only when he first read the *libelle* in London on about 2–3 July.

13 Beaumarchais' expense account is given by Donvez, (*Politique de Beaumarchais*, pp. 401–5), and Lever (*Beaumarchais*, II, 432–3n.). On Sartine's suspicions, see Huot, *Beaumarchais en Allemagne*, pp. 193–4, esp. the letter of Mercy to Kaunitz, 7 October 1774. D'Eon and Tort also made inconsistent allegations against Beaumarchais. See Burrows, *Blackmail*, p. 103.

14 This analysis of the pamphlet follows Huot, *Beaumarchais en Allemagne*, p. 184.

15 On the blackmailing of Beaumarchais, see pp. 100–1. On Morande's secret printshop see CPA 516 fos 219–28, d'Eon to Vergennes, 27 May 1776.

16 For the 'Lettre de Marly' see *Courier de l'Europe*, 12 July 1776, BCE, document 38. The original draft, CPA 518 fos 54–5, apparently escaped the attention of Gunnar and Mavis von Proschwitz (see *BCE*, I, 16–21). D'Eon claims that Morande also wrote paragraphs 'mistreating French ministers, particularly Sartine' in the *Westminster Gazette* in May 1776 (see BMT, R21).

17 On the early history of the *CE* see *BCE*; Hélène Maspero-Clerc, 'Une Gazette anglo-française pendant la guerre d'Amérique, *Le Courier de l'Europe*, 1776–1788', *Annales historiques de la Révolution française* 44, no. 226 (1976), 572–94; Gunnar von Proschwitz, 'Courier de l'Europe' in Jean Sgard, ed., *Dictionnaire de journaux, 1600–1789*, 2 vols (Oxford: Voltaire Foundation, 1991), I, 282–93. On its later history see Simon Burrows, *French Exile Journalism and European Politics* (Woodbridge: Royal Historical Society, 2000).

18 AN, 446AP/3, 'Mémoire pour J.-P. Brissot', fo 28.

19 *MSB*, IX, 24 September 1776; CPA 517 fos 204–5 and CPA 518 fo 53, letters of Beaumarchais to Vergennes, 8 September 1776, *BCE* documents 57 and 59.

20 Beaumarchais to Sartine, London, 14 October 1776, in Donvez, *Politique de Beaumarchais*, pp. 422–5, quote at p. 424; Gudin, *Histoire de Beaumarchais*, pp. 164–5. See also Vergennes to Louis XVI, 23 February 1776, *BCE*, document 17; *Louis XVI and the Comte de Vergennes: Correspondance*, edited by John Hardman and Munro Price, SVEC 364 (Oxford: Voltaire Foundation, 1998), pp. 221–2; Pomeau, *Beaumarchais*, p. 87. On Vignoles' journal see Beaumarchais to Louis XVI, 27 April 1775 (extract) in Donvez, *Politique de Beaumarchais*, pp. 411–15.

21 On Beaumarchais' lobbying campaign, see Spinelli, 'Beaumarchais and d'Eon', pp. 57–62. Beaumarchais' lobbying has gone unnoticed by most previous scholars, who assume he took the role unwillingly.

22 Gudin, *Histoire de Beaumarchais*, p. 168, citing an undated memorandum to Louis XVI.

23 Kates, *Monsieur d'Eon*, pp. 220, 333n.15.

24 ULBC, file 65 records social engagements on 15 July, 23 July, 8 September, 27 September, and 28 December. The heart cost a guinea in Birmingham.

25 The discussion of d'Eon's gender transformation in this and subsequent paragraphs draws heavily on Kates, *Monsieur d'Eon*, pp. 217–29. See also James Lander, 'A tale of two hoaxes in Britain and France in 1775', *Historical Journal*, 49:4 (2006), 995–1024. Both Lander and Kates note that the insistence that d'Eon dress as a woman only entered the negotiations once Beaumarchais was involved.

26   ULBC, file 1, Chap. VIII, 3.

27   On d'Eon's theology see Kates, *Monsieur d'Eon*, pp. 278–91.

28   Simon Burrows, 'The Chevalier d'Eon, media manipulation and the making of an eighteenth-century celebrity' in Burrows et al., eds, *The Chevalier d'Eon and His Worlds*, pp. 13–23.

29   For copies of the Transaction, see CPA supplément 16 fos 436–42 and BMT, R7; Pierre Pinsseau, *L'Etrange Destinée du Chevalier d'Eon*, 2nd edition (Paris: Clavreuil, 1945), pp. 184–90. Lever, *Beaumarchais*, II, 109, records the more extravagant aspects of d'Eon's claim, including 15,000 *livres* for lost rents and vines in Tonnerre and 100,000 *livres* for living and extraordinary expenses.

30   CPA 516 fos 219–28 and BMT, R. 22, d'Eon 'Campagnes du Sr Caron de Beaumarchais'; ULBC, file 65 p. 149. ULBC, file 3 fos 233–4 contains Ferrer's receipt.

31   On evidence for the cash offer, see below. Some discussion of the wagers certainly occurred at this time. In a letter of 25 September 1775 (AN, 277AP/1, dossier Morande fo 216), Morande told d'Eon that he had been approached for advice about the policies in view of d'Eon's possible return to France. Morande's gambit received a cold reception (see 277AP/1, dossier Morande fo 217, Morande to d'Eon, 26 September 1775), but on 27 September Beaumarchais returned with good news from Versailles and d'Eon, Morande and Francy all dined with him (ULBC, file 65 p. 149).

32   CPA 516 fos 233–4, 'Etat des pièces de . . . la correspondance entre Caron de Beaumarchais . . . Ferrers . . . et le Chevalier d'Eon', 28 May 1776.

33   *Morning Post*, 14 November 1775. The original French version appeared the previous day.

34   Frédéric Gaillardet, *The Memoirs of Chevalier d'Eon*, translated by Antonia White (London: Anthony Blond, 1970) [original French edition, Paris, 1866]), p. 265; Lever, *Beaumarchais*, II, 127.

35   ULBC, file 65 p. 153, entry for 28 December 1775.

36   CPA 516 fos 219–28 and BMT, R. 22, d'Eon, 'Campagnes du Sr Beaumarchais'. The passages quoted here use a slightly adapted version of the wording of Antonia White's translation in Gaillardet, *Memoirs of d'Eon*, pp. 265–6. The cause of the quarrel is confirmed by d'Eon's private memoir of the meeting in ULBC, file 65 p. 153. CPA 513 fo 433, Ferrers to Beaumarchais, Staunton Harold, 13 January 1776 [copy], records d'Eon's arrival at the Ferrers estate and subsequent illness.

37   ULBC, file 31 p. 154, Beaumarchais to d'Eon, 31 December 1775.

38   CPA 514 fos 24–33, d'Eon to Beaumarchais, 7 January 1776.

39   ULBC, file 31 pp. 146–53, Beaumarchais to d'Eon, London, 18 January 1776, translated in Kates, *Monsieur d'Eon*, pp. 235–6, [copy in BMT, R16 bis]. ULBC, file 31 pp. 140–2, contains a previous letter, dated 9 January, in which Beaumarchais accuses d'Eon of ingratitude, warns against his 'rage d'imprimer' and raises the question of missing documents.

40   BMT, R17 bis, d'Eon to Beaumarchais, Staunton Harold, 30 January 1776 (copy), translated in Kates, *Monsieur d'Eon*, pp. 237–40.

41   On this article see Kates, *Monsieur d'Eon*, p. 243; CPA 516 fos 233–4, 'Etat des pièces', 28 May 1776.

42   AN, 277AP fo 296, Morande to d'Eon, 4 March 1776; fo 293, Morande to d'Eon, 6 March 1776; ULBC, file 3 fo 181, note of d'Eon dated 16 March 1776; ULBC, file 65 p. 157, entry of 18 March 1776.

43   AN, 277AP/1, dossier Morande fos 286–7, Morande to d'Eon, 4 May 1776; fo 284, d'Eon to Morande, 5 May 1776 [copy]; fos 279–83, Morande to d'Eon, 5 May 1776; CPA 513 fos 421–3, d'Eon's information to King's Bench, at fo 421.

44   Several copies of the witness testimony exist. For the English text see CPA 513 fos 435–7; for French versions CPA 516 fos 51–3; BMT, R18 bis; BL, Add. MS 11,341 fos 191–2. The declaration, dated 8 May, was signed by La Chèvre, Vignoles and Jacques Dupré. The next day, Beaumarchais and d'Eon met one last time at the home of the banker Duval. According to d'Eon, they met by chance and only exchanged pleasantries (see ULBC, file 65 p. 160, entry for 9 May 1776; CPA 516 fos 219–28 and BMT, R22, d'Eon to Vergennes, 27 May 1776).

45   CPA 516 fos 233–4, 'Etat des pièces', 28 May 1776; BL, Add. MS 11,340 fo 8, *Westminster Gazette*, 20–24 August 1776 (cutting); AFB, Morande to Beaumarchais, 2 June 1776, *BCE* document 35.

46   CPA 516 fos 211–18 and 219–28, d'Eon to Vergennes, 27 May 1776. There are copies in BMT, R20 and R22.

47 Kates, *Monsieur d'Eon*, p. 242.

48 AN, 277AP/1, dossier Morande fo 266, Morande to d'Eon, undated, received 24 May 1776.

49 Ibid., fos 258–61, Morande to d'Eon, 4 June 1776 at fo 261.

50 CPA 517 fo 237, O'Gorman to Vergennes, London, 6 August 1776.

51 Ibid., fos 228, 'Copy of the Chevalier d'Eon's first Billet in answer to the libel, which . . . Morande addressed to Mademoiselle d'Eon on the third of August about noon.' [English]. For another copy see CPA supplément 17 fos 8–9.

52 *Westminster Gazette*, 6–10 August 1776.

53 CPA supplément 17 fo 10, Morande to d'Eon, 7 August 1776 [copy]. There is another copy in CPA 517 fo 238. On d'Eon's swords see ULBC, file 65 p. 166; on Eliza, AN, 277AP/1, dossier Morande fos 302–3, Morande to O'Gorman, 7 August 1776.

54 CPA 517 fo 242–4, 'A copy of the Chev. d'Eon's second message of the 8th of August 1776 to the Sr de Morande', quotes at fo 242 and 244 [English]. French version at CPA 517 fos 239–40; CPA supplément 17 fos 11–12.

55 CPA 517 fos 278–9, Pienne's annotation (dated 13 August) on O'Gorman's challenge to Morande, 12 August 1776.

56 Ibid., fos 308–9, Morande to Pienne, 16 August 1776 and declaration of Pienne, same date.

57 *Morning Chronicle*, 23 August 1776; ULBC file 65, p. 167. See also BL, Add. MS 11,340 fo 7, *Westminster Gazette*, 20–24 August 1776 (cutting).

58 CPA supplément 17 fo 6, O'Gorman to Vergennes, 20 August 1776.

59 BL, Add. MS 11,340, fo 10, *Morning Post*, 27 August 1776.

60 A note in d'Eon's private account books (ULBC, file 65 fo 333, 5 March 1786) states Morande was the *Westminster Gazette*'s publisher. For accounts of Morande's dispute with d'Eon in French sources see: Mairobert, *Espion anglois*, VIII, 1–29; IX, 1–19; *CSP*, IV, 125–31; VI, 3–6, 33, 82–105; Ange Goudar, *L'Espion françois à Londres, ou observations critiques sur l'Angleterre et les anglois*, 2 vols (London: aux depens de l'auteur, 1780 [original edition, 1779]), I, 203–40.

61 BL, Add. MS 11,340, fo 8, *Westminster Gazette*, 20–24 August 1776 (cutting). On the fabrication of evidence against Guerchy see Burrows, *Blackmail*, p. 92; Burrows, 'D'Eon, media manipulation and celebrity', pp. 18–20.

62 BL, Add. MS 11,340, fo 16, *Public Ledger*, 2 September 1776. Emphasis in original.

63 Ibid., fos 7–8 and 13, *Westminster Gazette*, 20–24 August; 24–27 August 1776; 27–31 August 1776 (cuttings).

64 Ibid., fo 6, *Morning Post*, 23 August 1776 (cutting).

65 Ibid., fo 13, *Westminster Gazette*, 27–31 August 1776 (cutting).

66 Ibid., fo 17, *Westminster Gazette*, 31 August to 3 September 1776 (cutting).

67 Ibid., fo 22, *Public Advertiser*, 6 September 1776 (cutting).

68 Ibid., fo 17 *Westminster Gazette*, 31 August–3 September 1776 (cutting). I thank Moira Bonnington for sending me her extensive researches on Horneck.

69 Ibid.

70 *Morning Chronicle*, 6 September 1776.

71 On the Horneck affair see *St. James Chronicle*, 1–4 March 1777; *Gazetteer*, 4 March 1777; *Morning Post*, 4, 5 and 8 March 1777; *London Evening Post*, 6–9 March 1777; *Morning Chronicle*, 10 March 1777.

72 *Morning Post*, 10 March 1777.

73 ULBC, file 65 p. 167, entry for 18 August 1776; CPA supplément 17 fo 6, O'Gorman to Vergennes, 20 August 1776; BMT, L102, d'Eon to Sir John Fielding, 28 August 1776.

74 If d'Eon did profit from the policies, he most likely received a commission (£400 p.a. according to Morande) from the underwriters to conceal his sex to prevent claims: see *Public Ledger*, 4 September 1776. This is compatible with d'Eon's behaviour and is supported by the existence of an account in d'Eon's papers (BL, Add. Ms. 11,341 fos 193–4) which calculates a commission on policies traded between 28 March and 19 June 1770 (see above Chapter 2, note 29). There is also the testimony of Beaumarchais and Hayes that d'Eon attended a party in the country with Samuel Swinton (who lent him £200 as an advance), Robert Ainslie (soon to be ambassador to Contantinople), Sir John Clark and Captain Chasley, who had offered him £10,000 to reveal his sex. According to Beaumarchais, the man bringing the money failed to show up, so d'Eon decamped and swore an affidavit that he had never had, and never would have, an interest in the policies. However, Hayes said in court that because d'Eon refused their blandishments, the

conspirators planned to ambush him while he slept, but d'Eon guessed their intentions and fled. D'Eon later borrowed £200 from Beaumarchais to repay Swinton's advance. Beaumarchais forwarded the receipt to Vergennes. See Beaumarchais to Vergennes, 12 July 1776, *BCE* document 39; ULBC file 27, 'extrait du procès sur le sexe du chevalier d'Eon', pp. 248–9.

75 BL, Add. MS 11,340 for 34, *Westminster Gazette*, 10–14 September 1776; CPA 513 fos 421–3, d'Eon's information against Morande; ULBC, file 65 p. 168.

76 BL, Add. MS 11,340 fo 44, *Morning Post*, 19 November 1776 (cutting). In fact, the hearing was delayed several days.

77 See *Morning Chronicle*, 29 November 1776 and BL, Add. MS 11,340 fos 45–8, *London Evening Packet*, 25–27 November 1776; *Morning Post*, 28 November 1776; *Public Ledger*, 28 November 1776 (cuttings).

78 On the Hayes-Jacques case, see ULBC, file 27 pp. 219–60; see also at pp. 261–83, d'Eon's letter to holders of policies on his sex and the jury that heard the case. An unidentified press cutting (ULBC, file 60 p. 201 bis) tells of Mansfield's disgust. See also Kates, *Monsieur d'Eon*, pp. 248–9.

79 *Morning Post*, 10 December 1777; Kates, *Monsieur d'Eon*, pp. 250–1. Intriguingly, four witnesses in this case insisted that d'Eon was male.

80 AFB fos 252–3, Morande to Beaumarchais, 14 March 1786.

81 ULBC, file 65 pp. 345 and 354, entries for 9 May 1787, 30 June 1788; AN, 277AP/1, dossier Morande fos 299, 300, 201, 202, 204, letters of Morande to d'Eon dated respectively 15 and 17 August 1786, 30 April and 3 May 1789 (both letters of this date).

82 ULBC, file 55 shows that d'Eon visited Morande's home on 3 May 1790, 9 and 18 January 1791, and 8 April 1791; see also AN, 277AP/1, dossier Morande, letters of Morande to d'Eon, 14 and 19 February 1791. [These two letters lack folio numbers].

83 *CE*, 16 July 1790; ULBC file 7, 'Mémoire pour servir de Préface ou d'Introduction [to d'Eon's unpublished memoirs], écrit en 1794', p. 36.

84 Kates, *Monsieur d'Eon*, pp. xii–xiii; see also Gaillardet, *Memoirs of d'Eon*, pp. 312–13.

85 ULBC, file 3 pp. 253–6, d'Eon to Drouin, 25 April 1777.

86 Anonymous letter to Franklin, [before 21 December 1776] at http://www.franklinpapers.org/franklin/framedNames.jsp on 10 October 2009. Franklin's editors tentatively attribute this letter to Lauraguais, but Tort or d'Eon seem likelier candidates. I thank Paul Agnani for this reference.

87 CPA 526 fos 416–17, Tort's list of points to discuss with Vergennes. CPA 523 fos 203–4, Tort to Raynach, 6 June 1777, insists that Tort was the first to denounce Morande's perfidy, but he was probably d'Eon's front man.

88 Pelleport, *Diable*, pp. 32–3.

89 CPA 515 fos 321–4, Beaumarchais to Vergennes, 16 April 1776, *BCE* document 20; NA, SP78/170, Horace St Paul to Weymouth, 1 May 1776, *BCE* document 25; Stormont to Weymouth, 21 August 1776, *BCE* document 52; Stormont to Weymouth, 25 September 1776, *BCE* document 64; SP78/300, Stormont to Weymouth, 6 November 1776, *BCE* document 68.

90 CPA 515 fos 321–4, Beaumarchais to Vergennes, 16 April 1776; CPA 515 fos 422–5, Lauraguais to Vergennes, 26 April 1776.

91 Hannah Barker, 'Henry Bate Dudley' in the *Oxford DNB*. Bate added Dudley to his surname after the period discussed here.

92 Information supplied by Nicholas Rodger.

93 *Gazetteer*, 27 August 1778, letter of Morande to the editor. Punctuation and italics as in original.

94 *General Advertiser*, 27 August 1778. The dispute and 'Queries' are briefly discussed in W. Hindle, *The Morning Post* (London: Routledge, 1937), p. 17.

95 *General Advertiser*, 27 August 1778.

96 The report appeared in the *Morning Post*, 29 August 1778, and the *Morning Chronicle, Gazetteer, General Advertiser, St James Chronicle, London Evening Post, London Chronicle, General Evening Post, Westminster Journal* and *Public Advertiser*. Details concerning Morande's hat only appear in the regional press: see *The British Chronicle or Pugh's Hereford Journal*, 3 September 1778 and the *Chester Chronicle*, 4 September 1778.

97 *Gazetteer*, and various other papers, 31 August 1778.

98 Letter of 'Test' to *General Advertiser*, 2 September 1778. See also the letter of 'The Town' to

General Advertiser, 3 September 1778, which remarks that though 'both [may] stand pistol shot as well as any highwayman in the kingdom', Bate and Morande are equally devoid of honour.

99   Pelleport, *Diable*, p. 115n.

100   Morande, *Réplique à Brissot*, p. 23. Morande says only that the meeting with Lord North took place in 1778 after the outbreak of war. However, his letter to the *General Advertiser* is dated from 40 Duke Street, so we can reasonably infer that the interview occurred before he left London and after the duel.

101   Morande, *Réplique à Brissot*, p. 23; Pelleport, *Diable*, p. 34; Manuel, *Police dévoilée*, I, 267. London Metropolitan Archives, G1/1, Surveyor of Highways accounts, 1772–1826; MR/PLT 1418–1420, Land Tax Assessments, Great Stanmore, 1780–1784; DRO 14/A1/5, St John the Evangelist Church, Great Stanmore, Register of Baptisms, Marriages and Burials, 4 April 1779. See also Court Rolls for the Manor of Great Stanmore in the County of Middlesex, 1764–1799, copies of which exist in the Percy Davenport manuscripts at Harrow Library, fos 145, 151–2, 153, 272. These reveal that Morande's property and two adjoining ones comprised a tenement covering two acres belonging to the local rector, Joseph Smith. Surviving records suggest that Morande's house stood on Church Road just East of where Pynnacles Close now joins it.

102   See p. 53.

103   Beaumarchais to an unknown correspondent, Paris, 24 January 1781, reproduced in *BCE*, I, 112–15.

104   Letters of Morande to [Sartine] dated 24 June, 15 July and 8 August 1780, *BCE* documents 241, 245, 249. The last of them appears to confirm that Sartine was the addressee.

105   The verses were doubtless scandalous and may have been the notorious anonymous *Amours de Charlot et Toinette*, which Beaumarchais may have written. See Burrows, *Blackmail*, p. 103. On this poem, see p. 132.

106   Beaumarchais to an unknown correspondent, Paris, 24 January 1781, *BCE*, I, 112–15.

107   Swinton to Philip Stephens, Rye, 27 April 1778, *BCE* document 162. Other letters concerning Swinton from around this time can be found in the Sandwich papers at the National Maritime Museum (SAN/F13/14, 16 and 114). I thank Nicholas Rodger for supplying details of these documents.

108   Swinton to Beaumarchais, London, 17 February 1781, *BCE* document 270.

109   Beaumarchais to unknown correspondent, Paris, 24 January 1781, *BCE*, I, 112–15.

Notes to Chapter 5: On His Majesty's Secret Service

1   *Public Advertiser*, 28 July 1781; *Morning Chronicle*, 28 July 1781.

2   *Morning Chronicle*, 9 January 1781.

3   The main sources consulted on La Motte's arrest and trial were NA, TS 11/793/2 and TS11/1116, Rex versus Francis Henry de La Motte; *Public Advertiser*, 4–20 January and 14–20 July 1781; *CE*, July 1781; *Morning Herald*, 4–31 January and 16 July–15 August 1781; *Morning Chronicle*, 8–20 January and 14 July–4 August 1781; *St James Chronicle*, 4–20 January and 14–17 July 1781; 'The trial of Francis Henry de La Motte for high treason', *The Proceedings of the Old Bailey* at http://www.oldbaileyonline.org/browse.jsp?id=t17810711-1&div=t17810711-1&terms=La|Motte#highlight on 10 October 2009. *The Burney Collection of Early English Newspapers* was also searched electronically for references to Morande. Of over 100 'hits', none linked him to La Motte.

4   CPA 563 fos 28–9, Barthélemy to Montmorin, 14 April 1787.

5   CPA 565 fos 103–9, Morande to Montmorin, 28 April 1788, *BCE* document 516.

6   Ibid., fo 178, Montmorin to La Luzerne, 14 May 1788. His first despatches to the foreign ministry (in CPA supplément 28) date from December 1786.

7   Manuel, *Police dévoilée*, II, 253.

8   Pelleport, *Diable*, p. 34.

9   Manuel, *Police dévoilée*, I, 267. The only ambassador who could conceivably have visited the gardens is the Count de Moustier in early 1783.

10   See H.M. Scott, *British Foreign Policy in the Age of the American Revolution* (Oxford: Clarendon Press, 1990), p. 214; Richard B. Morris, *The Peacemakers. The Great Powers and American*

Independence (New York: Harper and Row, 1970), p. 133. I thank Nicholas Rodger for these references.

11   Pelleport, *Diable*, p. 34.

12   On the redemption of Morande's annuity see: AFB, Beaumarchais to Sartine, [undated letter, Spring 1775], *BCE* document 4; CPA 511 fo 301, Vergennes to Louis XVI, 24 August 1775: CPA 521 fo 126, Beaumarchais to Van Neck, 15 September 1775; CPA 512 fo 64, Morande to Beaumarchais, 31 October 1775.

13   AFB fos 38–9, Morande to Beaumarchais, 7 August 1782, *BCE* document 324; NA, C12/440/25, Morande versus Woodifield, 28 July 1781; CPA 565 fos 103–9, Morande to Montmorin, 28 April 1788.

14   Beaumarchais to Morande, 29 May 1784, *BCE* document 384; Swinton's accounts with Beaumarchais, 7 September 1783, *BCE* document 347; AFB fos 171–2, Morande to Beaumarchais, 20 October 1787, *BCE* document 509; fos 51–2, Morande to Beaumarchais, 13 June 1788, *BCE* document 517; fo 275, bond of Morande to Francy, 10 July 1781. This bond was signed over to Beaumarchais on 29 July 1783 (AFB fo 274). Beaumarchais probably hoped to use it as a weapon of last resort against Morande.

15   CPA 565 fos 288–90, [Morande] to [Montmorin], 18 June 1788; CPA 550 fos 313–14, d'Adhémar to Vergennes, 7 December 1784; CPA 559 fos 224–5 and 228–9, d'Adhémar to Montmorin, 13 March 1787; fos 251–2, Montmorin to d'Adhémar, 25 March 1787; CPA 560 fos 141–2, Morande to Montmorin, 2 June 1787; AFB fos 53–4, Morande to Beaumarchais, 27 March 1789, *BCE* document 534.

16   Beaumarchais to Morande, 29 May 1784, *BCE* document 384.

17   The key documents concerning Francy's succession are ibid and AFB fo 289, Morande to Beaumarchais, 10 June 1784, *BCE* document 388; fos 298–9, Rose-Antoinette Théveneau Villedey to Beaumarchais, 10 June 1784; fos 292–3, [Jean-Bernard] Villedey to Beaumarchais, 18 June 1784; fos 294–5, 296–7, 300–1, 304–6, letters of Louis Théveneau to Beaumarchais, dated respectively 26 July, 3 August, 16 August and 2 November 1784; fo 291 bis, Guichot to Beaumarchais, Autun, 6 August 1784; fos 302–3, Philiberte Belin to Beaumarchais, Arnay-le-Duc, 20 August 1784; fos 43–4, Morande to Beaumarchais, 7 September 1784 (NB the abridgement of this letter in *BCE*, document 399, covers other matters); fos 14–15, Eliza Morande to Junquières, May 1785 [copy] and Junquières to Eliza Morande, 19 May 1785, which contains the quote. Jacques-Louis-Antoine de Junquières was a lawyer at the *Parlement* of Paris and *agent d'affaires* for the Prince de Conti (information communicated by Bernard Leblanc).

18   This total includes around £8,425 from his salary as a spy; £4,300 from Francy; £1,400 from the suppression of the *Secret Memoirs of a Woman of Pleasure*; £875 from selling half his government annuity; income from family annuities totalling approximately £3,250; at least £625 from Beaumarchais; £210 in gratuities; £800 profit from the *Gazetier cuirassé* and £1,466 earned as editor of the *CE*.

19   Swinton's account for Beaumarchais, 1783, *BCE* document 347; Swinton to Francy, 15 April 1784, *BCE* document 374; AFB fos 107/9, Morande to Beaumarchais, 17 August 1789; fos 176–7, Morande to Beaumarchais, 7 September 1789, *BCE* document 550; fo 275, bond of Morande to Francy dated 10 July 1781.

20   AFB fos 159–60, Morande to Beaumarchais, 15 December 1789, *BCE* document 557. On his £51 debt to Le Chevalier see fos 107–9, Morande to Beaumarchais, 17 August 1789 and fos 80–1, Morande to Beaumarchais, 1 September 1789.

21   AFB fos 16–17, Morande to Beaumarchais, 24 December 1789.

22   See Burrows, *Blackmail*, especially pp. 99–111

23   Morris, *The Peacemakers*, p. 113.

24   CPA 559 fos 224–5 and 228–9, d'Adhémar to Montmorin, 13 March 1787 at fo 229, *BCE* document 492 (abridged).

25   CPA 563 fos 28–9, Barthélemy to Montmorin, London, 4 July 1787.

26   CPA 541 fos 227–32, Moustier to Vergennes, London, 23 March 1783 at fo 231.

27   For 'States of the navy' in the foreign ministry archives see, for example, CPA 543 fo 355; CPA 567 fos 76–9, 259–69. Several documents concerning naval intelligence in AN, B^7 473 are almost certainly from Morande, including naval lists (pièces 49, 52, 55, 58, 59 and 60); pièce 57 (an unsigned letter dated 15 July 1787 in Morande's handwriting); and pièce 61, an undated 'Note

sur le devoir du contre-maître et second canonier'. Several documents in B^7 456 probably also originated with Morande.

28   CPA 566 fos 209–32, Morande, 'Etat actuel de la Marine d'Angleterre [etc.]' dated 24 August 1788. This document was enclosed in fos 246–8, Morande to Montmorin, 30 August 1788.

29   Nicholas Rodger, *The Command of the Ocean: A Naval History of Britain, 1649–1815* (London: Penguin, 2004), p. 361.

30   On tensions over India in 1788, see Jeremy Black, *British Foreign Policy in an Age of Revolutions, 1783–1793* (Cambridge: Cambridge University Press, 1994), pp. 163–4.

31   Nicholas Rodger, private email communication to the author, 22 April 2009.

32   Morande provided greater detail on this innovation in CPA 566 fos 102–3, [Morande] to [Montmorin], 25 July 1788. See also CPA 567 fos 341–2, [Morande] to [Montmorin], undated letter [August 1788]. Quote from Nicholas Rodger, private email communication to the author, 22 April 2009. On Morande's friendship with Douglas see CPA supplément 28 fos 199–200, [Morande] to [Montmorin], 22 July 1787.

33   Rodger, *Command of the Ocean*, p. 420.

34   This discussion of naval gunnery draws on ibid., pp. 420–1. The quotes in this paragraph come from the same source. Professor Rodger added (private correspondence, 22 April 2009) that he had not come across carronades mounted in the tops, which would be difficult to supply with ammunition. Morande records reporting the capture of the *Hébé* in CPA 565, fos 103–9, [Morande] to [Montmorin], 28 April 1788, *BCE* document 516.

35   The earliest of Morande's regular reports, addressed to Vergennes on 25 December 1786, is in CPA supplément 28 fos 177–8. A further 16 hitherto unknown reports from December 1786 to October 1787 survive at fos 179–214. Gunnar and Mavis von Proschwitz, who first noted Morande's spy reports, did not find these earliest reports. Further reports are found in CPA volumes 562 (3 reports, one of which is a summary copy); 564 (3 reports); 565 (2); 566 (6); 567 (20); 568 (11); 569 (14); 570 (2); and 577 (1 report). Morande's first use of the signature '#' is in CPA 567 fos 345–6, [Morande] to [Montmorin], undated letter [mid August 1788]. For earlier material that may be traced to him, see above note 27. His despatches to Launay do not seem to survive in the Bastille papers; nor has his correspondence with Baudouin been located.

36   CPA 566 fo 111, 'Note pour Morande', 27 July 1788. This note was read to Morande by Barthélemy in early August: see fo 170, Barthélemy to Montmorin, London, 12 August 1788.

37   CPA supplément 28, fos 194–5, [Morande] to [Montmorin], 3 July 1787.

38   CPA supplément 28, fos 189–90, [Morande] to [Montmorin], 22 June 1787.

39   *Annual Register*, 1774, p. 179.

40   CPA supplément 18 fos 284–5, 'Mémoire de Sr Barthélemy, joined to his letter of 1 June 1790; CPA 538 fo 239, Goëzman to Baudouin [?], London, 4 October 1782; CPA 541 fos 227–32, Moustier to Vergennes, London, 23 March 1783. Unaware that Morande was already employed by the navy, Vergennes decided that correspondence with the ports was too sensitive to be entrusted to refugees: CPA 541 fo 322, Vergennes to Moustier, 2 April 1783. For Pellevé's summary of his services see CPA 566 fos 262–3, Pellevé to Montmorin, London, 7 September 1788. His 'fresh' intelligence had already been provided by Morande, sometimes months earlier.

41   CPA 562 fos 26–32, 'Extrait d'une lettre de Sieur Morande de Londres', 13 October 1787.

42   See CPA 565, fos 103–9, [Morande] to [Montmorin], 28 April 1788, *BCE*, document 516 and Morande's correspondence with Montmorin in CPA supplément 28, fos 177–214 passim.

43   See CPA 565, fos 103–9, [Morande] to [Montmorin], 28 April 1788, *BCE*, document 516. CPA 565 fos 286–7, [Morande] to [Montmorin], 18 June 1788, records that Taylor (whose name neither I nor Nicholas Rodger know from other sources) no longer worked for the Admiralty but maintained the correspondence.

44   CPA 565 fos 286–7, 18 June 1788; CPA 569 fos 332–3, [Morande] to [Montmorin], 8 June 1789. On Forth see Marion Ward, *Forth* (London: Phillimore, 1982).

45   CPA 567 fos 42–5, Barthélemy to Montmorin, 21 October 1788; fos 55–6, [Morande] to [Montmorin], same date.

46   Ibid., fo 57, Barthélemy to Montmorin, 20 October 1788.

47   Ibid., fos 358–9, [Morande] to [Montmorin], undated letter [October or November 1788].

48   See in particular, CPA 567 fos 351–4, [Morande] to [Montmorin], undated letter wrongly ascribed to 1788 [actually written on 31 January 1789]. A reference to the previous day's being the feast of Charles I, king and martyr, fixes the letter's date precisely.

49 CPA 568 fos 19–20, [Morande] to [Montmorin], 6 January 1789.

50 CPA 569 fos 280–1, [Morande] to [Montmorin], 26 May 1789.

51 CPA 568 fos 220–1, [Morande] to [Montmorin], 17 February 1789.

52 Ibid., fos 267–8, [Morande] to [Montmorin], 24 February 1789.

53 Among evidence given to support this view of George III see CPA 567 fos 343–4 and fos 347–8, [Morande] to [Montmorin], undated letters [probably written 31 August 1788 and early September 1788 respectively] which assert that George III uttered 'horrors' against French ministers when he met the inventor Argand.

54 Except where indicated the material that follows comes from CPA 565 fos 103–9, [Morande] to [Montmorin], 28 April 1788, *BCE* document 516.

55 CPA 566 fos 102–3, [Morande] to [Montmorin], 25 July 1788; fos 246–9, [Morande] to [Montmorin], 30 August 1788. The Cairo to Suez route comprised a series of stations manned by Arabs. Morande learned of it from one of Baldwin's friends, though curiously he also announced Baldwin's intention to establish an overland communications route in *CE*, 27 July 1787. I thank Professor Edward Ingram for supplementary information on these routes. Ainslie was a friend of Morande's employer and associate Swinton: Morande offers a sensationalised account of his career in *AP*, 9 (7 July 1791), pp. 231–2. See also above Chapter 4, note 74.

56 Morande said his claims could be verified by consulting Baudouin's correspondence. Most of the items he mentions are found, unattributed, in CPA 540–7. Pereyra was almost certainly either Jacob Pereyra (1743–24 March 1794), the future Conventionnel who was executed with the Hébertists, or his brother. Pereyra apparently served as a messenger between Morande and Beaumarchais: see AFB fos 110–11, Morande to Beaumarchais, 26 December 1787.

57 J. R. Harris, *Industrial Espionage and Technology Transfer: Britain and France in the Eighteenth Century* (Aldershot: Ashgate, 1998) contains a chapter on Le Turc, including (at p. 452) the evaluation of his activities quoted here. The pulleys are discussed at pp. 439–44. Harris does not mention Morande, but CPA supplément 28 fos 177–8, [Morande] to [Montmorin], 25 December 1786 proves his involvement with the project and the workers, whom he names as Ross (the foreman), Dayet (the son of a pulley-maker), Ball and Brooks. Harris (p. 441) calls the first two Ross and Dyatt and mentions a third man, Lichfield, who accompanied them to France in August 1786. He does not mention Ball and Brooks. For Morande's recommendation for Le Turc (who was already involved in espionage), see AFB fos 240–1, Morande to Beaumarchais, 6 October 1785. See also CPA 565 fos 103–9, Morande to Montmorin, 28 April 1788, *BCE* document 516. In *BCE* Gunnar and Mavis von Proschwitz transcribe his name 'Le Ture' and seem unaware of his significance.

58 Harris, *Industrial Espionage*, pp. 501–2.

59 CPA 559 fos 226–7, Morande to d'Adhémar, 12 March 1787, asks d'Adhémar to confirm to Montmorin that Morande sent the memorandum that persuaded Vergennes to invite Boulton and Watt to France. CPA 567 fos 343–4, [Morande] to [Montmorin], undated letter [probably written 31 August 1788] suggests that Argand and Morande enjoyed close relations: see above note 53. Morande campaigned on Argand's behalf after a controversial British court judgment over a patent case: see *CE*, 28 February 1786; 12 May 1786; 19 and 23 January 1787.

60 CPA 569 fos 332–3, [Morande] to [Montmorin], 8 June 1789.

61 CPA 565 fo 122–3, [Morande] to [Menneville], 2 May 1788. Morande followed the crisis closely in his newspaper: see *CE*, 2, 6 and 9 May, and 6 and 24 June 1788.

62 CPA 571 fos 243–52, La Luzerne to Montmorin, London, 9 December 1789 [cypher]. Morande and La Luzerne denounced Shee and Morande's old friend Dr Saiffert as d'Orléans' agents in London.

63 See also CPA 564 fos 320–1, [Morande] to [Montmorin], 2 March 1788.

64 On British strategic thinking, see Rodger, *Command of the Ocean*, p. 366. Rodger does not mention New Zealand hardwoods.

65 See CPA 569 fos 36–7, [Morande] to [Montmorin], 31 March 1789; fos 204–5, [Morande] to [Montmorin], 5 May 1789; *CL*, 28 March 1789. The three earliest extant French-language reports on the Botany Bay colony are Morande's reports in the *CL* and CPA and La Luzerne's report enclosed with his ambassadorial despatch of 27 March 1789 (CPA 569 fos 28–31).

66 CPA 565 fos 288–90, [Morande] to [Montmorin], 18 June 1788.

67 On this man, who Morande says was born in Calais and supplied whatever he asked, see CPA 565 fos 246–9, [Morande] to [Montmorin], 30 August 1788; CPA 566 fos 102–3, [Morande]

to [Montmorin], 25 July 1788; CPA 567 fos 341–2, [Morande] to [Montmorin], undated letter [August 1788]; CPA 569 fos 85–6, [Morande] to [Montmorin], 7 April 1789. Morande reveals that he was brother-in-law of an MP called Kenwick (or possibly Fenwick or Kendrick).

68   CPA 565 fos 288–90, [Morande] to [Montmorin], 18 June 1788.

69   CPA supplément 28 fos 205–6, [Morande] to [Montmorin], 14 and 15 August 1787. On Saiffert's relations with Lamballe see Vircondelet, *Princesse de Lamballe*, pp. 161–5, 168–71. CPA 566 fos 289–90, [Morande] to Montmorin, 16 September 1788 reports completed or impending visits to Chatham and the Medway, Deptford, Woolwich and Portsmouth.

70   CPA 569, fos 332–3, [Morande] to [Montmorin], 8 June 1789, reports Hawkesbury was being marginalized for opposing the queen on key issues during the regency crisis.

71   CPA 566 fos 102–3, [Morande] to [Montmorin], 25 July 1788; fos 309–10, [Morande] to [Montmorin], 23 September 1788.

72   CPA 567 fos 343–4, [Morande] to [Montmorin], undated letter [probably written 31 August 1788].

73   CPA 570 fos 49–50, [Morande] to [Montmorin], 30 June 1789. Morande also mentions a conversation with a Scottish MP named Stewart without indicating his political affiliation (CPA 568 fos 40–1, [Morande] to [Montmorin], 13 January 1789).

74   CPA 568 fos 74–5, [Morande] to [Montmorin], 20 January 1789.

75   BL, Add. MS 35,118 fo 23, Morande to Sheridan, 7 March 1776.

76   CPA 564 fos 314–17, [Morande] to [Montmorin], undated letter [annotated February 1788]. For Morande's journalistic comment on British customs abuses see p. 182.

77   CPA 569 fos 119–20, [Morande] to [Montmorin], 14 April 1789.

78   CPA 568 fos 276–7, [Morande] to [Montmorin], 3 March 1789.

79   AFB fos 189–90, Morande to Beaumarchais, 2 June 1789, *BCE* document 539.

80   CPA supplément 28 fos 207–12, [Morande] to [Montmorin], 29 September 1787. I have found no evidence of such a campaign.

81   MD Angleterre 73 fos 125–34, [summary of the] Report of General Green on the work at Cherbourg, sent by Morande, 1784.

82   Ibid.

83   CPA 565 fos 286–7, [Morande] to [Montmorin], 18 June 1788; CPA 568 fos 40–1, [Morande] to [Montmorin], 13 January 1789. The only evidence of George's rank comes from Lavirotte, 'Notice sur Morande'.

84   CPA 566 fos 102–3, [Morande] to [Montmorin], 25 July 1788.

85   AFB fos 82–3, Eliza to Beaumarchais, 20 March 1789; fos 197–8, Morande to Beaumarchais, 16 June 1789, published in *BCE* document 540; fos 161–2, Morande to Beaumarchais, 10 July 1789 (cf. the account at fos 91–2); fo 77 bis, Morande to Beaumarchais, 9 October 1789. Morande claimed he paid Salisbury 100 guineas per year for George's equipment and maintenance, but according to Nicholas Rodger (private e-mail) 25 guineas would be excessive. Presumably Morande was exaggerating his expenses or Salisbury, suspecting Morande's game, was profiteering at his expense.

86   See letters of Morande to Beaumarchais, 11 March 1784, (*BCE* document 366); 17 August 1782 (AFB fos 38–9, *BCE* document 324); 29 August 1785 (AFB fos 18–19); 24 January 1786 (AFB fos 22–5, published [abridged] in *BCE*, document 460); 15 August 1786 (AFB fos 221–2, *BCE* document 471); 6 February 1787 (AFB fos 47–8). The abridgement of the last document in *BCE* document 484 lacks the relevant information.

87   AFB fos 149–50, Morande to Beaumarchais, 26 August 1785; fos 36–7, Morande to Beaumarchais, 12 December 1785 (the material used here is lacking from the published extracts in *BCE* document 454); fos 221–2, Morande to Beaumarchais, 15 August 1786, *BCE* document 471.

88   AFB fos 269–70, itemized school bill drawn on Francy's estate, August 1788; fo 235, du Bertrand to Morande, 8 July 1785.

89   AFB fos 47–8, Morande to Beaumarchais, 6 February 1787. On George's education see AFB fos 201–2, 131–2, 65–6 and 151–2, Morande's letters to Beaumarchais dated respectively 18 December 1786 (which includes the quotation) and 13 February, 13 March and 18 April 1787. The abridgements of these documents in *BCE* lack the information presented here.

90   AFB fo 267, account of Morande with Serani, 6 June 1788.

91   AFB fos 207–12, Morande to Beaumarchais, 7 September 1787.

92   AFB fos 173–4, Morande to Saiffert, 10 June 1788.

93 *CL*, 20 August 1788.
94 On *Termagent*'s exploits see: *CE*, 20 June 1788, 25 March 1789; *CL*, 19 July; 20 August, 28 October, 15 November 1788. On Salisbury see also *CE*, 13 March and 13 May 1788.
95 AFB fos 191–2, Morande to Beaumarchais, 23 June 1789. For the ship's cargo see *CE*, 20 June 1788.
96 Morande, *Lettre aux électeurs du département de Paris sur Jacques-Pierre Brissot* (Paris: Froullé, 1791), p. 20.
97 Manuel, *Police dévoilée*, II, 252–3.
98 Morande, *Réplique à Brissot*, p. 23. Morande was technically wrong about the date of Bedford's death, for it occurred on 15 January 1771, but Bedford retired from politics some years earlier. Morande claimed to have spoken to North on only three occasions.
99 On Goy's career and character see Manuel, *Police dévoilée*, II, 249–50.
100 MD Angleterre 73, fos 125–34, [summary of the] Report of General Green, 1784, at fo 134.
101 AN, 277AP/1, dossier Morande fo 178, Morande to d'Eon, 31 May 1789. On Goy see also *Lettre curieuse de Mlle Le Bac, autrement Mlle St Amand, alias Mad^e Lescallier, Londres, 17 Octobre 1763* (London, 1763). There is a copy in ULBC file 58 fo 2.
102 Morande was (first?) instructed to use the diplomatic bag for correspondence to Montmorin in CPA 566 fo 111, 'Note pour Morande', 27 July 1788.
103 CPA 564 fo 319, [Morande] to [Montmorin], 1 March 1788; CPA 568 fos 267–8, [Morande] to [Montmorin], 24 February 1789; and CPA 569 fos 70–1, [Morande] to [Montmorin], 4 April 1789, contain attestations of Menneville's services, submitted at Montmorin's request. They contend that he suffered 20,000 *livre* losses on speculations made as part of his cover. Menneville also apparently introduced Morande to his contact in the Bureau of Ordnance: see CPA 569 fos 85–6, [Morande] to [Montmorin], 7 April 1789.
104 CPA 565 fos 103–9, Morande to Montmorin, 28 April 1788, *BCE*, document 516.
105 Ibid.
106 CPA 565 fos 122–3, [Morande] to [Montmorin], 2 May 1788 [cypher] (for explanation of the cypher see fo 136, Menneville to Montmorin, Boulogne, 6 May 1788); CPA supplément 28 fos 199–200, [Morande] to [Montmorin], 22 [July 1787?].
107 This is probably a coded reference to the *CE* rather than the regular mail.
108 See CPA supplément 28 fos 178–82, [Morande] to [Vergennes], 24 January 1787 at fo 179. See also fos 201–2, [Morande] to [Montmorin], 21 August 1787.
109 CPA 568 fos 346–8, [Morande] to [Montmorin], 17 March 1789; Francy to Beaumarchais, 2 December 1783, *BCE* document 352.
110 See William Slauter, 'News and diplomacy in the age of the American Revolution', (unpublished PhD dissertation, Princeton, 2007), Chs 4 and 6 respectively for detailed discussions of the *Courier de l'Europe*'s portrayal as a spy and the translation of American constitutions.
111 Identification after Gunnar and Mavis von Proschwitz in *BCE*, document 516. MacMahon was a sub-editor at the paper.
112 CPA 565 fos 103–9, Morande to Montmorin, 28 April 1788, *BCE* document 516.
113 CPA supplément 28 fos 203–4, [Morande] to [Montmorin], 'CE 26' [probably 26 July 1787]. This letter clarified an earlier description at fos 191–3, [Morande] to [Montmorin], 1 July 1787.
114 See, for example, CPA 567 fos 351–4, [Morande] to [Montmorin], undated letter wrongly ascribed to 1788 [actually written on 31 January 1789].
115 CPA 568 fos 346–8, [Morande] to [Montmorin], 17 March 1789.
116 On Sainte-Foy see *BCE*, p. 153n. 3. Strangely, the authors of *BCE* do not pick up on the significance of Sainte-Foy's link to the navy.

Notes to Chapter 6: Poacher Turned Gamekeeper: Morande, Police Spy

1 On Jacquet see MO, MS 1422, pp. 53–5; Arsenal MS 12,453; Louis Charpentier (attrib.), *La Bastille dévoilée*, 9 livraisons (Paris: Desenne, 1789–1790), 3rd livraison, pp. 36–9; Manuel, *Police dévoilée*, I, 255–60; Pelleport, *Diable*, pp. 44–8; *MSB*, XVIII, 22 December 1781; XX, 26 January and 7 February 1782.
2 MO, MS 1422 pp. 54–5.

3　CPA 541 fos 50–1, [Lenoir?] to [Vergennes?], 24 February 1783; *MSB*, XVIII, 22 December 1781.

4　CPA 541 fos 50–1, [Lenoir?] to [Vergennes?], 24 February 1783.

5　Arsenal, MS14,453 fo 37.

6　On this pamphlet see Burrows, *Blackmail*, pp. 154–6.

7　Burrows, *Blackmail*, pp. 147–51. See also Vivien R. Gruder, 'The question of Marie-Antoinette: the queen and public opinion before the revolution', *French History* 16:3 (2002), 269–98. On sales of the *Historical Essay* see Henri d'Almeras, *Marie-Antoinette et les pamphlets royalistes et révolutionnaires* (Paris: Librarie mondiale, 1907), p. 403.

8　CPA 534 fos 158–61, Goëzman to Vergennes, Ostende, 10 August 1781; fos 162–5, Goëzman to Louis XVI, 10 August 1781; fo 303, Goëzman to Maurepas, Paris, 14 November 1781; fo 315, Goëzman to Vergennes, 27 November 1781.

9　CPA 541 fos 132–3, Goëzman to Baudouin, London, 7 March 1783.

10　CPA 536 fo 340, Baudouin to Vergennes, 22 Avril 1782; CPA 541 fo 24, Baudouin to Vergennes, Paris, 19 February 1783; fos 50–1, [Lenoir] to [Vergennes], Paris, 24 February 1783; fo 134, Baudouin to Vergennes, Paris, 7 March 1783; Morris, *The Peacemakers*, pp. 139–40.

11　CPA 541 fos 145–6, Goëzman to Baudouin, 12 March 1783; fos 346–9, Goëzman to Vergennes, 4 April 1783.

12　CPA 541 fo 61, Vergennes to Lenoir, Versailles, 25 February 1783; fo 71, Vergennes to Moustier, 26 February 1783; Manuel, *Police dévoilée*, I, 241.

13　CPA 541 fos 196–9, Moustier to Vergennes, London, 16 March 1783. This letter appears in Manuel, *Police dévoilée*, I, 242–9.

14　Morande's police plan does not survive: however, Gunnar and Mavis von Proschwitz speculate that an 'Essai sur la police de Londres' published in the *CE*, 18 June 1782 (*BCE*, document 317) may be Morande's work.

15　CPA 541 fos 196–9, Moustier to Vergennes, London, 16 March 1783.

16　Manuel, *Police dévoilée*, I, 139; Arsenal, MS 14,453 fo 42; Charpentier, *Bastille dévoilée*, 3rd livraison, pp. 55–6. Charpentier insisted Launay died of natural causes.

17　On Pelleport's career see Burrows, *Blackmail*, pp. 29–32; Darnton, *Bohemians*. Jacques-Pierre Brissot de Warville, *Mémoires de Brissot sur ses contemporains et la révolution française*, (ed.) F. de Montrol, 4 vols (Paris: Lavocat, 1830–1832), II, 191, implies Pelleport had homosexual leanings by comparing him to Alcibiades. On Alcibiades see above, Chapter 3, note 31.

18　On this pamphlet see Burrows, *Blackmail*, pp. 175–7.

19　CPA 542 fos 37–42, 'Moyens simples . . . pour prevenir . . . attentats semblable à celui de Boissière', at fo 38. This document is, in fact, Morande's memorandum on *libellistes*. It is written in his hand, and Morande (*Réplique à Brissot*, pp. 39–40) confirms that an extract (from fos 41–2) published by Manuel (*Police dévoilée*, I, 136–42) is an authentic part of his memorandum.

20　Cf. Robert Darnton's assertion that Pelleport's *Les Bohémiens* is a forgotten masterpiece. The best of Pelleport's works is *Le Diable dans un bénitier*. Both works are discussed later in this book.

21　CPA 542 fos 43–6, 'Case for the opinion of Mr Bearcroft', Lincoln's Inn, 15 April 1783.

22　D'Almeras, *Marie-Antoinette et les pamphlets*, pp. 45–6, 188–91 223, 236–40; Vincent Cronin, *Louis and Antoinette* (London: Collins, 1974), pp. 197, 402–5. *CSMT*, III, 458–9, suggests that in 1780 d'Artois corresponded with *nouvellistes* who denigrated the queen.

23　CPA 541 fos 234–7, Moustier to Vergennes, London, 23 March 1783; fos 239–40, Moustier to Vergennes, London, 23 March 1783; fo 251, Lenoir to [Vergennes], 25 March 1783; fo 305 and fos 309–10, two letters of Moustier to Vergennes, London, 31 March 1783. On Goëzman's career and the evidence against him see also Morris, *The Peacemakers*, pp. 136–45. Morris notes that Goëzman's reports seem designed to sow mistrust between France and her Spanish allies, but is uncertain whether he was a double agent. He also notes that Landis, who feared he had been supplanted in Shelburne's esteem by Goëzman, may have denounced him through malice.

24　CPA 541 fos 346–9, Goëzman to Vergennes, London, 4 April 1783.

25　CPA 542 fos 217–20, [Goëzman], 'Mémoire concernant les libelles du 9 mai 1783'.

26　For a copy of the *Alarm-Bell* see CPA 451 fo 378.

27　CPA 542 fos 285–9, 'Compte rendu de Receveur', 22 May 1783.

28　Ibid.

29　Ibid and fo 358, note of Receveur, 4 June 1783.

30　CPA 565 fos 103–9, Morande to Montmorin, 28 April 1788, *BCE* document 516; Morande, *Réplique à Brissot*, p. 40.

31 MO, MS 1422 p. 56.
32 The main evidence for this statement comes from preliminary findings of the AHRC funded project on 'The French book trade in Enlightenment Europe', which I am currently leading.
33 CPA 542 fos 402-3, d'Adhémar to Vergennes, 15 June 1783 (extrait).
34 CPA 543 fo 165, Vergennes to d'Adhémar, 4 July 1783.
35 See AFB fos 20-1, Morande to Philiberte Belin, London, 23 March 1786.
36 *BCE* document 328, Francy to Beaumarchais, 11 September 1782, reveals that Francy suggested the idea of a move to America first to Eliza. AFB fo 289, Morande to Beaumarchais, 10 June 1784, *BCE* document 388, asks whether Mme. Francy would exchange Morande's share of her husband's legacy for an American plantation. AFB fos 32-3, Morande to Beaumarchais, 10 February 1786, offers to serve as Beaumarchais' agent.
37 Pelleport, *Diable*, p. 5.
38 Ibid., pp. 22-3, 32-4, 83.
39 Ibid., pp. 61-72, 95 and passim. For Morande's memoir on *libellistes* see above, note 19.
40 Pelleport, *Diable*, p. 109.
41 CPA 542 fos 33-4, Moustier to Vergennes, 15 April 1783, reveals that Moustier introduced Morande to 'a young Senator', M. Pitt, who championed the plan; Morande, *Réplique à Brissot*, pp. 37-8, reveals that this was Morton Pitt rather than the Chancellor and soon-to-be Prime Minister, William Pitt.
42 Pelleport, *Diable*, p. 95.
43 Ibid., pp. 28-9.
44 Ibid., p. 61.
45 Ibid., pp. 66-7. On this print see also Paul Agnani, 'Libelles et diplomatie à la fin du dix-huitième siècle d'après la Correspondance Politique, Angleterre conservée aux Archives du Ministère des Affaires étrangères, 1771-1783' (unpublished *Mémoire de Maîtrise*: University of Besançon, 2004), p. 66.
46 Pelleport, *Diable*, esp. pp. 95-119.
47 Ibid., pp. 101-3.
48 CPA 542 fos 285-9, 'Compte rendu de Receveur', 22 May 1783.
49 Pelleport, *Diable*, p. 120.
50 CPA 545 fo 132, d'Adhémar to Vergennes, 4 October 1783.
51 Ibid., fos 170-1, Vergennes to d'Adhémar, 16 October 1783.
52 CPA 565 fos 103-9, Morande to Montmorin, 28 April 1788, *BCE* document 516; Morande, *Réplique à Brissot*, p. 42.
53 AN, 446AP/2, 'Mémoire pour Brissot', fo 3.
54 MO, MS 1422, p. 56. Records of Pelleport's interrogation do not survive in his Bastille dossier, Arsenal, MS 12,454.
55 For documents concerning Brissot's embastillement see AN, 446AP/2. See also Simon Burrows, 'The innocence of Jacques-Pierre Brissot', *Historical Journal* 46:4 (2003), 843-71. Jacques-Pierre Brissot de Warville, *Réplique de J. P. Brissot à Charles Théveneau Morande* (Paris: de l'imprimerie du *Patriote françois*, 1791), p. 25, and AN, 446AP/3 fo 153, 'Mémoire contre Desforges', affirm that Pelleport declared him innocent; fo 156 asserts that Desforges wrote to Brissot's mother-in-law on 18 July 1784 reassuring her that Brissot was no *libelliste*. We can assume that this letter existed, for having mentioned it in his judicial memoir, Brissot would be expected to produce it in court. There are no indications in Brissot's interrogations that Pelleport implicated him.
56 AN, 446AP/1, Brissot to 'le comte' [Moustier], London, 14 April 1783. During his Bastille interrogations, Brissot asserts that Serres de La Tour suggested that he wrote this letter: see 446AP/2, 'Deuxième interrogatoire du Sr Brissot de Warville', 21 August 1784, fos 1-2.
57 CPA 542 fo 81 billet [of Moustier for Vergennes], London, noon 21 [April 1783]; fos 187-8, Lenoir to Vergennes, Paris, 4 May 1783; fos 185-9, Receveur's 'compte rendu', 22 May 1783. Lenoir strongly suspected Pelleport, but doubted that Brissot was involved. See also Burrows, 'Innocence of Brissot', pp. 854-5.
58 Brissot, *Mémoires*, II, 175.
59 This testimony is suspect, as in 1783 Morande was not yet editor of the *Courier de l'Europe*. However, Morande regularly placed articles in the press before becoming a professional journalist. For apparent blackmail puffs, see the notices about an ambassador being robbed at the Pantheon, *CE*, 16 November 1784; an unnamed mesmerist seducer, *CE*, 28 September 1784;

and several extra-marital affairs in *CE*, 12 September 1784. Blackmail may also have motivated Morande's dealings with Cagliostro, Calonne and Mirabeau, see Chs 6 and 7.

60 Brissot, *Mémoires*, II, 186. For an original draft of this material see AN, 446AP/3, 'Mémoire contre Desforges' [1785], folio K [insertion].

61 AN, 446AP/2, Brissot to Martin [?], 20 August 1784. See also 446AP/3, 'Mémoire contre Desforges', fos 32-3.

62 Brissot, *Mémoires*, II, 188.

63 Ibid., II, 188-9.

64 AN, 446AP/2, [subscriber's prospectus for] 'The London Literary Lyceum, or an assembly and correspondence established at London'.

65 Morande, *Réplique à Brissot*, p. 70. This document was published by Morande and appears genuine. It was given to him by Desforges and Brissot never denied its authenticity.

66 AN, 446AP/2, [Morande] to [Receveur], undated letter received 8 August 1784.

67 The date is confirmed by Charpentier, *Bastille dévoilée*, 3rd livraison, p. 12.

68 AN, 446AP/2, [Morande] to [Guérin], 16 July 1784; 'Interrogatoire de Brissot de Warville à la Bastille', 3 August 1784, fo 1.

69 AN, 446AP/2, 'Deuxième interrogatoire du Sr Brissot', 21 August 1784, fos 6-7.

70 CPA 545 fo 132, d'Adhémar to Vergennes, 4 Octobre 1783 (extrait), mentions the recently published *Diable*. Thivars only arrived in London in November: see Burrows, 'Innocence of Brissot', p. 858, note 102.

71 AN, 446AP/2, 'Deuxième interrogatoire du Sr Brissot', 21 August 1784, fos 7-8.

72 Ibid., 'Note [of Lenoir] pour le Baron de Breteuil', 5 September 1784. The document was printed in Brissot, *Réponse*, in *Patriot françois*, 739 (18 August 1791), p. 203.

73 Charpentier, *Bastille dévoilée*, 3rd livraison, p. 12.

74 See Burrows, 'Innocence of Brissot', pp. 859-60.

75 AN, 446AP/2, 'Note [of Lenoir] pour le Baron de Breteuil', 5 September 1784. This document was printed in Brissot, *Réponse*, in *Patriot françois*, 739 (18 August 1791), p. 203.

76 *CE*, 18 February 1785.

77 *CE*, 1 February 1785. Cesare Beccaria (1738-1794) was the enlightenment's best-known penal reformer and author of *On Crimes and Punishments* (1764).

78 AN, 446AP/3, 'Mémoire contre Desforges', esp. fos 109-12; 446AP/4, 'projet des lettres'. Brissot cites as libels the aforementioned editions of the *CE* and that of 28 January 1785. For further calumny of Brissot see *CE*, 14 December 1787.

79 AN, 446AP/4, 'projet des lettres', fos 14, 18-19.

80 AN, 446AP/2, [Morande] to [Receveur], 8 August 1784.

81 Ibid., and Morande, *Réponse au dernier mot de Jacques-Pierre Brissot, et à tous les petits mots de ses camarades* (Paris: Froullé, 1791), p. 16; Charpentier, *Bastille dévoilée*, 3rd livraison, p. 101; CPA 565 fos 103-9, Morande to Montmorin, 28 April 1788, *BCE* document 516.

82 On 'Chamorand' / Fini's crime, see *Gazetteer*, 31 October 1785, translated in *CE*, 1 November 1785 and Louis Charpentier et al., *Bastille dévoilée*, 3rd livraison, pp. 101-4.

83 Ibid., and *CE*, 22 November 1785.

84 *CE*, 4 November 1785.

85 *CE*, 1, 4 and 8 November 1785.

86 See the letter of 'M' in *CE*, 29 November 1785 and the account of Fini's journey and arrest in *CE*, 25 November 1785.

87 CPA 565 fos 103-9, Morande to Montmorin, 28 April 1788, *BCE* document 516.

88 *CE*, 9 and 16 July 1784; 5 October, 25 November and 6 December 1785; 25 January 1788.

89 *CE*, 27 April and 19 October 1787; 25 April 1788; *CL*, 27 September, 3 and 12 December 1788. On 22 June 1787, Morande announced that he would not normally publish descriptions of petty criminals sent in by readers.

90 CPA 542 fo 358, [Receveur] note of 4 June 1783.

91 CPA 552 fos 74-5, Goëzman to Vergennes, 23 January 1785.

92 See CPA 542 fos 43-6, 'Case for the opinion of Mr. Bearcroft', 15 April 1783; fos 62-3, Moustier to Vergennes, 18 April 1783. CPA 541 fo 224, Barrington to Moustier, 22 March 1783.

93 Simon-Nicholas-Henri Linguet, *Mémoires sur la Bastille, et de la détention de l'auteur dans ce château royal, depuis le 27 septembre 1780 jusqu'au 19 mai 1782* (London: Spilsbury, 1783), pp. 36-7; CPA 541 fo 204, Moustier to Vergennes, London, 17 March 1783; CPA 541 fo 377,

Thomas Evans to Moustier, 7 April 1783. On the sting operation see Darline Gay Levy, *The Ideas and Careers of Simon-Nicolas-Henri Linguet: A Study in Eighteenth-Century French Politics* (Urbana, Ill.: University of Illinois Press, 1980), pp. 1–2.

94   On Morande's disgust at Linguet's 'defence of Tiberius and Nero' see AFB fos 40–1, Morande to Beaumarchais, 16 April 1784, *BCE* document 375.

95   Levy, *Linguet*, p. 227.

96   BL, Add. MS 11,341 fos 208–9, untitled, undated note in d'Eon's hand. D'Eon dates Linguet's partisanship back to 1777, but the only article concerning him in Linguet's *Annales* for 1777 refers to the Hayes vs Jacques legal case over his gender. It makes no mention of Morande or Beaumarchais.

97   Morande (attrib.), *Le Bon-homme anglois* (Amsterdam, 1783), pp. 12–13.

98   Ibid., p. 11.

99   *MSB* XXVIII, 23 April 1785.

100 See *CE*, 8 March 1785 and allusions to the incident in *CE*, 14 and 17 September 1784. See also Morande, *Réplique à Brissot*, p. 36; *MSB* XXVIII, 3 April 1785; XXIX, 30 May 1785; AFB fos 154–5, Morande to Beaumarchais, 3 October 1784, *BCE* document 403. The *Réplique à Brissot* reveals that Morande's sub-editor, M. de Morgan, was a witness to the spitting incident.

101 On Beaumarchais and the Kehl edition, and Morande's involvement, see *BCE*, I, 125–37.

102 See Linguet's *Annales*, X, 495, announcement after no. 80 [December 1783].

103 *CE*, 17 February and 5 March 1784, *BCE* documents 361 and 363.

104 *BCE* document 366, Morande to Beaumarchais, 11 March 1784.

105 *CE*, 4 May 1784, *BCE* document 377, qv. Linguet, *Annales*, XI, 189–92.

106 Linguet, *Annales*, XI, no. 85, p. 320. [July 1784]. *CE*, 31 August 1784, suggests that this letter was written by a 'female swordsman who wears a moustache [i.e. d'Eon], who served in London as secretary, as censor, and as cook to the political Annaliste [i.e. Linguet]'.

107 The delayed numbers were *Annales*, nos 85, 86, 88 and 89.

108 'Avis' in Linguet, *Annales*, XII, 59–67. At pp. 65–6, Linguet dates the writing of this advice to 30 January 1785. I have not identified Linguet's memoir to Vergennes, which he claimed to have sent in August 1784.

109 Ibid. Quotes at p. 60.

110 AFB fo 42, Abbé de C. [Calonne?] to [Beaumarchais or Swinton?], undated fragment pinned to letter of Morande to Beaumarchais, 16 April 1784 (which deals with Linguet). This document reads 'l'ab. de C. desirerait que M. Morande, le rédacteur actuel montrà [sic?] tremper [?] moins de partialité contre M. Linguet. Il prit aussi M de Warville a qui il fait mille compliments, de condescendre à cette demande s'il influe pour quelque chose dans le rédaction du *Courier*.'

111 For further attacks of Morande on Linguet, see *CE*, 10, 14, 17 September, 19 October, 16 November, 14 December 1784; 8 and 22 March 1785. NB the first attack on Linguet in Morande's *CE* is a letter to the editor published on 30 January 1784, which mocks Linguet's ignorance in confusing the Bank of England with the British national debt (qv. *Annales politiques*, no. 79). After 1785, mentions of Linguet in the *CE* tend to be mocking but less vitriolic.

112 Morande, *Réplique à Brissot*, p. 36. On this incident, see also *CE*, 8 March 1785, which asserts that everyone Buttet visited during her separation from Linguet would recall 'the benign nature of her reflections on his [moral] character and her libertine observations on his physique'.

113 René Nicolas Dufriche Desgenettes, *Souvenirs de la fin du XVIIIe siècle et du commencement du XIXe siècle, ou mémoires de R. D. G.*, 2 vols (Paris: Firmin-Didot, 1835), I, 140. I thank Laurence Brockliss for indicating this source.

114 Although some editions bear the date 1784, Morande announced that the pamphlet had only just appeared in CE, 28 January 1785.

115 Desgenettes, *Souvenirs*, I, 124–30. Desgenettes refers to the man as Frédéric, Morande's correspondence as Hardi. However, the *CE*, 1 March 1785, and Old Bailey records give his name as Jacques-Philippe Hardy.

116 AFB fos 22–5, Morande to Beaumarchais, 24 January 1786, *BCE* document 460 (abridged).

117 See the transcript of the trial at 'Jacques Philip Hardy, theft, grand larceny, 23rd February 1785' in *The Proceedings of the Old Bailey*, reference number: t17850223-15 at http://www.oldbaileyonline.org; *CE*, 1 March 1785.

118 AFB fos 22–5, Morande to Beaumarchais, 24 January 1786, *BCE* document 460.

119 Desgenettes, *Souvenirs*, pp. 132–3; *CE*, 1 March 1785.

120   AFB fos 22–5, Morande to Beaumarchais, 24 January 1786, *BCE* document 460 (abridged). AFB fos 36–7, Morande to Beaumarchais, 12 December 1785, *BCE* document 454 (abridged) suggests that Hardy himself supplied this information.
121   See pp. 184–6.
122   *MSB*, XXIX, 30 May 1785.
123   Burrows, *Blackmail*, p. 53n. 20; AN, 446AP/2, 'Interrogatoire de Brissot de Warville à la Bastille', 3 August 1784, fo 3.
124   This statement is based on preliminary analysis conducted using *Signature* author recognition software by Dr Peter Millican of the Leeds Electronic Text Centre and Hertford College, Oxford, on approximately 10,000 words of each text and comparisons with Pelleport *Diable* and several Morande texts. We intend to publish a definitive analysis of these and other texts in due course. I wish to thank Peter Millican for adapting *Signature* for this purpose; Paul Agnani and Nicholas Cronk for supplying digital texts; and Laura Mackie, Henry Merivale, Louise Seaward, and Sarah Taylor for preparing further texts.
125   *Le Portefeuille de Madame Gourdan, dite la Comtesse* (Spa [London], 1783), p. 31. While the *Portefeuille* hides the identity of most clients behind initials, the author says that there is no point hiding that our 'peacock' is a banker called M. Pexioto. It also alleges Pexioto has homosexual leanings.
126   Anon., *Joueurs*, pp. 8, 9, 43, 58.
127   See *CE*, 18 June 1784; 21 August 1787 and 22 April 1788; *AP* 40 (29 October 1791), pp. 381–4; 48 (26 November 1791), pp. 605–6; 62 (16 January 1792), pp. 105–6.
128   Arsenal, MS 12,453 fo 37. On the computer analysis see note 124 above.
129   Robiquet, *Morande*, pp. 108n., 125–6n.
130   For a more detailed discussion, see Burrows, *Blackmail*, pp. 108–11.

Notes to Chapter 7: The Magician, the Necklace and the Poisonous Pig

1   Many aspects of the diamond necklace affair remain mysterious. The best accounts are Frances Mossiker, *The Queen's Necklace* (London: Victor Gollancz, 1961); Evelyne Lever, *L'Affaire du collier* (Paris: Fayard, 2004).
2   [Morande], *Gazetier cuirassé*, pt I, pp. 98–9.
3   Ibid., p. 81.
4   AFB fo 235, du Bertrand to Morande, 8 July 1785.
5   See Burrows, *Blackmail*, pp. 131–2; Munro Price, *Preserving the Monarchy: the Comte de Vergennes, 1774–1787* (Cambridge: CUP, 1995), pp. 178–80.
6   *CE*, 8 September 1786. This source does not name Carbonnières, but he is identified in Morande, *Réplique à Brissot*, p. 43.
7   Jeanne de La Motte, *Memoirs of the Countess de Valois La Motte* (Dublin: John Archer and William Jones, 1790 [original French and English language editions London, 1789]), pp. 158–9. See also Marc-Antoine-Nicolas de La Motte, *Mémoires inédits du comte de Lamotte-Valois sur sa vie et son époque (1754–1830)*, edited by Louis Lacour (Paris: Poulet-Malassis et de Broise, 1858), pp. 67–8.
8   Jeanne de La Motte, *Memoirs*, pp. 159–60. For MacMahon's relations with Morande see *BCE*, I, 29–30.
9   Jeanne de La Motte, *Memoirs*, pp. 164–5.
10   Ibid., p. 183. Marc-Antoine de la Motte, *Mémoires inédits*, p. 90.
11   Jeanne de La Motte, *Memoirs*, p. 166.
12   Ibid., pp. 166–8.
13   Ibid., p. 177.
14   Ibid., pp. 171–9.
15   CPA 556 fo 275, d'Adhémar to Vergennes, 30 May 1786.
16   It is unclear when MacMahon befriended the count. He was probably the 'Irish priest' who was a go-between with MacDermott, mentioned in Jeanne de La Motte, *Memoirs*, pp. 158.
17   On Benavent's involvement in fraud see Mairobert, *Espion anglois*, II, 14; *MSB*, VIII, 23 August 1775; Maza, *Private Lives*, pp. 142–6.

18 Morande, *Réponse au dernier mot*, p. 15, gives Benavent's Paris address. *AP* 24 (2 September 1791), pp. 644–5, refers to a memorandum which Benavent had sent to Morande and the National Assembly. Morande declined to publish it.

19 See Joseph Balsamo, *Mémoire pour le Comte de Cagliostro, accusé, contre M. le Procureur-général, accusateur* (Paris, 1786); Jeanne de Saint-Rémy de La Motte, *Mémoire pour dame Jeanne de Saint-Rémy de Valois, épouse du comte de La Motte* (Paris: Cellot, 1785).

20 Iain McCalman, *The Seven Ordeals of Count Cagliostro* (London: Century, 2003), pp. 144, 157.

21 Balsamo, *Lettre au peuple anglois*, pp. 39–40.

22 McCalman, *Seven Ordeals*, p. 147; Anon., *A Life of the Count Cagliostro* (London: T. Hookham, 1787), pp. xxii–iii; Balsamo, *Lettre au peuple anglois*, pp. 39–43.

23 For similar articles, see *CE*, 10 and 31 May 1785.

24 *CE*, 23 December 1785; 3 and 10 March and 4 April 1786.

25 *CE*, 23 June 1786.

26 Balsamo, *Lettre au peuple anglois*, pp. 42–3.

27 *CE*, 8 September 1786.

28 McCalman, *Seven Ordeals*, pp. 151–2.

29 Ibid., p. 152.

30 CPA 557 fos 200–1, Barthélemy to Breteuil, London, 22 August 1786; Lever, *L'Affaire du collier*, p. 298.

31 *CE*, 24 June 1788, offers Morande's eyewitness testimony concerning the Gordon riots. See p. 190.

32 *CE*, 20 August 1784.

33 *CE*, 19 November 1784.

34 *CE*, 23 November 1784.

35 Quote from *CE*, 12 July 1785.

36 For Gordon's letter see *Morning Herald*, 13 August 1785.

37 *CE*, 12 August 1785.

38 *Public Advertiser*, 1 September 1785.

39 Ibid.

40 *CE*, 2 September 1785.

41 *CE*, 21 October 1785.

42 *CE*, 6 December 1785; 5 and 19 May 1786.

43 *CE*, 31 January and 9 May 1786.

44 *CE*, 15 August 1786.

45 CPA 557 fos 200–1, Barthélemy to Breteuil, London, 22 August 1786; NA, TS11/388, 'Brief for the Prosecution', p. 1; McCalman, *Seven Ordeals*, p. 157.

46 *CE*, 22 August 1786.

47 *CE*, 3 November 1786, alludes to visits to Cagliostro by 'members of the court'.

48 *Public Advertiser*, 22 and 24 August 1786, cited at CPA 557 fos 202–3, 207.

49 For documents concerning the case, including Gordon's handwritten drafts of the offending paragraphs and a copy of his pamphlet, *The Prisoner's Complaint* (London, 1787), see NA, TS11/388. On his trial, see: *The Trial at Large of the Hon. George Gordon* (London: R. Randall, 1787); *The Whole Proceedings on the Trials of George Gordon* (London: M. Gurney, 1787); *Annual Register* 29 (1786), p. 246. None of these accounts repeats Gordon's exclamations, which the *London Chronicle* (5–7 June 1787) considered 'too delicate to be repeated'. I have therefore retranslated Barthélemy's version from CPA 560, fos 160–5. The sentence is reported in CPA 564 fo 139, La Luzerne to Montmorin, London, 28 January 1788.

50 For Morande's take on the story see *CE*, 8, 19, 26 and 29 June, 3 and 27 July, 11 and 21 December 1787; 1, 4 and 29 January 1788.

51 *CE*, 5 September, 10 and 20 October 1786.

52 *CE*, 5 September, 24 October and 7 November 1786.

53 *CE*, 5 September 1786.

54 *CE*, 10 October 1786.

55 CPA 559 fos 224–5 and 228–9, d'Adhémar to Montmorin, 13 March 1787.

56 These included the memoirs of Carlo Sacchi, who had been Cagliostro's assistant in Strasbourg, and the Baroness von der Recke's account in the *Journal de Berlin* of Cagliostro's attempts to

summon her brother in a séance. For Morande's use of their testimony see *CE*, 15, 19, 22 and 26 September and 3 and 27 October 1786.

57 *CE*, 8 September 1786.
58 Lever, *L'Affaire du collier*, p. 67.
59 *CE*, 8 September 1786.
60 See below and AFB fos 182–3, Morande to Beaumarchais, 21 November 1786, *BCE* document 478; CPA 559 fos 226–7, Morande to d'Adhémar, 12 March 1787.
61 *CE*, 15 June 1787. See also the revelations in *CE*, 25 May and 12 June 1787, which detail the judicial investigation that resulted in Cagliostro's uncle's testimony.
62 MD France 1400, fos 305–6, Fontaine to Durival, 16 September 1786; fo 308, Crosne to Vergennes, 19 September 1786. See also fos 315–18, Crosne to Vergennes, 24 September 1786; *CE*, 10 October 1786. Morande denies that he was paid to attack Cagliostro in *CE*, 27 February and 24 August 1787 (*BCE* document 506).
63 CPA 559 fos 226–7, Morande to d'Adhémar, 12 March 1786; fos 251–2, Montmorin to d'Adhémar, Versailles, 25 March 1787.
64 *CE*, 25 August 1786.
65 The original appeared in the *Public Advertiser*, 5 September 1786. This translation from the *Daily Universal Register*, 8 September 1786. The challenge and Morande's reply appear in French in *CE*, 5 September 1786.
66 *Daily Universal Register*, 8 September 1786. For the original French version see *CE*, 5 September 1786.
67 *Public Advertiser*, 9 September 1786; *CE*, 12 September 1786. Cagliostro's letter was dated 6 September but was not published until three days later.
68 *Morning Post*, 11 September 1786; *CE*, 12 September 1786.
69 McCalman, *Seven Ordeals*, p. 168, claims, without giving a source, that Morande was 'a Modern Rite freemason'. Martin Cherry, the librarian-archivist at the Freemasons Hall Museum and Library, London, was unable to find any evidence to corroborate this statement.
70 *CE*, 24 October 1786
71 *CE*, 27 October 1786.
72 See Marsha Keith Schuchard, 'William Blake and the promiscuous baboons: a Cagliostroan séance gone awry', *British Journal for Eighteenth-Century Studies*, 18:2 (1995), 185–200. Both Schuchard and McCalman (*Seven Ordeals*, pp. 168–9) cite Constantin Photiadès as their ultimate source for saying that Morande spread the story (and McCalman says he did so in the *Courier de l'Europe*). In fact, Photiadès, *Les Vies du Comte de Cagliostro*, 9th edition (Paris: Grasset, 1932), p. 343, does not explictly source the story to anyone and I have not found it in the *CE*. As Schuchard notes, in the *Magic Flute*, Mozart's character Sarastro, who is usually taken to represent Cagliostro, leads the hero, Tamino, into the Egyptian Temple of Wisdom while playing his flute to summon animals portrayed by actors dressed as baboons and orang-utangs.
73 *CE*, 3 November 1786.
74 McCalman, *Seven Ordeals*, pp. 169–72, where the print is reproduced at p. 170. It was advertised in the *CE*, 21 November 1786.
75 For British press attacks, squibs or epigrams on Cagliostro, some doubtless produced in Morande's camp, see *Morning Post*, 29 and 31 August; 2, 8, 9, 11, 13, 14, 16, 27 and 29 September; 19 October 1786. *Daily Universal Register*, 18 and 20 September 1786; *General Advertiser*, 28 September; 3 and 18 October 1786; *Morning Herald*, 10 October 1786.
76 These creditors included Cagliostro's old assistant Carlo Sacchi and a Monsieur Silvestre from Cadiz who was seeking payment for a silver cane. See *CE*, 13 October 1786 and 3 April 1787; McCalman, *Seven Ordeals*, p. 173; Photiadès, *Vies de Cagliostro*, p. 339.
77 McCalman, *Seven Ordeals*, p. 177; *CE*, 3 and 10 April 1787.
78 *CE*, 18 and 25 May; 8, 12 and 15 June; 21 December 1787; 4 January 1788; *CL*, 15 October, 29 November 1788.
79 Robiquet, *Théveneau de Morande*, pp. 194–205; Roberto Gervaso, *Cagliostro*, transl. Cormac O'Cuilleanáin (London: Gollancz, 1974), pp. 167–77; McCalman, *Seven Ordeals*, pp. 159–73.
80 *Morning Chronicle*, 13 and 29 December 1786.
81 CPA 558 fo 315, Barthélemy to Vergennes, London, 26 December 1786.
82 See Burrows, *Blackmail*, pp. 134–5; for d'Adhémar's advice see CPA 559 fo 166, d'Adhémar to Crosne, London, 24 February 1787.

83   CPA 559 fo 166, d'Adhémar to Crosne, London, 24 February 1787. La Motte's publication appears to have been a newspaper article and is so obscure that contemporaries and historians have ignored it.

84   *CSCV*, II, 140, 154-5, 161, 166-7; Henry Vizetelly, *The Story of the Diamond Necklace*, 2 vols (London: Tinsley, 1887), II, 159-60. For the comtesse's narrative of her escape, see: Jeanne de Saint-Rémy de La Motte, *The Life of Jane de St Remy de Valois, heretofore Countess de La Motte*, 2 vols (Dublin: P. Wogan, P. Bryce, J. Moore and J. Rice, 1792), II, 154-220; *Morning Post*, 16 August 1787.

85 · Jeanne de Saint-Rémy de La Motte, *An Address to the Public* (London: Ridgway, 1789), pp. 7-10. Jean-François Georgel, *Mémoires pour servir à l'histoire des evenemens de la fin du dix-huitième siècle depuis 1760 jusqu'en 1806-1810*, 6 vols (Paris: Alexis Eymery, 1817-1818), II, 208-9, speaks erroneously of a pay-off following this negotiation: see Burrows, *Blackmail*, p. 144n.97.

86   Alphonse-Joseph de Serres de La Tour, *Appel au bon sens* (London: Kearsley, 1788), pp. 4-5: advertisements appeared in the *Morning Post* in late December 1787.

87   NA, C12/1389/27, La Tour versus de Callonne [sic], 5 December 1788; FO95/631/247-9, drafts of Calonne's 'Exposé des faits', 9 December 1788.

88   See Calonne's accounts in NA, FO95/631/248 pp. 33-6; *The Times*, 2 February 1789. See also NA, FO95/631/156, Calonne to Duchess de Polignac, 27 January [1788], and FO95/631/164, Calonne to Duchess de Polignac, 'pour vous seule', undated.

89   NA, PC1/129/151, Calonne to Duchess de Polignac, London, 16 May [1788].

90   NA, PC1/129/155, Calonne to Duchess de Polignac, London, 10 June 1788; PC1/129/157, Calonne to Duchess de Polignac, London, 8 June 1788; FO95/631/267, 'Copie de la gazette angloise', 2 February 1789; *The Times*, 2 February 1789.

91   NA, FO95/631/248, p. 38.

92   NA, FO95/631/248, pp. 38-41.

93   NA, C12/1389/27, La Tour versus de Callonne [sic], 5 December 1788. This file contains documents from both sides. La Tour's claims seem improbable, especially as he signed for the advances.

94   See Serres de La Tour, *Appel au bon sens* and Jeanne de La Motte's scathing *Detection or a Scourge for Calonne* (London, 1789) and *Address to the Public*.

95   CPA 563 fo 43, Montmorin to Barthélemy, 12 August 1787 (copy); fo 47, Montmorin to Barthélemy, 12 August 1787 (copy). Robert Lacour-Gayet, *Calonne: financier, réformateur, contre-révolutionnaire, 1734-1802* (Paris: Hachette, 1963); p. 247 dates Calonne's arrival in London to between 10 and 14 August.

96   AFB fos 217-18, Morande to Beaumarchais, 14 August 1787.

97   AFB fos 207-12, Morande to Beaumarchais, 7 September 1787

98   *CE*, 4 April 1788. AFB fos 207-12, Morande to Beaumarchais, 7 September 1787; fos 178-9, Morande to Sainte-Foy, 22 September 1788, appear to confirm that Calonne and Morande met face to face.

99   In *CE*, 15 February 1788, Morande claims he forbade himself from discussing Calonne and Necker's disputes, but perhaps he was following orders. *CE*, 22 February 1788, refuses to publish letters from partisans of either party.

100   CPA 562 fos 140-1, [Morande] to [Montmorin], 27 November 1787. See also Morande's account of his services to Calonne in *CL*, 4 October 1788. This claims that Morande provided some of the information on Britain in Calonne's *Requête au roi*.

101   AFB fos 103-4, Morande to Beaumarchais, 9 October 1787; *CL*, 4 October 1788.

102   On this close surveillance, which lasted from late 1787 until at least December 1789, see CPA 562 fos 140-1, [Morande] to [Montmorin], 27 November 1787; CPA 567 fos 347-8, [Morande] to [Montmorin], [September 1788]; CPA 571 fos 243-52, La Luzerne to Montmorin, 9 December 1789. See also CPA 572 fos 307-11, La Luzerne to Montmorin, 23 March 1790.

103   CPA 565 fos 288-90, [Morande] to [Montmorin], 18 June 1788.

104   CPA 566 fos 309-10, [Morande] to [Montmorin], 23 September 1788; CPA 567 fos 17-18 and 35-6, [Morande] to [Montmorin], 7 and 15 October 1788, make Montmorin's opposition to Morande's campaign against Calonne explicit. AFB fos 219-20, Morande to Beaumarchais, 27 January 1789 (*BCE*, document 527), asks Beaumarchais and Sainte-Foy to remain neutral.

105   CPA 562 fos 140-1, [Morande] to Montmorin, 27 November 1787.

106   CPA 567 fos 345-6, [Morande] to Montmorin, August 1788.

107 *CL*, 2 and 9 August 1788. Groubentall (1739–1815) finally published his ideas in his monumental *Théorie générale de l'administration politique des finances* (1788), but some chapters had been written several years earlier.
108 *CL*, 30 August 1788.
109 *CL*, 10 September 1788.
110 *CL*, 19 September 1788.
111 CPA 567 fos 347–8, [Morande] to [Montmorin], [September 1788].
112 Ibid., fos 17–18, 35–6, 191–2, Morande's letters to Montmorin, 7 October, 15 October 1788 and 30 November 1788. See also *CL*, 15, 18 and 21 October 1788. Morande was careful to observe a specific ban on discussing Calonne's most recent publication.
113 AFB fos 178–9, Morande to Sainte-Foy, 22 September 1788; CPA 567 fo 195, [Morande] to [Montmorin], 2 December 1788. See also CPA 569 fos 146–7, [Morande] to [Montmorin], 21 April 1789.
114 CPA 566 fos 309–10, [Morande] to [Montmorin] 23 September 1788; AN, 297AP/2 pièce 85, 'Contrat relative au *Courier de l'Europe*, 1806 [sic]' [draft].
115 BCE document 532, Beaumarchais to Eliza Morande, 11 March 1789; AFB fos 53–4, Morande to Beaumarchais, 27 March 1789, *BCE* document 534.
116 CPA 568 fos 346–8, [Morande] to [Montmorin], 17 March 1789; CPA 569 fos 36–7, [Morande] to [Montmorin], 31 March 1789.
117 CPA 569 fos 36–7, [Morande] to [Montmorin], 31 March 1789.
118 Ibid., fos 146–7, [Morande] to [Montmorin], 21 April 1789.
119 AN, 297AP/2 pièce 85, 'Contrat relative au *Courier de l'Europe*, 1806 [sic]' [draft].
120 AFB fos 187–8, Morande to Beaumarchais, 28 April 1789, *BCE* document 538.
121 See *BCE* document 545, Swinton to Beaumarchais, 24 July 1789; AFB fos 156/8, Morande to Beaumarchais, 2 October [1789], *BCE* document 553.
122 For complaints about Swinton's venality see AFB fos 197–8, Morande to Beaumarchais, 16 June 1789, *BCE* document 540; CPA 569 fos 332–3, [Morande] to [Montmorin], 8 June 1789. NA, PC1/127 piece 210, Swinton to Calonne, undated letter [June 1791], asserts that Morande never suspected Calonne's involvement in the paper.
123 *CE*, 30 August 1785; *CL*, 1 and 5 February 1788.
124 *CE*, 4 September 1787, 5 February 1788. See also *CE* 25 March 1788.
125 *CL*, 22 October 1788. The abolitionists actually succeeded in having this captain arrested and brought before the Privy Council. Morande's surviving (though fragmentary) correspondence with Montmorin suggests that the abolitionists only paid to place propaganda in the *Courier de l'Europe* from mid 1789.
126 On the Friends of the Blacks, see Marcel Dorigny and Bernard Gainot, *La Société des Amis des Noirs: contribution à l'histoire de l'abolition de l'esclavage* (Paris: éditions UNESCO, 1998).
127 AFB fos 197–8, Morande to Beaumarchais, 16 June 1789, *BCE* document 540; *CL*, 3 June 1789.
128 CPA 568 fos 96–7, [Morande] to [Montmorin], 27 January 1788; CPA 567 fos 351–4, [Morande] to [Montmorin], undated [31 January 1789]. He repeated his offer to refute La Motte's *Memoirs* on 3 March.
129 On this point, see Burrows, *Blackmail*, Chapters 2–5.
130 On La Motte's *Memoirs*, see ibid., pp. 152–4.
131 A catalogue of the secret dépôt drawn up by the Parisian bookseller Poinçot in 1790 appears in Robert L. Dawson, *Confiscations at Customs: Banned Books and the Booktrade during the last years of the Ancien Régime* (Oxford: Voltaire Foundation, *SVEC* 2006:7), pp. 243–76.
132 CPA 568 fos 144–5, 220–1, 276–7, Morande's letters to Montmorin, 10 and 17 February and 3 March 1789.
133 See Edmund Burke, *Reflections on the Revolution in France* (Harmondsworth: Penguin, 1969), pp. 168–70; Iain McCalman, 'Mad Lord George and Madame de La Motte: riot and sexuality in the genesis of Burke's *Reflections on the Revolution in France*', *Journal of British Studies*, 35:3 (1996), 364.
134 BCE document 531, Menneville to Beaumarchais, Paris, 10 March 1789. It was doubtless Morande who assured Menneville that 'the means exist' to have the La Mottes transported.
135 AN, F^7 4445/2 dossier 3 pièce 9, Jeanne de La Motte to unknown correspondent, 23 June 1790. This person was probably the younger Goy. This implies that the older Goy lived on into 1790. The ghost writer for La Motte's *Life* was Peter Stuart, who wrote in English.

136   Burrows, *Blackmail*, p. 136.
137   *AP*, 62 (19 January 1792), pp. 106–7 (quote p. 107).
138   Frantz Funck-Brentano, *Cagliostro and Company*, transl. George Maidment (London: Greening, 1910), pp. 167–8.
139   See ibid., pp. 136–7.
140   *CSCV*, II, 598; *AP*, 94 (31 May 1792), pp. 913–14.
141   Vercondelet, *Lamballe*, p. 249. Some historians believe the sexual atrocities to be mythical because an intact headless body, supposedly that of Lamballe, was deposited with the revolutionary authorities the day after her death. The evidence on this point is contradictory. However, stories of her rape and dismemberment circulated almost at once.
142   Mossiker, *Queen's Necklace*, p. 565.
143   Gérard Walter, *Actes du Tribunal révolutionnaire* (Paris: Mercure de France, 1968), pp. 96–7.

Notes to Chapter 8: *The First Revolutionary Journalist*

1   Cf. Peter Wagner, *Eros Revived*, p. 98.
2   Jeremy D. Popkin, *Revolutionary News. The Press in France, 1789–1799* (Durham and London: Duke University Press, 1990), pp. 106–68.
3   On the paper's circulation see CPA 560 fos 141–2, Morande to Montmorin, 2 June 1787, *BCE* document 498; AFB fos 45–6, Morande to Beaumarchais, 4 January 1787, *BCE* document 483.
4   See Swinton to Francy, 15 April 1784, *BCE* 374; AFB fos 45–6, Morande to Beaumarchais, 4 January 1787, *BCE* document 483; fos 49–50, Morande to Beaumarchais, 17 January 1788, *BCE* document 513; CPA 560 fos 141–2, Morande to Montmorin, 2 June 1787, *BCE* document 498.
5   Burrows, 'Cosmopolitan press', pp. 25, 34. See also Jeremy D. Popkin, *News and Politics in the Age of Revolution: Jean Luzac's Gazette de Leyde* (Ithaca, NY and London: Cornell University Press, 1989).
6   *AP*, prospectus [May/June 1791], p. 3.
7   AFB fos 254–5, Morande to Beaumarchais, 27 January 1786.
8   *AP*, prospectus [May/June 1791], pp. 3–4.
9   Ibid., p. 4.
10   See *CE*, 13 January to 6 February 1787. See also comments on venality of offices in *CE*, 2 and 9 July 1788. Morande, *Réplique à Brissot*, p.25, says the first *Lettres d'un voyageur* appeared in 1787, but he first signed himself 'un voyageur' on 19 December 1786.
11   See *CE*, 13 May 1785.
12   *AP*, nos. 64–75 (25 January–6 March 1792), passim. Morande promised to republish these articles in a pamphlet. CPA 590 fos 196–9, Lottin to Delacroix de Contaut [?], 16 pluviôse V [4 February 1797] says it was in press when Morande was forced to flee Paris. His address to the British is mentioned in *AP* 72–3 (double issue, 24 February 1792), pp. 365–6.
13   *AP*, 21 (18 August 1791), p. 567; CPA, 583 fo 155, François Noel to Lebrun, 2 November 1792; CPA 590 fos 196–9, Lottin to Delacroix de Contaut [?], 16 pluviôse V [4 February 1797]; fo 201, Delacroix de Contaut [?] to Lottin, 19 pluviôse V [7 February 1797]. It is unclear whether Delacroix wished to see Morande in person as he asked Lottin for copies of the *Argus patriote* before remarking ambiguously that he would doubtless find valuable information 'chez vous [Lottin] et chez lui [Morande]'.
14   *CE*, 1 January 1788. *CE*, 11 September 1787, contains an earlier attack on the *parlements*.
15   See *CE*, 14 March, 23 and 28 May, 3, 10, 13, and 20 June, 30 July and 9 August 1788.
16   *CL*, 11 January 1791.
17   See *CE*, 31 May, 24 and 27 June 1788; *CL*, 9 January, 6 February and 26 October 1790, 7 and 11 January 1791; *AP*, nos 53 (15 December 1791), pp. 736–40; 86 (1 May 1792), pp. 707–12; 87 (3 May 1792), pp. 729–33.
18   *CE*, 31 May, 15 January 1788.
19   I thank Claude Labrosse for drawing my attention to these essays.
20   CPA 565 fos 288–90, [Morande] to [Montmorin], 18 June 1788, at fo 289, and quoted in *BCE*, I, 186–7.

21   *CL*, 13 August 1788, p. 100n.
22   *CL*, 6 December 1788.
23   *CE*, 15 November and 16, 20, 23 and 27 December 1785. On this exchange see *BCE*, I, 163–6.
24   See Richard Livesey and James Whatmore, 'Étienne Clavière, Jacques-Pierre Brissot et les fondations intellectuelles de la politique des Girondins', *Annales historiques de la Révolution française*, 72:3 (2000), pp. 1–26.
25   See *BCE*, I, 166.
26   AFB fos 246–7, Morande to Beaumarchais, 17 January 1786; fos 32–3 Morande to Beaumarchais, 10 February 1786. Extracts of both these letters appear in *BCE*, I, 164. On the Hardy case, see pp. 150–1.
27   See Maza, *Private Lives*, pp. 295–311.
28   See especially *CE*, 8, 12, 15 June and 3 and 24 August 1787. Morande's friendship with Daudet is mentioned in AFB fos 139–40, Morande to Sainte-Foy, 19 June 1787, *BCE* document 501.
29   AFB fos 137–8, Morande to Beaumarchais, 6 July [1787], *BCE* document 504; fos 213–14, Morande to Beaumarchais, June 1787.
30   *Lettre de M. Morande, auteur et rédacteur du Courier de l'Europe, à M. de Beaumarchais* (Geneva 1787), republished in *BCE*, document 505.
31   AFB fos 184–5/6, Morande to Beaumarchais, 27 June 1787 (abridged in *BCE* document 502), invites Beaumarchais' opinion on what Morande has written about Kornmann.
32   *CE*, 24 August 1787.
33   *CL*, 13 September 1787.
34   AFB fos 155–6 *bis*, Morande to Beaumarchais, 10 March 1789, *BCE* document 530.
35   *CL*, 18 March 1789. Part of this article appears in *BCE*, I, 166–7.
36   AFB fos 26–7, Morande to Beaumarchais, 20 March 1789, *BCE* document 533. Morande does not name Nehra, but there is little doubt whom he meant. On Nehra's departure and the *Histoire secrète* see also Barbara Luttrell, *Mirabeau* (Carbondale and Edwardsville: Southern Illinois University Press, 1990), pp. 101–2.
37   Antonina Vallentin, *Mirabeau. Voice of the Revolution*, transl. E. W. Dickes (London: Hamish Hamilton, 1948), p. 292.
38   Ibid., p. 293.
39   *CL*, 6 May 1789; Vallentin, *Mirabeau*, p. 285, reveals that the proof corrections were not in Mirabeau's hand.
40   *CL*, 10 June 1789.
41   Vallentin, *Mirabeau*, p. 331.
42   *CL*, 12 April 1791.
43   *CL*, 16 July 1788. Although published in a 'contributed' article, this statement bears the hallmarks of Morande's style, and was the forerunner of many similar comments: see, for example, *CL*, 10 October 1789 (supplément) and 12 April 1791.
44   *CL*, 2 May 1789.
45   See Elizabeth Eisenstein, 'The tribune of the people: a new species of demagogue', in *The Press in the French Revolution*, ed. Harvey Chisick, *SVEC* 287 (Oxford: Voltaire Foundation, 1991), pp.145–59.
46   *CL*, 2 September 1789.
47   *CL*, 22 and 26 October 1790.
48   *CL*, 22 July 1789; AFB fos 55–6, Morande to Beaumarchais, July 1789, *BCE* document 544.
49   *CL*, 22 July 1789 and *CE*, 24 July 1789, which contains both the quotes.
50   See, for example, *CL*, 10 and 15 August 1789
51   See, for example, *CL*, 14 March, 4 April, 27 May, 11 July, 2 and 13 September, 3 October, 27 November 1789.
52   *CL*, 7 and 17 October 1789.
53   *CL*, 11 and 15 July 1789.
54   *CE*, 24 July 1789.
55   *CE*, 31 July 1789.
56   *CE*, 24 July 1789.
57   *CE*, 5 August 1785.
58   See, for example, *CL*, 7 November 1789.
59   See, for example, *CE*, 23 and 26 March and 4 and 13 April 1784; *CL*, 7 January 1789.

60 *AP*, 25 (5 September 1791), pp. 660-1.
61 *CE*, 5 October 1787.
62 *CL*, 7 and 11 March 1789.
63 See, for example, *CL*, 14 March, 16 September 1789.
64 *CL*, 8 and 29 August and 9 September 1789.
65 On the *monarchiens* see Robert Griffiths, *Le Centre perdu: Malouet et les monarchiens dans la révolution française* (Grenoble: Presses universitaires de Grenoble, 1988).
66 *CE*, 24 June 1788.
67 *CL*, 22 July 1789 and *CL*, 10 October 1789, supplement entitled *Courier extraordinaire*.
68 The allegation was decisively refuted by Robert Darnton, 'Marat n'a pas été un voleur: une lettre inédite', *Annales historiques de la Révolution française*, no. 185 (July–September 1966), pp. 447–50. Darnton (p. 447n.) and others have traced the allegation back to the *Glasgow Star* of 4 March 1793. However, it first appears in Morande's *CE*, 17 and 24 October 1789.
69 See *CL*, 2 and 23 January 1790. Morande's role is remarked in an intercepted letter sent to Favras in prison and published by his brother in Guillaume-François de Mahy de Comère, *Justification de M. de Favras* (Paris, 1791), pp. 191–5. It says Morande contradicted Provence's statement that he had not seen Favras since 1775 by declaring that Favras had shown Provence's promissory notes to all and sundry. This is a rather creative interpretation of Morande's *CL* articles.
70 *CL*, 2 March 1790.
71 His daughters' school is mentioned in AFB fos 84–5, Eliza Morande to Beaumarchais, 2 March 1789.
72 NA, PC1/127 piece 210, Swinton to Calonne, undated letter [June 1791].
73 His address appears in documents concerning Morande's imprisonment and in documents seized on Froullé, cited below.
74 *AP*, prospectus [May/June 1791], p. 6
75 This may explain the paucity of spy reports from 1790 and 1791. The latest (CPA 577 fos 122–3) is dated 8 April 1791.
76 *AP*, no. 22 (25 August 1791), p. 578.
77 'Notice sur la vie de Brissot' in Jacques-Pierre Brissot de Warville, *Correspondance et papiers*, ed. Claude Perroud (Paris: Picard, 1912), p. lviii; Brissot, *Réponse*, in *Patriot français*, 740 (19 August 1791), p. 211. See also Brissot, *Patriote françois*, 4 September 1791; Brissot, *Mémoires*, IV, 100–1.
78 AN, 446AP/7 pièce 6, Manuel to Brissot, June 1791.
79 *AP*, no. 70 (16 February 1792), p. 306.
80 ADCO, 2E26/10.
81 AFB fos 93–4, Morande to Beaumarchais, 17 April 1792, *BCE* document 593.
82 *AP*, prospectus [May/June 1791], p. 4.
83 *AP*, 1 (6 June 1791), pp. 1–9.
84 Ibid.
85 *AP*, 13 (21 July 1791), pp. 333–4.
86 See especially *AP*, nos. 16 (2 August 1791), pp. 414–22; 50 (3 December 1791), pp. 652–4; 52 (10 December 1791), pp. 710–12; 53 (15 December 1791), p. 751; 54 (18 December 1791), pp. 769–71; 55 (22 December 1791), p. 813; 57 (28 December 1791), pp. 845–52; 58 (31 December 1791), pp. 879–81.
87 Timothy Tackett, *When the King Took Flight* (Cambridge, Mass: Harvard University Press, 2003), p. 102.
88 *AP*, 6 (26 June 1791), pp. 137–52.
89 *AP*, 7 (30 June 1791), pp. 165–74.
90 Manuel, *Police dévoilée*, II, 250–3.
91 AN, 446 AP/7 pièces 7 and 8, letters of Manuel to Brissot, undated [summer 1791] and 3 September 1791. The evidence Manuel passed to Brissot included 446AP/2, Morande to Guerin, 13 July 1784; Morande to Guerin [?], 16 July 1789; Morande to Receveur, 8 August 1784.
92 *AP*, 2 (12 June 1791), pp. 40, 41.
93 *AP*, nos. 9 (7 July 1791), pp. 220–1; 11 (14 July 1791), p. 270.
94 *AP*, 11 (14 July 1791), pp. 261–3.
95 These foreigners included Clavière, Anarcharsis Clootz, Jean-Jacques Rutledge, Etta Palm, Virchaux, Pio, Jean-Baptiste Rotondo, Dignam Brown, John Oswald and the Prussian Jew Ephraim.

96   See Brissot's *Patriote françois*, 26 July 1791.
97   *Patriote françois*, 31 July 1791; *AP*, 22 (25 August 1791), pp. 579–82; Brissot, *Mémoires*, IV, 98–102.
98   *Patriote François*, 7 August 1791; Brissot, *Mémoires*, IV, 102,105.
99   *AP*, 22 (25 August 1791), p. 581; Morande, *Lettre aux électeurs*, p. 19.
100 Brissot, *Réponse*, published in *Patriot français*, 740 (19 August 1791), quote at p. 211.
101 Morande, *Réplique à Brissot*, p. 24.
102 Ibid., pp. 39–45.
103 Ibid., pp. 5–6. Cf. Manuel, *Police dévoilée*, II, 265.
104 AN, 446AP/3, Brissot, 'Mémoire contre Desforges' [1785], fos 67; Morande, *Réplique à Brissot*, p. 105.
105 Morande, *Lettre aux électeurs*, p. 17; *AP*, no. 15, 29 July 1791, p. 392.
106 Moreover, in *AP*, 23 (29 August 11791), p. 614, Morande said the documents were available for inspection and claimed over 50 people had seen them.
107 On the charges against Brissot see Burrows, 'Innocence of Brissot'.
108 See ibid., p. 850; Brissot, *Mémoires*, II, 64–273 passim; Brissot, *Correspondance*, pp. 46–78, AN, 446AP/1, Brissot to Félicité Dupont, undated letter. See also Brissot, *Réplique*, pp. 2–25.
109 AN, 446AP/3, Brissot, 'Mémoire contre Desforges', fos 50, 55. David Williams, *Incidents in my Own Life which have been Thought of Some Importance*, ed. Peter France (Brighton: University of Sussex Library, 1980), p. 24, castigates those who 'unjustly impeached his [Brissot's] integrity' on these grounds.
110 *Patriote françois*, 28 August 1791.
111 *AP*, nos. 22 (25 August 1791), pp. 579–80; 26 (8 September 1791), p. 618. The other pamphlets were the *Lettre aux électeurs* and *Réponse au dernier mot*.
112 Lanthénas to Bancal, Paris, 29 August 1791, in *Lettres de Madame Roland*, edited by Claude Perroud, 2 vols (Paris: Imprimerie nationale, 1900–1902), II, 361–2.
113 On the elections see Etienne Charavay, *Assemblée electorale de Paris*, 3 vols. (Paris: Quantin, 1890–1905), II, pp. i–xlii, 512–38. See also Brissot, *Mémoires*, IV, 106–12.
114 Morande in *AP*, 55 (22 December 1791), p. 790, condemns those who used the veto as a pretext for such attacks.
115 *AP*, 37 (17 October 1791), pp. 307–10. Quote at p. 309.
116 *AP*, 43 (9 November 1791), pp. 461–6. See also the contributed pieces in *AP*, 45 (15 November 1791), pp. 521–33, and *AP*, 52 (10 December 1791), pp. 701–6.
117 *AP*, nos. 45 (15 November 1791), pp. 513–20; 48 (26 November 1791), pp. 593–6.
118 *AP*, 49 (30 November 1791), pp. 617–24. See also *AP*, 40 (29 October 1791), pp. 384–7.
119 *AP*, 44 (12 November 1791), pp. 495–503.
120 *AP*, nos. 27 (12 September 1791), pp. 29–30; 37 (17 October 1791), p. 311.
121 *AP*, 39 (25 October 1791), pp. 353–66.
122 *AP*, nos. 52 (10 December 1791), pp. 701–6; 53 (18 December 1791), pp. 757–67.
123 *AP*, nos. 59 (7 January 1791), pp. 2–13; 79 (23 March 1792), p. 541; 52 (10 December 1791), p. 721.
124 *AP*, 63 (21 January 1792), pp. 116–17.
125 *AP*, 85 (26 April 1792), p. 686. See also *AP*, 84 (21 April 1792), pp. 657–65.
126 See, for example, *CL*, 23 February 1790; 11 April 1790. For attacks on the Belgians see *CL*, 3 February, 16 and 20 April, 7 May and 15 June 1790.
127 Morande's visceral hostility to Pitt is explicit from the very first *Argus patriote*. However, it was stepped up from *AP*, 63 (29 January 1792), pp. 184–6.
128 *AP*, 4 (19 June 1791), pp. 94–101.
129 *AP*, 81 (11 April 1792), pp. 585–90.
130 *AP*, 84 (21 April 1792), pp. 670–1.
131 *AP*, 87 (3 May 1792), p. 735.
132 *AP*, nos. 39–46 (25 October 1791 – 19 November 1791) and passim.
133 See Archives départementales de la Seine, DQ[10] 103 dossier 1814, which includes a document, dated 14 February 1793, by which Morande and Eliza recognize their debt to Froullé; AFB fos 8–9, Beaumarchais to Morande, undated [annotated 1792], *BCE* document 594.
134 William J. Murray, *The Right-Wing Press in the French Revolution: 1789–92* (Woodbridge: Boydell, 1986), pp. 96–7, 154–6, 177.

135 AFB fos 97–8, George Théveneau to Beaumarchais, 16 August 1792; fos 99–100, Morande to Beaumarchais, 15 August 1792, *BCE* document 596.

136 Camille Desmoulins, *The History of the Brissotins* (London: Owen, 1793), p. 35n. As the ultimate sources for Brissot's words are his enemies Chabot and Danton, some historians doubt that he uttered them. The timing of Morande's arrest and Morande's relationship with Brissot, as recounted here, suggest otherwise.

137 AN, W251 dossier 27 pièce 1, *procès-verbaux* of searches of Morande's apartment, 19–22 September 1792; pièce 2, 'Interrogatoire du Sr Théveneau de Morande', 10 September 1792; pièce 4, 'Extrait du registre des déliberations du Conseil-Général du Commune', 21 September 1792; F^7 4774 dossier 3, 'Section de Montblanc: Extrait du Procès-Verbal de l'Assemblée Permanente', 10 September 1792.

138 David Andress, *The Terror* (London: Little, Brown, 2005), pp. 113–14.

139 Desmoulins, *History of the Brissotins*, p. 35n. 'M. Demorande' in *Biographical Anecdotes of the Founders of the French Republic* (London: R. Philips, 1797), pp. 131–2, suggests that Morande's survival under Robespierre stemmed from a mutual dislike for Brissot.

140 AN, F^7 4774 dossier 3, Delainville, *fondé de pouvoir* of the Section of Montblanc to the President and deputies of the Convention, 17 December 1792.

141 CPA supplément 30 fo 5, Pereyra to unnamed correspondent, 1 January 1793. On Pereyra see above, Chapter 5, note 56.

142 Lavirotte, 'Notice sur Morande'.

143 Jules Parthiot, *Episodes de le Révolution dans les baillage et district d'Arnay-le-Duc* (Dijon: Venot, 1901), p. 48. I thank Bernard Leblanc for this reference.

144 AN, W292 dossier 204, 3e partie, pièce 6, Siessel [or possibly Teissel or Geissel] *fils* to Fouquier-Tinville, dated 7th day of the 2nd *décade* of the 2nd month of the One and Indivisible Republic. The meaning of this date is ambiguous: the obvious choice is 17 Brumaire of the year II [7 November 1793], but this was a week after Brissot was executed.

145 *Jugement rendu par le Tribunal Criminel Révolutionnaire* [against the Girondins] (Paris, 1793), pp. 6, 18.

146 'M. Demorande' in *Biographical Anecdotes*, p. 132. An exactly analogous phrase appears in J.-B. Sault, *Receuil d'anecdotes biographiques, historiques et politiques sur les personnages les plus remarquables et les événements les plus frappants de la Révolution française* (Paris, 1798), p. 183.

147 ADCO, L 195, Lists of electors, Arnay-sur-Arroux.

148 An inventory prepared after his death (see below note 152) shows that Morande's personal library comprised almost 700 volumes of books and several crates of foreign newspapers.

149 Lavirotte, 'Notice sur Morande'.

150 Ibid.

151 *BCE* document 620, Swinton to Beaumarchais, 25 October 1795; document 621, Beaumarchais to Swinton, 23 February 1796; document 644, Gudin de la Ferlière and Beaumarchais to Morande, 8 November 1798; AFB fos 259, Delarue to Morande, 27 January 1804.

152 ADCO, 3Q1, lists the value of his '*meubles*' [goods other than real estate] at 1,768 *livres*. However, the summary of an inventory of Morande's effects in the Archives départementales de Saône et Loire in Mâcon published by Michel Naudin in *Pays d'Arnay*, no. 150 (October 2004), p. 1,501, lists just 653 francs [*livres*] worth of '*effets délaissés*' [items left] by Morande and 667 *livres* of debt owed to 53 creditors. I thank Bernard Leblanc for communicating this article. The Mâcon document appears to detail goods provided by the estate to clear debts, especially as the items are all portable and no furniture is included. It also appears to have been misdated.

153 Archives de la Préfecture de la Police, Paris, Aa 429, dossier on Adolphe-Charles Théveneau de Morande, pièces 213, 214, 226 and 228.

Notes to Chapter 9: Afterlife: Morande in Fiction, Myth and History

1 Lavirotte, 'Notice sur Morande.'

2 Brissot, *Réplique*, p. 28; Morande, *Lettre aux électeurs*, p. 20, denies ever saying this.

3 Pelleport, *Les Bohémiens*, I, 51.

4   Ibid., I, 196–8.
5   Only six copies of *Les Bohémiens* are known to survive. Robert Darnton, who views it as an unsung masterpiece, attributes its lack of success to the revolutionary climate's making depictions of the world of the London pamphleteers obsolete (see Darnton, *Bohemians*). This is surely erroneous. Revolutionary readers read avidly about this world, but it was in the *exposés* of Charpentier's *Bastille dévoilée* and Manuel's *Police dévoilée*, rather than Pelleport's spiteful and sordid allegorical fantasies.
6   The quoted phrase is probably the author's own. It is taken from an article in the *Süddeutsche Zeitung*, 8 December 2006, but similar phrases appear in other interviews with Morchiladze. A translated version of the article appears at http://www.signandsight.com/features/1094.html (consulted 19 May 2009). Morchiladze's novel has been translated into German but not English or French.
7   Morande, *Réplique à Brissot*, p. 20.
8   Ibid., pp. 25–6.
9   The police spy claim was championed by Darnton in 'The Grub Street style of revolution: J.-P. Brissot, police spy', *Journal of Modern History*, 40:4 (1968), 301–27. It has been the subject of a long controversy. For the debate and latest evidence, see Burrows, 'Innocence of Brissot'.
10   M. Foisset, 'Théveneau de Morande' in *Biographie universelle*, XXX, 68–70, at p. 68.
11   Alfred Franklin, 'Théveneau de Morande' in *Nouvelle Biographie générale*, XXXVI (1865), cols. 450–3 at col. 453. Cf. Loménie, *Beaumarchais et son temps*, pp. 381–2 and 382–4n.
12   Robiquet, *Théveneau de Morande*, p. 307, partially quoted in Prologue, above.
13   Darnton, 'High enlightenment', pp. 115, 110.
14   Ibid., p. 109.
15   For a detailed critique of Darnton's arguments, see Burrows, *Blackmail*, esp. pp. 10–18.
16   See Burrows, 'Literary low-life' and Burrows, *Blackmail*, pp. 26–9.
17   McCalman, *Seven Ordeals*, p. 148
18   *BCE*, I, 180–96, quote at p. 195.
19   See Burrows, *Blackmail*, ch. 1, esp. pp. 51–2.
20   In the *Iliad*, Cassandra possessed the gift of prophesy and the curse of never being believed. The image is Morande's own, used to express fears that his *Lettres d'un voyageur* would not be heeded: see AFB fos 47–8, Morande to Beaumarchais, 6 February 1787, *BCE* document 484 [abridged].

Sources

MANUSCRIPT SOURCES

FRANCE

Archives du Ministère des affaires étrangères, Paris
Correspondance politique, Angleterre, (CPA) volumes 497–577.
CPA supplément, volumes 13–14, 16–18, 28, 30.
Mémoires et documents (MD), Angleterre, volume 73.
MD, France, volumes 1398–1400.

Archives nationales, Paris
Series AP: Archives privées:
277AP/1 – D'Eon papers, dossier Morande.
297AP/2 – Calonne papers.
446AP/1–4, 7 & 13 – Brissot papers.
Series B^7: Marine:
B^7 456 – correspondance arrivée, Angleterre, 1693–1788.
B^7 473–5 – Angleterre.
Series F^7: Police générale:
F^7 4445^2 – Affaire du collier.
F^7 4774^{51} dossier 3 – arrestation de Morande
Series K:
K 157.
Series T: Séquestre.
T 489/2 – papiers d'Alexis Guinet.
Series W:
W 251 dossier 27: procès verbal de la perquisition faite chez le Sr Morande.
W 292 dossier 204: affaire des Girondins.

Bibliothèque de l'Arsenal, Paris
Bastille papers
MS 12,247 – Théveneau de Morande.
MS 12,345 – Théveneau de Morande.
MS 12,451 – Samuel Swinton.
MS 12,453 – Jacquet, Duvernet, Marcenay.
MS 12,454 – Pelleport, Chamorand.

Service historique de la défense, Château de Vincennes, Paris
$4YC^{11}$: Contrôle des troupes, dragons de Bauffremont, 1748–1760.
$6YC^{73}$: Contrôle des troupes, Carabiniers, 1763–1776.
$7YC^3$: Contrôle des troupes, dragons Bauffremont, Lorraine 1763–1776.
YB^{104}: Contrôle des officiers: contrôles collectifs – Cavalerie et Dragons, 1748–1763.
YB^{605}: Contrôle des officiers: Bauffremont.
YB^{839}: Nomination des officiers: 'Enregistrement de Cavalerie et de Dragons commencé le 1 juin 1760 jusqu'au 1er May 1763'.

Archives de la Préfecture de la Police, Paris
Aa 429, pièces 213–28, dossier on Adolphe-Charles Théveneau de Morande.

Archives départementales de la Seine, Paris
DQ^{10} 103 dossier 1814, papiers de Froullé, libraire, condamné.

Archives départementales de la Côte d'Or
C7836 – Contrôle des Actes, Arnay-le-Duc, 1772–1773.
C7904 – Table de testaments d'Arnay-le-Duc.
L195 – list of electors, Arnay-le-Duc.
L 1274 – census of the revolutionary district of Arnay-sur-Arroux.
2E26/4-24 – Etat civil, Arnay-le-Duc, 1737–1858.
4E64/261 – notaire Gaspard Bresson, Arnay-le-Duc, 1772–3.
3Q1 – Table des successions directes et indirectes, 1 vendémiaire X-1 janvier 1807.

Bibliothèque municipale, Dijon
Liasses F.8, F.11–14, F.19 – materials relating to Collège Godrun and Collège Martin.

Archives communales, Arnay-le Duc
Etat Civil; Tables des mariages; Tables des baptêmes; Tables des sepultures.

Bibliothèque municipale, Tonnerre
D'Eon Manuscripts, B 27; H 117–19; J 62–3; J 153–67; K 9–12; K 124–5; L 11–22; L 26–8; L 41; L 54;
　L102; O3; R1–2; R 7–10; R 18; R 20–22; R 24; Y3.

Mediathèque d'Orléans
MS 1421–3, Mémoires of Jean-Charles-Pierre Lenoir, 1732–1807.

Archives privées
Archives de la famille Beaumarchais: Morande-Beaumarchais correspondence.
'Notice sur M. de Morande' par César Lavirotte, présentée par Claude Guyot.

GERMANY
Bayerisches Hauptstaatsarchiv, Munich
Politische Korrespondenz des Herzogs von Pfalz-Zweibrücken, Kasten blau 405/34.

UNITED KINGDOM
British Library, London
Add. MS. 11,339–41 – d'Eon papers.
Add. MS. 35,118 – Sheridan papers.

City of Westminster Archives
Printed marriage registers, parish of Saint-George Hanover Square, vol. 16, 1768–1771.

National Archives, Kew (formerly Public Record Office)
C12 series: Chancery Court papers.
C12/440/25 – Morande versus Woodfield, 28 July 1781.
C12/1389/27 – Latour versus de Callonne [sic], 1788.
C12/2114/28 – de Morande versus Simond, 22 June 1778.
FO 95: Foreign Office papers, miscellaneous.
FO95/630–32 – Calonne papers.

PC series: Privy Council Papers:
PC1/124–31 – Calonne papers.
SP78 series, State papers, France:
Volumes 285, 300.
TS series, Treasury Solicitor's papers:
TS11/388 – trial of Lord George Gordon, 1787.
TS11/793/2 – trial of François-Henri de La Motte, 1781.
TS11/1116 – Rex versus François-Henri de La Motte, 1781.

London Metropolitan Archives
Parish records of Saint John the Evangelist, Great Stanmore:
A1/5 – baptisms and burials 1765–1796.
F1/1 – overseers of the poor, accounts.
G1/1 – surveyors' accounts, surveyors of highways, 1772–1826.
MR/PLT 1418–68 – land tax records, 1780–1832.

Brotherton Library, Leeds University
Brotherton Collection, d'Eon papers.
Ernest Alfred Vizetelly, *The True Story of the Chevalier d'Eon* (London: Tylston and Edwards and
A. P. Marsden, 1895), 'extra illustrated' edition compiled by A.M. Broadley, bound in seven folio
volumes.

Harrow Public Library
Percy Davenport Collection, hand copies of original documents:
Court rolls of the manor of Great Stanmore, 1764–99.
Land Tax assessments, manor of Great Stanmore.
Surveyor of Highways Accounts, 1772–1826, Great Stanmore.
Great Stanmore Parish Registers.

PRINTED SOURCES
BOOKS AND PAMPHLETS DEFINITELY ATTRIBUTABLE TO MORANDE

Le Gazetier cuirassé ou anecdotes scandaleuses de la cour de France, 1st edn (imprimé à cent lieües de
la Bastille à l'enseigne de la liberté [i.e. London], 1771).
Le Gazetier cuirassé, ou anecdotes scandaleuses de la cour de France, 1777 edn (n. p.).
Lettre aux électeurs du département de Paris sur Jacques-Pierre Brissot (Paris: Froullé, 1791).
Ma Correspondance avec M. le comte de Cagliostro (Hambourg, 1786).
*Réplique de Charles Théveneau Morande à Jacques-Pierre Brissot: sur les erreurs, les infidélités et les
calomnies de sa Réponse* (Paris: Froullé, 1791).
Réponse au dernier mot de J.-P. Brissot et à tous les petits mots de ses camarades (Paris: Froullé, 1791).

BOOKS AND PAMPHLETS PROBABLY ATTRIBUTABLE TO MORANDE

Morande, Charles-Claude Théveneau de (attrib.), *Le Bon-homme anglois* (Amsterdam, 1783 [1785?]).
—— *Historical Remarks and Anecdotes on the Castle of the Bastille*, trans. by John Howard (London:
T. Cadell and N. Conant, 1780).
—— *Mandement du Muphti*, in Morande and Voltaire (attrib.), *Le Tocsin des Rois Par M. De
VOLT**** suivi d'un Mandement du Muphti, ordonnant la SUPPRESSION de cet Ouvrage; et d'un
Decret du DIVAN, qui condamne l'Auteur à être empalé*. Imprimé à Constantinople: L'An de l'Égire
1168. Se trouve à LONDRES, chez BOISSIÈRE, (London: Boissière, [1772]).

—— Rémarques historiques et anecdotes sur le château de la Bastille et l'inquisition de France (London: n. p. 1774).

BOOKS AND PAMPHLETS ATTRIBUTED SPURIOUSLY OR PROBABLY MISTAKENLY TO MORANDE

Anon., Le Désoeuvré, ou, l'espion du boulevard du temple (London, 1782).
—— La Gazette noire, par un homme qui n'est pas blanc ([London]: n. p. 1783).
—— Les Joueurs et M. Dusaulx (Agripinae [London]: N. Lescot, 1781 [1st edn, 1780].
—— Lettre de M. Morande, auteur et rédacteur du Courier de l'Europe, à M de Beaumarchais (Geneva 1787).
—— Le Portefeuille de Madame Gourdan (Spa [London], 1783).
—— La Vie privée ou apologie du très sérénissime prince Monseigneur le duc de Chartres contre un libelle diffamatoire écrit en mil sept cent quatre-vingt-un, mais qui n'a point paru à cause des menaces que nous avons faites à l'auteur de le décéler, par une société d'amis du Prince (London: n. p., 1784).
—— Le Vol plus haut, ou l'espion des principaux théâtres de la capitale (Memphis: Paris, Chez Sincere, 1784).

BOOKS AND PAMPHLETS BY OTHER AUTHORS

Andrea de Nerciat, André-Robert (attrib.), Julie philosophe, ou le bon patriote, 2 vols (Paris: Le Coffret des Bibliophiles, 1910 [original edition, 1791]).
Anon., Les Amours de Charlot et Toinette (Paris: 'à la Bastille', 1789).
—— Essai historique sur la vie de Marie-Antoinette d'Autriche, Reine de France, pour servir à l'histoire de cette princesse, (London: n. p., 1789).
—— A Life of the Count Cagliostro (London: T. Hookham, 1787).
Bachaumont, Louis Petit de, (attrib.), Mémoires secrets pour servir à l'histoire de la république de lettres en France, depuis 1762 jusqu'à nos jours, 36 vols (London: John Adamson, 1777–1787).
Balsamo, Joseph, Lettre du Comte de Cagliostro au peuple anglois (1786).
—— Mémoire pour le Comte de Cagliostro, accusé, contre M. le Procureur-général, accusateur (Paris, 1786).
Beaumarchais, Pierre-Augustin Caron de, Correspondance, ed. Brian Morton and D. Spinelli, 4 vols (Paris: Nizet, 1969–78).
—— Lettres à Madame de Godeville, 1777–1779, ed. Maxime Formont (Paris: Lemerre, 1928).
—— Les Lettres galantes de Beaumarchais à Madame de Godeville, ed. Maurice Lever (Paris: Fayard, 2004).
Biographical Anecdotes of the Founders of the French Republic and other Eminent Characters who have Distinguished themselves in the Progress of the Revolution (London: R. Philips, 1797).
Brissot de Warville, Jacques-Pierre, Correspondance et papiers, ed. C. Perroud (Paris: Picard, 1912).
—— Mémoires de Brissot sur ses contemporains et la révolution française, ed. F. de Montrol, 4 vols (Paris: Lavocat, 1830–1832).
—— Réplique de J. P. Brissot à Charles Théveneau Morande (Paris: de l'imprimerie du Patriote françois, 1791).
—— Réponse à tous les libellistes qui ont attaqué et attaquent sa vie passée (Paris: de l'imprimerie du Patriote françois, 1791).
Broglie, Charles-François, comte de, Correspondance secrète du comte de Broglie avec Louis XV, ed. Didier Ozanam and Michel Antoine, 2 vols (Paris, Klincksieck, 1956–1961).
Burke, Edmund, Reflections on the Revolution in France (Harmondsworth: Penguin, 1969).
Charpentier, Louis, et al., La Bastille dévoilée (Paris: Desenne, 1789–1790).
Correspondance secrète entre Marie-Thérèse et le comte Mercy-d'Argenteau, ed. A. von Arneth and M. Geoffroy, 2nd edn, 3 vols (Paris: Firmin-Didot: 1874–1875).
Correspondance secrète inédite sur Louis XVI, Marie-Antoinette, la cour et la ville de 1777–1792, ed. M. de Lescure, 2 vols (Paris: Plon, 1866).

Correspondance secrète, politique et littéraire, ou mémoires pour servir à l'histoire des cours, des sociétés et de la littérature en France, depuis la mort de Louis XV, 18 vols (London: John Adamson, 1787–1790).

'M. Demorande', in *Biographical Anecdotes of the Founders of the French Republic and other Eminent Characters who have Distinguished themselves in the Progress of the Revolution* (London: R. Philips, 1797), pp. 131–2.

Desgenettes, René Nicolas Dufriche, *Souvenirs de la fin du XVIIIe siècle et du commencement du XIXe siècle, ou mémoires de R. D. G.*, 2 vols (Paris: Firmin-Didot, 1835).

Desmoulins, Camille, *The History of the Brissotins; or Part of the Secret History of the Revolution and of the First Six Months of the Republic* (London: Owen, 1794).

Dutens, Louis, *Mémoires d'un voyageur qui se repose*, 3 vols (London: Dulau, 1806).

Georgel, Jean-François, *Mémoires pour servir à l'histoire des evenemens de la fin du dix-huitième siècle depuis 1760 jusqu'en 1806–1810*, 6 vols (Paris: Alexis Eymery, 1817–1818).

Gordon, George, *The Prisoner's Complaint to the Right Honourable George Gordon, to Preserve their Lives and Liberties, and Prevent their Banishment to Botany Bay* (London, 1787).

Gotteville, Anne Latouche de, *Voyage d'une françoise à Londres ou la calomnie détruite par la vérité des faits* (London: Mesplet, 1774).

Goudar, Ange, *L'Espion françois à Londres, ou observations critiques sur l'Angleterre et les anglois*, 2 vols (London: aux depens de l'auteur, 1780 [original edition, 1779]).

Gudin de La Brenellerie, Paul-Philippe, *Histoire de Beaumarchais*, ed. Maurice Tourneux (Paris: Plon, 1888).

Hardy, Siméon-Prosper, *Mes Loisirs*, ed. Maurice Tourneux and Maurice Vitrac, 2 vols (Paris, 1912).

Imbert, Guillaume, (attrib), *La Chronique scandaleuse ou mémoires pour servir à l'histoire de la génération présente*, 3rd edn, 4 vols (Paris: n. p. 1788).

La Motte, Jeanne de Saint-Rémy de, *An Address to the Public Explaining the Motives which have Hitherto Delayed the Publication of the Memoirs of the Countess de La Motte* (London: Ridgway, 1789).

—— *Detection, or a Scourge for Calonne* (London: n. p. 1789).

—— *The Life of Jane de St Remy de Valois, heretofore Countess de La Motte*, 2 vols (Dublin: P. Wogan, P. Bryce, J. Moore and J. Rice, 1792).

—— *Mémoire pour dame Jeanne de Saint-Rémy de Valois, épouse du comte de La Motte* (Paris: Cellot, 1785).

—— *Memoirs of the Countess de Valois La Motte* (Dublin: John Archer and William Jones, 1790).

La Motte, Marc-Antoine-Nicolas de, *Mémoires inédits du comte de Lamotte-Valois sur sa vie et son époque (1754–1830)*, ed. Louis Lacour (Paris: Poulet-Malassis et de Broise, 1858).

La Tour, Alphonse-Joseph Serres de, *Appel au bon sens dans lequel M. de La Tour soumet à ce juge infaillible les détails de sa conduite relativement à une affaire qui fait quelque bruit dans le monde* (London: Kearsley, 1788).

Lauraguais, Louis-Léon de Brancas, Count de, *Mémoire pour moi, par moi* (London, 1773).

Le Bac, Mlle., [pseud.], *Lettre curieuse de Mlle Le Bac, autrement Mlle St Amand, alias Mad^e Lescallier, Londres, 17 Octobre 1763* (London, 1763).

Linguet, Simon-Nicolas-Henri, *Mémoires sur la Bastille, et de la détention de l'auteur dans ce château royal, depuis le 27 septembre 1780 jusqu'au 19 mai 1782* (London: Spilsbury, 1783).

Louis XV, *Correspondance secrète inédite de Louis XV*, ed. M. E. Boutaric, 2 vols (Paris: Plon, 1866).

Louis XVI and the Comte de Vergennes: Correspondance, ed. John Hardman and Munro Price, *SVEC* 364 (Oxford: Voltaire Foundation, 1998).

Mahy de Comère, Guillaume-François de, *Justification de M. de Favras, prouvée par les faits et par la procédure* (Paris: chez l'auteur, 1791).

Mairobert, Mathieu-François Pidansat de (attrib.), *Anecdotes sur Madame la comtesse du Barri* (London: n. p. 1775).

—— (attrib.), *L'Espion anglois, ou correspondance secrète entre Milord All'Eye et Milord All'Ear*, nouvelle édition revue, corrigée et consideralement augmentée, 10 vols (London: John Adamson, 1779–1785).

—— (attrib.), *Journal historique de la révolution opérée dans la constitution de la monarchie française par M. de Maupoeu* (London, 1775).

—— (attrib.), *Letters to and from the Countess Du Barry, the Last Mistress of Lewis XV of France*, translated from the French (Dublin: P. Higly, 1780).

Manuel, Pierre-Louis, *La Police de Paris dévoilée*, 2 vols (Paris: Garnery, l'an II de la liberté [1791]).
Pelleport, Anne-Gédeon de La Fite de, *Les Bohémiens*, 2 vols (Paris: Rue des Poitevins, hôtel Bouthillier, 1790).
—— *Le Diable dans un bénitier et le Gazetier Cuirassé transformé en mouche, ou tentative du sieur Receveur et de la cour de France pour établir à Londres une police à l'instar de celle de Paris* (London: n. p., 1783).
—— *Les Petits Soupers et nuits de l'hôtel de Bouill-n. Lettre de Milord Comte de ****** à Milord ******** au sujet des récréations de M. de C-stri-s ou de la danse de l'ours, anecdote singulière d'un cocher qui s'est pendu à l'hôtel de Bouill-n, le 31 décembre 1778 à l'occasion de la danse de l'ours* (Bouillon [London], n. p., 1783).
Piton, Camille (ed.), *Paris sous Louis XV: rapports des Inspecteurs de police au roi*, 5 vols (Paris: Mercure de France, 1906–1914).
Ravaisson, François (ed.), *Archives de la Bastille*, 19 vols (Paris: Durand et Pedone-Lauriel, 1866–1904).
The Register Book of Marriages of the Parish of Saint-George Hanover Square in the County of Middlesex (Harleain Society, 1886).
Roland, Jeanne-Marie Phlipon, *Lettres de Madame Roland*, ed. Claude Perroud, 2 vols (Paris: Imprimerie nationale, 1900–1902).
Sault, J.-B. *Receuil d'anecdotes biographiques, historiques et politiques sur les personnages les plus remarquables et les événements les plus frappants de la Révolution française* (Paris, 1798).
The Trial at Large of the Hon. George Gordon (London: R. Randall, 1787).
Voltaire, *Correspondence*, ed. Theodore Besterman, 107 vols (Geneva: Institut et musée Voltaire, 1953–1965).
—— *Questions sur l'Encyclopédie par des amateurs*, nouvelle édition soigneusement revue, corrigée et augmentée, 9 vols (1771–1772).
The Whole Proceedings on the Trials of Two Informations Exhibited Ex-Officio against George Gordon (London: M. Gurney, 1787).
Williams, David, *Incidents in my Own Life which have been Thought of Some Importance*, ed. Peter France (Brighton, 1982).

NEWSPAPER AND PERIODICAL SOURCES

Annales politiques, civiles et littéraires du dix-huitième siècle (ed. Linguet)
Annual Register
Argus patriote (ed. Morande)
British Chronicle or Pugh's Hereford Journal
Chester Chronicle
Courier de l'Europe (ed. Morande)
Courier de Londres (ed. Morande)
Daily Universal Register
Extraordinary Intelligencer
Gazette britannique
Gazetteer
General Advertiser
General Evening Post
Gentleman's Magazine
Lloyds Evening Post
London Chronicle
London Evening Packet
London Evening Post
Morning Chronicle
Morning Herald
Morning Post
Patriote françois (ed. Brissot)
Political Register
Public Advertiser

Public Ledger
St James Chronicle
The Times
Universal Magazine
Westminster Gazette

ELECTRONIC PRIMARY SOURCES

The Benjamin Franklin Papers at http://www.yale.edu/franklinpapers/project.html
The Burney Collection of Early English Newspapers
Eighteenth-Century Collections Online
Gallica at http://gallica.bnf.fr
The Proceedings of the Old Bailey at http://www.oldbaileyonline.org

SELECTED SECONDARY SOURCES

(NB. Only published secondary works mentioned more than once in the notes
are listed here)

Albrier, A., 'Charles Théveneau de Morande', in *Bulletin du Bouquiniste*, 15 December 1875, 1–4.
Almeras, Henri d', *Marie-Antoinette et les pamphlets royalistes et révolutionnaires* (Paris: Librarie mondiale, 1907).
Arneth, Alfred von, *Beaumarchais und Sonnenfels* (Vienna: Wilhelm Braumüller, 1868).
Barker, Hannah, and Simon Burrows (eds), *Press, Politics and the Public Sphere in Europe and North America 1760–1820* (Cambridge: CUP, 2002).
Burrows, Simon, *Blackmail, Scandal, and Revolution: London's French Libellistes, 1758–1791* (Manchester University Press, 2006).
—— 'The Chevalier d'Eon, media manipulation and the making of an eighteenth-century celebrity', in Simon Burrows, Jonathan Conlin, Russell Goulbourne and Valerie Mainz, (eds), *The Chevalier d'Eon and His Worlds: Gender, Espionage and Politics in the Eighteenth Century* (London: Continuum, 2010), pp. 13–23.
—— 'The cosmopolitan press', in Hannah Barker and Simon Burrows (eds), *Press, Politics and the Public Sphere*, pp. 23–47.
—— 'The innocence of Jacques-Pierre Brissot', *Historical Journal* 46:4 (2003), 843–71.
—— 'A literary low-life reassessed: Charles Théveneau de Morande in London, 1769–1791', *Eighteenth-Century Life* 22:1 (1998), 76–94.
—— Jonathan Conlin, Russell Goulbourne and Valerie Mainz (eds), *The Chevalier d'Eon and His Worlds: Gender, Espionage and Politics in the Eighteenth Century* (London: Continuum, 2010).
Darnton, Robert, *Bohemians before Bohemianism* (Wassenaar: NIAS, 2006).
—— *The Corpus of Clandestine Literature in France 1769–1789* (New York: Norton, 1995).
—— 'The high enlightenment and the low-life of literature in prerevolutionary France', *Past and Present* 51 (1971), 81–115.
Donvez, Jacques, *La Politique de Beaumarchais* (Leiden: IDC, 1980).
Foisset, M., 'Théveneau de Morande', in *Biographie universelle, ancienne et moderne*, 85 vols (Paris: Michaud, 1811–65), XXX, pp. 68–70.
Franklin, Alfred, 'Théveneau de Morande', in *Nouvelle biographie générale depuis les temps les plus reculés jusqu'à nos jours* (Paris: Firmin Didot, 1852–65), XXXVI, cols. 450–53.
Funck-Brentano, Frantz, *Cagliostro and Company*, transl. George Maidment (London: Greening, 1910).
Gaillardet, Frédéric, *The Memoirs of Chevalier d'Eon*, translated by Antonia White (London: Anthony Blond, 1970, [original French edition, Paris, 1866]).
Harris, J. R., *Industrial Espionage and Technology Transfer. Britain and France in the Eighteenth Century* (Aldershot: Ashgate, 1998).

Huot, Paul, *Beaumarchais en Allemagne, révélations tirées des archives de l'Autriche* (Paris: Librairie internationale, 1869).

Kates, Gary, *Monsieur d'Eon is a Woman: A Tale of Political Intrigue and Sexual Masquerade* (New York: Basic Books, 1995).

Lacour-Gayet, Robert, *Calonne: financier, réformateur, contre-révolutionnaire, 1734–1802* (Paris: Hachette, 1963).

Lever, Evelyne, *L'Affaire du collier* (Paris: Fayard, 2004).

Lever, Maurice, *Pierre-Augustin Caron de Beaumarchais*, 3 vols (Paris: Fayard, 1999–2004).

Levy, Darline Gay, *The Ideas and Careers of Simon-Nicolas-Henri Linguet: A Study in Eighteenth-Century French Politics* (Urbana, Ill.: University of Illinois Press, 1980).

Loménie, Louis de, *Beaumarchais et son temps*, 2 vols (Paris: Michel Levy frères, 1856).

Lüsebrink, Hans-Jürgen, and Rolf Reichardt, *The Bastille: A History of a Symbol of Despotism and Freedom* (Durham, N.C.: Duke University Press, 1997).

Maza, Sarah, *Private Lives and Public Affairs: The Causes Célèbres of Prerevolutionary France* (Berkeley, CA: University of California Press, 1993).

McCalman, Iain, *The Seven Ordeals of Count Cagliostro* (London: Century, 2003).

Merrick, Jeffrey, 'The Marquis de Villette and Mademoiselle de Raucourt: representations of male and female sexual deviance in late eighteenth-century France', in Jeffrey Merrick and Bryant T. Ragan Jr., *Homosexuality in Modern France* (Oxford University Press, 1996), pp. 30–53.

—— and Bryant T. Ragan Jr., *Homosexuality in Modern France* (Oxford University Press, 1996).

Morris, Richard B., *The Peacemakers. The Great Powers and American Independence* (New York: Harper and Row, 1970).

Mossiker, Frances, *The Queen's Necklace* (London: Victor Gollancz, 1961).

Photiadès, Constantin, *Les Vies du Comte de Cagliostro*, 9th edn (Paris: Grasset, 1932).

Pomeau, Réné, *Beaumarchais ou la bizarre destinée* (Paris: PUF, 1987).

Proschwitz, Gunnar and Mavis von, *Beaumarchais et le Courier de l'Europe: documents inédits ou peu connus*, *SVEC* 273–4 (Oxford: Voltaire Foundation, 1990).

Robiquet, Paul, *Théveneau de Morande: étude sur le XVIIIe siècle* (Paris: Quantin, 1882).

Rodger, Nicholas, *The Command of the Ocean: A Naval History of Britain, 1649–1815* (London: Penguin, 2004).

Spinelli, Donald, 'Beaumarchais and d'Eon: what an affair' in Simon Burrows, Jonathan Conlin, Russell Goulbourne and Valerie Mainz, (eds), *The Chevalier d'Eon and His Worlds: Gender, Espionage and Politics in the Eighteenth Century* (London: Continuum, 2010), pp. 57–71

Vallentin, Antonina, *Mirabeau. Voice of the Revolution*, transl. E. W. Dickes (London: Hamish Hamilton, 1948).

Vircondelet, Alain, *La Princesse de Lamballe: l'ange de Marie-Antoinette* (Paris: Flammarion, 2005).

Vizetelly, Ernest Alfred, *The True Story of the Chevalier d'Eon* (London: Tylston and Edwards and A. P. Marsden, 1895).

Vizetelly, Henry, *The Story of the Diamond Necklace*, 2 vols (London: Tinsley, 1887).

Wagner, Peter, *Eros Revived: Erotica of the Enlightenment in England and America* (London: Paladin, 1988).

UNPUBLISHED SECONDARY SOURCES

Agnani, Paul, 'Libelles et diplomatie à la fin du dix-huitième siècle d'après la Correspondance Politique, Angleterre conservée aux Archives du Ministère des Affaires étrangères, 1771–1783' (unpublished *Mémoire de Maîtrise*: University of Besançon, 2004).

Slauter, William 'News and diplomacy in the age of the American Revolution', (unpublished *PhD* dissertation, Princeton, 2007).

Acknowledgements

This biography has been a labour of love over 20 years. As a result I have many debts to acknowledge, not all of which can be mentioned here. This book would have been poorer without the input of all those named below and many others besides. Its faults, needless to say, are entirely my own.

I would like to thank the following for financial assistance: The Humanities Research Centre at the Australian National University; the British Academy; the Faculty of Arts at the University of Waikato; the School of History and Humanities Research Leave Scheme at the University of Leeds; and the Arts and Humanities Research Board Research Leave Scheme.

I would also particularly like to thank staff of the Archives du Ministère des affaires étrangères; the Bibliothèque municipale de Tonnerre, especially Marie-Christine Beccavin; the Médiathèque d'Orléans; the British Library; the Brotherton Library at Leeds University; the Australian National Library; Philippe Henrat at the Archives Nationales; Bob Thomson at Harrow Library; Martin Cherry at the Freemasons' Hall Museum and Library; and I. A. Mayr at the Bayerisches Hauptstaatsarchiv.

I would also like to thank the following for providing guidance, support or references, or for commenting on drafts of material for this book and related projects: Moira Bonington; Laurence Brockliss; Kimberly Chrisman; Jonathan Conlin; Nicholas Cronk; Mark Curran; Simon Dixon; Alan Forrest; Russell Goulbourne; Michael Gregory; Vivian Gruder; William Jennings; Colin Jones; Tom Kaiser; Andrew Lambert; Kevin Linch; Iain McCalman; Laura Mackie; Valerie Mainz; Anne-Marie Mercier-Faivre, Claude Labrosse and the rest of the LIRE research team at Lyon-2; Roger Mettam; Peter Millican; David Parker; Jeremy Popkin; Munro Price; Nicholas Rodger; Guy Rowlands; Louise Seaward; Barry Shapiro; Chris Sheppard; Jenny Skipp; Will Slauter; Sarah Taylor; and Christopher Todd.

Special thanks to my French friends Bernard Leblanc, *savant* and historian of Arnay-le-Duc and Paul Agnani for sharing their time, knowledge and resources. I am also deeply grateful to the custodian of the Beaumarchais family papers, who wishes to remain anonymous. I am indebted to the Brotherton Library, the British Library and the Department of Prints and Drawings at the British Museum for allowing me to reproduce visual materials from their collections.

I am deeply grateful to Ben Hayes at Continuum books for his enthusiasm and support for my projects and to my father, Peter Burrows, my indispensable proof-reader, critic and indexer. I am also grateful to Martin Sumpter for his hospitality in Paris and my wife Andrea for acting as an unpaid research assistant and sharing her husband with a long-dead scoundrel.

Finally I would like to acknowledge the kindness and hospitality of my younger cousin Danalee Burrows on my research trips to London. Sadly, she died of cancer while I was writing this book, which is dedicated to her memory.

Simon Burrows
Leeds, October 2009

Index

Notes: (1) Illustrations are indicated by italics. (2) 'n.' after a page number indicates the number of an endnote on that page. (3) Morande's relationships are classified under the names of the people involved; other entries involving him appear under the appropriate entry e.g. 'youth'.